CREATURES BORN OF WAR

A Novel About the Korean and Vietnam Conflicts

Bruce Wm. Taneski

Forward By
Jeff Beck MFTI

ISBN 10: 1533305919
ISBN 13: 9781533305916

Edited by Valerie Rans & Suzy Eyler

Other books by the author;

FORWARD

*C*reatures Born of War *"A Novel about the Korea and Vietnam"* is a compelling and historically accurate story that focuses on the evolution of the Korean War and the Vietnam War. This book is a continuation of the author's first novel *Creatures Born of War "A Novel about the World Wars* that portrays an accurate depiction of the psychosocial impact of war; not only for the veterans who served during these wars but also the lasting impact post war for the service member and their families. This psychosocial impact is presently known as Post-Traumatic Stress Disorder (PTSD).

Post-traumatic Stress Disorder was added to the third edition of the Diagnostic and Statistics Manual of Mental Disorder (DSM-III) in 1980 by the American Psychiatric Association (APA). According to the United States Department of Veterans Affairs, "The framers of the original PTSD diagnosis had in mind events such as war, torture, rape, the Nazi Holocaust, the atomic bombings of Hiroshima and Nagasaki, natural disasters (such as earthquakes, hurricanes, and volcano eruptions), and human-made disasters (such as factory explosions, airplane crashes, and automobile accidents)." The diagnostic criterion for Post-Traumatic Stress Disorder has been revised multiple times throughout the years. In 2013, the American Psychiatric Association revised the diagnostic criteria for PTSD in the fifth edition of the Diagnostic and Statistics Manual of Mental Disorder (DSM-V). In the latest revision, PTSD is no longer categorized as an Anxiety Disorder.

It is now classified as a Trauma and Stressor Related Disorder.

The author, Bruce Wm. Taneski, served in the United States Army during the Vietnam War. Throughout his combat experiences, he endured a significant amount of trauma; which led to his diagnosis of Post-Traumatic Stress Disorder. It was not until 2014 when he began to seek treatment for his PTSD. That's over 40 years of living with this diagnosis without any assistance from a licensed mental health professional.

Unfortunately, this is very common for individuals during the Vietnam War Era and the generations of veterans who served in combat prior to him. The idea of this novel was developed as a direct result of the author's exposure therapy and cognitive restructuring. As he engaged in his treatment, he was encouraged to write a detailed narrative associated with one of his traumatic events. This led to the development of his first book, *I Came Home, But It Wasn't Me Memoirs of a Combat Recon Scout LRRP*. Writing now became a source of coping with his symptoms. It encouraged him to research and write about other wars for the purposes of providing insight and education into the true cost of war.

This novel illustrates a variety of character driven narratives that are not only historically accurate but also, in some cases, real-life experiences. I truly value and appreciate this author's efforts to bring more awareness into Post-Traumatic Stress Disorder and its effects on our past, present, and future "Creatures Born of War".

Jeff Beck
MFTI

TABLE OF CONTENTS

The Primary Fictional Characters;

Joseph McMullen NYPD (Retired)
Margaret McMullen
Michael McMullen NYPD (Retired)
Susan McMullen (nee Kennedy) Captain
USN (Retired)
Kevin Brogan ESQ.
Marguerite (Maggie) (Nee McMullen)
Brogan
Dylan Brogan USMC / CIA
Dorothy Brogan

Steve Bush

Colleen Costigan
Hope Ann Costigan USA / NURSE CORPS
Jack Randall Jr. USN

Caroline Grindell OSS/CIA

Charles Randall ESQ
Kathleen (Kay) (Nee Laudisio) Randall
Joyce Randall
Michael Jack Randall CAPTAIN / USA

Eilis McDevitt

Duy Minh VIET MINH/ Viet Cong / NLF
Huyen Trang VIET MINH / VIET CONG /
NLF
Nguyen Hung VIET MINH / VIET CONG /
NLF
Phan Duong, Viet Minh/ NVA

The Secondary Fictional Characters;

Dave Solomon NYPD/OCPD
Grant Williams
Detective Meziaz RPD
Detective Breaker RPD

Colonel Jessup USA
Major Todd USA / Nurse Corps
Corporal Tom 'Doodles' Dudal
Captain Selleck / USA
Captain McCauley USA

Sean Murphy
Mary Murphy

Michael Costigan Jr.
Tom Brady

Vang Bo VIET MINH / VIET CONG / NLF
Vang Mei
Vang Meilin
Nguyen Tam VIET CONG / NLF

Primary Historical Characters;

Steve Cahill CORPSMAN / USN
Michael Rans CORPSMAN /USN
Charles 'Bobby Boot Camp' Gallagher PFC
USMC
John 'Hollywood' DeFelice CORPORAL /
USMC
Tom Corbett SERGEANT / USMC

PROLOGUE

World War II is over as the story about the McMullen, Costigan, and Brogan Families continue from the first book "Creatures Born of War", A Novel about the World Wars.

An old man and his wife are in Washington DC. They have driven from their home in New Jersey this Memorial Day 2018 weekend to participate with other Vietnam Veterans commemorating the fiftieth anniversary of the Tet Offensive of 1968 and to "Honor Memorial Day". He had been a Navy Corpsman assigned to the 1st Battalion, 4th Marine Regiment of the 3rd Marine Division at Con Thien. He arrived in Vietnam in January of 1970. He was awarded the Purple Heart just three weeks after his arrival and would leave Vietnam with his second Purple Heart in June 1970.

The old man had never been to the wall. He had never attended any of the reunions of his unit. The only place that would welcome his membership upon coming home was a Detachment of the Marine Corps League. He had been turned away from the American Legion and the Veterans of Foreign Wars. Twenty-four years later the South Jersey Vietnam Veterans Association would form and the man was impressed with the service that group did with assisting veterans and their families. These men were his only contact with other veterans of Vietnam. He was active with the programs in the South Jersey Vietnam Veterans Association. His Purple Heart orders were accepted as proof of his Vietnam service.

The Marine Corps League and the SJVVA group had no knowledge that he had been awarded the Medal of Honor when he first joined. That had changed over the years, but he was not one to speak about his combat experience. Like the Marine Corps League, he was welcomed with open arms and he found a sense of brotherhood.

At dawn on this Memorial Day morning, he and his wife made their way down the path leading to the apex of the wall. A US Park Policeman stood nearby. He stopped at Panel 6W. There etched into the black granite wall were the names of the Marines he tried to save that day. A day that is forever etched into his mind. A day that he wore on his lapel in the form of a small blue rosette.

His wife stood quietly beside him. His hand reached out and touched the cool black granite. Memories he could never bury flooded his mind. The horror of that day gripping him, never letting go. His big shoulders shook as the he wept for them, and himself. He had tried. He had done everything he could, but could not save them. They died in front of him as the enemy killed them one by one.

They died as he desperately tried to shield the bodies of the last of his wounded comrades. Some of them would have died anyway, others watched helpless as their lives were taken with such cruelty. His Lieutenant ordered him to stay put. His Lieutenant would write in his after-action report that his valor on the battlefield that day was above and beyond the call of duty. A General would push the paperwork through. President Nixon would clasp the nation's highest award for courage under fire, around his neck. Why? He could not save them. He saw their faces everywhere. The last words of a dying Marine playing in his head over and over. "Am I Ok Doc? Don't lie to me, is it bad?" Tell my wife I love her." Stop the pain, Doc, please stop the pain."

He composed himself. He allowed the tears to stay and fall down his cheeks. He reached up to his lapel and pulled the blue rosette from the lapel of his jacket.

Bending over with some effort he placed it gently at the base of the wall. Then with a little help from his wife he stood up and came to attention and saluted the Marines he loved and lost.

Together they walked toward the center of the wall and up the incline to the statue of the three soldiers who watch over their fallen comrades. "I think adding the statue was a good idea. They look so proud to be here.

It's as if they know why they are here. The same space is shared by them all. The names seem to embrace them and say welcome home. The three men seem to tell all the names we will never forget you," the woman told her husband.

They turned away then and walked back down the path. As they approached the panel where they had stopped he saw the Park Policeman come to attention and salute. He returned his salute. His wife smiled at the Policeman. They continued up the path into the bright sun of a new day, turning right onto the path to see the Women's Memorial Statue.

Once there, he reached into his pocket and took out a quarter. He placed the coin gently into the outstretched right hand of the fallen soldier. The significance of the gesture, was the same as leaving a coin on a head stone.

The quarter symbolizing that the person leaving the coin was with the deceased when he was killed. A final salute and then they left. Surrendering the hallowed ground to the throngs of visitors who would come that Memorial Day in 2018.

CHAPTER 1

RETURNING HOME

The war was over. The victors were squabbling over the wreckage of Europe and the Far East. Since the start of the first World War and the end of World War II, more than 100 million people lost their lives. The war years in America were like living with a couple of two-year-old's in a large room full of toys and other things. Everything was scattered about the room. Family members were in different parts of the country and the world. People returned home and everything needed to be picked up and put away. The routines of daily life without the war would be renewed. People put their lives back together. Businesses changed from war time production back to normal operations. The greatest generation would produce a whole new generation of Americans. They would fight their own war. Its cause and purpose would tear at the very fabric of the nation. They would have their creatures too. The mystery of who the creature was and how it came to be would be answered. Their pain would be special in so many ways.

Sitting on the aft observation deck of the ocean liner SS Monterey, Mike McMullen lit his cigar. The double bourbon on ice and another glass of bourbon neat sat on the table. He was waiting for his wife, Lieutenant Commander Susan (Kennedy)

McMullen. She was now retired from the Navy after twenty years of service. They had departed Hawaii that afternoon, and had just finished dinner. While waiting, he watched the sun set over the now peaceful Pacific.

He was retired from the NYPD. Her last duty station was the naval hospital at Pearl Harbor, and they were going home. She took the chair next to his having arrived from freshening up after dinner. They sat in silence each lost in their own thoughts of the last six years. Mike was anxious to see his sister's boy, Dylan. He had not seen him since he joined the Marines in 1937. He had been on Luzon when the Japanese invaded the Philippines. He was later rescued from Cabanatuan prison camp by the Army's 6th Ranger Battalion.

He had been beaten and starved but somehow managed to survive the Bataan death march and the prison camp. He had been home just about a year now, but still suffered from his experience.

Mike had survived France in the first World War, and had been awarded the Distinguished Service Cross. He too suffered from his war service. He lost his best friend Jimmy to the aftermath of war. So many other young men would return to their families different and broken. With so many coming homes there could never be a peaceful night anywhere in the country. The war would live on with the returning heroes of Guadalcanal, Tarawa, Iwo Jima, North Africa, Italy, Normandy and Bastogne. The families would suffer as well. Like Mike, the men would escape to their own world of isolation and depression. They would never speak of the terrible things they saw. Some would try desperately to bury the terrible things they did. Those evils would return in the night and torment them for the rest of their lives. The marriages and personal relationships would pay the price.

Susan sat quietly drinking her bourbon. She had not seen her family since she and Mike had left for Hawaii, just before the war started. She had enlisted in the Navy to escape the sleepy little town of Arlington Texas, just outside of Fort Worth. She had traveled the world, but now she would settle down with Mike and have a home of their own. He wanted to look at homes along the southern Jersey shore. His old NYPD partner Dave Solomon had settled there.

The letters they received from home indicated that Dylan needed help for his nightmares, explosive anger and isolation issues. His readjustment to peacetime and civilian life was not going well.

In addition, she thought about the feisty little Irish woman, Rose Costigan who had passed away in Havana just a few weeks ago. She and Mike had missed the funeral. Her oldest son Michael Jr. had her body returned to New York so she could be laid to rest with her husband and youngest son Jimmy. "I wish we could have left earlier. It would have been nice to attend Rose's funeral. She was quite a character," Susan said to Mike.

"Yea, I wish we could have been there. We can go to New York and pay our respects at the grave site. We are going to the city anyway to see Hope, and Colleen's parents," Mike replied.

"So much has happened, so many lives changed. You and I have seen two world wars. I hope the world can be at peace now," Susan said.

"Not likely. We are already bickering with the Soviets in Europe. French-Indo-China has declared their independence from France. We are already supporting the French war against some guy named Ho Chi Minh. The communist Chinese and the Soviets are expanding their influence in South East Asia including Korea. World War II might be over, but the aftermath will most likely set up the next war we get involved in," Mike said angrily.

"Well for now it's a beautiful night and we are together," Susan said standing. "Come on, let's go to our cabin."

"I haven't finished my cigar," Mike said.

Susan lifted her leg unto Mikes chair exposing her thigh and said, "You want to sit here with that stinky cigar or do you want to play?" Mike stood throwing the cigar overboard, and said, "Lead the way, my love."

Five days later they arrived in San Francisco. They both stood on the deck with many other passengers to see the Golden Gate Bridge. Many of these people like Mike and Susan had not been home in years.

From here they would use train service to Fort Worth Texas. Susan knew when they were leaving that she would see her parents again. They were both up in their years but their health was excellent.

Hard work built strong bodies and minds. Promises were made to visit her once she and Mike were settled. A week in Texas with her parents and then they were back on a train to Philadelphia.

Caroline Grindell grew up in Philadelphia and was already home. She had spent the last four years in London. She was employed by the US State Department. Her sister Charolette helped her get the job. Charolette was already working for the State Department in Paris when the war broke out. She was relocated to London before the Germans seized control of Paris. Caroline spoke French fluently and was used as a translator. Later she would be used to send coded messages via short wave radio to the French resistance operating in France.

These operations where run by the State Department with assistance from the OSS. (Office of Strategic Services) She was home on leave now and employed by the newly formed Central Intelligence Group. She would be home for a few weeks before reporting to Washington. Today was her second day home and she had made arrangements for lunch with the boy next door.

His name was Dylan Brogan. He had enlisted in the Marines in 1937 and was interned in a Japanese prison camp on Luzon. She had not seen him since he was home on leave after completing Marine Recruit training. Before he enlisted their relationship was flirtatious and later became physical. She was not in love with him, but there was a strong physical attraction.

She had seen him briefly the day before when she arrived home. He was quite different from the young man she remembered. She first encountered him as an inquisitive young boy who watched her undress from his window next door. Then the relationship grew to a sexual one before he left for the Marines. When he returned again after his training the relationship continued.

The difference was he was no longer a young boy learning to be a man. The Marines had transformed him into a confident and somewhat cocky young man. His shoulders no longer drooped as they used too, as the young boy unsure of himself. The Marines taught him to stand up straight.

He moved with a sense of confidence and strength, like a leopard ready to seize his prey when he was so inclined.

Yesterday when she saw him he was no longer that stealthy predator. The shoulders he had as a young boy had returned. They were slouched and his overall posture was submissive. Yet, at the same time there was an air of hostility that could present itself at the drop of a hat. He was still the leopard, but this predator's behavior was one of a cornered cat.

She knew very little about his war time service as a POW under the Japanese. Reports in the news media about the experience of these men was well known by now. The country still held the Japanese in contempt.

The sneak attack at Pearl Harbor and the stories of the atrocities of the Bataan Death March still lingered. They took the bus together into Center City. It was a short ride into town down

Pennsylvania Avenue, and then along the Benjamin Franklin Parkway. He boarded first and took the side seat towards the rear of the bus on the driver's side. Just past the rear side door she noted he could observe every one getting on and off. It also presented an opportunity to make a quick exit out that rear door if needed. Every action on his part was to take in all of his surroundings. He appeared to be a man on edge, yet at the same time there was still this sense of submissiveness.

They got off the bus at 13th and Market and went into Wanamaker's department store. Passing through the stores Grand Court and the 2500-pound bronze eagle statue they boarded elevators for the ninth floor. Once off the elevators they entered the Crystal Tea Room, one of the largest dining facilities in the world.

They ordered cocktails and club sandwiches. Although they were seated half way into the large dining room, he insisted that their table be against the wall. He sat at the table with his back to the wall and his eyes scanned the dining room constantly.

"So, how did you like London?" He asked, once their sandwiches arrived.

"It was an interesting city. There was a lot of damage to it during the bombings by the Germans," she replied.

He asked, "Were you ever near any buildings damaged by falling bombs?"

"Not really," she replied, "The building I was working in had its own underground access to the subway system. I lived in an apartment building just a few blocks away. Charolette and I shared a flat together. I'm sure your time in the war was quite different from mine."

"You could say that. It's funny, I spent the entire war in the Philippines, and never experienced combat. I never fired a weapon. The so called gracious Japanese were anything but," he said.

"Tell me about that stick you always keep with you. It looks as if you can walk all right without it," she inquired.

"My buddies gave it to me after a Jap officer broke my foot. I did need it then to move around. Now I've gotten used to it. I still have a slight limp without it. I guess it's more of a psychological crutch. It's important to me, though. I don't know why but, not having it with me is something I don't want to do," he said.

"Speaking about what you want to do, what are your plans? Are you looking to work at your father's firm?" Caroline asked him.

"No, I'm not interested in being a lawyer. The Marines are letting me go for medical reasons. Maybe I could go to work with you in DC. What exactly do you do now and who are you working for?" he asked.

"I work for the CIG. It's a new group working foreign intelligence. I have no idea what I am supposed to do yet. I'll find out when I get down to Washington," she replied.

"I was in intelligence with the Marines in China. I even had an agent working for me. He was Chinese and hated the Japs. He would go to the docks and track incoming shipping. Just before we left China, he got caught by the Japs. I never did find out what happened to him. I'm sure the Japs tortured and killed him," he said sadly.

"What was his name?" She asked.

"His name was Vang Bo," he replied.

"Maybe the new Central Intelligence Group could use you. Looks like you have the experience," Caroline told him.

Michael Costigan Jr. handed over the keys to his prized 1921 Cadillac Suburban. He brought the car with him when he relocated to Havana to live. The car was garage kept, and Michael took care of it mechanically as well as inside and out. Every spot on the car glistened as if it were brand new.

He loved the car, but getting it back to New York would be an expense that was more than the car was worth. He had also sold his night club, "Danza Cubano." The only thing left to sell was his house. Over the years, he had made deposits to a bank account in the Cayman Islands. The profits from the club were deposited into a local Havana bank. The Cayman deposits were all large sums of cash he had brought with him when he left the states. A mob connected business partner ran a bootlegging operation from Cuba to Atlantic City. Michael and his partner were hauling in large amounts of money from the operation.

Michael was a homosexual and had a relationship with this man. The man's mob associates could not accept this from one of their own, so someone ordered a hit. The murder itself was a classic job, but the body was left in a most graphic and gruesome fashion. The mob was sending a message. It was a message that Michael understood.

His relationship with the victim became known to his family. As devote Irish Catholics, his life style was a source of unbearable shame to them, so he left his New York home.

His mother, Rose, eventually came to Havana to live with her son. She passed away in Cuba a few weeks ago. She made her son promise to bury her with her husband and youngest son Jimmy. Michael loved and respected his mother, and made all the arrangements. Everyone in the family and all of her friends attended the service.

The only people not attending was Mike and Susan McMullen. They were still in Hawaii but would be home in a few more weeks.

After his mother's funeral, Michael rented a small apartment on the 300 block of East 8th Street in the East Village. The area would soon be occupied by artists, musicians, and a new phenomenon, beatnik's.

Coffee houses would spring up and poets would join with the other artists. As the area developed the old slums of the lower east side gave way. This was the new area for the new post war crowd. As a homosexual, Michael would fit in here. Once again Michael found himself starting over.

The spring of 1946 seemed to offer a new beginning for everyone. So much had happened to them all over the years.

With the end of the war and a new year everything looked promising. They would all start new chapters of their lives, but one old curse would still be with them. It could never be broken or cured.

Their futures would insure the survival of this curse. It had infected the last generation, and would renew itself into the current generation. The prosperity of the current generation would suffer as well.

One of them was determined to find out why. Hope Costigan had learned about the affliction from her mother. The father she never knew had died as a result of it. Her Uncle was also a victim, and now her cousin whom she had grown up with, suffered as well. She was determined to find out why it existed and how to defeat it.

To defeat this, she would have to go into the belly of the beast. A student at NYU, she was immersed in her studies. Once she completed her college studies, she would enter the advanced nursing program at NYU. Then she would enlist in the Army, like her father. With so many young men home from Europe and the Pacific, she was sure that the military would care for these men. Her mother would be furious. What she did not know, was the embers of another two wars were slowly smoldering.

Hope Ann Costigan would find out for herself and bring home her own curse, a creature all her own. Hope was already attacking a full academic load of studies at NYU. Living with her mother's parents, in lower Manhattan she started her day early and returned home at the end of the day with her text books and notes from the day's lectures. Easter break was just a week away and today she was in a hurry to get back to her grandparent's apartment. Her Uncle Mike and Aunt Susan were arriving this afternoon.

They were not her real Aunt and Uncle. Mike McMullen was her father's best friend in the army during WWI. Their friendship continued after the war. After a flirtatious relationship with her mother, Colleen, he finally found a woman who could deal with him. Aunt Susan was a Navy nurse at the Brooklyn Naval Hospital.

She was in charge of a ward of men who had trouble readjusting to civilian life. The military called it 'Shell Shock.' Mike and Susan had spent the war years at Pearl Harbor. It was five long years since she had seen them and she was looking forward to seeing them again.

She loaded the basket attached to the back wheel and fender of her bicycle and headed south on Broadway. She reached the apartment and left her bike in the rear storage room behind the building's foyer and raced up the steps with an arm load of text books. Bursting into the door of the apartment she dropped the books and her notes scattered into the hallway. Her grandparents were sitting in the parlor with Susan. Mike was back in the kitchen making drinks. "Well, hello there, college girl. How are you?" Susan asked getting up to greet Hope.

"Oh, my God, Susan I'm so happy to see you," Hope exclaimed embracing Susan. The two women started to pick up the books and papers laughing over the mess.

Mike entered the parlor from the hallway leading to the kitchen. He set the tray with the drinks on the coffee table and watched them picking up the books and papers. Hope was in the door way with a bundle of loose papers in her arms when she saw him. She dropped the papers and started towards him when he held up his hand and ordered her to "Stop. Just stand there. My goodness, I can't believe it's you. You're, well… you're just as beautiful as your mother."

She could bear it no longer and raced into his arms saying. "Uncle Mike, I have missed you so much. I really like the cheesy mustache. It makes you look…"

"Old and as ornery as Yosemite Sam," Susan chimed in chuckling at her joke.

"Who is Yosemite Sam?" Hope asked.

"A short ornery old train robbing cartoon character in a Bugs Bunny show," Susan said. "Your Uncle Mike fell in love with the little guy and grew that stupid mustache."

"That's right, I am the rootiness, shootiness, meanest hombre in the west, darlin. Don't ever forget that," Mike declared.

Hope responded, "Well I think it's cute. My goodness, I really missed you two. I'm really happy to see you both. How does it feel to be back in New York?"

"The city has really changed quite a bit. In fact, the whole country seems different. There seems to be an air of anticipation here. Almost like everyone has been waiting to get out and do something," Susan said.

Sean Murphy added, "Well, the war is over now. People are getting back to their lives. All the boys are coming home from overseas."

"It will be like a new and fresh start for a lot of people," Mary Murphy added.

"So many of these boys coming home will have a hard time of it. That's what I want to study about. Susan, you've worked with these men.

That's what I want to do once I finish college and the nursing program.

I want to find out what happens to them and why they have such problems," Hope said excitedly.

"How are you going to do that?" Susan asked.

The room was quiet. Sean and Mary Murphy knew the answer and had kept the secret, hoping it would fade away. "When I have my RN and my Associates Degree, I'll join the Army," Hope said.

"Whoa, slow down honey. What are you going to do in the Army? Maybe you should consider a veteran's hospital," Mike added.

"I thought about that. It's not just the aftermath of the war experience that is causing the men to behave the way they do."

"It's the entire military experience. If I am going to study about these men, I need to be able to have some military background. Don't you think?" Hope answered.

"Does your mother approve of this?" Susan asked.

"My daughter doesn't know about the Army plans. She only knows Hope is studying for her degree and her RN," Sean said.

"If I know your mom, she will be very upset," Mike added.

"Everyone, please calm down. Hope has to finish her studies. Maybe some other means will present itself in the next few years. For now, let's just enjoy that we are all together again," Mary said.

"Mike, what are your plans?" Sean asked.

"First thing in the morning Susan and I will go to St. Patrick's to pay our respects to Rose. Then we can take the afternoon train down to Philly, after lunch," Mike said.

"I'm all caught up on my studies, but I do have a history paper to write over the break. I can't wait to see my mom and Dorothy," Hope said.

"How is your mom? Does she still work at city hall?" Susan asked.

"She is doing well, and yes she still has the same job. She is still working for Mr. Carter. He has really been a great boss. When Aunt Maggie was not well he allowed my mom to take a lot of time off to help take care of her."

"She really went through a rough time knowing Dylan was in a Japanese prison camp. Now, Aunt Maggie is dealing with his nightmares. They beat him, you know like an animal. He has scars all over his back. He had lost so much weight. You would not have known him. Aunt Maggie walked right past him in San Francisco when he came home. The Marines gave him a medical discharge" Hope explained.

"I'm looking forward to seeing him. It seems like it was just yesterday I was playing and wrestling with the little guy. Hard to imagine he is a grown man now and a war veteran at that. I have my demons and now he has his own to live with," Mike said.

"I can't wait to see Dorothy. We write each other often, she's in love with Villanova. It will be great to have everyone back together again. Oh, I almost forgot. Uncle Michael is relocating back here. He has left Havana and has an apartment in the East Village."

"We should try and see him before we leave for Philadelphia. Maybe we could try to go to his place when we go to St. Patrick's," Hope said.

"How far is it?" Susan asked.

"About ten blocks or so from St. Patrick's. He is on East 8th Street," Hope replied.

"OK, we can get a cab, your Aunt Susan and I are out of shape for walking in the city like we used too," Mike said.

Then Susan said, "Mike and I want to take you all out to dinner tonight. We will all be going to the restaurant where Mike and I met in Brooklyn. I just hope our waiter is still there."

That night they arrived on Court Street and entered the restaurant. The old Maître D, Sam was not there. A young and very pretty girl greeted them instead. "Table for five please. Is Franklin still working here?" He asked.

"Yes sir, he just started his shift. I can seat you in his section, if you would like," she answered.

"That would be fine," Mike replied.

They were seated and Susan was looking around for Franklin when she spotted him coming towards the table. On his tray was a single glass of bourbon, neat. Susan stood to greet him and after placing her drink on the table she embraced him warmly. "Franklin, it is so nice to see you again," she said.

"I am so pleased to see you too. I see you have brought some other fine people with you and a hobo from the train yards,"

Franklin said smiling broadly. "Behave yourself, you, old sailor. This pretty young lady is my niece and her grandparent's," Mike said standing.

"I am so pleased to meet you fine folks; my name is Franklin. If you need anything, you just let me know," Franklin declared.

"Miss Kennedy, who is this cantankerous old man at your table. Please inform him that pets of any kind are not permitted on the premises," Franklin said his smile still beaming.

"Franklin, it's no longer Miss Kennedy. I am now Mrs. Michael McMullen. You do remember my husband?" Susan said playing along.

"Well, now, I am so pleased this old dog soldier finally did the right thing for once in his miserable existence. But, I digress. The caterpillar on his lip will still have to wait outside," Franklin replied.

Susan smiled and laughed as the two men embraced as old friends. "Good to see you again old friend. You're not getting a tip and my fuzzy pal stays with me," Mike said.

Introductions were made around the table and Franklin took the drink orders. Returning with the drinks he took everyone's dinner order except Mike's. When the food arrived, Franklin placed a plate of meat loaf and mashed potatoes in front of Mike. It had always been his favorite meal.

When dinner was concluded, it gave everyone a chance to talk and catch up. Franklin had served in WWI in the Navy as a steward on the USS Oklahoma. The ship had been badly damaged in the Pearl Harbor attack and was to be decommissioned and sold for salvage. The news was well known but it was still sad for Franklin. "I'm just glad that she had two of my favorite people with her in the end. She was a fine ship, with a great history," Franklin said.

When the dinner was finished, Franklin escorted his old friends to the door. "Miss Hope, you stop in with your friends to see me now and then. I know college people are always hungry," Franklin said.

"I will Franklin, it was a pleasure to meet you," Hope replied.

"We will be in from time to time as well, Franklin," Sean Murphy said.

"It will be my pleasure to see you both again, Mr. Murphy," Franklin said shaking his hand.

Susan stepped forward and hugged Franklin and said, "Whenever I am in New York, I will be by. Take care of yourself."

Then Mike shook his hand and Franklin said, "I see there was no tip again with the check. You have not changed your ways. Shave off that squirrel's tail, it makes you look uglier than you already are."

"I got a tip for you. Don't let old cop's in here. They're lousy tippers," Mike joked. Mike and Susan hailed a cab and returned to their hotel. The Murphy's and Hope took a cab back to Tribeca.

The next morning Hope met them at St. Patrick's at the grave site of Michael, Rose and James Costigan. She remembered her grandmother, Rose. She never met her grandfather. Her own father, she was told never held her as a baby. He died shortly after her birth. Mike talked about his friend Jimmy, from WWI. Hope listened to the stories. Uncle Mike rarely talked about the war. As he spoke she noted the pained expression on his face. Even when he told the funny stories, his eyes still revealed a sadness. Aunt Susan never interrupted him and gave Hope a look that said let him talk. She seemed to know that these were things he needed to get out. Hope made mental notes to herself. She was learning that the best way to deal with men like her Uncle Mike was to let them speak. It was as if they were sweating out the pain in their hearts. The things they saw and did stayed with them. Hidden deep inside of them as much as they wanted or tried to bury the pain, it kept coming back. It was something that had to come out no matter how hard they tried to keep it away.

They stayed for about an hour. Hope had heard many times, the story of when her Uncle Mike had first met her grandmother, Rose. He recalled that day when speaking of her. They laughed at the absurdity. All of five feet tall and weighing a hundred pounds, she had punched the big young man in her doorway. Her father Jimmy, hiding behind the door laughing at his predicament.

They took a cab to the 8th Street address Hope had for her Uncle Michael. With no way to alert him they would be there, they found no response at Michael's door. Left with no options they got another cab to the train station and started for Philadelphia.

Susan soon fell asleep to the rocking of the train and this gave Hope an opportunity to speak with her uncle. "Uncle Mike, I've heard all the stories about my dad, before and after the war. You knew him in France. What was he like?" Hope asked.

Mike answered, "He was very easy going. It was hard to get him to lose his temper. We had another buddy, his name was Tom O'Brian. Tom and I would argue over the Giants and the Dodgers. Your dad would bait us with stories about the Yankees. Turns out he knew more than we did. Your dad was generous to a fault. He would help anyone. Tommy and I would play practical jokes on each other. Your dad always got punished with us because we were all friends. He was a good soldier too. He would tell us stories about your mom. He really did love her. She was all he ever talked about. He was so proud of his brother. He enlisted you know to save your Uncle Michael from the draft. I miss him. After he came home he became different."

"What happened to him?" Hope pursued.

"Your dad was wounded in one of the attacks. Tommy was listed as missing. Your dad got separated from his us and had to find his way back to our lines in the dark. I never saw him again after that attack. I thought he and Tommy were both dead. I found out later that your dad was in the hospital and that Tommy had been killed. War changes a man. The things you see and do, affect you for the rest of your life. It's something no one ever forgets. Your dad was no different than anyone else.

He lived with his own demons and it hurt him inside. It changed him. It changed us all," Mike said sadly.

"Was he brave, in the war?" Hope asked.

"Oh, yes, your dad was a crack shot too. Everyone respected him. Our platoon sergeant, would always have him up front to pick off German officers. He took out a German machine gun position by himself, with only two shots," Mike said.

"But, what was he like, just every day?" Hope asked him.

"I don't understand. What do you mean every day?" Mike inquired.

"You, know, what was he like when there was no fighting?" Hope continued.

"Well, it's kind of hard to answer. I don't remember the everyday stuff. It was boring. Just sitting around waiting, or cleaning weapons. We filled sandbags, dug foxholes. I really only remember the bad times.

Or the fun times we had. I remember I painted the tip of Tommy's nose red on the ship going over. We got in trouble for a lot of goofy things. Most of that was me and Tommy. Your dad was guilty by association. He took it all as good fun. We took some prisoners back to headquarters and got to spend a night behind the lines. We ate until we were all sick. Your dad was just a normal guy. We were buddies," Mike told her.

Susan woke when the train bounced over some track junctions. "How much further to go?" Susan asked.

"We just left Trenton, I guess about an hour to go," Mike answered.

Mike was right, they arrived at 30th Street Station an hour later and took a cab to the Brogans home on Olive Street. The next round of long awaited reunions was about to begin. The Brogan's had been called and were expecting the long-awaited arrival of Mike and Susan. It had been five long years since they all had seen each other. The war kept them apart, but it was now over and the spring of 1946 was to be the start of new experiences for all of them.

17

CHAPTER 2
NEW PLANS

Maggie was wrapping up her dinner preparations assisted by her mother Margaret and Colleen. Mike and Susan were returning from New York with Colleen's, daughter Hope. Hope was the first one in the door followed by Susan and then Mike. The reunion was loud and animated. Tears were shed, but the most noticeable part was Maggie's reaction to Mike's moustache. "Oh, my God, what is that? She cried.

Mike was clearly uncomfortable now and his mother was pulling at the ends of it. Margaret cried, "Susan, how could you allow this. He looks so foolish, like he has two squirrels up his nose. Joseph say something."

"What do you want me to say? He's a grown man with a caterpillar on his face," his father replied laughing.

"You know I think it has potential. Susan, I believe we can fix that thing and make it more presentable," Collen added.

Susan replied, "What do you have in mind?"

"I believe with a little trimming…it might just look good on him," Colleen said.

"Don't be silly dear. What could you possibly do with that… that furry thing?" Margaret retorted.

"Well, whatever we decide to do it will have to wait until after dinner," Colleen remarked.

"Hey, don't I get a say in this?" Mike asked nervously.

"NO," all the women replied.

Kevin and Joseph, laughing at Mike's situation, tried to encourage him.

"Don't worry old man, we are on your side in this. We men have to stick together. Kevin and I will be right here, to hold you down," his father laughed.

"Everybody sit and eat, enough of this foolishness," Margaret declared.

"Wait, where is Dorothy and Dylan?" Hope asked.

Maggie replied, "Dylan is in Washington, looking at a new job. He will be home tomorrow. Dorothy won't be home for another two hours."

Everyone sat and enjoyed their first meal together in years. When dinner was finished, the women cleaned up and the men retired to the parlor for coffee and cigars. Kevin asked Mike, "What are your plans?"

"Tomorrow, Susan and I will look into a furnished apartment at that new building on the Parkway, 2601. Once that is done we want to look at homes at the Jersey shore. We both like living near the water. We had a great little cabin on the bay overlooking Pearl Harbor," Mike replied.

"You watched the attack, as it happened, according to your letters. That must have been rough," his father said.

"I thought I had lost Susan. Those were some bad days," Mike replied.

"The war is over now son. We can all try to get back to our normal lives again," Mike's father said.

Dorothy came home from school and she and Hope made a show of their reunion. The girls were very close and had not seen each other in months. Dorothy was excited to see Mike and Susan as well.

Once the greetings were finished the two girls bounded up the stairs to Dorothy's room. Both girls were eager to catch up. They talked about school, the courses they were taking and of course boys. "So, what's new and exciting in your life?" Dorothy asked.

"Nothing, just working hard on my studies. My days are full with lectures and other class work. Staying with my grandparents has been great. They are very supportive, and the city is wonderful," Hope replied.

"That's good. Anybody special in your life?" Dorothy asked.

"Who has time for boys. A lot of the boys I see in class are really returning from the war. They take advantage of their benefits under the GI Bill. They seem to be detached and dedicated to their studies. Some are there just chasing girls. I'm steering clear of dating, I just don't have the time," Hope answered. "Are you dating anyone?" Hope asked.

"I'm dating anything that moves. Even though Villanova is a Catholic University, there is plenty to do socially," Dorothy replied.

"How are your courses doing?" Hope asked.

"I do alright. I have a B average for now. I am really just enjoying the whole college experience. There always seems to be a party somewhere. A lot of the other students live off campus. The fraternity parties are the best. I'm getting plenty of chances to fool around," Dorothy replied naughtily.

"Oh really. You haven't done it yet, have you?" Hope asked with anticipation.

"No silly, I want my husband to be my first. But that doesn't mean I can't have a little fun. I learned that guys are always after one thing. So, the trick is to just get them off. The quickest way is to just go down on them. Let them get all worked up and play with your sweater puppies. Then once they get all moaning and try to get to your pants, drop down and blow them," Dorothy replied excitedly.

"DOROTHY! You really do that? What's it like? Sounds kind of... I don't know icky! What do you do when they finish?" Hope asked bewildered.

"Remember how when we were with boys and we gave them hand jobs? You had to keep a handkerchief or tissues with you. Even then it was still kind of messy. This way you just swallow and it's over."

"The first couple of times I spit it out. But then I thought, what the hell, gulp gulp." Dorothy declared giggling.

"Oh, my God, I... Dorothy, you're so bad," Hope said.

"It's really no big deal. Quick and easy. Then you can just spend the rest of the night not having to worry about getting overcome with desire, and doing something you will regret," Dorothy said amused.

"That is always something I found was so hard. I used to get all worked up with Bobby. You told me that you and Tom used to get pretty far. Remember that night I slept over and we masturbated? You were moaning so loud, I thought your mom was going to catch us," Hope said.

"That was the first time I ever came. I once let this guy finger me, and I got off," Dorothy said dreamily.

"I've done that with Bobby, but never got off. Oh, well, I'm just too busy to think about that stuff. I'm not sure if I could ever blow a guy. Maybe if we were really in love, or getting married," Hope said.

"Trust me, honey once you get past the thought of it being icky, you'll do it to save your virginity," Dorothy said.

Downstairs, Mike's mother came into the parlor and ordered him to sit on a dining room chair. Then she wrapped a towel around his neck as Maggie, Colleen and Susan approached him with a razor and scissors. Kevin and his father, Joe were encouraging him, yet at the same time laughing at his dilemma. The women were intent on trimming his overgrown mustache. "Hold still, Michael," his mother commanded as she cut off the two ends of the extended handlebars. Joe and Kevin cheered while Mike sat in the chair embarrassed. "How should we do the rest of it?" Colleen asked.

"Make it look like Hitler," Kevin suggested.

"NO, now hold on," Mike protested.

"Sit still your big baby," Susan said as she used a comb and the scissors to trim it down. Colleen added, "That's good Susan thin it out a little more."

When Susan finished, the four women stood back eyeing their work. "You know he doesn't look half bad now.

Kevin and Joe were still laughing and applauding their work. "Should we leave it like that or do you think maybe we could go for the Clark Gable look?" Susan asked.

"If you ask me, take it all off," Margaret declared.

"I think it looks pretty good," Maggie added.

"I like it too," Colleen said.

"Mike, you look so handsome and sophisticated," Kevin taunted.

"Aw, shut up. You guys were no help. What was all that sticking together stuff. You two left me high and dry," Mike said dejected.

"Go look in the mirror, Mike. I really do like it now," Susan told him.

Mike got up and looked in the mirror. The once bushy and long mustache that he had grown and nurtured was now trimmed down to almost nothing. The mustache covered his upper lip with closely cropped but even hairs and ended at the corners of his mouth. He had to admit it did look better.

But he was not going to admit it. "It took me a long time to get it just right. Look at what you all did to it," he said sadly.

"Come sit down, sweetheart. I'll make you a fresh drink," Susan said.

Reluctantly, he sat back down and accepted the fresh drink. "Here's to Yosemite Sam, I'm going to miss him" he toasted. "To Sam, everyone replied laughing.

At the end of the evening Mike and Susan were going back to their hotel. Mikes parents walked with Colleen and Hope as far as Parrish Street and then they split up. Walking on Parrish Street Hope, asked Colleen, "Mom, when was the first time you did it with Dad?" Colleen stopped walking stunned by the question. "Why...have you?" Colleen let the question hang there. They started walking again.

"No, mother I am still a virgin. To answer the next question, I know you will ask, no I'm not seeing anyone. I don't have the time for boys. I'm just curious, that's all," Hope stated.

"Why?" Colleen asked.

"Like I said, I'm only curious." Were you married for the first time with Dad?" Hope inquired, pressing the issue.

"Your father and I were very much in love. I knew that I wanted my first time to be with your Dad. He was going to France. I knew that it was possible that I might not ever see him again. So, before he left we made love together. Funny, I've had this same conversation with your grandmother. Wait, you were talking with Dorothy. Has she...?" Colleen stopped walking again.

Hope laughed and said, "Will you please keep walking. No, Dorothy is still a virgin as well. Besides, that would really be none of your business."

"You're right. It is none of my business. I know you two are close and most likely share everything. Just that... you know you can come and talk to me too. I love you honey, and I will always be there for you," Colleen told her daughter.

Hope put her arm around her mother's arm and said, "I know, don't worry, and I love you too. I promise if and when I do anything I'll tell you. Every graphic detail."

"Oh, good God, spare me the details," her mother responded. Hope laughed as they came to 29th Street. It was late and the streets were deserted.

Crossing over 29th Street they encountered a Negro man walking north. He tipped his hat and said, "Good evening, ladies."

"Good evening," Colleen responded.

They continued towards the house and unlocked the door to go inside.

Hope was looking forward to sleeping in her own bed that night.

The next day Mike and Susan were successful in renting a small one bedroom furnished apartment at 2601 Parkway. Their next task was to buy a car. They visited the Scott Smith Cadillac dealership at Broad and Ridge. They picked out a used 1940 Ford De Luxe convertible. It had a saddle brown leather interior and canvas top. The boot for the top when it was down being missing wasn't an issue for them. Susan liked the garnet color which was a deep marron. The car had 15000 miles on it and was owned by a pilot who had been killed over Germany. It reminded them of the old Ford they had in Hawaii, but this car was in much better shape. They paid $550 for it and had 4 new tires installed. They were now settled into an apartment and had their own mobility. The next project was to find a permanent home on the New Jersey shore. They made plans to drive down on Sunday morning. It was getting warm enough to drive with the top down. So, they did. They took a short drive up and down the East and West river drives enjoying the new car and the spring weather. After their drive, they went to Kevin and Maggie's to show off the new wheels. Dorothy was out on the front steps reading a text book when they drove up. "Wow, fancy new wheels," Dorothy remarked. Maggie heard her from the parlor and went outside and commented on the new car. "Oh, it's so cute, I love it," she cried.

"It's not cute. It's stylish," Mike defended.

"Dylan is in the back yard, Mike. He'll be thrilled to see you," Maggie offered.

Mike went inside and passed through the house spotting his nephew sitting in a chair smoking a cigar. He stepped into the yard looking his nephew over. He had still not regained all his weight. He was keeping a steady 180 pounds. What disturbed Mike was how old he looked?

He looked ten years older than his real age of twenty-seven. "Hey kid, how the hell are you?" Mike asked as Dylan stood to greet him.

"Uncle Mike, I'm ok. You look great. I heard about the mustache. They ganged up on you," Dylan said embracing his uncle.

"One thing I've learned about women kid, is that they're always right. You look a little thinner but no worse for wear. What's with the stick?" Mike asked.

"I got this from some of my buddies in Luzon. It helped me get around when my foot was broken. I've had it ever since. Where is Susan?"

Dylan asked.

"Right here handsome. Come over here and give me a hug," Susan said coming out to the yard. "Wow, you look great. I think you have gotten prettier over the years," Dylan flirted.

"Don't go and try to sweet talk me young man. Dylan, I'm so happy to see you again," Susan said.

Maggie and Dorothy brought out some of the kitchen chairs so they could all sit and talk. Maggie also brought out some ice tea and a couple of beers for the men. "Dylan, tell everyone about your job interview in Washington," Maggie said with some excitement.

"Yeah, it went great. I got the job. I start the first of next month. I get to go to Maryland for my training. I really think I'm going to like it," Dylan said.

"Where in Maryland? What kind of job did you get?" Mike asked.

"I will be working for the Central Intelligence Group. After my training, I will go overseas and be assigned to a US Embassy. The job is very much like the one I had in the Marines, so I'm a perfect fit," Dylan replied proudly.

"Do you know what embassy they will send you to?" Susan asked.

Dylan replied, "I have no idea. Based on my previous experience, I'm gonna guess the Far East again. Lots of stuff happening in Korea and French Indo-China."

"Great, I just get him home and he's off to the other side of the world again," Maggie protested.

"I know Mom, but this time there is no war. I'll be at an embassy, and most likely living on the grounds. You can come and visit," Dylan added.

You two are lucky. You don't have any children to worry over," Maggie said to Mike and Susan.

"Oh, I don't know, I'm thinking a girl," Susan said humorously.

"What, what the hell are we… are you… when were you gonna tell me?"

Mike blurted.

"Relax, dopey. I'm talking about a dog. You know once we get settled into the new house at the shore," Susan laughed.

"Oh, for Christ's sake, you scared the hell out of me," Mike exclaimed.

Maggie scolded her little brother, "And what is wrong with having children? The whole world does not revolve around you, you know. Some of us like the idea of a family."

Mike started to reply before Maggie cut him off, "But, you just said…"

"I know what I just said your big goof. Don't you go telling me what I said,"

Dylan leaned towards his uncle and whispered in his ear, "Remember what you said about women a few minutes ago."

"I'll have you know that a lot of people have families and sacrifice everything for their children," Maggie continued not noticing Dylan whispering in his uncle's ear. Susan and Dorothy grinned at each other enjoying Mikes discomfort. Mike finished his beer and said, "I need something stronger."

"Oh, sure, drown your troubles in alcohol," Maggie continued.

"Mom, calm down. Are you all right.?" Dorothy asked.

"Yes, I'm fine," Maggie said getting up to go back in the house.

"She's upset with me. Mom does not like the idea of me going back overseas. That won't happen for another year or so but, I guess she is still upset about the war," Dylan said.

"I would say she has a point. For years, she had no news. She did not know if you were alive or dead. She went through a lot Dylan. Try to be closer to her as much as you can," Susan offered.

"I know, and I will. But like I said, even if there is to be an overseas posting it's more than a year away," Dylan replied.

"Do you get any kind of travel allowance?" Mike asked.

Dylan answered, "I really don't know. I'll find out more information once I get down to Maryland."

Mike asked, "How long will you be in Maryland?"

"Just a couple of days. Some type of orientation. After that the real training will begin," Dylan replied.

Susan asked, "How long will the actual training be, and will it be in Maryland too?"

"I'm not real sure. The orientation is supposed to clear up all the foggy details," Dylan answered.

Mike and Susan left to unpack some things and get settled into the new apartment. Dorothy stayed with Dylan in the yard while her Mom prepared dinner. Her father came home a while later and noticed that Maggie was upset. "Something bothering you?" He asked.

"It's Dylan. He got the job he applied for in Washington. He is going overseas again. Why is he doing this? He's only been home for a year and now he's off again. I don't know if I can do it all over again," she started to cry but composed herself.

"Maggie, you have got to understand. He's a grown man now. If he had stayed in the Marine's, he could be sent anywhere. This is his life now. We have to let him live it. Maybe he will go far away. But, the war is over. He will not be in danger anymore," Kevin consoled her.

"I know. I know. Go and talk with him. He's anxious to see you. He and Dorothy are in the yard," Maggie told him.

Kevin hugged his wife, and took three Ortliebs out of the ice box. He uncapped the bottles handing one to Dorothy and Dylan. "I hear congratulations are in order," Kevin stated.

"Yes sir, got the job. Going to Maryland for a couple of days the first of the month," Dylan replied proudly.

"Fill me in on the details," Kevin said.

Michael Costigan Jr. had broken all ties to his business and homes in Havana. He was back in New York for good. He walked around the neighborhood to get a feel for it. Every neighborhood in New York had its own culture and personality. The city was diverse. His apartment on East 8th Street was a few doors from Avenue B. Across the avenue was Thompkins Square Park. He made a point to get to know the beat cops.

A little advice from Mike McMullen. Sitting on his stoop he would engage the policemen in conversation. Before long all of the cops assigned to walk a beat knew that they could use a bathroom, or get a cup of coffee or a cool drink at Michaels door. Michael looked out for them, they looked after Michael. He tried some of the cafés and restaurants and picked his favorites. It was spring in New York. The days were warm and the nights cool. With the war over and many of the men returning home, housing was in great demand. Michael was very comfortable financially and could buy a house or even a building. Instead he chose the care free life of renting an apartment.

This gave him the ability to move whenever he wanted and helped to conserve his wealth. After a week or so he walked back to the Tribeca section of the city and paid a visit to Colleen's parents. They were thrilled to see him. He and the Murphy's exchanged all the news about everyone.

Unfortunately, Hope was at class at NYU, so he missed her. He was happy to hear that Mike and Susan had returned from Hawaii and thought about making plans to see them soon. After his visit, he walked back home and sat in the park.

Surrounded by the trees and the buildings around the park, Michael felt alone and isolated. He missed his mother. He knew people in the city before he lived in Havana but that was more than ten years ago. He had no need or desire to work.

He knew he had to get something in his life or he would fall into a deep depression. In Havana, he would lounge on the beach during the day, and work at the club at night.

He watched a young man painting, and walked over to him and introduced himself. The younger man's name was Tom Brady. He was a student at Coopers Union School of Art located just three blocks west at 3rd Avenue and Seventh Street. He was in his second year of school. His painting almost completed was an abstract of a park bench and tree. They talked about the painting and the school.

Tom worked as they talked and Michael found him to be friendly and outgoing. Michael learned that Tom came to the park often after classes and spent his time either painting or sketching.

Tom showed some of his drawings to Michael, and he saw that Tom was quite talented. He mentioned that he had a niece who was also very talented. He remembered the sketch she had done for Dylan in Havana. Tom was about the same age as Hope. Michael noted that Tom did not seem to be interested in talking about Hope. Michael thought to himself, that maybe he had a girl friend or was dedicated to his studies.

Tom finished the painting and offered it to Michael, who was pleased to have it. He had just the spot for it in his apartment. The two parted ways and Michael returned to his apartment and promptly hung the painting in the parlor. He thought it looked great, but it just needed a frame. Something he thought he would have to look into.

He was not lonely but he found himself excited about this talented young man. He decided that pursuing a relationship with him was desirable. Michael was confused. He was not sure of Tom's sexual leanings. Some of the ways he carried himself and his soft-spoken voice led Michael to think he might be a homosexual.

With no immediate plans, Michael was free to be in the park any afternoon. He decided that he would visit the park in hope of seeing Tom again.

He arranged his very flexible schedule to insure he was in the park each day in the mid-afternoon. Before long the two men became friends.

Michael observed Tom looking for clues about this handsome young man's preferences. He also noted that when pretty girls passed them as they walked by that Tom would notice them. Sometimes he would make a comment. Her hair was too long or she should wear heels to make herself taller. Sometimes the comments would be sexual in nature. He especially liked to comment on a girl's breasts.

Michael would watch him paint or draw. Before long they were having coffee or drinks in any of the small coffee shops or bars around the park.

As the two men became more comfortable around each other, Michael noticed that Tom also watched some of the younger men and boys in the park. Tom cleared the air one day by mentioning a couple he saw. "I could enjoy those two between the sheets," he said.

Michael somewhat surprised replied, "You mean both of them at once?"

"Sure, why not. Life has to be explored. We are all born with a clean canvas. What we leave on the canvas is up to us, and those who want to make their impressions with us."

Eventually Michael invited him home for dinner. Michael was a decent cook and after broiled salmon and several bottles of wine the two men became intimate.

CHAPTER 3

INDEPENDENCE

Emerging from the cave, Vang Bo sat in the morning sun on an old tree stump. Ho Chi Minh and the Viet Minh had seized control of the northern part of Vietnam after the Japanese deposed all French Colonial rule over Vietnam in March of 1945. Hidden on a hilltop overlooking an airfield at Kien An, was a small maintenance installation. The primary job for Vang and his unit was the repair of small arms captured from the French or the Japanese. The hill was 140 meters high and covered in tall grass and scrubs. A few huts were on top of the hill but served no purpose except for shelter from the sun and rain. The real facility for his unit was underground. The old cave entrance had been dug out and there was a large shop area built into the mountain. The large room was reinforced with timbers and had electricity provided by a generator hidden in one of the huts. It was not bomb proof, but it had provided cover from the prying eyes of Japanese aircraft. Now they hid from the French.

The conference in Potsdam last July of 1945 split the country in two. The arrival of British and French troops in the south took control of those regions while here in the northern section the Viet Minh under Ho Chi Minh and the Democratic Republic of

Vietnam had control of Hanoi, and the surrounding provinces. Ho Chi Minh held negotiations with the French over the disposition of Southern Vietnam but the talks failed. In just a few more weeks the French and the new independent state of North Vietnam would be at war. The Viet Minh had been making preparations for months after the August Revolution of 1945. A letter from Ho Chi Minh in February of 1946 to President Harry Truman begging for US intervention was ignored setting the stage for the French War in December of 1946.

On this morning, his old friend Nguyen Hung, who had befriended him after his escape from the Japanese came for a visit. Hung was a small man and looked much older than his forty years. He was very intelligent and spoke Chinese, English, French and some Japanese. Bo had learned Vietnamese from this man and a little French during the war years. The two men had not seen each other since the August Revolution. "It is good to see you again my friend. How have you been?" Hung asked.

"My health has been good. I don't like the cave room. It is very damp inside. My only pleasure is to warm myself each morning in the sunlight. I sit here and drink my tea, preparing myself for a new day," Bo replied.

"Yes, the sun rises each day to warm mother earth, bringing new life and nourishment to all living things. New beginnings start with each new dawn. That is why I am here. You and I will leave today for Hanoi. You have other talents to be utilized in our struggles with the French. Soon we will be at war again," Hung said.

"From what you taught me, your people have been at war for years. When will it all end?" Bo asked.

"Our struggle will be over, but it will take many years. We have a grip on our freedom and independence here in the North. We will not let that go."

"The French and their western allies will have to be pushed out of the South. Our people in the South have lost their way.

They have been corrupted by western colonialism. This is system-ic in the larger cities, like Saigon, Hue, and Da Nang. The real Vietnamese people that live in the country have no interest in who governs them. They are already free and independent. Their families have lived in the same villages for centuries. They plow their fields, feed their families and worship their ancestors. This is their way of life. The colonist steals the resources produced by the labor of the people. They get little in return. Once we unify all of Vietnam all will be peaceful and prosperous," Hung stated.

"What would I do in Hanoi?" Bo asked.

"You told me that when the Japanese captured you, that you were giving military information to the American Marines. How did you do this?" Hung asked him.

"I would go to the docks. I would make note of the name of ships and what they carried. How many trucks. How many troops," Bo replied?

"This is what you will do for us," Hung told him handing him an envelope.

Inside the envelope was a worn Chinese Passport with his name and home city of Changchun. There were also other docu-ments, all listing him as Vang Bo. He looked at his old friend, a hundred questions coming to him at once. "You are, Vang Bo. A citizen of China from Changchun City. You are a professional machinist. You are employed by the province of Long Khanh, to teach the trade in the school in Dinh Quan. Your wife and chil-dren died at the hand of the Japanese in the war. As you can see you have been in Vietnam for many years. All of this information is verifiable, because it is true.

Your students will be young men wishing to be machinist. Some of them will be NLF. They will be your agents. They will advise you of French troop movements. You will give this infor-mation to your case officer. You will be seeing him in Hanoi. You remember Duy Minh?" Hung asked him.

"Yes, of course. He was the one who brought me to you," Bo answered.

"He will be your case officer. All of this will be explained to you by Minh when you travel south. Finish your tea. Take with you any personal items you want to keep. Everything else will be provided to you in Hanoi," Hung stated.

He went into the cave and packed a small canvas bag with the few books he cherished. He packed a clean shirt and pants and went outside to his friend. Together they walked down the hill where there was awaiting Citroen. The drive took almost three hours. It gave the two men time to talk of other things, besides Bo's new assignment. Bo hated the Japanese for what they did to his family. He also hated the French. The French government in Vietnam capitulated to the Japanese. Bo believed the French were spineless men with no moral character. French government officials in Vietnam were powerless to do anything without the permission of the Japanese during the war. They were simply puppets that seized power again when the Japanese surrendered to the allies. The Vietnamese gave him food, clothing, and medical care. He was as devoted to their cause as they were. Someday he hoped to return to China and find out what had happened to his twin daughters. He knew his wife was dead. Major Sasaki had shown him the pictures of her body.

Sasaki was with the Kempeitai (Japanese Secret Military Police). Sasaki was the one who brought him to China. After his escape from the Japanese base where he was kept, he was brought to a secret camp of the Viet Minh. It was here he met both Minh and Hung. They provided him with everything he needed, all they asked from him was his ability to repair the rifles and pistols they had that needed repair. Some of the weapons he was able to repair, others would need to be repaired in a proper machine shop. These weapons were kept for spare parts. He worked at his craft to the best of his ability despite the fact he did not have the proper tools or machines. Hung talked with him for hours at a time and taught him Vietnamese and some French.

He was a free man and he had a purpose in his life. The Viet Minh treated him as one of their own and their desire for independence and control over their own country was something he shared.

The re-union with Minh was like the greeting of two brothers who had been separated for some time. He liked Minh very much. Minh was a dependable and dedicated soldier. He was calm in situations and had a clear head. He had been in charge of a squad of other men who raided Japanese bases and convoys. They also ambushed Japanese patrols during the war. They showed no mercy to the enemy and always returned with a new cache of weapons. Minh helped him with his Vietnamese during the war years, and the two men became good friends. Minh gave him a suitcase which Bo filled with new clothes. He was also provided toiletry items and he found his books fit into the suitcase as well. The three men would spend a week in Hanoi getting briefings on French troop units and command structures. The briefings were conducted by members of the DEER Team commanded by Major Allison Thomas of the American OSS. Thomas and a dozen other team members had parachuted into North Vietnam in July of 1945. They had trained the Viet Minh in tactics and military intelligence. With war on the near horizon with the French to liberate South Vietnam, the People's Army of Vietnam (PAVN) was in it's infancy. Vang Bo was not a member of the Communist Party. Now he was and an intelligence operative of the Viet Minh.

Bo did not like communist in general but the new leader of North Vietnam, Ho Chi Minh seemed to have the backing of the American government.

Ho Chi Minh had photographs taken of him and other Viet Minh officials with American officers including General Claire Lee Cheenault of the now famous 'Flying Tigers'. The Viet Minh had been instrumental in the recovery of Allied pilots who had been shot down during the war. When Ho declared absolute independence for Vietnam he quoted passages from the American Declaration of Independence.

Hung said his goodbyes and wished them both well. It would be many years before they saw each other again. Minh and Bo would travel back to Haiphong and board a modified fishing boat that would take them south to Cam Ranh Bay. From there they would travel by bus and on foot to Dinh Quan, some seventy-five miles north east of Saigon.

Once they arrived they were met by the local communist cadre and taken to a house on the outskirts of the town. This was to be Bo's new home. Located on QL20 at the intersection of Gia Canh Road the home was located on the southwest corner. It was modest in size but of good construction. Minh would live eight miles to the northeast in the smaller village of Xa Phu Lam. The school that Bo would be teaching was just half mile up the road from Bo's home. Bo was shown two photographs of students who would be attending his class. These two were his agents who would give him their reports of troop movements in the area. Bo would then relay the information to Minh. The two men would meet once per week at a local café. A local pedal cab driver would introduce himself to the men by using his code name of Osprey. He would relay any priority reports to each of them as needed. In turn, they were each assigned a code name while they were in Hanoi. Known only to them and their superiors in Hanoi they would only use them in an emergency. For this operation, they would be using new code names known only to them the two students, the pedal cab driver and the cadre member. Use of the code name in a sentence would identify them. Bo selected 'Gayal' as his code name. A large wild water buffalo that weighs in excess of a ton and travels in herds across the central highlands. Minh selected 'Bishop' as his code name.

Bo might say to Osprey, "I want to see a bishop." This would mean he had hot new information that needed to be delivered. Bo had a new purpose and was anxious to begin his new role. He slept well in his new home, and woke early and walked to the school.

Congress passed the National Security Act of 1947. It was signed into law by President Harry Truman. Within its provisions was the creation of the Central Intelligence Agency as part of the National Security Council. The existing Central Intelligence Group was disbanded and the new agency took its place. Dylan and Caroline were now part of the new agency. They had both finished a year of training under the supervision of the old OSS and CIG. Housed in Bethesda Maryland, the training took place in location designated only as Area 'F'. During the course of that year they saw little of each other. Even when they did cross paths it was only for minutes at a time.

Caroline was assigned to a nondescript office outside of Washington in Roslyn Virginia. As an analyst, her primary duties were the breakdown of intelligence reports received from around the world. Because of her background in Europe, the UK and France she was assigned to the western European group. Intelligence reports that were shared by the British SIS, (Special Intelligence Section) MI6, (Military Section 6) and the French SDECE, (Foreign Documentation and Counter-Espionage Service) crossed her desk on a regular basis. All of this information was shared. British and French agencies would hold back on their secrets to protect their own interests. The US would do the same once they developed their own agents and case officers to process their own intelligence.

New employees came into the office on a regular basis. These employees were recruited from around the country from colleges and universities. Some of these people had military backgrounds and had served in the war. Secrecy was the one doctrine they all lived by. Employees were told to refrain from using the word agency as their place of employment.

Instead, they were encouraged to use the word company. She was one of four section managers. Her immediate supervisor was Kevin Murray, a discharged Army Air Corp Colonel, who served as a P-38 Lightning pilot.

Murray had spent the war years flying over the UK, France, Belgium and Germany taking reconnaissance pictures. He had the ability to look at high altitude photographs and be able to identify the area in any of these countries. He was of average height and build with dark hair just starting to gray at the temples. He was handsome and looked distinguished. He was also a flirt. Caroline thought he was cocky, but he was still her boss.

She had an apartment that she shared with one of the other women, Barbara Graham. Barbara was also a section manager and worked another shift. The apartment was in Roslyn, Virginia just outside of Washington. The apartment and the office were in walking distance of each other. Barbara was younger, just twenty-four years old. She was a graduate of Princeton with a major in history. She also spoke French. They became friends but saw little of each other during the week. They did share their days off together, Sunday and Monday. Caroline worked Tuesday to Saturday and Barbara worked the same days, but Caroline had the day shift and Barbara worked the second shift. Barbara had lived in Mooretown, NJ and had done well in school. Her father was a doctor with a successful practice in town. Because Caroline would spend her summers with her aunt and uncle in Maple Shade, NJ both women had a connection. They were familiar with the same movie theaters, lakes and playgrounds.

On Sundays both women would sightsee in Washington. Neither of the women was involved romantically, although there were plenty of young men posted to Fort Meyer, not far from the office and their apartment. Both women were focused on their work and knew that what they were doing was important. The work itself was tedious. Because this new agency was just starting, they had to improvise and learned things as they went along.

The French had an uprising in Indo-China. The SDECE was providing reports about communist expansion and military activities in the northern provinces of Vietnam now declared as independent from French rule.

By the end of the year, war would break out, as the French made an attempt to stop the insurrection from invading the southern part of Vietnam.

Dylan Brogan stood between the close walls of his firing position at the range. Located in Bethesda Maryland in a place known only as Area 'F'. He was taking his last pistol qualification. He had already qualified with other weapons but today he was demonstrating his proficiency with the Soviet Tokarev TT-33. He had also trained with other Soviet weapons. The thought of going to Russia especially in the winter was not appealing to him. Why there was so much emphasis on the Soviets was frustrating. He was hoping for a far east posting in a warm climate. After firing his last magazine, he was given his scores. He rated as an expert with most of the weapons he trained with and the Tokarev was no exception.

Returning to his room in an old apartment house he was in a standby state to see where he was to be posted. He would spend the next week waiting for orders and they finally came on a Saturday morning. He learned that he was to report to the embassy in Manila. He was going back to the Philippines. At first, he was excited, but then the thought of returning to a place where he and many of his friends had suffered so much worried him. Still it was a warm climate and he was familiar with the people and the country. The people of the Philippines were very appreciative of the Americans.

He was given train tickets from Philadelphia to San Francisco. Once there he would travel by commercial air to Hawaii. Military transport would then take him from Henderson Field to Manila. He had a two week leave before he was due to leave. Packing his bags, he was thinking of his mother. She was sure to be concerned with his orders. He knew that the place he was going was no longer a threat, but trying to convince his mother was going to be a task. Leaving the billet, he signed out and took a cab into Washington to get a train to Philadelphia.

He also had left a message for Caroline to contact him at his home. The train ride home gave him time to think. He was starting out on his new life. He was returning to a place where his old life would certainly remind him of the suffering and death endured by him and the men he had served with. The old life never seemed to leave him. It was always there.

Arriving at 30th Street Station in Philadelphia, he took a cab home to Olive Street. His mother and sister were home and about to order their Saturday night dinner from the local cheese steak and hoagie shop. When he walked in the door he was greeted warmly. "We were just about to order sandwiches, what do you want?" His sister asked.

"Italian hoagie with oil, and peppers," he replied.

"They let you go for the weekend again?" his mother asked.

"Actually, I'm here for two weeks. I got my orders. I'm on leave before I go back to Manila," Dylan said.

"Oh, dear God, after all you have been through in that country. Why on heavens earth would they send you back there?" Maggie asked.

"Experience mom. I know the country and the people. The Philippines are independent now. The country is trying to rebuild itself with our help. I'll get four weeks leave every year. The war is over, there is nothing to worry about. This is who I am, Mom, this is what I do," Dylan replied.

"Sounds exotic to me," Dorothy exclaimed.

"It is, and the people love Americans. I thought about it on the train up here. I kind of go back to my old life and start a new one in the same place. Maybe it will help me to be my old self again," Dylan said.

"I just wish it wasn't so far away. I was hoping they would keep you in Washington, like Caroline," his mother said.

"That reminds me, I'm expecting a call from her," Dylan told them.

"So, what's the deal with you two. Any special plans we should know about. When are, you going to make it all official?" Dorothy asked him in a mischievous tone.

"There is nothing between us. We are just good friends. Besides anything involving me and a colleague is strictly 'Top Secret'. You want to get arrested?" Dylan mocked.

"Eww, top secret. It's all so intriguing. Secret rendezvous' in places only spies go too. Dark smoke-filled rooms, sitting in corners wearing nothing but their trench coats and sun glasses. Hiding, or trying to hide from everyone. Passing messages, pitching woo in seedy hotels," Dorothy laughed.

"DOROTHY, that will be enough of such talk. You were raised better," Maggie scolded.

"I'm just having some fun with my big brother. Let's order the sandwiches. Daddy will be home soon," Dorothy said.

Maggie picked up the phone and called the shop to order the food. Dorothy and Dylan would walk up to pick up the order. This gave them both time to talk as brother and sister. Dorothy had known about Dylan's relationship with Caroline before the war. For now, he was looking for news about Villanova and her studies. She was busy and doing well. Her grades had improved.

College life agreed with her. She was still single. Dorothy had no desire to get tied down in a relationship with one man. She was having too much fun playing the field.

Arriving at the shop they paid for the food and returned home. Kevin had returned from work and Maggie had informed him of Dylan's job assignment. He was not surprised at the idea of returning him to Luzon. It was the one place other than China where he had any practical experience. He wondered however how returning to the place where he endured the terrible traumas that affected him would be for him. Dylan and Dorothy returned with the sandwiches and they all sat together to enjoy the evening meal. As they ate they discussed and planned a going away party. Family and friends would once again see Dylan off, as he left for another trip back to the Far East at the pleasure of the government.

CHAPTER 4

SUNRISE OVER THE OCEAN

Susan was putting the drapes up in the living room of the small Jersey bungalow she and Mike had purchased. The home was located on Waverly Boulevard at the end of Sea Spray Rd. The little house was small and reminded them of their old house at Pearl Harbor. The front door opened to the small living room. The kitchen was the same size and sat at the right-hand side of the home. A small corridor led to the only bathroom with a bedroom on either side. A ladder in the corridor was mounted to the wall and was the only access to the attic. They had a small yard in front and the dunes and the beach with the ocean served as their back yard. They loved it.

Mikes old partner Dave lived a few blocks away on Seacrest Rd. Dave managed to get a job with the Ocean City Police Department as a detective. Dave was trying to get his old partner a position with the department. Susan thought it would be a good idea. It would be something to occupy his mind.

After twenty years of service with the NYPD and his involvement during the war with the Civil Defense group Mike was more than qualified. They had met this morning and then went to headquarters so that Mike could be interviewed by the Chief of Police.

Susan expected them home for lunch and after hanging the curtains she went into the kitchen to prepare the meal. A casserole of macaroni and cheese with fresh crab meat was her plan. After starting the oven all she needed to do was wait for the guys to come home. She was sitting at the kitchen table when the men arrived.

"Honey, I'm home and I got a job," Mike announced as he came in through the side door in the kitchen. Dave was with him and grinning broadly.

"He is now the protector of the sand and wood of Ocean City," Dave proclaimed.

"What in the world is that?" Susan asked.

"My job is to walk the boards and patrol the beach. Protecting the citizens from violent horseshoe crabs, food stealing sea gulls, and ensuring that no one is drinking the devils brew next to the ocean," Mike declared.

Susan laughed as she hugged her husband.

"If he does well, the Chief will promote him to orderly duty at headquarters. His new position of responsibility will be to take complaints, write daily reports and sweep out the lobby," Dave proclaimed with enthusiasm.

"Well, in my mind he will be Chief of Police in no time. Now sit down and we can have lunch," Susan said.

Mike had another week before he started. The beach and boardwalk job would not start until the beginning of May. The summer season began on Memorial Day and people from Philadelphia and New York came to vacation in the family friendly town. The city itself was dry, no booze could be sold within its borders. This appealed to many people looking to just relax and enjoy the beach and the ocean.

With an extra bedroom in their small little bungalow Mike and Susan anticipated visitors. Hope and Dorothy had already made plans for July. A week at the beach soaking up the sun and watching life guards was something they both looked forward too. Colleen also made plans for the end of July.

Mike and Susan purchased a double bed and a small night stand and dresser. The second bedroom did not have a closet. With more than four people in the house things could be crowded. There was room for four people at the small kitchen table.

Mike noted that he could put small twin beds upstairs in the attic but it was too hot during the summer months and downright freezing in the winter. During the winter months Dave told them that the small inlet was deserted. Now that the war was over expansion and the construction of new homes started. During the new decade that was fast approaching the entire New Jersey shore would see an abundance of new construction.

Mike started his new job the following Monday. He was given an old Army surplus jeep to patrol the beach and the boardwalk. He took the jeep home each day and started his tour of duty from the north end of the inlet. Driving south along the beach he would stop in at the Police Building and check in. The boardwalk contained numerous shops and small restaurants. During the summer season people road bicycles in the morning until ten AM. With the morning bikers gone people began to stroll on the boardwalk visiting the shops. He found the beach and boardwalk patrol boring.

The only excitement he could experience was driving the jeep along the surf line. Splashing the incoming waves under his wheels and chasing the birds along the water's edge. Strolling along the boardwalk with the rest of the people as they shopped was monotonous. The only upside to his day was watching young women in their bathing suits headed for the beach. This was not New York City. Crime was for all practical purposes being non-existent. The only hardship was the sun. It was hot, and relentless. Even in the shade of a shop awning, the reflecting sun light off the ocean and sand was a constant torture. Still it gave him something to do. He was earning his keep although he did not need the money. He had lunch each day at home with Susan. When the tour of duty was over she greeted him each day with a cold bottle of Ortliebs beer. The summer season started in May and continued until Labor Day in September. The big event in town in the summer was the 4th of July parade and fireworks. Dave's job as a detective was not any more exciting. The occasional burglary was the biggest crime he would deal with. The city was growing and with growth there was always more crime. Ocean City seemed to defy the fates and crime rates stayed the same. The two friends boasted that Ocean City was crime free because they enforced the law so well. Criminals stayed away, McMullen and Solomon had control of the city.

One afternoon while Mike went was at work, Susan drove the convertible down Route 9 to the town of Rio Grande. Mike would have lunch with Dave today at the police station. She had made arrangements with a local breeder to purchase a puppy. The puppies were now ten weeks old. She had already made her pick of the litter. The plan was to surprise Mike when he returned home from work. Susan had picked a male.

He was the smallest of the litter, but he was also the most active. He chased his mother constantly wanting to feed off her. Susan had already purchased a leash, food and water bowl, and a bed. After paying for the pup she drove back to Ocean City.

The new addition to their home ran around with his nose to the ground. He was exploring all the rooms. Susan thought he might need to do something. She snatched him up and took him out the side door and put him down. Susan had guessed right, the puppy sniffed a little then urinated on the dirt drive way. Just as he finished Mike returned from work with the jeep. The puppy looked at Mike and the jeep. Mike stepped out of the jeep and asked Susan, "Where did that come from?" The pup barked and jumped back and forth at the jeep. Not sure what this strange creature was he was letting it know he was not afraid of it.

Mike reached down picking up the pup and looked at it face to face. "What happened to your face? It's all pushed in," Mike said.

The puppy barked his response and wiggled in Mike's hands. They took him inside and Mike put him down. As soon as his short little legs hit the ground he had his nose to floor and resumed his exploration of his new home. "We should come up with a name," Susan said.

The pup was now standing up pulling at the table cloth on the kitchen table. Still grasped in his mouth he fell over pulling the cloth.

Susan had a plate of cupcakes on the table and they fell on the floor. Mike's only reaction seeing the cakes all over the floor, and the puppy grabbing one was, "CUPCAKE!"

Susan and Mike grabbed the cakes and the plate and picked everything up laughing. The puppy had his face buried in one of the cakes and had frosting and what was left of the cupcake all over his face. Susan declared, "I think that is the perfect name for the puppy. Cupcake!"

Mike picked up the puppy and wiped off the frosting from its face. "I'm not so sure. Cupcake sounds a little to girly for an English Bull Dog. How about, Lady or Gracie, something like that," Mike said.

Susan laughed and said, "I like Cupcake!"

"Well, all right. If you want her name to be Cupcake then that will be her name," Mike gave in.

He held the pup up again looking at it face to face and told it, "Your name is Cupcake. I am your master. You will obey me. You will...Hey, wait this dog is a guy"

Susan was laughing hard. "Yes, sweat heart he is a boy, and his name is Cupcake." Mike put the dog on the floor.

"Aww, come on that's just not right. How about Major, or Spike. Maybe we could go with something a little more man like?" Mike said.

"No, we agreed and like Cupcake," Susan declared.

"But, he's a boy. You can't call him Cupcake. Look he won't even answer to it. Here, Cupcake!" Mike said stooping down.

Cupcake stopped sniffing and ran right to Mike as Susan laughed.

"I think he likes his new name. Susan sat on the floor and called the puppy. "Here Cupcake, come to me sweet baby boy." Cupcake left Mike and bounded straight to Susan. "See, he likes it, don't you baby boy. Yes, you know your new name," Susan cooed and played with the pup.

Mike went to the ice box and took out a bottle of beer and went out the side door. "Where are, you going?" Susan asked.

"Outside to shoot myself. I am the master of a male English Bull Dog named Cupcake. Life is cruel," Mike said.

Susan laughed and played with the new dog. She thought to herself, we are a family now.

Susan was good at training the dog. She had him house broken in about a week and was working on walking him off leash. There were some children on their block and Cupcake was a big hit. Cupcake really loved to run on the beach and chase the birds from the surf line. Still young and ungainly on his short legs the occasional wave would knock him over if he went into the surf too far. Despite his name, Mike loved the little guy and would sit on the beach with him. For whatever reason, Cupcake did not like the jeep and would growl and bark at it when Mike left or returned from work.

Memorial Day arrived and with-it vacationers from the city. Even with all the additional people in town things were still peaceful. Most of the police calls over the new radios dealt with rent disputes and the occasional fight. Mike made a plan to get to know all the shop owners and their employees. Patrolling the boardwalk took up most of his time that was passing a little quicker now. Talking with the shop owners he learned about their families as well as their business. The department was operating on a post war budget. Mike was never issued a department side arm but he carried his old reliable Colt 1911 he brought home from France. The department installed a radio on his jeep and he carried an old walkie-talkie while on the boardwalk. The old walkie-talkie was a hassle to carry and often Mike left it in the jeep.

Mike was on the south end of the inlet when a radio call announced he was needed at 9th Street and the beach. He knew there was a life guard stand there and they often called for police backup whenever bathers ignored their instructions. Driving up the surf line with his red light on he used the horn instead of his siren. People moved out of his way and when he arrived the lifeguards were arguing with a man. The man was obviously drunk. He was also holding a bottle wrapped in a brown bag. All the lifeguards knew Mike by name. "Mike this guy is drunk and he has an open container," one of the guards informed him.

"Look, I ain't hurtin nobody. So, I got a beer, big deal. What's the beef?" The man asked.

"The beef, my friend is that the city is dry. No booze is sold in town. You can only have drinks in your house. No booze on the beach, either."

"So, give me the bottle and I'll take you back to wherever you're staying," Mike declared.

"Bullshit, you not getting my beer. I bought it legal outside town," the man slurred.

Mike getting his dander up said, "Look pal, give me the bottle and get in the jeep or I'm gonna have to run you in."

The man looked at Mike sizing him up. They were about the same size. What stood out was Mike's Colt. "What kind of cop carries a .45.

You an MP, or something?" The man asked laughing. Mike was dressed in his beach uniform. He wore boots with khaki shorts and a white short sleeve shirt. His badge was pinned to the pocket of the shirt. He had a regular policeman's cap that he never wore. Hearing what the man said Mike guessed he was about thirty years old and most likely a vet. "Where were you in the war?" Mike asked.

"Yea, 6th Marines, I was on the Canal. Got malaria, went to Pearl, then they sent me back. Got hit going up Surabachi on Iwo." The man said proudly.

Mike saw his opening. "I was at Pearl, when the Nips hit us. But, my .45 was brought home from France in 1919. Now, how about we get you back to where you're staying Marine?" Mike said to the man.

"OK Mac, anything you say," the man slurred.

Mike found the rooming house where the man was staying and drove him to the house on 10th Street. Once they arrived the man went to his room and slept off the beer. Mike drove over to headquarters and filled his report. His report would get him into trouble later in the week.

Finishing his tour, he drove up the beach to his house. Driving over the dunes he parked the jeep. Cupcake growled and barked at the jeep as he always did. Then seeing Mike, he dashed up to him. Susan standing in the side door to the kitchen greeted Mike. "I almost made an arrest today," he said kissing her as he entered the house.

"Really. What happened?" Susan asked.

"Just a drunk Marine from the war with a bottle of beer on the beach. I took him back to his boarding house to sleep it off," Mike explained.

"Wow, sounds exciting," Susan joked.

"What's for dinner?" Mike asked.

"Nothing special, burgers and dogs on the grill," Susan replied.

A week later Mike reported for duty in the morning. The desk Sergeant told him that the Chief wanted to see him. Arriving at the Chiefs office Mike was told to take a seat. "I read the incident report you filed last week about the intoxicated man at 9th Street. I also read the report filed by the life guards. I also checked with the duty desk and you have not filed any citations since Memorial Day started. An open container on the beach is a $50.00 fine. Public intoxication on the beach is also a $75.00 fine.

This city thrives on its summer season. Vacationers come here spend their money and that supports local business. Those business owners pay taxes to the city. Taxes that pay your salary. Fines we collect supplements the budget of this department. This man should have been issued citations for these offenses. Explain to me why you did not write him up, and based on the life guard reports should have been arrested as well," the Chief demanded.

"The guy was a Marine vet. Rather than escalate the incident into an arrest I got the situation under control and closed it peacefully," Mike replied.

"OK, this is not New York. We live on the citations we write. If things start to get out of hand, make an arrest. People who come here expect a nice peaceful vacation. Trouble makers and people who do not obey the law are not tolerated," the Chief said.

"OK, Chief anything else?" Mike asked.

"No that will be all. Check with the desk sergeant. He will give you a list of codes and violations. Start writing citations," the Chief said.

Mike left the Chiefs office and reported to the desk sergeant. He had already been briefed and handed Mike two pages of mimeographed papers. Mike went out to his jeep and sat there reading the two pages. Great he thought I've become a glorified meter maid. He started the jeep and drove to the southern end of the beach. Sitting there in the jeep he lit a cigar and thought about the meeting that morning.

The job was bad enough with all the boredom but to be ordered to write citations to generate revenue for the department was too much. Beach goers walking past him smiled and said good morning. None of this did anything for his sour mood. Finishing his cigar, he started to drive up the beach. It was early for lunch but he decided to go home anyway.

Arriving at his house he was greeted by the growling and barking Cupcake. He really did not like the jeep. Once the dog saw Mike though it changed his aggressive demeanor into a happy dog, glad to see his masters return. Mike's mood had not changed and he ignored the dog.

Going into the house through the side door into the kitchen he found Susan washing something at the sink. "Hi, you're here early," she said turning towards him for the kiss she expected. Mike ignored her as well and sat at the table stewing. "What's wrong you look like an old wet hen," Susan asked.

"I'm supposed to be a cop. The Chief let me know today that I'm really nothing more than a meter maid," Mike told her, dejection in his voice. Then he told her about the meeting he had that morning.

"I know you think of yourself as a cop, but this Ocean City, New Jersey. We are not in the big city. Look at the bright side of things. You don't have to deal with hard dangerous criminals. The occasional drunk and people on the beach after curfew is what you have to deal with. You're no spring chicken either. Relax and try to enjoy it. You get paid to go to the beach and the boardwalk all day. The people you deal with pay to go to the beach and boardwalk. Go with the flow, Mike," she told him.

"I guess you're right. What's for lunch?" He asked.

"Well, Officer I may need to be arrested for indecent behavior towards a public official," she said taking off her t-shirt exposing her breasts.

"I'll have to frisk you first," Mike said getting up from the table.

"I was hoping you would say that," Susan laughed. They went into the bedroom and lay on the bed. Cupcake joined them standing against the side of the bed barking.

June passed quickly, Mike wrote the citations he was supposed to write and things settled into a routine. Susan and Mike were now expecting their first guests of the summer season. Hope and Dorothy would arrive at the bus station later in the day. Mike would pick them up and bring them to the house. Two weeks on the beach was just what the girls needed. Both had finished the second year of college and needed a break from all the hard work. The bus arrived from Philadelphia on time and Mike met the girls as they got off the bus. Dressed in shorts and a blouse each of the girls had their hair up in pony tails. Some of the young men arriving on the bus stood close by until the girls each gave Mike a kiss on the cheek. Mike just glared at the younger men knowing full well what they were after. Once the girls had their bags in the jeep Hope climbed in back and Dorothy sat next to Mike up front.

He could have taken the city streets but decided to drive up the beach splashing his tires in the surf. The girls got a big kick out of it and when they arrived over the dunes at the house Cupcake was there to growl and bark at the jeep. Both girls got a big kick out of the bulldog attacking the jeep and Cupcake was happy two new people showed up that loved to give him attention and belly rubs. Mike had pointed out all the life guard stand locations during the drive. Mike was concerned for their swimming safety; the girls were interested in only the life guards themselves.

Once inside they greeted Susan and quickly changed into their new two-piece bathing suits. They were off over the dunes and on to the beach. "Hey, how are you? How have you been? I like what you've done with the place," Mike said sarcastically.

Susan laughed and replied, "Don't be a grumpy old uncle. They're young and excited to be here. There will be plenty of time to talk over dinner. To answer your next question, we're having chicken," Susan said.

"Did you see those bathing suits? I may need to work with a shotgun while they're here," Mike complained.

"Funny when we go to the beach and men look at me, you don't seem to mind," Susan laughed.

"Who looks at you. I mean I know why they look at you. I mean..." Mike stammered.

"Quit while your ahead sweetheart, you're getting in too deep to climb out," Susan told him somewhat angry.

"You know what I mean. I...we are responsible for those two. Those life guards and every other guy out there are going to be after those two like wolves after a deer," Mike said concerned.

"Oh stop. You sound like an over protective father. They will be fine," Susan assured him.

Hope and Dorothy ran onto the beach dropped their towels and bags and went straight at the water. Splashing in the surf this far north they basically had the beach to themselves. They sat in the surf and talked excited to be on the beach. "Did you see some of those yummy life guards? Maybe we should go down the beach further and pretend to drown," laughed Dorothy.

"I think this is a pretty good spot," Hope said.

"One thing for sure, we can work on our tans," Dorothy replied.

"I hear that Stevie Bush has been hanging around when you're at home," Hope said.

Dorothy responded, "Yea, he has always had a crush on me since we were little."

"Did he ever ask you out?" Hope asked.

"That's funny. He never has. I know he wants too. Maybe he is just too shy," Dorothy answered.

"If he did would you go out with him?" Hope asked.

"I guess. He is kind of cute. I think when I'm home the last thing I think about is boys. I do have a few suiters on campus you know. When I get home I just want to hang out and relax. My Mom likes him," Dorothy said.

"Well, maybe if you gave him some encouragement you two could get together," Hope said.

"You trying to get me set up? You're starting to sound like my Mom. What's the deal with you? Anyone ringing your bells lately?" Dorothy asked playfully.

"No not really. Next semester is going to be busy. I'm taking my nursing courses, plus my other studies," Hope said.

Dorothy sat up and said, "Let's make a pack. First one to loss her virginity even if it's by marriage buys lunch somewhere fancy."

"Ok. You can take me to the Tavern on the Green in Central Park," Hope said with excitement.

"What makes you think I'm gonna loss the bet?" Dorothy asked.

I'm just going on a hunch here, but the bet is on. Pinky swear," Hope said holding out her finger.

"Pinky swears." Dorothy said.

The girls lay in the sun until dinner time. Then they returned to the house. Cupcake was excited to see his new friends return and the girls were eager to oblige his desire for belly rubs. Chicken off the grill and homemade potato salad was served. The girls ate heartily and shared with Cupcake. The next two weeks the girls enjoyed the beach and the ocean. They flirted and talked with the life guards but surrendered to no dates. They were on vacation, all that mattered was the sun, sand and the ocean. The only man in their lives for those two weeks was Cupcake.

CHAPTER 5

OLD & NEW ATTRACTIONS

Dylan got a call from Caroline. He informed her of his orders and told her about the upcoming going away party. Dorothy and Hope had returned from Ocean City last week and would also attend. Caroline asked if her roommate Barbara could come that Sunday and was pleased to learn she would be welcome. Maggie and Colleen would prepare homemade coleslaw, potato salad and macaroni salad. Burgers and hot dogs would be cooked on Kevin's new charcoal grill. Three cases of beer were ordered and delivered by the local distributor. Uncle Mike and Aunt Susan would drive up from the shore with Cupcake. The Murphy's would take the train to Philadelphia the day before and stay with Colleen for a week. Colleen was scheduled to spend a week with Mike and Susan after her parents returned to New York. Dylan was looking forward to seeing Caroline. Their postings would keep them far apart so he was hoping for another sexual encounter with her. He and Caroline were not in love but they both had a strong physical attraction to one another. When he finished the call, Stevie Bush arrived to see if he was needed to help with any party preparations. Stevie lived up the street and was Dorothy's age. He was also devoted to her, but never once pursued her. Everyone knew how he felt about Dorothy. Dylan was a few years older. Stevie had been rated as unfit for military duty due to heart murmur. During the war years, he performed volunteer work for the USO. He held a factory job at the Budd plant on Hunting Park Avenue. He and Dylan had always been friends.

"Dorothy and Hope went shopping down town. They should be back soon with some party decorations. I'm sure they will appreciate your help," Dylan said.

"OK, I'll wait for her," Stevie said.

Dylan was the only one who called him Steve. To everyone else he was Stevie. "Steve, when are you going to ask my sister out? I know you like her. I'm pretty sure she would say yes," Dylan stated handing Stevie a beer.

"I don't know. I mean look at me. Why should she want to be seen with me as her as her boyfriend," he asked Dylan sheepishly? He wore thick horn-rimmed glasses that partially hid his bushy eyebrows. He kept his dark brown hair neatly trimmed with a weekly haircut. He dressed neatly and conservatively. He was frugal and had accumulated a good savings account. In the minds of most girls he would be a good catch. He just had a low opinion of his own looks. Dorothy on the other hand was stunning.

"It's not always about looks. You've known each other since you were kids. I know she likes you. My Mom and Dad like you. Shit, I even like you," Dylan told him laughing.

Stevie said, "I don't know. I'm just scared she might say no. Or worse laugh at me."

"Trust me she would never do that to you. You have to face your fears if you two are ever going to be together."

"You have to give yourselves a chance. The life you want could be taken away at any time for any reason. Think about it, Ok," Dylan said to him.

The girls came home with large shopping bags and Stevie went straight to Dorothy to help her. Hope made note of the fact she was left on her own but laughed about it to herself. Maggie came downstairs to see what the girls had bought. "Oh, let me see what you two have. Hello Stevie, I had no idea you were here," Maggie said.

"Hello Mrs. Brogan. Dylan and I were just talking. I'm also here to help out if I can," Stevie replied.

"Well of course. We can use all the help we can get," Maggie told him.

All the hard work paid off and the party day had arrived. Everyone went to early Mass.

Cupcake was a big hit with everyone and the dog loved all the attention and treats he was getting throughout the day. People moved from inside the house out to the backyard and even the front step. Caroline had brought Barbara with her and she was happy she came. Caroline had told her about Dylan but left out their sexual history. As far as Barbara knew Dylan and Caroline were just good friends. Barbara was very much attracted to him. Dylan could not keep his eyes off her. Barbara was the same size as Caroline. She had blond hair that she kept long just past her shoulders. She had a great figure and piercing blue eyes. Her lips turned up at one end when she smiled, looking as if she were smirking. Caroline stayed close to her roommate until she noted that Dylan was definitely interested in her. She let nature take her course. Caroline was not jealous. She had not anticipated a sexual encounter with Dylan this weekend. She spent time with her parents and only spoke briefly with Dylan.

Dorothy was sitting with Hope in the yard when Stevie Bush approached them. He had a small bowl of chips and pretzels with him. "Hi girls. Dorothy, could I speak with you please," he asked?

"Of course, here sit down," Dorothy said.

"If you two will excuse me, I'm going to powder my nose," Hope declared.

Stevie sat next to Dorothy and offered her some snacks from the bowl. She declined and asked him, "What do you want to talk about?"

"Well...I mean...I have tickets for the Phillies game next Saturday against the Dodgers. Can we... or I mean will you... would you want to?"

"Dodger tickets. Count me in pal. I'll buy the beer and hot-dogs," Mike interrupted as he passed by. "How many tickets do you have?" Mike asked sitting in Hopes old seat.

"Just the two tickets sir," Stevie replied.

"Well we should be able to get more. Let's check around and see if anyone else wants to go," Mike said. Hope had returned and grabbed her uncle.

"Let's get you inside before you do any more damage," she said quietly pulling him away.

"What," he started to question.

Hope cut him off by squeezing his arm hard. "Shoosh, your big dope. Come with me and be quiet," she added sternly pulling him towards the house. Susan was in the kitchen and noticed her husband being pulled inside by Hope. Once inside Hope turned to her uncle and told him, "Stevie was about to ask Dorothy on a date.

You should not have interrupted. Now go inside and behave yourself," Hope instructed him.

Susan laughed and added, "Lay off the beer, it's still early."

Mike went into the parlor and continued outside to sit on the step. Hope noted he was talking with someone and she went to see who, when her Uncle Michael walked in the door.

"Uncle Michael," she said excitedly running into his arms.

"Hello sweat heart, my goodness, look at you. Your just as gorgeous as your mother," Michael said proudly.

Hope noticed the young man behind her Uncle. "This is my friend, Tom Brady. I hope it's all right that he came with me, Michael said to her.

"Hello Tom and welcome, I'm so glad to meet you," Hope addressed Tom.

"Hello and thank you for such a warm welcome. Michael has told me so much about all of you. I can't wait to meet everyone. If Michael is right, I look forward to meeting your mother. If she is only half as beautiful as you I am sure to be pleased," Tom said.

Hope noticed a slight lisp in Tom's speech. He was also very soft spoken.

"Come inside and see everyone," Hope said to them.

As Michael made his way around the house he was greeted warmly by everyone. He introduced Tom and they were given drinks. Caroline slipped up to Hope and asked, "Who is that pretty thing with your uncle?"

"His name is Tom Brady, and your right about his being pretty in so many ways," Hope said with a little sarcasm.

"Pity," Caroline responded.

"I would say, what a grand challenge. A noteworthy quest, if one were so inclined," Hope said.

"Your uncles not half bad either. Maybe I could bag both birds with one shot," Caroline teased.

"CAROLINE, how wicked of you," Hope laughed.

Dorothy felt sorry for Stevie. Uncle Mikes interruption drained any courage he had worked up. She knew what he was getting too. She was about to start the conversation again when her Uncle Michael came into the yard. "My God, your stunning. How you have grown. I'm so happy to see you again," Michael said approaching Dorothy.

Michael introduced Tom and they both were introduced to Stevie. "If you all would excuse me I need to freshen up," Stevie said.

Dorothy took notice of Toms soft spoken lisp and concluded that he was more than just a friend to her uncle. Michaels homosexuality had always been an issue with the family. Exiled by his parents to Florida and Cuba he was still part of the family.

61

Dylan was stationed to Guantanamo Bay when he was in the Marines prior to the war. Colleen and Hope had visited with him in Havana. Hopes grandmother, Rose moved to Cuba to be with her son. Now he was home again, back in New York.

He was always nice and polite with everyone and generous to a fault whenever someone had a birthday. Her grandfather and Uncle Mike tolerated him. They knew about some incident that happened in New York that was never spoken of.

One of those family secrets that would die without ever being revealed.

Tom as always had a soft leather case with him containing pencils and a drawing pad. As an artist, he was constantly working on his talent. Sitting now in the yard he was sketching Dorothy. His pencil moved across the page and captured her perfectly. When he was finished, it looked like a black and white photo graph. Cupcake was lying in the yard and he became the latest work. Caroline walked up to him and looked over his shoulder.

"Do you mind if I watch you work," she asked?

"Not at all. If you like I could draw you next," he replied smiling.

"Now would that be a facial portrait or a full body work," Caroline asked teasing?

"In this company, I think a facial portrait would be more appropriate. I think a more in-depth work could be done later, if a lady were so inclined," Tom replied looking into her eyes. Caroline was surprised and confused.

This handsome young man was obviously a homosexual yet he flirted like a brazen man confident around women. "Well we will have to see how well the portrait comes out," Caroline replied.

Dylan and Barbara were sitting on the step-in front of the house. They had met Michael and Tom when they arrived. Mike was with them sitting on the fender of his car smoking a cigar and telling Army stories. The beer he drank was catching up to him. Dylan a veteran himself recognized the pain in his voice when Mike spoke about Tommy and Jimmy. Dylan carried his own bag of bricks. Barbara learned he had been on Luzon when the Japanese captured the Philippines. She also knew he had been on the Bataan Death March and was rescued at Cabanatuan. Listening to the two veterans swapping stories saddened her.

Yet at the same time she was overwhelmed with pride for all these two men had done in defense of the country. Dylan convinced Mike to lend him the car and he and Barbara left the house in the convertible. He took a leisurely drive up and down the East and West river drives. He finally parked the car on Lemon Hill in Fairmount Park. The sun was going down and they talked about their lives. Eventually they were kissing and petting heavily in the car. Barbara was not going to surrender herself in an open convertible to the man she had just met. Dylan started the car and drove back to the house. The party was still going well and no one noticed their absence.

Colleen and Susan were in the kitchen talking. They spoke about the upcoming visit to the shore when Colleens parents returned to New York. Colleen had been working hard and needed the vacation.

"Just to lay on the beach put my toes in the sand and soak up the sun sounds just delicious," Colleen said.

"Well we are happy to have you visit. You said you have one of those new two-piece bathing suits. Where did you get it?" Susan asked.

"Wanamaker's. The bottom fits perfectly but the top I think is a little too revealing. Still and all it's my vacation and all I want to do is relax," Colleen replied.

"When the girls were with us, they had the two-piece suits. Mike was frantic. The life guards moved the stand they use on the beach closer to the house. He was so cute, like an over protective father," Susan said smiling.

"I promise not to get in your way at night if you know what I mean. Just give me a heads up and I can retire for the night or go for a walk," Colleen informed Susan.

"Nonsense, he will just have to adjust when we have visitors. Although I did notice he was a little more attentive when the girls were there," Susan said.

"He does have a wandering eye when it comes to women," Colleen noted.

"That's true but he is also not the type of man who is a womanizer. He knows what side of his bread is buttered. He'll watch these young girls on the beach and I'll catch him. It's so cute when he tries to defend himself.

I'm an officer of the law, I have to be observant, he'll say. I just laugh at him and that upsets him more. He tries so hard to rationalize his looking," Susan said happily.

"Let's have some fun with the old boy when I'm visiting," Colleen said mischievously.

Susan looked at Colleen and smiling replied, "Sounds like the fun we had in the old days. I'm in, what do you have in mind?"

"What kind of suit do you have?" Colleen asked.

"A full suit, but I see a two-piercer in my future," Susan giggled.

"Excellent, here's what we can do," Colleen smiled.

Mike sat with his father and talked about the old days on the job at the NYPD. Joe McMullen was looking his age. He was tired all the time and slept most of his time. Mike informed his Dad about the boring work he was assigned to do in Ocean City. It was easy work and the pay was all right. Sean Murphy joined them. He was using a cane now and was slightly bent over when he stood.

Mike thought to himself that his parents and other people in his life were getting old. Sean had a glass of Irish Whiskey in his hand. Something he was forbidden to have but would never give up. Setting the glass down he said with a naughty smile, "If anyone asks Mike this is yours."

"Ok, Sean no problem." Mike replied.

"Getting old is a blessing and a curse. You don't have to work anymore. You can sit back and enjoy your family. Watch your children and grandchildren grow and become the type of people that they should be. The body though does not co-operate. The mind says yes and the body says, who the hell are you kidding. I'm too old to fight ya, to slow to chase ya," Joe said.

"Well then Pop the only thing left is to shoot the son of a bitch," Mike laughed.

"I'll drink to that," Sean Murphy declared.

"Sean Murphy as long as I've known ya, ya would drink to Hitler's birthday," Joe declared laughing.

"And to many more," Sean laughed raising his glass.

Mike lit a cigar. "Pop, I have to tell you, I'm proud of you. Always have been."

"I'm proud of you too son. Now when the hell will your mother and I see some grandchildren from you," Joe demanded.

Mike laughing replied, "What's wrong with Cupcake?"

"I'll drink to that, "Sean declared finishing the whiskey.

CHAPTER 6
TEASING & TERROR

Mike escorted his parent's home to their house on 25th Street. He took note of how tired his father looked. Once they were inside the house Mike kissed his mother goodnight and hugged his father. Returning to the party he sat with Michael Jr. and Tom Brady on the front step. Tom talked about his studies and Michael praised his talent and work. Tom showed Mike the portrait of Dorothy and the one he had done of Cupcake. Mike wanted to buy the drawing of Cupcake but Tom insisted on giving to him without charge. Tom had also done a profile drawing of Caroline. Mike learned that Tom was also a painter and invited them to the shore house. Tom was excited about the beach scenes he could do. "Hope can draw fairly well too," Mike told Tom.

"So, I've heard. I saw the Marine Corps drawing she had done for Dylan," Tom replied.

The drawing was now framed and hung in the living room of the Brogan home. "Maybe someday she will take up the talent again. Right now, she is focused on her studies to become a nurse," Mike said.

"Yes, I spoke with her earlier. Is she really considering a military career after college? She seems obsessed with finding out what was wrong with her father," Michael responded.

"What happened to her father?" Tom asked.

Mike responded to his question, "Jimmy changed after the war. We served in France together. He would burst into anger for no real reason. He had nightmares and he sat in that damn humidor by himself for hours at a time.

When Hope was born, he was not there at the hospital. He drank too much.

He never once held his child."

"God, that sounds terrible," Tom replied.

"It was like he became someone else. I did not know him before the war. Michael could tell you more," Mike said.

"My brother was so easy going and soft spoken. He was generous to a fault. He enlisted in the Army so I would not be drafted. He was wounded and spent a night alone isolated from his unit. That night changed him. The changes started slowly. The whiskey seemed to bring his bad behavior out more quickly. It's almost as if he was fighting a war with himself. He was trying desperately to be himself, but this other person that he could become just took over. He had no control, but control was something he was obsessed with. He would sit in the humidor for hours and just stare into space. I still miss him," Michael said sadly.

"How about you Mike? You were there with him. Did the war change you too?" Tom asked.

"I have my days. Sometimes at night I can't sleep. If I do sleep, I have nightmares. I like to be alone at times. Susan worked in the naval hospital with some of these men before the war. She knows how I am. There's times she knows just to leave me alone," Mike replied.

Susan and Colleen came outside. "Time to go lover we have a long drive back to the shore," Susan told Mike.

"I don't see any reason to feed this guy for a least a week," Colleen stated holding on to Cupcake.

Susan replied, "So I guess when you arrive next week we will start feeding him again."

"Looking forward to it. Bye bye, Cupcake. Be a good boy. Here take the leash and get your doggie," Colleen said giving Mike the, leash.

"I guess we are leaving. Tom nice to meet you. Michael, take care of yourself," Mike said.

Susan said goodbye to everyone and she and Mike left.

Caroline stayed with her parents and Barbara joined them. The Murphy's left with Colleen. Hope would stay with Dorothy. Michael and Tom took the last train back to New York. Dylan sat in the yard thinking about his future. He was attracted to Barbara but knew there was no future there. He was off to the Philippines and she would return to Washington. Whatever romance he was to have it would be waiting for him half way around the world.

Colleen arrived at the bus station and Susan met her as she got off the bus. She was looking forward to a much-needed vacation. The two women rode back to the house with the top down and Cupcake sitting happily in the back seat.

Colleen loved the house. It was small but nestled along the dunes with the beach and the ocean for a back yard made up for any complaints about its size. Mike showed up for lunch and the women were alerted by Cupcakes barking and growling at the jeep. Dave was with him and the two of them were comical looking in Colleens opinion. Dave was dressed with slacks, tie and sport coat, while Mike wore his boots, shorts, and his new uniform shirt. "You two look like different bookends," Colleen joked.

"Well, I am a well-dressed detective while Mike here is a beach bum with a badge," Dave replied.

"A very handsome beach bum, right Honey?" Mike asked Susan.

"Quit while your ahead, Sweetheart," Susan quipped.

They sat and had lunch and discussed Colleens plans for her time at the shore. Relax, soak up the sun, ~~swim in the surf~~ and eat and drink were her only plans.

After lunch, the men returned to work and the women changed into their bathing suits and went to the beach. "I could do just this for the rest of my life," Colleen said. She was laying on her back outstretched on a large blanket Susan used for the beach. The only sounds were the pounding surf, seagulls and Cupcakes heavy panting. "It's not bad. There is such much new building though I fear the tranquility will fall victim to bigger crowds," Susan replied.

"Well it's working for me now, so let's enjoy it while we can," Colleen added.

"Mike does not work tomorrow, so let's have some fun with him," Susan said.

"You think he's going to fall for our old pranks again?" Colleen asked.

"Only one way to find out," Susan replied.

Mike had been the object of pranks and jokes played on him since Colleen and Susan had become friends. Susan knew about his old attraction to Colleen, and knew they had almost had sex once.

Colleen would flirt and be very touchy with Mike around Susan. Susan would either ignore the behavior or would feign anger. Then Susan would do the same and Colleen would react the same ways. Mike was never sure how he was supposed to act or react and he always felt confused and uncomfortable. It was the discomfort the two women were driving at. They always kept him off guard and guessing.

Cupcake announced Mike's arrival from work. He came into the house found both women in the kitchen and kissed Susan. "Hey, no kiss for me?" Colleen pouted.

Confused and worrisome, Mike kissed her on the cheek and took off the gun belt he wore. Dinner was being prepared and Mike was already hungry. Taking the evening paper off the table he sat on the end of the sofa and started reading. Both women still wore their bathing suits. The new two-piece suits were brightly colored and showed off the figures of the two women. Colleen briefed by Susan took two bottles of Ortliebs out of the ice box and sat down next to Mike. She handed him his beer and while running her fingers in his hair asked provocatively, "How was your day?"

"Boring as usual, nothing special," Mike replied.

"We fixed a nice dinner, hope you're hungry," Susan announced from the kitchen.

"I'm starving," Mike said.

"Good it's ready so come and get it," Susan said.

Mike stood put down the paper and heard Colleen say, "A little help please."

She was holding out her hand indicating that Mike should help her up off the sofa. Mike took her hand and as she stood pressed herself into him.

"Excuse me." She cooed, walking past him smiling at Susan. Barely able to contain herself Susan sat down at the table. Mike took his usual seat and started to fill his plate. They were having his favorite meal of meat loaf and mashed potatoes. Eating his dinner Mike watched the two women eat theirs as they sat smiling at him. It was going to be a long week, he thought.

After two days of this Mike realized they were teasing him. They had done this before. He decided that this time would be different. He was going to turn the tables on them. Coming home from work and feeling a little cocky he saw the girls still on the beach.

Susan was on her stomach and Colleen was sitting with her legs stretched out and her arms behind her propping her up.

He greeted both of them and noticed the sun tan lotion on the blanket. Picking it up he put some on his finger tips and began to apply it to the front of the shoulders of Colleen. "You're gonna get a burn. You need to be careful," he said.

"Thank you, mmm, that feels nice," Collen said.

Emboldened Mike moved his hand to the top of her suit revealing the white skin at the top of her breast. "See, you already are getting a little red," Mike declared.

Surprised Colleen took his hand away and stood up. "Maybe we should go back to the house and get dinner started," she said. Susan had watched from her position on the blanket and gave Colleen a questioning look. "You two want to ride or walk?" Mike said with confidence. "We can walk," Susan said.

Mike drove the jeep over the dunes towards the house with Cupcake barking and running after the jeep.

"What was that all about?" Colleen asked.

"I don't know. He's never acted that way before. Maybe we are going too far, sending him the wrong signals," Susan answered.

"You don't think he actually would consider me having...or us having sex with him?" Colleen asked worriedly.

"He's up to something. That has to be it. Let's keep an eye on him. How far are you willing to go?" Susan inquired.

"I'm not sleeping with him or either of you for that matter. If that is where he thinks all of this is going we need to be careful," Colleen stated.

"I don't know. He would never cheat on me. But if he thought I was in on it...he might just try something," Susan said.

"Maybe he's playing us now," Colleen said.

"That sneaky son of a bitch. Maybe he is. OK, let him play his cards. We'll see what he's up too," Susan declared.

Caroline and Barbara returned to Washington on Sunday after Dylan's party. Anxious to get back to work the two women arrived at their apartment. Caroline would be the first to return to work. Europe was starting to rebuild itself under the Marshall Plan. So many towns, villages and even cities had been destroyed. Allied forces were still rounding up Nazi officials for trial. The world was coming to grips with what Hitler and his henchman meant by the final solution. The world watched in horror as the truth about the death camps was being revealed. The European desk was busy. Intelligence reports about the whereabouts of wanted Nazi officers and party officials were given top priority. Some of the internal dispatches were coming in from Argentina and other South American countries.

Kevin Murray, Caroline's immediate supervisor was in charge of the European desk. He communicated to her that all communiques from the field desks in Argentina and Germany were to be cross referenced and documented. The hunt was on and Caroline felt good to be a part of it. She was not a field operative. As a supervising analyst, her job was very important. She thought about Dylan. He was case officer and heading for the Philippines. Keeping track of communist insurgents and running a network of agents sounded mysterious and exciting to her. The reports she read came from other case officers and their agents. It was becoming a dangerous world again. The new agency was developing its procedures and protocols to keep the nation's foreign secrets safe. Some of the reports they received had been redacted. Lines of information would be blacked out. Although she and all the people she supervised had the highest security clearances they could not be privy to certain information about operations. In addition, people involved or their assets of some operations had to remain secret.

Only those individuals involved with the operations could read the blacked-out information.

This was called compartmentalizing the intelligence. People would be given tasks to complete for an operation but would have no idea why they were given the task or what other unknown people would do with the completed task. The right hand had no idea what the left hand was doing and vice-versa. Only the case officers, station chiefs and directors knew it all.

Dylan said goodbye to his mother, and hugged his sister. His father would drive him to the train station. He had a ticket that would take him too San Francisco California. Once there he would travel by commercial air to Hawaii. Military transport from Henderson Field would finish the trip to Clark Air Base in the Philippines. He was looking forward to the trip. He said goodbye to his father and boarded the train. He put his luggage away in the berth and headed for the club car. The train left on time and sat back and relaxed with a drink. He looked around the club car and stared scrutinizing the other passengers. He was using his field training or trade craft. He made note of a flirtatious blond-haired woman that had removed her wedding rings. The small tell-tale white ring on her wedding finger revealed her secret. The overweight balding man at the end of the car wore a messy suit. The bulge of a snob-nosed revolver on his right hip showing. More than likely a railroad dick. Another man standing at the bar was clean cut. His clothes were pressed. The broad shoulders and athletic build indicated a man to be watched. The low quarter brown shoes were military issue. A soldier on leave or returning to a post. A middle-aged couple sat in a booth looking at pictures. Vacationers on their way home. The most interesting was the man who served the drinks and made the sandwiches. An older negro this man had a wealth of stories to tell. The button on his lapel said his name was Henry. Dylan decided he would befriend Henry and learn about all the trips he had taken.

Henry was a wealth of information. The guy in the rumpled suit was indeed a railroad cop. The blond travelled between New York and Chicago on a monthly basis. Going to New York she was always married. Going back to Chicago she was always single. There in and of itself was a story.

The athletic man was on his way home on leave from Fort Dix NJ.

One other stop would be made in Pittsburgh before the train went non-stop to Chicago. From there it would go to Denver and then on to San Francisco. Dylan would trade craft the new passengers and found out he was getting good at spotting the regular passengers. These people seemed more relaxed and at ease. They also knew Henry's name. Dylan's story was he was a salesman for a fictitious company called American Publications. He sold text books to school districts around the country. Most of the people ignored his work. It was dull and boring. Which was what he wanted.

He was more interested in their work and lives. Information that might be used later was gathered from those conversations. He also learned it was a small world. He met an attorney that knew his father. He got on the train in Denver. He lived in Carmel south of San Francisco. Dylan never let on he was Kevin's son. The attorney was an opponent in a case his father worked on and won. He had nothing but good things to say about his father.

Arriving in the early morning in San Francisco he took a cab to the airport. He had an afternoon flight to Hawaii. He practiced his trade craft while waiting for the flight. He was not armed but he looked for the weapons that were always available to him. He still had his walking stick but he noted the brooms and mops that could be broken and used for Kendo fighting. Because he always had his walking stick when he was at Area F he took an interest in Kendo. He mastered the Japanese art while there. He had been trained to fight with his body. All of the most vulnerable points on the body were specific targets for different parts of the body. Fingers and thumbs were used to gouge the eyes.

The soft web of the hand between the thumb and the index finger was used to hit a man in the throat. The heel of the hand was used instead of a fist. Elbows and knees could deliver a powerful blow. The heel of the foot could break a man's leg. Even a rolled-up newspaper or magazine could become a weapon. He found this part of his training fascinating. He had lunch and boarded the aircraft just before 2PM. The plane took off twenty minutes later and he settled in to his seat for a nap.

Grant Williams had been in and out of reform schools and orphanages all his life. Now at the age of nineteen he was free. He was a dangerous young man. Originally from Baltimore he eventually made his way to Philadelphia on a freight train. He had been arrested shortly after being released from the last reform school he was in. The charge was indecent assault. He met a girl at a dance hall on a Saturday night and she found him very aggressive with his hands. He was given a summons and was instructed to go to court that following Monday. He hopped a train to Philly instead. Technically he was a fugitive from justice. He settled in the suburb of Colwyn just outside of Philadelphia. He had a room and a job at a sandwich shop on Main Street.

Tonight, he was on the prowl for a victim. He had been watching a certain trail that went through some woods and under a trolley trestle near the 69th Street Terminal in Upper Darby. The trail started at the edge of an athletic field next to Arch Bishop Prendergast Catholic High School for Girls. It emptied out on to Garrett Road and was a favorite short cut. It was late afternoon on Friday and just starting to get dark. He had planned this for some time. A sophomore named Julie Tanner made her way to the trail. She was on her way home after practice with the chess club.

Waiting for her he hid behind a large tree and as she passed he grabbed her. He had a five-inch Barlow knife in his hand. The blade was closed but the knife in his fist emphasized the blow as he punched her in the face. He had worked the action on the knife so that he could open it with the flick of his wrist. Once open the blade locked in place. He had honed the edge of the knife in work and it was now razor sharp. He pulled the stunned girl into the brush and flicking his wrist he opened the knife. Pulling up the skirt of her uniform he cut off her panties. He ripped the blouse open and cut her bra exposing her breasts. Still stunned from the punch she offered no resistance. He opened his pants and tried to enter her. Waking now she struggled. He was getting harder and pushed his way into her. She cried out in pain. He grabbed her by the throat with his left hand and pushed in to her over and over. She trashed beneath him and was clawing with both of her hands at his hand clasped around her throat. He held the knife close to her face and felt the orgasm beginning to build. The more she struggled the more excited he became, finally exploding his semen into her as he finished. He lay over her exhausted. She was very still. He got up and looked at her. Her eyes were lifeless staring straight up into the top of the trees. He fixed himself put the knife away in his pocket. He started back to the trail. One of her books was there. He picked it up and looked at the cover. It was titled 'Your Life with Christ'.

He threw it back on the ground and laughed to himself. Where was Christ when you needed him most he thought. He came off the trail on Garrett

Road and started walking towards the 69th Street Terminal. Thinking about what he had done he felt no regrets or shame. He only thought about his orgasm. It felt so good. It was nothing like when he masturbated. It was all so exciting. I need to do that again he thought. I need to plan a new attack. The night is young, let's see what we can find, he thought.

It rained that Saturday. Sunday started out raining and then cleared. No one had used the path until early Monday morning. Three girls walking to school took the path they used every day.

First, they found a book in the path. More books led into the brush. They found Julie Tanners body as he left her, on her back her legs wide apart with her shirt ripped open. Screaming and crying the three girls ran to the school. The first victim of a long series of assaults had been found.

CHAPTER 7

SILLY MAN, SAD MAN

Susan and Colleen noticed the change on the beach, and saw the same cockiness at the house. Mike was getting very touchy with Colleen.

Sitting down to dinner, Mike helped serving and he would put his hand on her shoulder while she sat at the table. He sat on the end with both women on his right side. Colleen was closest and he played footsie with her as they ate. Colleen played along but managed to alert Susan. After dinner Mike sat outside with his coffee and a cigar. "What the hell is he doing?" Colleen asked.

Susan replied, "I think he's trying to turn the tables. Why else would he be acting this way? For the last few days he's been stumbling around here like a blind mule. Every time you went near him he got nervous. Now today he's coming on to you like a love-sick school boy. I have an idea. We can call his bluff. Tonight, after his shower I'm willing to bet he will go into your room. Only instead of you he's going to find me."

"OK, what if he just goes to bed like normal?" Colleen asked.

"Then he will crawl into bed with you. Either way he's going to get a surprise," Susan added.

"But what if he...you know starts getting frisky?" Colleen asked.

"Play along a little and make some noise, then I will come in," Susan said.

"Then what?" Colleen asked.

"We can let him know we are on to him. But after tonight whatever happens we can't tease him anymore. If he really thinks sex is a possibility, we have to stop before we go too far. Agreed?" Susan explained.

"I just hope we don't hurt his feelings or his pride," Colleen said.

"He's a big boy. Besides I'll make it up to him," Susan giggled.

Mike finished his coffee and cigar and came back into the house.

He sat in the middle of the sofa and turned on the radio. Music was playing and he started to read the paper. Susan and Colleen still in their bathing suits on either side of him. Mike continued to read the paper and folded it so it could be held in one hand. His other hand was on Colleens thigh. He switched the paper occasionally from one hand to the other. His free hand was either on Colleen or Susan's thigh. They made small talk through the evening then Colleen announced she was going to take a shower. "Need any help?" Mike asked.

"Maybe, I'll call you if I do," Colleen said looking back at Susan.

Mike and Susan sat there for a few minutes and then Susan said suddenly. "You know I think maybe I'll see if she does need help." She got up and went to the bathroom door and knocked. Colleen poked her head around the door surprised to see Susan. "What are you doing?" Colleen asked.

"We have to finish our showers together. I'm not leaving you two alone while I'm getting mine," Susan whispered taking off her bathing suit. Colleen had already started the water and was naked. Susan pulled back the curtain and stepped into the tub. "C'mon, we have to hurry," Susan said.

"You want me to shower with you?" Colleen asked.

"It's no big deal, get in," Susan said. Colleen stepped into the tub and the two women began to wash. They were on the beach most of the day and they had sand and sun tan lotion on. The shower space was small and the two women bumped into each other. This caused them to laugh and whisper to each other. Mike got up and heard the women whispering but the shower made it hard for him to make out what they were saying. "You two all right in there?" Mike asked as he tried the door. Poking his head inside he saw Susan peak from behind the curtain. "Get out we don't need any help."

Mike closed the door and thought about what was going on. His wife and Colleen were naked in the shower together. The water stopped and Colleen came out first followed by Susan. Both women had towels wrapped around them as they ran into Colleens bed room laughing.

Colleen took off her towel. She put on her pajamas, which was a pair of shorts and a top that buttoned down the front. "Shit my pajamas are in my room. What do I do now?" Susan asked.

Colleen pulled off Susan's towel and shrugged her shoulders.

"Right, I'll make him get a shower. When he's in there we switch rooms. Got it?" Susan asked. Colleen nodded her approval.

Susan then walked out of Colleens room bare ass naked. Mike was standing in the living room totally confused. The thought of Susan and Colleen naked in the shower excited him. The site of Susan however gave him primal clarity and he followed her into their bedroom. "Hi there, good looking," he said.

"Never you mind, go get your shower. I'm going to sleep she said pulling a night gown over her head.

Mike grabbed his pajama pants and went into the bathroom. Colleens door was closed but the light was still on. He took off his clothes and got into the shower. What were these two up too, he thought? He started to think about all that had happened all week and tonight. Susan was not the kind of women to get sexual with another woman.

Neither was Colleen for that matter. These two were up to something. They had a long history of teasing him and being flirtatious. They're baiting me he thought. Susan walks naked into the bedroom and declares she's going to sleep. Colleen is in her room with the light still on. They want me to go into Colleens room. He was washing the whole time and noticed he had an erection. He rinsed and dried himself and put on his pajama pants. Well if that's what they want then I'm going to call their bluff. I'll get into bed with Colleen and then we'll see what happens. Wearing his pajama pants he noted he was still excited as he peeked into his bedroom. Susan was in bed and appeared to be sleeping.

Colleens door was closed but the light was still on. He took a deep breath and tried the door knob. It turned in his hand just as the light went off.

Susan and Colleen switched bedrooms. "Fake like your sleeping and lay still. I'll be in your room," Susan told Colleen.

"I hope this works," Colleen replied. Colleen got into Susan's bed on her side and laid there very still. Susan looked around the room and then at her night gown. She decided to take off the gown at the last minute. She would be naked in Colleens bed. Susan was by the door when Mike came out of the bathroom. She heard him try the door to her bedroom. She turned off the light switch just as Mike turned the door knob.

She was under the sheets waiting for him in the darkness. Mike couldn't see a thing. He took a deep breath and thought it's now or never. Wearing only his pajama bottoms he crawled into bed with Susan. He was surprised that she was naked. Holly crap, he thought Colleen has no clothes on. Then he felt her grab him as she whispered seductively. "Someone's happy to see me," she said.

"What… what the hell. Susan what are you doing here?" Mike yelled.

"I might ask you the same thing. What are you doing here?" Susan demanded. Then the door opened and Colleen switched the light on. Mike had gotten out of bed and was standing there.

"Yea, Mike why are you and your friend in my bedroom?" Colleen demanded pointing at his pajama's. Mike looked down his erection poking at his pajama's. He grabbed a pillow from the bed and covered himself. "You're supposed to be in that bed naked," he exclaimed and pointing at the bed.

"Oh, really and why would I be naked?" Colleen demanded.

Mike ignored her and stated, "You're supposed to be in there sleeping."

"And if I were sleeping, just where would you be?" Susan exclaimed sitting on the bed not covering herself.

"I would be in here with you, no I mean you," Mike said pointing back and forth between Colleen and Susan.

"So, if I had been in my own bed without my clothes on, just what were you expecting?" Colleen demanded.

"I know just what he wanted. After all it was my naked body he snuggled up to with that… thing," Susan said.

"Hey, you grabbed me, but it was supposed to be her grabbing me," Mike cried pointing at Colleen.

"Oh really," Susan said feinting shock.

"You two switched beds. So even if I did go to my own bed you would have been there. Waiting for me," Mike exclaimed pointing to Colleen.

"So, you were looking for Colleen?" Susan asked.

"Yes...no...I mean. You're supposed to be in there, in your own bed. And you are supposed to be in here," Mike declared confused.

"So again, you were here looking for me," Colleen said triumphantly.

"Michael McMullen, after all these years you still think that I would have sex with you?" Colleen asked indignantly.

"That's what you wanted. And you too. You two have been screwing with me all week. But, I was going to call your bluff. Tonight, I was going to be the one to screw with both of you," Mike said, and even after the words came out he knew he was doomed.

"Well I must say, I'm ashamed of you. To think that you thought you were going to have sex with both of us. Shame, shame on you Michael," Susan declared. She got out of bed and put her night gown on."

"C'mon Colleen let's go to bed. I'm not staying one more minute with this pervert," Susan said leaving the room. Mike was left standing there by himself. He was still holding the pillow, although by now it wasn't necessary. He was completely confused. What had gone wrong. "So, does this mean I'm not having sex tonight?" He asked.

"YES." Both women replied loudly.

Mike went into the living room and sat on the sofa. What the hell happened he thought. He looked at Cupcake and said, "A lot of help you were." The dog rolled over ignoring him.

Susan and Colleen lay in bed using their pillows to stifle their laughing. "I told you. He was trying to turn the tables on us," Susan said.

"Waiting in bed without your clothes on, that was the best," Colleen declared.

"Poor Mike. I hope he isn't mad in the morning," Susan said.

"Tell you what. Set the alarm an hour earlier and I'll take a walk on the beach before breakfast.

That will give you enough time to make it up to him," Colleen offered.

"What am I supposed to do for the other fifty-nine minutes?" Susan asked. Both women started laughing again.

Colleen and Susan woke to the alarm. Colleen got dressed and took Cupcake to the beach. Susan looked into Colleens room. Mike was sleeping on the bed snoring. She got into bed and woke him the way he liked to be woken.

Colleen and Cupcake returned just as breakfast was ready. Mike sat sheepishly at the table and shared a piece of sausage with the dog. Susan had woken him and they made passionate love.

He was still worried that he was in trouble. Based on Susan's actions that morning he thought he might be off the hook. He was about to beg for forgiveness when Susan said, "Mike, Colleen and I want to apologize. That was a nasty trick we pulled on you. I promise there will be no more teasing or pranks anymore."

Colleen added, "We are very sorry. It was unfair to do that to you. Please forgive us."

Mike was surprised, but cautious. Why were they apologizing. He thought he was the one in trouble. Suspicious he said, "OK, I forgive you. Does this mean the three of us are still having sex?"

"NO". Both women replied.

Margaret McMullen took her shopping cart and left for the super market on Girard Avenue. As she crossed Poplar Street the wheels of her cart got caught in the trolley tracks. The east bound PTC (Philadelphia Transit Company) trolley operator was talking with a passenger. He never saw Margaret as he came around the curve. Margaret realizing, she was about to be hit let go of the cart but ran the wrong way. The trolley struck her on the operator's side and pinned her under the wheels. She died before the trolley stopped.

Joe McMullen sat in his chair reading the morning newspaper. He heard the sirens as police and fire equipment arrived on the scene. He went outside and looked down the street. He saw the trolley stopped in the intersection. A red car (Police Car) could not make it down the street and stopped in front of his row home. One of the officers got out and started to walk down the street. "What happened Officer?" Joe asked.

"Trolley ran someone over," he replied.

Joe went back inside to finish his paper. What a shame he thought to himself. Twenty minutes later the doorbell rang. The same policeman was there with another cop and Lieutenant from the fire department. One of the neighbors Mrs. Naughton was with them. She was crying. "Are you Joseph McMullen?" The officer asked.

"I am, Captain McMullen retired NYPD," Joe replied formally.

"Captain I regret I have to inform you that your wife Margaret was killed in the trolley accident. I'm very sorry sir," the policeman said.

Joe stood there. He had done this sort of thing many times in his career. He never thought that someday he would be answering the door. "You're positive you have the right identification of the deceased?" Joe asked.

"Yes sir. Mrs. Naughton witnessed the accident. We also recovered the victims purse," the officer said. The fire department Lieutenant handed the purse to Joe. There was no doubt. It was Margaret's. "I assume the remains are going to the ME (Medical Examiner)?" Joe asked.

"Yes sir. As soon as the victim's body is recovered it will be turned over to the ME," the officer said.

Joe turned and went inside. He left the door open. A Police Lieutenant walked up to the group outside his door. The officer briefed him on the incident. The Lieutenant walked into the house and found Joe sitting on the couch holding his wife's purse. He stood before Joe and saluted. Joe looked up with tears in his eyes and returned the salute. "Captain, my name is Lieutenant Billings. I'm very sorry for you. Is there any one we can call for you?" Billings asked respectfully.

"My son is on the job in Ocean City New Jersey. My daughter lives on Olive Street. Can someone take me to her?" Joe asked.

"Yes sir. I want you to know we will treat this as if it was one of our own, Captain. Anything you want or need we will be there for you and your family. Can you give me your son's full name?" Billings asked.

"Mike, Mike McMullen OCPD (Ocean City Police Department)," Joe replied standing. He put out his hand to shake hands with Billings. "Thank You." Joe said.

"I can take you to your daughter's house. Please come with me," Billings said. They went outside and Joe saw the street had been cleared. The trolley was still blocking the intersection. He got into the Lieutenants car and sat up front in the passenger seat. Billings turned to one of the officers that was inside with him and ordered, "Call in to the district and have them notify OCPD. Then right up your report and leave it on my desk. Have the ME expedite the case. I'll be back at the district after I take Captain McMullen to his daughter's home." Billings got into the red car and backed up the street. Then he drove to Maggie's house. When he arrived at Maggie's Joe went inside. He was still holding Margaret's purse. Maggie was home about to have lunch. She saw her father holding her mother's purse. The look on his face told her something was terribly wrong. Then she saw Lt. Billings. At first, she thought something had happened to Mike but then her father told her the news.

Mike climbed into the jeep and started his usual morning patrol. After making a complete tour of the beach he drove to headquarters. He greeted the desk sergeant as he checked in for duty. He went upstairs to say good morning to Dave. They had coffee and discussed some of Dave's cases. Mike had been in the station for about an hour and decided to go back to the beach. The shops on the boardwalk would be opening soon.

The desk sergeant had just hung up the phone when he saw Mike at the bottom of the stairs. "Hey Mike," he called. Mike stood before the sergeant's desk responding to his call. Mike noticed the sergeant who was usually jovial was upset about something. "Mike, I just got off the phone with Philly PD. They told me…well, your mother was killed in an accident this morning. I'm sorry," he stated sadly.

Mike startled replied, "What? An accident? What sort of accident? My mother doesn't drive a car. How could she be in an accident? Are they sure it's her? Sarge what did they say?"

The sergeant answered, "Your mother was struck by a trolley car while she was crossing Poplar Street. They told me she died instantly at the scene. Your father was informed and he is at your sister's house. I'm sorry, Mike.

Take as much time as you need, I'll square it with the Chief." Mike went outside and sat in the jeep. He was stunned. He headed for the beach to drive home. Colleen had just left a few weeks ago. Susan would be home alone. The Labor Day weekend was just a few days away.

He drove up the beach fighting back the tears. He pulled up over the dunes behind his house. Susan was outside hanging sheets on the clothes line behind the house. Cupcake growled and barked at the jeep as he came to a stop. Susan saw the look on his face and knew that something bad had happened. He walked up to her and holding her finally let the grief out. It was a few minutes before he was able to tell her the news. Then they cried together.

They packed some clothes and drove to Philadelphia. It was a long silent drive. Arriving at Maggie's later that afternoon the whole family had assembled. Maggie ran to Mike as he entered, "Mike I can't believe it. We have been trying to call you all day," she said crying.

"I'm sorry, they told me at headquarters what happened. Susan and I drove up right away," he replied crying with her.

Joe McMullen was in the kitchen. He was drinking a cup of coffee. The look on his face was sullen. He was lost in his own thoughts. "Pop, are you, all, right?" Mike asked.

"I should have gone with her. She always went shopping by herself. I cannot believe this. It's not right. She was such a good woman. How will I live without her," he replied starting to cry again?

"I know Pop. I'll take care of everything. You need to take care of yourself," Mike replied.

"No. I'll do it. She was your mother. She was everything to me. I know how she wanted this to be, we discussed it. We both thought it would be me first. We went out to Calvary Cemetery up in Conshohocken. She loved it there. We have a four-grave plot. Dinan will handle the funeral. We already made arrangements last year," his father answered.

While the family grieved, Cupcake went to everyone in the house. He knew something was wrong. The humans in his life were all sad and upset. He pawed and wined at each one trying in his own way to help them. He did not understand, but he knew they were all hurting.

The funeral was a week later. The ME had expedited the return of the body. Everyone attended except for Dylan. Logistically he would not be able to return from the Philippines in time.

He grieved by himself over the loss of his grandmother. He did manage to get a long-distance connection from the embassy in Manila. The call was faint and full of static, but he was able to speak with his grandfather and his mother.

After the funeral, the family returned to Maggie's house. Along with some friends and neighbor's members of the 9th Police District had attended the funeral. Joe had to face a new chapter in his life. As much as he appreciated everyone's concern, he decided to return home. He needed to be alone.

CHAPTER 8
TIME MOVES ON

Grant Williams was a hunted man. Police Departments up and down the Main Line and smaller towns in Delaware County were actively looking for a man responsible for attacks on young women. There was no consolidated investigation between the departments. Eleven young women had been brutally beaten, raped and killed. The only common denominator was the killer took a trophy from each of his victims. He cut a portion of their hair for his own keeping. All of the attacks occurred on or near the trolley lines that left the 69th Street Terminal in Upper Darby Pa. The last attack happened in Media Pa. near the Providence Road Station. Four of the women were victims along the high-speed train route from the terminal to Norristown Pa. The Delaware County Times reported each of the incidents but no one in law enforcement connected the attacks to a single perpetrator. That would soon change.

Dorothy and Hope had completed their course of studies. Dorothy wanted to take an additional course at Villanova over the summer. Hope was looking to join the Army Nurse Corps. She had passed her boards and was an RN. The recruiter told her she would have to pass a physical, some other tests required by the Army and then she would be off to training.

Once she completed those tasks she would be commissioned a 2nd Lieutenant. The biggest obstacle was telling her mother Colleen. She passed her tests and her physical and signed the final enlistment documents. She received orders to report to Fort Devens in Massachusetts in the late summer of 1949. Another large family and friend graduation party had been planned and everyone had a good time. The future was looking brighter.

Hope and Colleen spent a weekend in early August with Mike and Susan. Mornings on the beach with coffee and a picnic breakfast were the best times of the day. Sitting on the beach on a large blanket they all watched the sun rise. Cupcake was happy to chase sea birds from the surf until the food came out of the basket. Once breakfast was finished they drank the last of the coffee from the three thermos containers Mike had. "Any job prospects coming your way Honey," Colleen asked Hope.

Hope was dreading this conversation but now was as good a time as any.

"I have a job. It's in Massachusetts. I enlisted in the Army," Hope said with as much enthusiasm as she could muster.

The silence that followed was deafening. Mike stood and called Cupcake to come with him. He walked to the surf with the dog happily chasing birds again. "Maybe I should leave you two alone," Susan said.

"Not at all. Please stay," Colleen replied.

"Mom this is really important to me...I" Hope said as her mother cut her off.

Colleen sighed and replied, "I know. It's just that I see how hard it is on Maggie with Dylan so far away. I've had you to myself all of your life. I always knew the day would come when I would have to let you go. I guess I always hoped that it would never be far away."

"Mom Fort Devens is in Massachusetts, not Manila," Hope said.

"Is that permanent?" Colleen asked.

"No. I'll just be there for training. After that I just don't know. The Army will put me into the best schools. I'll be working with the latest equipment. Maybe I can get assigned to Walter Reed General Hospital in Washington," Hope replied.

"Sounds very exciting. I guess I always hoped those questions about your father would eventually go away. If your happy sweetheart, then I will be too. You have to promise me that I will have grandchildren. Oh, I'm sorry Susan. I know that has always been a sore subject with Mike's parents," Collen said.

"It's all right. Just remember Hope, don't get so immersed in your career that you forget about a husband and a family. I don't regret any of my decisions. After all I have my own two children right there," Susan replied pointing to the surf line.

The rest of the weekend went well and Colleen and Hope boarded the bus for the trip back to Philadelphia. Once back in the city Colleen returned to work and Hope prepared for her trip to Fort Devens. Dorothy stopped by after her summer class and the two girls talked about their futures. "So, your Mom knows about the Army. I'm happy she took it well. When do you plan on popping out babies?" Dorothy laughed.

"Not any time soon. Don't forget about our bet. I imagine you'll be the one having children before me," Hope replied.

"The bet is not about children. The girl that loses her precious flower first buys lunch," Dorothy answered foolishly.

"So, did you get the job in Germantown at John Jenks Elementary?" Hope asked changing the subject.

"Yes, I did. I start at the end of August for faculty orientation. I start out as an assistant teacher with first graders. I can't wait to get my hands on those little munchkins. They'll all so cute. I am looking forward to it," Dorothy replied with enthusiasm.

"How's the summer class going?" Hope asked.

"It's easy. I have a final test on Thursday, then I'm done. Hey, do you think we can get down the shore to see Mike and Susan? That would be cool. Our last fling together before we start our careers," Dorothy asked with anticipation.

"I'm sure they would not mind. We could have breakfast on the beach and watch the sun rise," Hope replied.

"I was thinking more on the lines of late nights with muscle bound hard bodies of lifeguards. A little romp in the dunes, then sleeping until noon" Dorothy said mischievously.

"Dorothy, I swear you have a one-track mind. Don't forget the school Principal will not appreciate a flirty girl with a sordid reputation teaching his first graders," Hope said.

"Don't you worry darling. I am good at what I do. Ask anyone. I am also very discreet. I have seen and met the principal. He is a very handsome man," Dorothy said lustily.

The two girls laughed and waited for Colleen to come from work.

Dinh Quan was a small village northeast of Saigon. A trade school for machinist was established a few years ago, by the Province of Long Khanh. Most of the financing secretly came from the Communist Government in Hanoi. Province and other local officials had been bribed. The school operated with no oversite other than the man who was the school master. His name was Vang Bo a Chinese nationalist who was now a part of the intelligence arm of the Viet Minh. The school had just ten students. They came from the village and surrounding hamlets.

All but three were young men approaching military age. Of the three students spy one was a girl and two of the older men were committed Viet Minh apprentices. They reported French military movements to Bo. He passed the information to a pedal cab driver known to him only as Osprey.

During the day, Bo, would conduct his classes. All of his students learned their trade with enthusiasm. All of his students were in their teens. Full of youthful anger over the re-occupation of their country by the French, his students talked of Vietnamese independence often. Soon they would be of military age. Bo knew that most of these young boys would become members of the Viet Minh or the new National Army of South Vietnam. The subject was never openly discussed with him. He was Chinese, but he would overhear the conversations. He knew they would be surprised to know who he really was. His three counterparts stayed together.

They were friendly with the other students but kept mostly to themselves. The other students had no idea who they really were. They walked to school each day from three separate locations. It was during these walks that they made note of any French troop movements. The French were also supported by Moroccan and Algerian troops under the command of the French Foreign Legion. Although most of the fighting between the combatants was in the north around Tonkin, the south saw heavy guerilla fighting in and around Saigon. French troops were routinely ambushed by Viet Minh forces. People in the southern provinces living in hamlets and villages would be happy to learn that French or especially the Moroccan troops were ambushed and killed. The Moroccans were especially hated by the population because of their brutality.

Truck convoys of military supplies routinely passed through Dinh Quan. The convoys would pass the front of the school and Bo would allow his students to stand out front. They would wave and smile at the troops passing by the school. Bo would remain inside, knowing his three special students would count the number of vehicles and troops heading north on route QL20. One was tasked to count the number of vehicles. Another would only count the number of soldiers. The girl who was the youngest of the three would count the type of weapons. Once the convoy passed the three would each give Bo a number. He already knew what the numbers meant. Osprey would be outside the school and once the students returned inside the numbers would be relayed to the pedal-cab operator in order. He would then leave and pass the information to Dui Minh code name Bishop. On some days, the convoy would be ambushed miles north of the school.

There was a small French garrison in Dinh Quan. Ironically, French soldiers would bring in pieces of machinery or parts of weapons that needed repair or re-fabrication. Bo was always delighted to help the soldiers, and made sure that any work was completed with the highest standards. The soldiers would speak freely around him and he passed on any usable intelligence to Osprey. Bo's operation was but one of many all over the southern provinces.

The French garrison commander learned of the excellent work performed by the students at Bo's school. He sent a cable to his headquarters to have the Groupement de Commandos Mixtes Aeropotes check him out. The report he received back indicated everything about Bo was accurate. The French GCMA had no indication he was anything but who he said he was based on the information they could find. Bo would soon be invited to dinner parties at the French garrison. Learning that Bo was Chinese and not politically active in the affairs of the new French Republic of Vietnam, he was considered to be no threat to French military operations in the country. Bo never indicated that he had a knowledge of French other than a few phrases. Officers in the garrison would speak freely about operations in his presence never knowing he was listening to every word. His operational duties would be expanded. Counting of French troop movements along with the information he learned around the French officers would be delivered by Osprey to Bishop. Before long he was invited to Saigon. Social gatherings exposed him to other prominent South Vietnamese officials as well as members of MAAG (US Military Assistance Advisory Group). He was now a more than just a field operative for the Viet Minh. He had become a professional spy. Upon learning of his new activities Hanoi was considering moving him from the school.

New York City was becoming a post war bustling metropolis. Michael Costigan and Tom Brady saw each other on a regular basis. Tom had completed his studies at Cooper Union School of Art. He was making good money in Times Square drawing caricatures for tourists. It was an all cash business and Tom kept every penny. He copied the style of Al Hershfeld and did all of his work with a black pen. Hershfelds work was becoming famous and he had done work for the New Yorker Magazine as well as the New York Times. Tourist were eager to pay three dollars for the Hershfeld look alike drawings. Tom on a busy day could make six to nine dollars an hour. Making thirty to forty-five dollars a day he was doing quite well. Michael being well off himself was helping him look for an artist's studio in the East Village. Tom's social life had also expanded. He would make several tips to Washington by train to see Caroline Grindell.

They had developed a friendship at Dylan's going away party. That soon turned into a romantic relationship. The first time he saw her socially they had dinner and returned to her apartment. Sitting on the couch in her living room they shared a bottle of wine. As always Tom had his sketch pad and started a portrait of her. "You know, I think I would like you to draw all of me," she said.

She stood up and motioned him to sit on an adjoining chair. Then she stripped and laid down on the couch. Tom was enthused. His pencil started to fly across the page. Before long he could stand it no further and stripped off his own clothes. Standing before her he said, "You are so beautiful."

"You're not half bad yourself. Can you draw with this thing too?" Caroline asked grabbing him and stroking him. They spent the night together and after making love and finishing another bottle of wine he said to her, "This time I want to really concentrate on drawing you. She laid on the bed with the sheets around her. He moved the sheets to where he wanted them and then told her, "Don't move, this is going to be marvelous." After an hour, he was finished. Caroline looked at the drawing. It had been meticulously done. It was very sensual and erotic. She liked it. "Tell me. Who is going to see this?" She asked.

"I'm going to take it back to New York and paint it. With any luck, everyone will see it," he responded.

"I find that prospect very exciting. Who knows maybe someday me and the Mona Lisa will be on the same wall," she said enticingly. They made love again exploring each other's body and fell asleep.

Tom saw Caroline two to three times per month and usually for days at a time. He coordinated his visits with her days off. Sometimes she came to New York. He had a small one room one bath apartment on Avenue B south of Thompkins Square Park. He was also just a few blocks away from Michaels apartment. Tom was a typical artist. A free spirit in many ways including his sexual activities. Born in the wrong generation he would have been happier in the free love, love the one you're with generation of the sixties. There was nothing exclusive in his life other than his art.

He spent most of his time perfecting his talent. With Michaels help he was able to find a loft style artist studio at 13th and Avenue D. He grew a beard and let his hair get longer than it should. Tom also found himself immersed into the beat-nick scene that was starting to develop in the Village.

Aside from alcohol he started smoking marijuana, Michael and Tom would often go to coffee houses and bars were poetry was read.

All of this was a concern for Caroline. Her association with them was a threat to her security clearance. The FBI watched these groups and the new internal security office within the CIA kept tabs on all their employees.

Tom did finish the painting of Caroline. It was a very erotic piece and when she first saw it she was pleased. A few weeks later she was shocked to find out it had been sold to one of the underground clubs in the Village. Tom and Michael took her to the club one weekend and there she was. Hanging on the wall over the bar. There could be no mistake as to who the woman was. It was the last straw. She knew she had to break off her relationship with Tom and told him that night. She was somewhat surprised he took it so well. It was almost as if he could have cared less. She took the last train back to Washington that night. She was not in love with him, so the break up did not affect her. She decided she needed to be more careful about her personal life. She smiled to herself thinking about the painting. It was quite good and she looked terrific.

CHAPTER 9
TRAGEDY & TRAINING

The library at Villanova was almost empty except for a few students. Summer classes were still in session. Most of them were sitting at tables in the center of the library their heads buried in books or bent over note pads. On the second floor of the library back in the southeast corner there was a theological section of books. Dorothy and a young man named Ted were kissing. The encounter was getting a little heated as Ted fondled her breasts and he tried to get his hand up under her dress. She fought him off easily enough telling him, "Ted, stop this is not the time or place. Besides I need to get home and I do not want to miss my train." Disappointed and clearly aroused, she promised him, "You can wait baby, I'll make it well worth your while." She kissed him quickly while she grasped his erection bulging in the front of his khaki's and broke away before he could respond. Tucking at her dress and smoothing her hair she made her way down the steps and went into the ladies' room. Just as she thought her lipstick was smudged. She washed and touched up her makeup and made her way across campus to Lancaster Avenue. Adjusting the canvas bag over her shoulder that held her books, she saw the single car southbound train sitting at the station about seventy yards away. Damn, she thought as she raced across the street I've missed the train. As she reached the other side of the avenue the train pulled away from the station.

She knew it would be another twenty minutes before the next train came along. The spring evening was turning cooler and dusk settled over the pathway to the platform.

Just as she reached the stairs to the five-foot-high platform she sensed movement behind her and to her right. A hand grabbed her by her ponytail and pulled her off the stairs back onto the pathway. At first, she thought that Ted had followed her to the station. He was usually not this rough and she started to protest but did not scream. Before she knew it, she was being pulled by the strap on the canvas bag under the wooden platform.

Pushed to the back of the structure she found herself pinned to the ground and her attacker was sitting on her. This was not Ted she realized. She started to protest when the unknown as-sailant slapped her hard across the face. Her face was on fire from the slap and this angered her. She started fighting back. "Get off me you bastard," she said defiantly. Instead of just flail-ing with her hands she made a fist with her right hand and hit her attacker with a right cross. The punch surprised the man and he was stunned at first, but he quickly recovered. Slapping her again, he stunning her, he grabbed the front of the button-down dress ripping it open to her waist. In his left hand, he had a knife that she had not seen. He used it to cut her bra and in the process, she was cut along the right side of her left breast. "Aughh," she screamed from the pain.

Now she panicked and trashed around and flailed her arms to stop the attack. It was dark, damp and dusty under the platform. Inhaling the dust choked her and made her cough and gag. She crossed her ankles and locked her legs, making them as straight as she could but he still managed to get her legs open pushing hard with his knees. Regaining herself the struggle continued as he lifted the skirt and cut the panties open at the crotch. The knife tip caught her across the vagina and cut her. She screamed out in pain again, and the man told her, "Shut up you bitch." Then he punched her in the mouth. She tasted her blood in her mouth and felt some of her teeth coming out. Drawing from her last reserves of strength, she spat her teeth and blood into his face and once again started to fight him in earnest.

She started by attempting to gouge and scratch at his eyes with her left hand as she hit him with her fist over and over with her right hand. He brought his hands up to ward off her attack and she was able to knock the knife from his hand. She felt as if she was gaining the advantage and she was able to sit up somewhat. She grabbed his hair and repeated her punching. He managed to get ahold of both of her hands as they struggled and he hit her with a head butt as he pulled her up at the same time. The blow hit her across her nose. The pain was incredible and she was blinded and stunned. Having regained the advantage, he looked down on her as she lay motionless. Her face was bloody and he gazed at her exposed breasts. He undid his pants quickly and tried to enter her. She got her wits back and started to try to move him off her. "NO, NO...Stop," she cried. Her cries of protest only emboldened him. The more she whimpered and cried the more excited he became. He entered her tearing at her insides and the cut from the knife. "Aughh, NO...NO, please oh God NO!" Dorothy cried. He continued his thrusts, she felt as if he was tearing her insides apart. Crying out in pain she was now helpless. Her agonizing cries only made him more excited. She felt like she was drifting away.

She was losing consciousness. Lying still now she only whimpered softly to herself. This enraged him. If she did not cry out and beg him he would not be able to dominate her and finish. He felt his erection losing its ability to push into her. Finally, his limp member simply slipped out. Enraged at his inability to climax he lashed out at her. He punched her over and over. Finally exhausted he fixed his pants, crawled from under the station and ran north up the tracks.

She laid there for more than an hour unconscious and bleeding. She heard voices and she could see out of her right eye the southbound train sitting in the station. Her left eye was swollen shut. She could only breathe through her mouth. Blood had crusted and dried in her broken nose and the swelling closed off her ability to breathe. Her torso was covered in blood from the cut on her breast. The insides of her thighs were bruised and sore from her attackers repeated attempts to push open her legs. She was also bleeding from her vagina, both from the cut of the knife and his brutal rape of her. Her right hand hurt. It was badly swollen and looked more like the end of a club. She could not move her fingers. The nails of her left hand had been pulled out or broken to the quicks. The southbound train pulled away and she tried as hard as she could to cry out but could not. She started crawling towards the open end of the platform to the tracks. It took every ounce of what little strength she had to reach the tracks. She had no idea how long it had taken her to get out from under the platform unto the northbound track. She felt herself losing consciousness again and was about to pass out. She was cold and she shivered. The pain was winning overtaking her. There was nothing left. Dorothy collapsed on the tracks. She heard a loud piercing noise and then there was a bright light as the ground shook beneath her. Then there was nothing but darkness.

Wiping the sweat and blood from his face, Grant Williams stopped running and rested in the woods next to the tracks. He was angry. The bitch fought like a tiger. He tried to comb his hair and felt the pain on his scalp where she had torn at his hair. His lip was cut and he could feel his left eye starting to swell. Rested he walked into the woods away from the tracks and exited on Aldwyn Lane. Walking north he came to the intersection of Lancaster Avenue and Sproul Road. He needed to get cleaned up. There was a small pizza shop on the corner. He went inside and headed straight to the back to the restroom. Looking in the mirror he could see the damage she had done. His left eye was red, bruising and swelling shut. Blood had dried and crusted around his nostrils. She had also scratched him badly on the side of his head and neck. The tan colored t-shirt he wore under his jacket was covered in sweat and spattered with blood. He took off his jacket and shirt and began to wash himself.

Joey Lambert was working the evening shift making pizza's. A student at Villanova he was working his way through school. He saw the man enter the shop. Clearly, he had been in some kind of fight. The recent news stories about a mugger attacking young women around the school came to his mind. He talked with his boss. The boss had not seen the man enter the shop but agreed with Joey. He picked up the phone and called the police. Five minutes passed when two officers arrived. Joey directed them to the restroom. The two policemen opened the door and found Grant washing his face. The t-shirt he had taken off was in a bunch on the floor. They asked him for his identification and questioned him about his clothes and his face. He told them that some boys from the school had jumped him and beat him up.

The police found more blood on his jacket and the knees of his blue jeans were caked in dirt. Suspicious about his story they took him into custody over his protest that he had done nothing wrong.

Putting him the back of the patrol car they drove to Police Headquarters in Radnor. Once they arrived they learned of the attack of a young women at the Red Arrow Station at Villanova. Grant was placed in a holding cell. He sat there alone for hours. He was worried. The girl may be able to identify him. Then he remembered he had lost his knife. He was thinking to himself that he was going to get caught for this attack. He thought about the others. Would the police also be able to charge him with those as well. He had already given them a false name. He had to get away. There was a door he saw at the end of the hall where the cells were located. Perhaps he could make a break for it.

Detective's Mike Meziaz and Bill Breker arrived at the scene of the attack. They began the investigation by interviewing the northbound train operator, Bill Long. The man was still emotional and shaken by what had happened. "Try to take it easy, Mr. Long. Take a deep breath and tell us what happened," Detective Breker said. Long took the breath and started his statement. "I came up on the station right on time. When I got to the end of the platform I could see someone lying across the tracks. I hit the brakes hard then and the train came to a jolting stop. Some of the passengers screamed when they got jostled. One woman fell in the aisle. I told everyone to stay put and then I looked down at the track. I could not see the person. I jumped down, and that's when I saw her. She was almost under the wheels and the axle. Then I saw all the blood. I thought my God I've killed her. I got back on the platform and backed the train up and then climbed out the other side. The southbound train was coming into the station. I could see the girl. Like I said she had blood all over her. I turned her over and she moaned. That's when I called for the ambulance. I didn't see her until it was too late. Is she going to be all right? Please tell me I didn't kill her," Long said.

Meziaz had taken a short hand course and wrote everything down as Long spoke. Breker said, "We don't know yet. She was pretty bad. We are going to the hospital in a few minutes. Try to take it easy, this was not your fault. Thanks for your help."

Meziaz told a uniformed policeman to get the operators contact information when another officer approached. "Found this under the platform," he said holding a knife up with the ends of his fingers. Meziaz and Breker looked at the bloody knife. They both knew this was another attack by the man they were actively hunting. Another attack happened six weeks ago, near the County Line Station north of Villanova. Meziaz told the officer to book it as evidence as well as anything else they found. "Let's get to the hospital," Mike told his partner. They drove down Lancaster Avenue to Lankenua Hospital. Arriving outside the emergency room they went inside and checked in with the nurse in charge. She informed them that the girl they were looking for was in bad shape but alive. She had been badly beaten, cut and raped. She was not conscious when they ambulance people brought her in. Doctors were still attending to her. More than likely they would not be able to speak to her until tomorrow. Disappointed they could not speak to the victim they left to return to Police Headquarters.

On the way, out they bumped into a detective from the Bridgeport Police. He was there to pick up medical records from another victim killed just three days ago. The three detectives talked about their cases and discovered some similarities. Both of their victims had been assaulted with a knife. The bra and panties had been cut by the attacker. He also took a long lock of the victim's hair.

When they arrived at headquarters the desk sergeant informed them a man was in custody in a holding cell. He had been picked up near the campus by patrol officers responding to a call of a man in bloody clothes. "No shit. Get him into interrogation," Breker said cheerfully.

The desk sergeant made a call and the two detectives retrieved their case file. They waited in the interrogation room.

Five and then ten minutes passed. Meziaz went to the cell block and found the cell door open. He found the officer in charge of bookings lying on the floor unconscious.

The suspect was gone.

Grant looked at the cell he was in. It was five feet wide and about seven feet long. The door swung out into a single narrow hall way. A door at either end of the corridor was the only way in and out. The door to the right led to the offices. The door to the left led outside.

The office door opened and an overweight older officer came into the corridor. He hung up a jacket he was wearing on a coat hook on the wall. He took out a large key ring with just two keys on it and opened Grants cell door. Grant braced himself against the back wall of the cell. "OK bud, detectives want to talk with you so let's go," the officer said opening the door. Grant lunged with all his weight pushing against the door. The force of his movement on the door knocked the officer down and he struck his head on the opposing tile wall. The blow left the officer unconscious and Grant grabbed the keys from the cell door. He also took the jacket off the hook. He hesitated and then took the officers Smith & Wesson Model 10 from its holster. Running to the door on the left he found the only other key and pushed it into the lock. The door opened and he was outside. He put the oversized jacket on stuffed the four-inch revolver into his waist band and ran until he reached Lancaster Avenue. He was close to the Radnor Station of the Norristown line and ran to the platform. A south bound train was coming in and he boarded and sat in the rear.

The trip to the 69th Street Terminal took about twenty minutes. Exiting the train, he crossed the terminal and took the bus to the Darby Colwyn Station. He had to walk several blocks from the station to his small room in the rear of a sandwich shop at the corner of 3rd and Main Street. The room had room enough for a bed and a table on the opposing wall. A bath room had a toilet, a sink and a shower. He took a quick shower and changed his clothes. He packed clothes, the gun, and his belongings into a gym bag and left the apartment. He worked in the shop and had a key. The shop was closed.

Going straight to the register he found the cash from the day's sales in the drawer. The owner of the shop always left the money in the register. He found $44 and put the money in his pocket. Knowing the last number eleven trolley was leaving the Darby Colwyn station he started to walk east on Main Street towards Philadelphia. He boarded the trolley at Island Road. The trolley would take him into Center City Philadelphia. Once there he took a New Jersey Transit bus from the Reading Terminal to Wildwood New Jersey.

Meziaz and Breker sent teletypes out to surrounding departments regarding their escaped suspect. They also made inquiries about any unsolved Rape homicides. The following morning, they had a response from seven different police departments. They were from as far south as Sharon Hill and west to Media Pa.

All of the victims had a lock of hair removed, and the assailant used a knife. Cause of death was always strangulation.

The other staggering similarity was the attacks always occurred in or around Red Arrow Transportation Company rail lines. They were all in Delaware County with the exception of the Bridgeport attack. That was in Montgomery County. Within a week, a task force was formed. It would do no good. The attacks stopped and the man they all wanted had left the state. He was called the Red Arrow Rapist.

CHAPTER 10
TEARS SORROW & WAR

Colleen and Hope sat at the kitchen table making up a list of things needed for Hope's going away party. Colleen had been reading about new hostilities on the Korean Peninsula. The UN was working for a peaceful solution. Hope was going into the Army. Colleen knew that she would never be assigned to a combat unit. If war did break out she knew Hope would be caring for the wounded men. Where was the only concern? She and her daughter had made peace with her decision to join the Army. Hope never knew the father that had never held her. She knew her father was a troubled man. The war in France in 1918 changed him from the man her mother fell in love with to a cold and distant bitter man. The answer seemed so simple. The horror of war and men in close combat with each other was the obvious cause. The pressing question was, why these men could not put the trauma they experienced behind them and return to their normal lives. Men who had endured so much suffering should be overjoyed to be home and away from war. Hope would get her chance to try and find the answers to all of these questions. Colleen was proud of her. Hope had worked hard.

She finished college and a nursing program. The door to her life was just opening.

Kevin and Maggie were upstairs at home preparing for bed. The doorbell rang. "Dorothy must have forgotten her key again," Maggie said brushing her hair. "I'll go let her in. Don't forget we have to get a cake for Hopes party on Saturday," Kevin said going down the stairs. He opened the door and was about to complain about forgetting her key again when he saw the policeman standing on his front step. "Are you Kevin Brogan?" The policeman asked.

"Yes Officer, I am Kevin Brogan," he replied worried.

"Sir I am sorry to inform you that your daughter Dorothy was injured tonight. She is in the emergency room at Lankenua Hospital. I have been instructed to tell you her condition is serious but stable," the policeman told Kevin.

"Why? What happened to her? How was she injured?" Kevin pleaded looking for more information.

The policeman responded, "I'm sorry Mr. Brogan. I don't have any details. The doctors at the hospital will have all of that information. Good luck, sir," the policeman said stepping onto the sidewalk and getting back into the police car.

Kevin closed the door and ran back upstairs. "MAGGIE," he hollered.

After dressing they drove out to the hospital on Lancaster Avenue. They went straight to the emergency room and pleaded with the nurse at the desk, "We are the Brogans. Our daughter Dorothy Brogan was brought here. Where is she?

"Yes, sir she was. Please have a seat over there. I'll call the doctor for you," the nurse replied.

"Is she, all, right? Please tell us what happened?" Maggie cried.

"The doctor will speak with you about her condition. All I know is that she was admitted," the nurse answered hoping to ease their concerns.

The nurse picked up the phone and made the call. Kevin and Maggie sat in a small seating area by the desk. A few minutes later a doctor appeared and introduced himself. "I'm Dr. Samuels. Are you Mr. and Mrs. Brogan?" He asked.

"Yes, yes we are the Brogans. What happened to our Dorothy," Maggie asked desperately? The doctor sat with them and started giving them the news about their daughter.

"First of all, Dorothy's injuries are not life threatening. She has been admitted. She is sedated and you can see her. The police were here. Dorothy was attacked by a man at the train station outside her school. I don't know anything about their investigation. I can tell you that she was beaten and raped. She will recover from her injuries. There was no permanent damage except for her teeth. She will need extensive dental work. I expect she will be here for at least a week. I can take you upstairs to see her, but I must warn you she looks worse than what she is," the doctor said standing.

Maggie upon hearing the news burst into tears. Kevin held her and helped her up. They went to the elevators down the hall and went up to the third floor. Exiting the elevator, they walked down the hall to her room. A uniformed policeman was outside her door. At the request of the police she was placed in a private room. Maggie went straight to her daughter as she entered the room. Dorothy's face was badly bruised. She looked as if she were bandaged from head to toe.

Kevin stood next to Maggie fighting back his tears. "She is resting comfortably and I assure you she is in no pain. Do you have any questions for me?" Dr. Samuels asked.

"Her eye is badly swollen. Was there any damage to her sight?" Kevin asked.

"We don't think so. Once the swelling goes down we can do a more thorough examination. She will be awake in the morning. If you need anything else just ask the nurse at her desk down the hall. I'll check in on her later," Dr. Samuels said.

"Thank you, doctor," Kevin managed to say.

Kevin stood at the foot of Dorothy's bed. Maggie was sitting in a chair next to her. Kevin went into the hall and spoke to the policeman. "I'm Kevin Brogan. Can you tell me what happened to my daughter?" He asked.

"I'm sorry sir. I don't know. I was called in to stand guard and to notify the detectives working her case when she wakes up. That's all I know," the officer replied. Kevin went back into the room and sat in another chair. It was going to be a long night. He knew he should be telling family and friends but decide it would wait to be done in the morning.

It was mid-morning when Dorothy awakened. The police officer outside her door had been relieved and another officer was there. Hearing the Brogan's speaking to the victim he went down the hall to notify the detectives that Dorothy was awake. Meziaz and Breker would arrive at the hospital within the hour.

Upon their arrival, they introduced themselves. "Mr. and Mrs. Brogan, would you please step outside the room. We need to interview your daughter. There is a cafeteria downstairs. They have very good coffee. And you two look as if you can use some. We won't be long and we will talk with you there and answer your questions," Breker said to them.

Dr. Samuels had also arrived looking tired. "I'll stay with her during the interview. I wanted to check her now that she is awake," the doctor said reassuring them. Kevin walked down the hall with Maggie and stepped on the elevator.

Meziaz and Breker entered the room and informed Dorothy who they were and why they were there. "Do you feel up to answering some questions?" Breker asked.

"Yes," Dorothy replied weakly nodding her head.

"Did you know the man who attacked you?" Breker asked.

"No," Dorothy replied.

"Had you ever seen him before?"

"No"

"Do you think you could describe him?"

"It was getting dark. He grabbed me from behind. Then he dragged me under the station. It was dark and dusty. I did not get clear look at him," she replied.

"Did he say anything?" Breker asked patiently.

"I don't know. I can't remember. I'm sorry. I just fought back. I kept hitting him, and hitting him," Dorothy said starting to cry.

"That's all right. You did great. When you were fighting him, did you punch him on the left side of his face?" Breker asked.

"Yes, I think so. I did. I kept hitting him but he would not stop. Then he...he...he...raped me..." Dorothy cried. Her emotions catching up with her.

Breker held her left hand and tried to calm her. "Shhh, it's all right. Your safe now. He cannot hurt you."

Dorothy sobbed some more and then remembered, "He was angry. He couldn't finish. That's when he beat me more. That's all... I don't remember anymore."

"You did just fine. We are going downstairs to talk with your mom and dad. Dr. Samuels wants to examine you. There's a policeman right outside your door. Your safe. Try to get some rest. If you remember anything tell the policeman outside. We will be back tomorrow," Breker said.

The two detectives left the room and gave instructions to the officer at her door. Then they went to the cafeteria to meet with Dorothy's parents.

They sat in the back of the cafeteria away from other people and Meziaz started his briefing. "This is what we know so far. Dorothy was attacked by a man that has been attacking young women all over the county. There have been eleven other attacks. Your daughter was lucky. She fought with him. She put up a good fight and she survived. The other eleven victims were all killed by this man. Every police department in Delaware, Montgomery and Philadelphia county is looking for this guy.

We have blood and hair samples from him, thanks to your daughter. We also have his finger prints from the knife he left behind. It really is just a matter of time before we get him." Meziaz left out key points on their investigation. That information was protected and known only to the police departments that had an open file for the man they hunted.

He left out the fact that hair samples had been collected from each victim by the attacker. He also left out that they had him in custody before he escaped. He had attacked a police officer and fractured the officer's skull. He also had that officers service revolver. The important fact was that every police officer in southeast Pennsylvania was hunting this man, a man who was no longer there.

Kevin and Maggie sat in shocked silence at the report the detective just gave them. Dorothy had fought back. It was the only reason she survived.

Susan heard Cupcake barking outside. Mike was home from work. She was sitting at the kitchen table drinking coffee. Mike came in through the side door that came into the kitchen. "Hi Susan. How's my girl? He asked bending to kiss her. She kissed him back but the look on her face told him something was wrong. "What? Is it my father?" He asked her concerned. His father had been having issues since the loss of Margaret a few years ago, "No. Pop is fine. Please sit down," Susan said.

Mike sat waiting for what had to be bad news. "Kevin called this morning. Dorothy was beaten and raped last night. She is in Lankenua Hospital.

She's doing fine, Kevin told me that she will be home sometime next week.

Hope's party has been cancelled. We should still go up this weekend to see her," Susan told him.

Susan looked into Mike's eyes. What she saw frightened her. There was a menacing look as he stared at nothing on the table. She had seen this look before with many of her former patients. It was a look of murderous determination.

She knew from experience that what she said and what she did she had to do carefully. She knew Mike would never hurt her. But she also knew that anyone or anything crossing his path at this moment would be in trouble. He broke the silence, "Did they catch the Goddamn son of a bitch?"

"No. But the police all over Pennsylvania are looking for him," she replied. Mike sat stone still the anger in him flowing through every cell of his body.

Susan asked, "I have dinner ready. Your favorite. Meatloaf."

Mike stood and grabbed a beer from the ice box. He took a cigar from the box where he kept them. "Not hungry. I need to be alone to think about this," he told her getting ready to go out the door.

"Mike wait," she said standing and walking to him. "Let's leave this here," she said taking the big old Colt .45 from the holster on his hip.

He looked at her and said, "Ok, good idea."

He went outside and Susan pushed the button on the left side of the grip to release the magazine. Then she pulled the slide back and ejected the round that was in the chamber.

She reseated the slide and pulled the trigger. The click on the empty chamber seemed to be so loud. She put the Colt away in the drawer and then slipped all of the rounds from the magazine into the drawer. He had to process this and get control of himself. Solitude was the best therapy.

The phone rang as Hope and her mother finished breakfast. They were going into town to buy things Hope was told she would need when she arrived at Fort Devens. Hope answered and sobbed listening to the news from Kevin about Dorothy. Colleen knew something bad had happened. When Hope hung up the phone she told her mother. They cancelled their shopping trip and took a cab to Lankenua Hospital.

When they arrived on the third floor they saw the policeman outside the door. Kevin saw them and let them into the room. Colleen hugged Maggie and the two women cried together. Hope went to Dorothy's side. She had been sedated again to help her with the pain. Dorothy was a little groggy. She greeted the younger girl she thought of more as a sister than just a friend of her family. Crying Hope stroked the top of Dorothy's head. "I'm so sorry. You will get past this; I know you will." Dorothy turned her head towards Hope and whispered something. Hope did not hear her so she put her ear close to Dorothy's face and said, "I could not hear you, honey. Say it again."

Dorothy repeated, "You win."

Hope was surprised and confused. Then she remembered their bet. Overcome with grief she shook her head no. "No. This doesn't count. No. No." Dorothy speaking louder said, "I'm gonna miss the party. I'm going to miss you too, Lieutenant. The two girls embraced and cried together. Colleen and Maggie watching the two of them cried with them.

Mike and Susan arrived the next morning. They met with Kevin and Maggie. The policeman was still outside her door. Mike had noticed a large gathering of police in the intersecting corridor when they got off the elevator. After meeting with Kevin and Maggie they sat with Dorothy for a while. Then surprisingly Stevie Bush showed up. He sat with Maggie while Mike, Susan and Kevin went to go to the cafeteria for coffee. Mike excused himself as they got on the elevator. "I'll see you downstairs, get me a large coffee," he told Susan. The elevator doors closed and Mike went down the hall to the gathering of officers. He noted two men in sports coats. Detectives he thought. He approached

115

one and showed his badge, "Mike McMullen, OCPD. Is this the guy?"

Meziaz looked at Mike as he approached. Definitely a cop he thought. The bulge on his right hip convincing him. "Did you just say OCPD? Where is OCPD?" Meziaz asked him.

"Ocean City Police, New Jersey. Is this the guy?" Mike asked again.

"This guy...is Officer Merv Boyd. What guy are you looking for?" Meziaz asked.

Mike replied, "Oh sorry. I thought this might be the piece of shit that rapes and beats up young girls."

"So why would OCPD in New Jersey be interested in a rape assault in Delaware County Pennsylvania?" Meziaz asked.

Mike knew he was stepping on this detective's case. "Sorry. I'm not trying to get into your case. The girl around the corner is my niece. I'm not here officially. Are you involved in her investigation? He said.

Meziaz held out his hand, "Detective Mike Meziaz. This is my partner Bill Breker. We're with Radnor PD."

"There's an entire task force working your niece's case. The guy you're not...officially asking about is on the lam. We'll get him though."

Mike knew he was not going to get any additional details. "OK. Thanks. What happened to Merv?" Mike asked.

"Some piece of shit fractured his skull. Merv's got almost forty years on the job. He's gonna be all right. When he gets out of here he's gonna retire," Breker told Mike.

"Give him my best. Thanks again." Mike said shaking the hands of both men and leaving. As he rode the elevator down to the cafeteria floor he thought about what Breker had said. "Some piece of shit." The exact phrase Mike used when he asked about Dorothy's rapist. Was Breker trying to tell him something on the QT, or was he just repeating what he heard. If he was trying to tell him something that meant they had the guy and lost him. Either way Meziaz was confident they were going to get their man. Neither of them knew that a strange turn of events would bring them all back together.

CHAPTER 11

HEALING LOVE & BROKEN PEACE

The time in the hospital for Dorothy extended to three weeks. Hope had left for Fort Devens two weeks ago. During her second week, a dental surgeon saw her and set up a schedule for treatment. Extractions were completed and after healing fittings for dentures and a partial was also done. Stitches had been removed and the swelling and bruising were all but gone. She suffered no permanent damage to her right eye. She saw a counselor in the hospital during her second week. Appointments were scheduled to see a physiologist when she returned home and the following week Dorothy had been released.

Mike and Susan had returned to the shore and brought Mike's father with them. He would be living with them now. His overall health was not bad, but he missed his wife.

He was depressed and being alone with his grief was not doing him any good. Living with Mike and Susan gave him a sense of a normal life surrounded by love one's. Pop and Cupcake were regular walkers on the beach each day. Both enjoyed their mornings. Joe McMullen and the Police Chief became good friends.

The retired NYPD Captain was respected throughout the small city department.

Dave's much older partner Joe Rullo was retiring. He had twenty-five years on the job. Mike learned that he would be promoted to Detective and be Dave's partner. The promotion and the job which no one else wanted was a paperwork nightmare. There was no Gold Shield, like New York City and the increase in pay was just ten dollars a month. OCPD only had four Detectives within the department.

The biggest adjustment for Mike was the change of clothes. Detectives were required to wear a suit or sport coat and tie. Then there was the paperwork. Reports for the numerous burglaries that occurred during the off season. People were having homes built and they used them during the summer. The majority of burglaries were hobo's looking to get out of the harsh winter elements. Some would wind up in county jails. The work was routine and monotonous. Still Mike and Dave were back together as partners. The department also issued Mike a Smith & Wesson Model 36. It was a small frame snub nosed .38. Mike called it the mouse killer. He left it home and still carried the big Colt .45 from France. His skills as a two-finger typist improved and he found he type faster than Dave who was happy to leave the report writing to Mike. News of Dorothy's release from the hospital was received and plans were made to drive up in a week or two to visit.

Fort Devens was a quiet little post northwest of Boston. It initially opened during World War One and was now used a reception base for new Army recruits. Hope adjusted to the new regimented Army life. She learned about military laws and procedures. She was trained to march, dress and to clean everything in her world. She found the barracks she lived in to be spotless. The latrines they used were as clean as any operating room. Despite the conditions, they wiped, moped and shined everything until it gleamed brighter than they found it. Shoes, belt buckles and the brass on their uniforms were meticulously shined. She was ready for her new permanent assignment.

By the end of the year she would be assigned to the newly formed 8044ᵗʰ Mobile Army Surgical Hospital. It was a new Army concept to deliver wounded soldiers from the battlefield to the MASH unit quickly.

Once there, this is where the surgeons would stabilize their patients so they could be transported to hospitals in Japan. Saving the lives of the incoming wounded and prepare them for transport to a permanent and safe medical location was the mission. They were trained to tear down and reconstruct their facilities in a new location. The front lines of the battle field were fluid and could move in any direction. The MASH units were set up about twenty miles to the rear of the front line. The unit itself consisted of about one hundred people. It was self-contained with their own transportation, mess hall, laundry facilities, engineers and doctors and nurses. When orders came in to 'Bug Out' the unit could be torn down in a matter of hours. Once at its new location the unit could rebuild itself and be ready to receive patients. Depending on how far the unit had to move it could all be accomplished within a day. The training was hard and labor intensive. They lived and worked in tents that had prefabricated wooden frame work. The large tents could be torn down and rebuilt in under an hour.

She was fascinated by the new UCMJ. In May of 1950, President Truman signed the law and the Uniform Code of Military Justice was established. She quickly learned Army Regulations and knew this was going to be a useful tool in her quest to find out how war and military life affected men like her father. Medical care and patient treatment and evaluations were covered extensively in regulations and the UCMJ.

Her unit would join the 8055th, 8063rd and 8076th MASH units already deployed in Korea. Her unit would arrive in Korea in September of 1950. The training of tearing down, relocating and rebuilding paid off. The front line moved frequently. During 1950 and 1951 that line moved in both directions.

No one was happy about Hope's new assignment. Hostilities between North and South Korea started in June of 1950. The US sent its troops to the peninsula. War had broken out again just five years after World War Two ended. The public was weary of war and this new conflict was labeled as a police action. For the next three years, the only people affected were those who were sent to serve and their families. It would become the forgotten war. The rest of the population was busy rebuilding their lives after the end of WWII. Men and women who served in Europe and the Pacific would be busy getting married, building homes, staring families. They would be going back to school under the new GI Bill.

The country was reconstructing itself and transforming from a war time economy to a peacetime economy despite what was happening in Korea. Supplies and munitions left over from the global conflict would find its way to the Korean peninsula. In addition, new innovations would be utilized. Jet engines were re-placing prop driven fixed wing aircraft. The helicopter would make a debut and would begin to re-shape the battlefield. The men and women who served in this new conflict would tell you that the battlefield was just as horrific as any in the Europe or the Pacific theaters. It was also environmentally unforgiving.

The winters would be brutal and the summers unbearable. Another change in warfare was the human wave attack. Nothing the Germans or even the Japanese did in the global war could ever compare.

The 8044th arrived in Korea in late August of 1950. Hope had trained stateside and in Guam with her unit. She liked the people she was working with. Colonel Jessup was in command of the unit. Major Todd was in command of the nurse's. Todd made it clear to her nurses not to fraternize with the enlisted men. She also stressed not to get sexually involved with the doctors or other officers. She earned the nickname of 'Old Iron Pants'.

The other nurses were all highly trained and motivated. Hope was assigned to post-op. It was here that the wounded men who had surgery would recover before being moved to Seoul or Japan.

During her first eight months, the unit seemed to move constantly. UN forces comprised mainly by US troops were pushed back to the Pusan Province of South Korea. General MacArthur would make an amphibious landing on the western side of the Korean peninsula at Inchon in September of 1950. Catching, the North Korean advance behind the lines and cutting off needed supplies the North Koreans were pushed back. US forces had advanced into North Korea by November of 1950. Just short of the Yalu River the Chinese entered the war. US forces once again were pushed back and the North Koreans and the Chinese were successful in retaking Seoul. The front lines moved back and forth but stabilized in early 1951 along the 38th Parallel. The war became a stalemate as UN forces battled both North Korean and Chinese troops in a war to occupy the ridges along the 38th Parallel.

Stevie Bush was a constant figure in the Costigan household. Dorothy had been released from the hospital and was recuperating at home. He was there in the morning when she woke. He was there in the evening when she went to bed. He was still very much in love with her. The pain she had endured was his pain. He was determined to make her life happier. He would make her breakfast and sit with her until lunchtime. He had a job at the Philadelphia Gas Works. He worked in town and worked from one to eight-thirty. He made good money the job had benefits and the work was easy. Stevie still lived at home so he was able to save his money. After work, he would return to the Costigan home and sit with Dorothy. They would play cards, assemble puzzles or just talk. Dorothy was conscious about her appearance and always had been. The bruising and swelling were gone but she still had stitches on her chest. The cut on her vagina was not as long or deep and had healed well. Still, she was still sore. Lying in bed for so long she was out of shape. She decided she would start walking in the morning and get herself moving again. Stevie would be there to protect her. They strolled at a leisurely pace along the Benjamin Franklin Parkway. On the first day, they made it down to Logan Circle towards the city. Dorothy recovered quickly and after a month they were able to change their route and walked along the East River Drive. It was during those morning walks that Dorothy saw Stevie in a different way. She knew that he was in love with her. He had always felt that way since they were kids. He had never made any overtures. Now when they talked she would look into his eyes. What she saw was a kindness and a look of anticipation. He finally made a move one morning as they walked along the pathways and held her hand. She held his hand firmly and moved closer to him as they walked. Approaching a bench, they sat along the river and she snuggled in closer to him. As if on que he put his arm around her. She looked up at him and magically both knew what was about to happen. The kiss was just a few seconds but she was amazed at how natural it felt when their lips touched.

It felt like wearing a warm oversized sweater on a chilly day. That one kiss made her heart flutter. Despite the horrible attack, she was recovering from new desires were washing over her. Not the sexual desires she played at with the handsome guys in college. It was a desire to be so close that the two of them would become one. Without ever realizing it she had fallen in love.

Hope was exhausted. Everyone in the 8044th felt the same. Casualties seemed to be continuous, no matter how many times they moved, or 'bugged out'. The early stages of the war saw the front lines move steadily from the Pusan Peninsula back towards Seoul. To add to the misery winter was coming. As more and more UN troops arrived the pace of the war increased. During any of the lulls everyone in camp caught up on much needed sleep. Physical conditions in camp were as bad as they come. An army of rats seem to follow them wherever they went. Flies and mosquitos buzzed throughout the camp and got into everything. During that first winter in Korea no one was ever warm. The wind howled and found its way into every tent crevice it could find. It was impossible to stay warm no matter how hard they tried. Post-op had portable heaters. Every available unit was used to keep the recovering wounded as warm as they could. During the surgical sessions, the doctors would warm their fingers in the bodies of their patients. The war was taking its deadly toll. The living conditions never improved.

Moving from patient to patient Hope and the other nurses attended to their duties. The only reprieve from the misery of Korea was work. For those patients that were awake a brief conversation with a pretty nurse was uplifting. They spoke about their homes and families. Some required help to write letters home. Most of the men were just young boys.

At nineteen and twenty years of age they had survived the worst of what the war had to offer. Some of them were so young and innocent talking with a pretty girl had them stumbling over their words. Others were confident and would make their intentions known. A few could be downright vulgar. The women took it all in stride. They loved them all. Reassuring each one that they would be getting better. Most would be transferred to an evacuation hospital and sent home. Others would recuperate at the 8044th and be returned to their units. The amputees were especially hard. Learning of their fate some would give up and become bitter. The nurses paid close attention to these patients. Athletes lost their legs. Artists and musicians would lose their fingers or their hands. For some death, would have been a mercy.

Once the shift was over Hope returned to her tent she shared with, Joyce Smith, Nancy Peterson and Mary Cantrell. During the winter months, they pushed their cots together in the middle of the tent so they could huddle together to stay as warm as they could during the night. As small stove sat off to one side of the tent. No matter how much fuel was fed into it, it could never keep the cold out. Its primary purpose was to boil water for tea or coffee. The four women were close friends and knew every intimate detail about each other's lives. In this environment, personal secrets were impossible to keep. Not far from the lines they occasionally received incoming artillery fire. The possibility of death was always there and broke down any barriers to keeping personal secrets. They knew each other's families as if they were their own.

Hope often talked about her father. The other women were shocked to learn he had never held her as a baby. They did know all too well the changes that happened to men who had seen combat. It was not uncommon to see a patient sleeping with an angelic and youthful face. When he woke, the expression changed. The eyes went hard and calculating. The expression was cold and devoid of feeling.

Unknowingly the women were also the same. War and the horror of combat touched everyone. For those patients that had real problems there was Major Sam Mason. He worked at a psychiatric hospital at I Corps. Hope was excited whenever he came to the 8044th. They would sit and talk for hours in the mess tent over coffee. The Army was still referring to this condition as 'Battle Fatigue'. It would be another thirty years before it would be properly diagnosed.

Day in and day out the casualties arrived by ambulance and helicopters. Some days the number of wounded coming in seemed to stagger the mind. Men with very serious wounds that would require hours of surgical time were passed over. Doctors and nurses had to decide which patients could be saved based on the amount of time required to surgically treat them. It was heart breaking. Morphine was used to keep the troops passed over as comfortable as possible. Cooks, motor pool and other support personnel all chipped in wherever they were needed. Hope and the other nurses kept post-op running. Men would be moved constantly. Those wounded coming from surgery that were considered intensive care were kept right outside the surgical room. Many of them would return to surgery after the massive number of wounded were tended too. Twelve fifteen and twenty hours of continuous surgery was never uncommon. Once everyone was treated the medical and support staff moved about the compound in an exhausted trance. Those on duty would need food and massive amounts of coffee to keep going. These were the toughest and physical demanding days. Other days when the number of wounded was not as overwhelming took their toll emotionally. The ability to interact with wounded young men made it more personal.

Hope on many occasions held the hand of a dying soldier. She was experiencing firsthand the trauma of war. It would change her forever but at the time she never knew it was happening. Those days would come soon enough when the memories haunted her.

The holidays came and Christmas in Korea was more depressing than joyous. Despite attempts to celebrate everyone was thinking of home and family. Hope's thoughts were like everyone else. They sat together in the mess tent on Christmas morning talking about all the things they did to celebrate the day. Food was always a topic of discussion and not just for the holidays.

On this Christmas morning, it was talked about in detail. Roast turkey with all the fixings as well as ham or goose. Apple pie. Pumpkin pie as well as cakes and ice cream. In the mess tent, it was powdered eggs, stale toast and a concoction they named 'Rat Chowder.'

It consisted of meat and a cream sauce. It was the cooks attempt at creamed beef. They washed it all down with coffee that at times resembled watery pudding. Colonel Jessup tapped his cup with a spoon to get everyone's attention. The tent was animated with conversation and the only way to get their attention was when Doodles hollered, "At ease."

The tent went silent and Colonel Jessup addressed his troops. "Good morning and Merry Christmas. Today is special to all of us. I know that everyone is thinking of family and home. Hopefully we will all be back home soon. I hope everyone enjoyed your holiday breakfast."

Groans and comments flooded the tent. Jessup, let it go for a minute and then continued, "All right, all right. I've been told that Christmas dinner will be special. Thanks to our talented company clerk we will be having powdered mash potatoes, canned beats and…real roast turkey. Followed by pumpkin pie. So, three cheers go to Doodles." Cheers went up throughout the tent as well as some sarcastic comments about the cook's ability to deliver the meal. "That's enough I have some other news. After the New Year, we will be getting R&R allotments. Tokyo, Japan will be the destination and the trip will last a week, Jessup announced."

Everyone cheered. The thought of a weekly break from the war in Japan was a God send. Hope and her tent mates quickly sat together and started making a list of items to be brought back. Oddly, toilet paper and tissues were the most requested item. Shampoo and scented soaps were next on the list. All of the girls were excited and eager to go. Allotments would be announced after the New Year. Jessup withheld the list deliberately. The news of R&R allotments was a gift enough for Christmas. Announcing the list after the New Year gave his people something to look forward too.

New Year's Eve was celebrated with wounded. They started to arrive around 4PM. The number of wounded was not overwhelming but the steady flow continued to after 7PM. Surgeries were all done by 2AM. Post-op was filled to capacity. Hope had the mid-night shift with her tent mates. There would be no celebration in the camp tonight. The drudgery of the war had returned them all to reality. When the shift was finished, Hope returned to her tent and bunk exhausted. She slept with the other girls. A new year and a new hope was something they would all wake too. Hope learned she would go to Tokyo in late March. She would be the first of her tent mates to make the coveted trip. Other people in the unit would go sooner but early spring in Japan sounded heavenly. It was almost three months away, but it gave all of the girls something to look forward too.

Dorothy and Stevie waited for the clock to count down to the New Year. They were both very much in love. Stevie always had been. For Dorothy it was a new experience. She had always been attracted to men, but with Stevie it was more. Stevie as opposed to other young men in her life was genuinely concerned for her wellbeing. He was the one man that was always there for her. He was the one who understood when their kissing and petting became too intense for her.

She was still recuperating from the vicious attack last summer. She desperately wanted to be with him. The flash backs to her horrible experience was just too much for her. Stevie never complained. For Dorothy, it was hard to break away from this young man who had always wanted her heart. This however was a new year. She was determined that on this night she would surrender herself. They were dancing when the count down at Maggie's house began.

When the clock struck twelve they kissed and she held him close and whispered in his ear that tonight she wanted him to make love to her. His response only reassured her, "If that's what you want we will, but if you can't go thru with it I will understand. I love you and always have and always will. I can wait until time stops if need be."

She knew then that she would need to call up every bit of her strength to face this last hurdle that she and her physiologist had discussed.

When the party was over they went back to his house. His parents were visiting family in West Chester. They had the house to themselves. Once inside she held his hand and took him upstairs to his room. They both laid on the bed and began kissing. Soon things were getting hot and heavy. He lay on top of her and she rolled him back over so that she was on top. It was something she had always done with other young men. It was her way of taking control. She pulled her dress over her head. Then she unhooked her bra. Sitting on top of him she could feel his erection. He looked at her naked breasts. To him they were beautiful. The scar next to her left breast was still there. It always would be. He sat up and kissed and fondled her breasts. She was moaning with pleasure. His hands went from her breasts to the top of her panties. He pushed the top of the panties past her buttocks. She allowed him to remove her panties. This was further than they ever had been. Naked except for her stockings and garter belt she started to unbuckle his pants. He got off the bed moving her to her side and undressed himself. Laying side by side they continued kissing.

His hand moved down her side and found its way to her. She tensed. Sensing her apprehension, he spoke to her softly. He told her how much he loved her. How much she meant to him. "We can go as slow or as fast as you like," he said. This gave her new courage. She was determined to get past this. She needed to get past this. It was the only way to get her life back. His finger found its way inside her. Instead of fear she felt desire. His touch was soft and gentle. His purpose was to arouse her and get her past her fear. She was no longer feeling fear. She loved him more than ever. She wanted him now more than ever. Rolling him unto his back she grabbed him and guided him into her. Surprisingly she felt no pain. Sooner than she would have liked he finished. She was not done however and she kept moving above him. He never lost his erection and the two of them were lost in each other. A few minutes later she felt an entirely new sensation take her over. Her body shuddered with her own orgasm as he had his second, making him cry out. Exhausted they lay in each other's arms. "Happy New Year," she whispered in his ear.

"I love you. I've always loved you. I want to be with you forever," he said.

"I love you too," she said.

"No, I mean I really do love you. I want us to be together forever," He replied.

"Stevie, what are you saying?" She asked.

"I want us to be together. Let's get married. There really is nothing more in my life that I want more," he said laying on his back looking up at her.

Lying on her side facing him stroking his chest she pouted and said, "You're supposed to be on your knee with a ring in your hand."

Stevie jumped off the bed and ran into his parent's bedroom. Startled Dorothy called after him, "Where are you going?"

She was sitting up in bed when he returned. He fell on both knees holding a small ring in his hand. "Marry me Dorothy. I don't want to share my life with anyone or anything. Just you, that's all I want," he said holding out the ring. It was a small thin gold band, with a tiny diamond. It would only fit on her pinky finger.

"Where did you get this?" She asked.

"It was my great grandmother's; I want you to have it. We can get it fixed so it fits. Say yes, Dorothy. No one will ever hurt you again. Marry me," he said.

"How could a girl say no?" She replied.

They fell into each other's arms and talked until they fell asleep. Waking the next morning they cuddled in bed and talked. Suddenly Dorothy sat up in bed startled. "Oh shit," she said.

"What? What's wrong?" Stevie asked.

"I lost the bet," she replied.

"What bet?" Stevie asked.

CHAPTER 12
PREDATORS & SPIES

Wildwood New Jersey was preparing for a new summer season. The boardwalk was expanding. Boarding houses and small cottages were being built. The small post war city was expanding. Grant Williams got a job quickly in construction. He had learned carpentry in reform school and did well in those classes. Now he was framing small vacation homes around town for a local builder. He made good money and was able to upgrade his living conditions. Arriving in town he took a small room in a boarding house with a communal bathroom. Now he had his own apartment over a salt water taffy shop on the boardwalk. Stashed under a step that led up to his private bath he kept a small metal tool box.

Inside was .38 Special, cash bound by rubber bands, and ten locks of hair; each tied with a red ribbon. He often took these out at night alone in his room. Holding the bundles of hair up to his nose he believed he could still smell his victims. There was supposed to be eleven. The last bitch had fought like a tiger. The thought of her angered him. Because of her he had almost been caught. That night he was unfulfilled. He needed to hunt again. Masturbation did not satisfy his needs. He would have to wait. Winters here in the shore town was desolate. Soon the summer months would come. He was expecting a target rich environment. He had already searched out the best spots. Today he would return to the dive shop in town to purchase the knife. It was a Muela diving knife. The blade was seven inches long and had a serrated cutting edge on the top of the blade. It was expensive but he knew it would be worth the price. Leaving his apartment from the back of the building he checked the chain and lock on the 1945 Indian Scout motorcycle he purchased last month. Dark gray in color it was perfect for his night time activities. It was a three-block walk from his apartment to the shop in town. He purchased the knife and a sheath that he could strap to his calf. The shop owner knew this young man was not a diver but he had the cash for the expensive knife. The sheath had a pocket for a wet stone. He spent hours sliding the edge back and forth until the edge was like a razor. Summer was coming and soon he would satisfy his needs.

On the job, he kept to himself. He did his work and the boss had no complaints. His carpentry skills were never an issue. To the rest of the men on the site he was just a very quiet and shy sort of guy. He took coffee breaks and ate his lunch with the other workers. He listened to their conversations about sports, cars and their favorite subject; women. Occasionally he might ask a question, but for the most part he just listened. He always declined an offer to join them at the local bar for an after-work beer. Alcohol clouded the mind and effected his reflexes. He liked to keep his head clear. He was always on time, and always completed his work.

Sunday was his usual day off. This was the day he used to ride his bike and scout the locations for the attacks he planned. Cape May had the most deserted beach locations with lots of dunes to hide in. Atlantic City had a boardwalk and was popular. There was also Steel Pier. Under the pier, it was dark, deserted and very noisy. Any screaming by his victims would be drowned out by the amusement rides and bands playing. He was eager to begin. He also found dune covered beaches in Stone Harbor, Avalon and Sea Isle City. Ocean City also had a boardwalk and the southern area of the city was still under developed. He was ready. The Jersey shore was not.

This Sunday evening, he rode his motorcycle south down Route 9 to Cape May. He parked the motorcycle along Sunset Boulevard back by the old observation tower used during WWII to watch over Sunset Beach. There were just a few homes back towards town. Walking along the road he noted several places where he could make his attacks. He passed a small bungalow and saw a pretty young woman kissing her husband goodbye. He drove a pickup truck that was part of the Cape May Fire Department. He was close enough to hear him tell her that he would see her again in two days. He was going to work. The man drove off and Grant crossed the road and made his way alongside the house through high grass. He sat in the grass watching the house. Several times he saw the woman pass a window as she moved through the house. She was alone. The urges began to swell.

As it got darker she turned on a light in a room at the back of the home. Making his way towards the back he crept up to the window. The shade was down but at the bottom of the shade he was still able to see inside. She was undressing and the bath was filling. He had not planned anything for this night. The knife he would use was back at his apartment. Walking around the side of the house there was a door leading into the kitchen. He tried the knob, it turned and the door opened. Stepping inside he pushed the door shut as gently as he could. The only sound he could hear was the running water filling the tub. He moved silently to the bathroom door.

Nguyen Hung was reviewing the reports from his agents in the south of Vietnam. All of them had provided valuable information and were believed to be loyal to the cause. A few however came under question.

They were suspected of being double agents working for both sides for their own benefit. A question about the loyalty a Vang Bo was raised, not because of his behavior, but due to the fact he was Chinese. As much as Hung vouched for his old friend he was still ordered to look into Bo's activities. He also knew another way to ensure that Bo's loyalties would never again be questioned. He had made arrangements to meet a counterpart from the CCID (Chinese Central Investigation Department) in a park close by his office. The two men met and Hung made a request from the man. "I assume this is something you can do for me?" Hung asked.

The man replied, "I am confident that the information you seek is available. I will not insult you by asking why you have such a strange request. I will remind you though that we are very active in assisting your government and its cause. Moscow has committed to supporting my Government with money and supplies. We are already engaged with western powers in Korea. Let us hope the peoples fight in Vietnam is accomplished more peacefully. Perhaps the Americans will learn that Asian matters should be left to Asian people. I will call you when I find the information you seek."

Hung's counterpart stood and casually walked out of the park.

Hung had two agents that were suspected of being double agents. Each had different case officers. Two sets of false information would be channeled to the case officers. They would pass the information on to the suspected double agents. When French and South Vietnamese forces reacted to the information they would have the proof he needed. Decisions on their fate would be made by higher authority's. Hung knew what their fate would be. As for Vang Bo, his information had always been accurate. He fit into his role perfectly. Hung never doubted him.

Dylan sat reading his paper and drinking his coffee. He was at a table on a patio of a downtown Manila restaurant. He was watching a man waiting for a bus. On the bus was a communist rebel. The rebel would exit the bus at this corner and pass a folded newspaper to the man waiting for the bus. He was an undercover agent employed by Dylan and the CIA.

Dylan would follow the communist where he would be arrested a block away. The man was part of the Hukbalahap or Huks. This group was active in the attempt to overthrow the government of President Quirino. The US had granted Philippine Independence in April of 1946. The Soviet Union and Communist China were both active in solidifying Communism in South East Asia. The Cold War had begun and it was now global.

A short and very thin man in his forties got off the bus and passed the folded newspaper to Dylan's undercover man. The exchange was so subtle the untrained and waiting eye would never have seen it. Inside the folded paper was an envelope with cash. The undercover man would ride the bus for several more blocks and deliver it to the office of an attorney. National Intelligence & Coordinating Agency (NICA) agents would then raid and arrest the attorney and his staff. The rebel walked down the block away from the bus. At the next corner, he was accosted by another man who appeared to be drunk. A struggle ensued the rebel desperate to get away from the man. The struggle continued when the rebel finally punched the man. Manila police officers across the street witnessed the incident. Both men were arrested and taken into custody. The drunk was actually a Manila policeman. Once at the police station the men were separated. The rebel was turned over to agents of the NICA. Dylan returned to his office in the embassy. He sat at his desk to write the report that would indicate another successful operation. He worked closely with his counterpart from the NICA. They would have dinner that night in a downtown hotel.

Alone in the house he knew this was a special opportunity. He left the bathroom door and went back to the kitchen. Grant hung his denim jacket on a chair in the kitchen. He quietly removed his boots tee shirt and jeans. He looked in the drawers and found what he wanted, a large carving knife. Silently he crept back to the bathroom door. He could hear her bathing. She was humming to herself. He grasped the knob on the door and slowly turned it. Bursting into the bathroom she looked up in surprise. Soap covered her face. The wash cloth in her hands was at her neck. Grant grabbed the cloth and roughly pushed it into her mouth to stifle the scream that was coming. The force of his attack as he entered the room caused him to slip and fall into the tub on top of her. He lost his grip on the knife and it fell into the water. She was under the water struggling to get out of the tub. The soapy water made getting a grip on anything difficult for both of them. Grant grabbed her by the hair and pulled her out of the tub. Falling on the tiled floor she struggled and fought with him. The soapy bodies slipping on the tiled floor. She made it into the hall way starting to get to her feet when he caught her from behind. Turning her over on her back he pushed his legs inside hers and pushed hers open. He had lost the knife it was still in the tub. He slapped her with his right hand hard, the sound of it echoing through the hallway. He grabbed her neck with his left hand like he always did. Her legs were trying to push away and her hips were thrashing but he still managed to enter her. "GOD, oh God no, stop, please stop, AUUGH!" She cried. He tightened his grip on her throat silencing her screams. The eyes started to bulge, her face turning red. He thrust into her faster now knowing the moment was coming. His hand squeezed even harder and he could feel her neck muscles collapsing.

He arched his back as he finished exploding into her. She was still beneath him. He looked down at her. The eyes stared at the ceiling but they saw nothing. He knelt in front of her, pulling at himself. His semen still dripping to the floor.

He stood over her. She was very pretty and had a great body he thought. He stepped into the bathroom slipping slightly. He chuckled to himself. Reaching into the tub he tried to retrieve the knife when he heard her desperately trying to get air into her lungs. "Euogh, Euogh."

He turned and saw her on her side fighting for air. He reached into the hall and grabbed her by the hair. Pulling her back into the bathroom he pushed her into the tub. He climbed back in with her. She had trouble breathing. Between her damaged throat and the tub water she was coughing and gasping. Her body and his were slippery again from the soapy water. This excited him and he entered her again. He did not choke her he just thrust into her over and over. She had no strength left for a fight. Breathing was all she could hope for. She arched her hips and shoulders trying to stay above the water. He finished again groaning loudly. He stood up and looked down on her. Tiny bubbles forming around her nose rose to the surface of the water. She was very still. He got out of the tub and went down the hall to the kitchen. He took out his cigarettes and lit one. Then he went back to the bathroom. She had not moved. "You were the best one ever darling." Grabbing a towel, he dried himself. He watched her the entire time. He had to be sure she was dead. Satisfied she was gone he returned to the kitchen and dressed. He opened the ice box and saw the beer. Grabbing a bottle, he used his belt buckle to open the bottle of Schmidt's. He drank it all down and finished his cigarette. He went back into the hall. He looked for the knife. Then he remembered it was in the tub. She was still there silent and still. The knife was down by the drain. Grabbing it he took a very long strand of her black hair and cut it. This was the longest piece ever. This one he would cherish more than the others. He put it carefully into his jeans pocket and looked at her one last time. Then he left by the same door he entered. It was very dark now. He found his motorcycle where he left it and road slowly past the house on Sunset Boulevard. Everything was quiet and still. Then he revved the motorcycle breaking the silence as he left.

Audrey Miller was found on Tuesday when her husband Albert returned from a forty-eight-hour tour of duty with the Cape May Fire Department. The closest neighbor was more than 500 yards away. Police that canvassed the area learned that no one heard or saw anything. There was an abundance of forensic evidence in the house. Police retrieved finger prints on the side door and the bathroom door. The bathroom also had an abundance of prints. The empty bottle of beer also had fingerprints. A semen stain on the floor in the hallway would give them a blood type. Detective Joe Cox of the Cape May Police was assigned to the case. It was the first time in sixteen years on the job that he was investigating a homicide. He had the training now it was time to use it. Collecting all the forensic evidence he knew would be the keys to unlock the mystery. The county medical examiner (ME) placed the time of death sometime Sunday night. "What else can you tell me, Doc?" Joe asked.

Cause of death at first glance could be drowning, but she also has bruising on her neck. That indicates she was strangled. The victim had a large piece of her hair cut off. Once I get her on the table I can give you more detailed info," the ME stated.

"Ok Doc, thanks."

"You looking at the husband for this?" The ME asked.

"Naw, he's clear. Works for the fire department. He was on duty. His alibi is solid. That's what has me worried. I think we are going to be seeing more of this. Hope I'm wrong," Cox said.

Vang Bo sat drinking his tea. The work day was over. All of the students had left leaving him alone in his office. Without a sound, Nguyen Hung was standing in the doorway. Bo was surprised and happy, you startled me old friend. I am pleased to see you. Why are you here? It must be dangerous for you to be here," Bo declared.

The two men embraced each other smiling. "There is no danger for me my friend. I am like a gentle summer breeze. Sometimes I am there, and sometimes I am not. I want to tell you that we will meet in Saigon soon. You should prepare for the trip that is three weeks from now. We will meet on the third of the new month. Alert your students that school will be closed for three days. I will send you more details soon," Hung told his old friend. Bo had no idea that Hung had been ordered to verify his loyalty. Hung had made the argument many times that loyalty was always bought with blood or love. Money was never a medium to purchase loyalty. Whomever had the most cash always bought the false loyalty of a person. Hung knew first hand that Bo had proved his loyalty on more than one occasion. Still orders were orders. Hung had devised a plan that Bo's loyalty to would never be questioned again.

Two weeks after meeting with his Chinese counterpart in the park Hung was given a message from an old woman outside of his house in Hanoi.

Another meeting was arranged in the same park, on the same bench in thirty minutes. Hung went straight to the park and sat on the bench. Watching the entrance, he saw the man he was waiting for enter the park. His name was Wang Gie. "Good morning Comrade Hung. I have found what you asked me to find. What am I to do now?"

"Thank you, Comrade. Can you arrange for shipping to Saigon?" Hung asked.

"Of course, Such things can always be accomplished. I don't suppose you want to share your motives?" Gie asked.

"Sorry. I am not permitted to discuss the details. You understand?"

Gie responded, "I understand all too well, my friend. Secrets are the flowers of our spring. We must nurture and care for them. They blossom all summer and eventually die in the fall and winter. Give me a few weeks. A transport ship from Manila is arriving in Saigon on Thursday the twentieth of next month. Your cargo will be delivered then."

"Please be careful. These are very delicate. Handle with respect and the utmost care," Hung said.

"Consider it done, my friend," Gie replied.

Hung left the park to go to his office. Arriving a few minutes later than usual no one took notice. Hung had a lot to do today. He would have to travel south. He decided to notify only his contact in Saigon about his arrival in a few weeks. He would be travelling as a business manager of the Michelin Rubber Plantation in Xuan Loc. It was a cover he had used before.

CHAPTER 13
EXOTIC ROMANCE

Tokyo was fascinating to Hope. The streets of the city were filled with cars, Pedi cabs and bicycles. Her taxi dropped at the door of her hotel. The door man retrieved her bags and she paid the cabbie. Registering at the desk she was escorted to her room. The accommodations were simple and comfortable. She unpacked her clothes and decided to go downstairs to the bar she saw when she arrived. Sitting by herself at a small table in a sitting area she looked around the bar. A waiter approached and asked her if she wanted to or der a drink. Normally when she drank it was normal for her to just have beer or wine. This however was her R&R.

She should have a real cocktail but she was confused about what to order. The only thing that came to mind was 'Bourbon Neat'. She said it before she even realized it and the waiter left to fill her order. Oh, well, she thought, why not. I'm a big girl and I should be able to handle it. She looked around the bar and noted a very handsome Army Captain sitting at the end of the bar. He was still in his uniform as she was. She made note of the ribbons and badges on his blouse.

He was a combat veteran of the war and served in Europe. He was an Infantry Officer and had been wounded.

The waiter arrived with her drink. Looking at the small amount of liquid in the glass she thought how bad could it be. Picking up the glass she swirled the liquor around in the glass. She did not know why. She was simply mimicking what she had seen her Aunt Susan and Colleen doing with they're drinks. Then she raised the glass to her lips and drank a good portion of the bourbon. Swallowing the liquor, she was surprised at its potency. Her eyes watered as she was trying to catch her breath. It felt like she had swallowed a lit match as the warmth of the liquor spread inside her stomach. She coughed. Taking a deep breath, she regained her composure. Whoa, she thought, I did not expect that. Looking around she noticed the Captain smiling at her. He was clearly amused at her. She flushed somewhat embarrassed. When she looked up again he was standing by her table. "Good afternoon Lieutenant, allow me to be of assistance," he said gesturing for the waiter. When the waiter responded, he ordered a martini for himself, a glass of ice and a glass of water. The waiter left and then the officer extended his hand. "Captain M. Jack Randall." he declared introducing himself.

"Hello Captain, I am 1st Lieutenant Hope Costigan," she responded formally. The waiter returned and Captain Randall poured the rest of her drink into the glass with the ice, and then poured some water from the other glass. I think that will improve your drinking experience," he said. She tried the drink and nodded her approval. "That is much smother, sir. Thank you," she said.

"How about we drop the military protocol, and just be Jack and Hope," he said.

"All right, Jack. What does the M stand for?" Hope asked.

"Michael. I have a cousin named Michael. So, my family uses my middle name," he replied.

Hope asked. "Are you on R&R too?

No, actually I'm in transit. I have to report next week to 2nd Division Headquarters in Seoul," he replied.

"I guess you already know I'm on R&R. I'm assigned to MASH 8044th in Mubong-Ri," Hope informed him.

"Where are you from in the states?" He asked.

"I live in Philly with my Mom, although I'm originally from New York City. We moved to Philadelphia after my dad died. Before I joined the Army, I was living with my grandparents in Manhattan. I attended NYU," Hope informed him.

"Wow, how about that I live in Media Pa. in Delaware County. We are neighbors," Jack said with enthusiasm.

"I've heard of it but have never been there. My best friend went to Villanova. I'm afraid that's as far as I've ever been outside of the city. I have an Uncle that lives in New Jersey. We spend time there in the summer. He has a little cottage right on the beach in Ocean City," Hope said.

They continued to talk all afternoon. Jack had another martini and Hope had another bourbon and water. She was not used to the liquor and noticed her speech was getting a little slurred. Jack suggested that they get something to eat and told her of a restaurant nearby where they could get a couple of steaks.

Jack paid the tab for the drinks and they went outside and walked to the restaurant nearby. They ordered dinner. Hope found that she was famished from the booze and ate heartedly. Jack ordered a bottle of Cabernet Sauvignon with dinner. They sat in the restaurant and finished their meal and the bottle of wine. Jack wanted to pay for dinner but Hope insisted they go 'Dutch'.

Hope was feeling the alcohol as they walked back to the hotel. They each had rooms on the same floor and as they stopped at the door of Hope's room Jack took the key and opened her door.

During dinner, they had made plans to meet the next day and go site seeing together. She felt a little awkward and extended her hand to say goodnight. Jack took her hand told her they should meet at eight the next morning for breakfast. Hope agreed and said "Good night." She went into her room after closing the door and lay on the bed. The room was spinning so she got up, undressed and showered. As she lay in bed she thought about the man she had just met. He was handsome, charming and every bit of a gentleman. She knew she was very much attracted to him. That night she slept fitfully.

Jack shook her hand and said "Good night as she entered her room. He went done the hall and went into his own room and took off his uniform. He sat at the small writing desk in his room and wrote a quick letter to his Mother. Then he showered and went to bed. He was looking forward to the next day. Hope was beautiful he thought. He was captivated by her face and her eyes. He also felt as if he had known her forever. He soon fell asleep thinking and dreaming of her. It was a restless night. He could not get her out of his head.

The next morning, he woke early and dressed in slacks and a shirt with a sweater. He stopped at her door thinking that maybe he should knock or just go down stairs to meet her. She had finished dressing. She wore a new dress, she had purchased. Looking in the mirror she felt a little uncomfortable. The dress was a good fit but it was a little low cut and she was concerned about the cleavage she was showing. Like her mother, she was full breasted. She did not want to seem as if she was coming on too bold. Still she was excited about the coming day.

Deciding, well this is it she went to the door just as he knocked softly. Opening the door, she saw him in the hall. He was just as handsome in civilian clothes and he was thrilled to see her. "Good morning, you look beautiful out of uniform. I mean to say you look nice in a dress instead of a uniform. I wasn't trying to imply you were undressed. I just...well I am pleased..." he stammered.

She laughed at his dilemma and said "Good morning Jack, shall we have breakfast?" She asked.

They had breakfast in the hotel restaurant and went into the city to explore. They found a Japanese garden and walked around the grounds. The garden was filled with flowers and other plants. Each plant was hand attended and the aroma of the flowers filled the air. Some of the plants had sand or small cobble stones around them. It looked as if each stone had been placed just so and the sand had been racked to perfection. They came upon a large bonsai tree in the center of the garden. It stood about four feet tall. The tree was a cherry blossom and it was in full bloom with its tiny pink blossoms. The tree was displayed on a pedestal so that you could walk around the entire tree. Lush green moss covered the ground around the tree. Hope could not take her eyes of it. The tree had been sculptured by hand so that you could see each branch of the tree no matter where you stood. It was mesmerizing. Jack watched her as she was captivated by the beauty of the tree. He was captivated by her. She came back to where he was standing and said, "I don't think I've ever seen anything more beautiful in my life," she said looking up at him.

"I could not agree more," he said looking at her. She flushed, knowing he was not talking about the tree. He took her hand and they continued walking around the garden. Walking hand in hand they came back to the tree. An attendant of the garden approached them. She was an older woman and explained to them the history of the tree. She spoke very good English.

"This tree one hundred seventy-year-old. You can see the roughness of the bark. Most bonsai are much smaller."

"We call it Sofu or Grandfather. You are fortunate to see it today. Each flower and petal is in its finest today. Each spring it out does itself," she said.

"It is very pretty. It's perfect. I am very fortunate to see it, and all the other beautiful things surrounding it" Jack said looking into Hopes eyes.

Hope looked at Jack and felt lost in the moment. My goodness, what is happening she thought. Today at that moment there was no war. No Army. There was just this handsome charming man, and the smell of flowers in the air. They left the garden and had lunch. Jack ordered a martini and Hope decided to stick to wine. They talked again for hours over drinks. She felt so comfortable with him and he felt the same way. After lunch, they did some more site seeing and finally went back to the hotel. Hope was thinking about her mother and the circumstances surrounding the first time she had made love with her father. She knew she was falling for this man. She also knew she may never see him again. I may never have another chance at making love. Is this the time for me she thought? I want this man. The desire in her was building. When they arrived at her door he took her key and opened the door. This time she turned to him and they kissed for the first time. Hope could no longer fight the desire she had. The kiss was long and passionate. She looked up at him as he asked, "What shall we do for dinner?"

Pulling him inside she said, "How about room service."

Inside the room, they lay on the bed kissing and petting. She knew that this was the day she would surrender herself to this man. "Jack, I want you to know I have never done this before. I'm not the kind of girl who beds a man I've just met. I don't know why but something in me wants to be with you," she said standing and taking off her dress. Standing before him in her bra and panties she stripped before him. Standing naked in front of him she felt no embarrassment or inhibition. He was looking at her not lustfully at a naked woman but at a woman he knew he wanted to be with.

"I have never done this before either. I mean to say... I've never felt this way either."

She pulled him off the bed kissed him and began to undress him. He stood there letting her take his clothes off. Standing before her naked she touched his body. He was very fit. The shoulders and chest were rippled with muscle. There was a scar on his left shoulder. The bullet that struck him in Germany had gone clean through. She kissed the scar and reached down to touch him. He moaned with pleasure and fell back unto the bed. She thought about what Dorothy had said and began kissing his chest then his stomach. Holding him in her hand she kissed him there and then took him in her mouth. He was moaning again. He pulled her up and turned her gently unto her back. He kissed her ear and neck fondled her breast as she was breathing heavily. Working his way down on her he found she was moist with desire. He kissed and licked her as her hips moved beneath him. She shuddered with the orgasm. She pulled him up and he entered her. Moving together she felt another orgasm coming over her as he finished. Lying together they kissed and held each other. Hope could not believe how quickly it all had happened. Lying together they talked away the afternoon. He knew she had been his first. It made him feel closer to her than any other woman he had been with. They fell asleep in each other's arms. They woke later that night and made love again. This time it was longer as they explored each other's body. They never did order room service.

Waking very early the next morning they showered together. They were famished and finally ordered breakfast. Jack went to his room for clean clothes. When he returned, they ate breakfast consuming everything. They had eggs and sausage with toast. There was also fresh fruit. When breakfast was over Jack asked, "What shall we do today?"

"Let's see if we can find a Japanese tea ceremony," Hope said.

"You mean like at a Geisha house?" Jack asked.

"I don't know. Maybe someone at the front desk can help us," Hope answered. They made some inquiries at the front desk and made plans for the day. They did some more site seeing. To anyone who saw them they appeared to be lovers and they were. The week went fast. When it was over Hope learned that Jack would have to leave. The parted company and said their goodbyes. Hope would leave the next day. Her last day was filled with a longing for Jack.

She arrived in Seoul and got a jeep taking supplies back to the 8044th in Mubong-Ri. Arriving back at her MASH unit she was greeted by Major Susan Todd. "How was the R&R?" Major Todd asked.

"It was wonderful," Hope answered.

The Major noted the excited and happy mood. She had been in the Army since WWII and knew what could happen on an R&R.

"Well it's back to work. Post-op is filled with patients and we are expecting more casualties. Your scheduled for duty in the morning. Stash your bags and get into your fatigues," the Major said.

Hope was assigned too post-up duties. She was not trained to be a surgical nurse, but everyone worked where they were needed. She went into her tent and met Mary Cantrell who was writing a letter home. "Hi Hope. How was your R&R?" She asked.

"It was great. I met this wonderful Captain. We shared the week together. He is being assigned to the 2nd Infantry Division. I have pictures," Hope said with excitement.

"Oh good, let me see," Mary said with anticipation.

Hope showed the pictures she had and Mary was impressed with the dashing young man she had met. Leaving out the intimate details she described her week with Jack. It was not necessary to paint Mary a picture. She could read behind the lines. "So, are you two in love?" Mary asked.

"No silly, we are just friends. He lives in a small town outside Philly. I must admit, that I think if we get home something could be possible," Hope replied.

Two of the other nurses came into the tent and the girls were excited to hear about Hope's R&R. Mary was quick to establish that Hope had a new lover. Hope shared the tent with three other nurses. There were two tents assigned as nurse's quarters. Hope and Mary shared the tent with, Lieutenants Joyce Smith and Nancy Peterson. "Well I hope you two behaved yourselves. You know how 'Old Iron Pants' feels about men and sex," Joyce said.

Major Todd was very strict about the nurses having sexual relations in camp. The unit was comprised of officers and enlisted men. Personal interactions between officers and enlisted personnel was forbidden by the Army. Mash 8044 had seven male officers. Colonel Lee Jessup was the commanding officer. He had been in the infantry in France during the first world war. He went to college and medical school and went back into the Army. During WWll, he served with General Patton in Europe.

Colonel Jessup would retire from the Army when his Korean tour was completed. In addition to the camp Chaplain, Captain Peter McCauley there were five surgeons all of them held the rank of Captain. The surgeons had all been drafted into military service and in no way where they considered to be dedicated to the Army. To a man, they all hated that they had been drafted and pulled away from their families and being sent to Korea. The experience they would get here however would surpass any working skills they would have gotten at home. Their job would be to surgically repair the horrific wounds of soldiers brought to them by ambulance and helicopters. Once they were stable they would be transferred.

Those patients would be sent to Seoul or to Japan for further treatment. The overall mission was to get them in and out as quickly as possible. The surgical tent was large and was attached to the post-op or post-operative tent. Post-op could hold as many as a hundred patients.

The real commander of the unit was Corporal Tom Dudal, or 'Doodles'. He was the unit clerk and was Jessup's right-hand man. Everything the unit needed or wanted crossed his desk. He had contacts from a variety of units across Korea. The unit ran smoothly and was considered to be one of the best MASH units in the theater. "Doodles' was the hub; all of the other personnel were simply spokes of the turning wheel.

Major Todd had spoken to each of the nurses about sexual interactions with any of the men, officers or enlisted. A nurse who became pregnant while assigned to combat support would be discharged from the Army. All of the nurses had enlisted. The Army was their chosen career path. Not one of them was married. A shortage of nurses to work in the newly established MASH units could not afford to be taken away from her duties due to a pregnancy. Major Todd a career officer herself kept a tight rein on her nurses. Her own conduct in camp was legendary, thus the name 'Old Iron Pants'. All of the doctors and nurses were assigned regular shifts. Once casualties arrived everyone worked. Sometimes the number of wounded coming into camp was light and sometimes they unit was overwhelmed. The most critically wounded were treated first.

Hope had also done some shopping for the other nurse's and the doctors. While she was away she was able to fulfill everyone's request. The items she was tasked to obtain were shampoo's, skin lotions, books and the number one item, toilet paper. She had packed an extra duffle bag to take with her just for the coveted paper. The next slot for a nurse to take an R&R was two months away. The unit was flush with bandages, towels, sheets and surgical masks but the Army could never seem to get enough toilet paper into the camp. Even Doodles was constantly wheeling and dealing for the precious paper.

The next morning Hope reported for duty in post-op. The one hundred bed tent had only six patients. Two were scheduled to be transferred to Seoul later that day. Captain Selleck was the doctor on duty. He was from Florida. Professional in all of his interactions with the nurses he was a man dedicated to his patients. One of the men had a bad stomach wound. During surgery, he had to repair the man's badly torn bowel and lower intestines. He was watching him closely. Infection was now the patient's worse enemy. The other three men had shrapnel wounds to their extremities. Awake but resting these men would be transferred to Seoul the next day. For now, the sleeping PFC (Private First Class) was the big concern. "Good morning Lieutenant. Keep a close eye on this one. Check his vitals every thirty minutes and note them on the chart. We'll change his bandages after lunch. I'm going over to the mess tent for coffee. If anything develops call for me. How was the R&R?" Selleck asked.

"I had a great time, and I was able to get that book you wanted. I left it with Doodles," Hope replied.

"Thank you, you're the best. I can finally read something other than last month's Stars & Stripes, Selleck exclaimed leaving the tent. Hope checked the other patients then turned her attention to the badly wounded man. She noted from her chart he was a Marine. Looking at his face she thought how young he seemed to be. Checking the chart, she saw he was only eighteen years old. Why in the world is such a young man here? He should be home chasing girls and playing sports. She thought about her own father who had enlisted at this age to save his brother from the draft during the first world war. So many of these young boys have passed through here. We can only hope we did our best and they are well.

During the next two weeks, the unit saw few wounded. Fortunately, those that had been brought in by ambulance had minor shrapnel wounds. The lull in activity was a blessing. Everyone was content to catch up on sleep, write letters home or just have time to unwind. Major Todd kept a close eye on her nurses and informed Colonel Jessup in the weekly briefing that she wanted the doctors to train her staff in Triage techniques. Jessup said he would look into that possibility.

A few days later the training would have been beneficial. The camp was notified to be on alert for heavy casualties. The North Korean's and the Chinese had started a new fall offensive. A few ambulances showed up with badly wounded soldiers. Colonel Jessup and Captain Bourne worked triage as they came in. The other surgeons were already in the operating tent tending to their patients. Hope was on duty in post-op, preparing for more patients. Then it seemed as if all hell had broken loose. The ambulances that came in had wounded men packed in the back. Choppers were arriving as fast as they could land. Before the day was done post-op would be filled with all one hundred beds taken. Some of the less seriously wounded sat in the mess tent waiting for transport to Seoul. They had all worked twenty-four hours straight. Everyone in the camp was exhausted.

Hope, Mary, Joyce, and Nancy had twenty-five patients each in post-op. All of the men had sustained serious wounds. All of Hope's men were sedated or sleeping. Across the aisle, Joyce was talking with one of her patients. He was a sergeant from the 2nd Infantry Division. Joyce learned that all of the men here were in his unit. The North Korean's had over run their position on a hill they were defending. One of the three companies defending the hill top position had been wiped out. The 8063rd, 8076th, and the 8055th MASH units had also been swamped with casualties from the battle. Knowing that Hope's Captain was assigned to the 2nd Division she let Hope know the situation. "Cover for me, I need to find out if Jack is all right," Hope told Joyce. She left post-op and went to see Doodles. Entering the office, she said, "Doodles, please I need to know if Captain Randall of the 2nd Division is all right."

"You're going have to be more specific Lieutenant. What company is he in, what battalion?" Doodles asked.

"L Company, 1st Battalion," she said excitedly, tears starting to form in her eyes. She was worried sick.

"Ok, what regiment?" Doodles asked.

"Damn it Doodles, I need to know," she shouted. "Wait I'm sorry 23rd" she said regaining her composure.

Colonel Jessup heard the exchange outside of his office and left his desk.

"Calm down Lieutenant. What's the trouble?" he asked.

"Sir, my friend Captain Randall...I fear he may have been involved in this latest action...I need to know if he is all right," she started to cry.

"I have the Captain's unit sir, I could check," Doodles interrupted.

"All right Doodles, do that voo doo thing that you do and find out what the status is of this Captain," Jessup said as Major Todd came into the clerk's outer office. "Costigan, what are you doing here? You're supposed to be in post-op," she barked.

"I'm sorry Major, the other nurses are covering for me. I needed to know if Jack is all right. The Colonel said..." Hope said as she was cut off by Major Todd.

"Lieutenant everyone has worked all day and night without a break. What makes you think you can leave your post to attend to a personal matter? If we were not so busy I might be inclined to court martial your ass. The nurses that are covering for you have been relieved. They and you will report back to post-op in six hours. I suggest you get some sleep during that time. If you ever leave your post again..."

"Now hold on just a minute Sue. If her shift is being relieved, then it's ok for her to be here. Doodles find out about the Captain. Let's all go to the mess tent for some coffee. I'm buying," Jessup stated.

Major Todd knew this was not a request. It was an order. The old man had a way about him. He was as gentle and sweet as a lamb, but if he got his temper up you knew it. He was somewhere in between right now. The three officers left and entered the mess tent. Sitting down over coffee, they were interrupted by Captain Sawyer. "Colonel that patient with the head wound is taking a turn for the worst," Sawyer stated.

"Ok, I'll be right there Charles," Jessup said leaving.

Major Todd and Hope were alone now drinking their coffee. "I'm sorry Major. It won't happen again, I promise," Hope said.

"Forget it. We're all tired. It's been a long day and night. Hope you're the best post-op nurse on the staff. You take care of the patients and your bed side manner is terrific. That pretty face of yours is a blessing for these men. They're tired, scared, and hurt in way's no one should ever experience," Todd told her.

"Thank you Major, I don't know what to say," Hope replied.

"I know what it's like. You come to place like this and get a week in an exotic country to relax. You meet a handsome young man and nature takes its course. You cling to that. It is the one thing you have left as a young woman that makes any sense. Are you in love with him? I mean really in love him, or just the idea of him?" Todd asked her.

Hope thought about the question. It made sense. She did love Jack. But only in a different way. She had never been in love, but she knew that this was a fleeting kind of love. "I do love him. I think the war the far away romantic place and the circumstances affect that love. If we were home, it would be different. I think it could turn to real love, but we are not there. We are here. I guess the only way to know is let fate see it through," Hope answered.

"Get some sleep Lieutenant, you go back on duty in six hours. If there is any news, I'll let you know. I pray your Captain is all right," Todd said softly.

"Major. Thanks...I mean you are not as bad as everyone makes you out to be. The things they call you. I'm sorry...I have said to much," Hope said.

"What, you mean 'Old Iron Pants'. I've been called worse, believe me," Todd said laughing.

"You know about that?" Hope asked surprised.

"Trust me Lieutenant, there is nothing going on in my nursing staff that I don't know about. Now go and get some sleep," Todd said.

Hope left the mess tent and went to her quarters. The other girls were sound asleep. She lay on her bunk thinking about Jack.

I don't know if I can sleep she thought. Her mind and body said otherwise and within seconds she was in a deep sleep.

Six hours later she was in post-op when Colonel Jessup and Major Todd approached her. The look on their faces said it all. "I'm sorry Lieutenant your friend has been listed as MIA (Missing in Action). The North Korean's and the Chinese attacked a ridge he and his company were defending. The enemy still controls some of that area. We can only pray at this point that if he is alive he's getting proper treatment," Jessup told her.

"Costigan if you want to take some time for yourself I can cover you for a while," Major Todd added.

"Thank you, I think I will be all right. The reports have been confirmed? I mean there is no mistake?" Hope asked.

"Afraid not Lieutenant, Doodles confirmed it with I Corps," Jessup responded.

Hope left them and continued to take the vitals and recorded them in the chart for the sedated patient she was with. She moved to the next bed checking the bandages on the leg and hand of the next soldier in her care. "How do you feel Corporal? Are you having any pain?" She asked.

"No, I'm ok Mam. Could you help me write a letter home to my folks? I have a little bit of a problem here," the Corporal said holding up his right hand.

"I think we can help you with that. Just let me finish up the rest of my patients and I will be right back," Hope said smiling.

Hope moved to the next bed tending to her duties.

As Jessup and Todd left the tent, Jessup asked, "She going to be all right Sue?"

"Costigan is a trooper sir. She will be just fine. If things quiet down I'll see if I can get her relieved earlier," Major Todd said.

Hope finished her shift. She returned to her tent and quietly cried herself to sleep. She was allowed to sleep in and woke in mid-morning.

She checked the duty roster and saw she had the next two shifts off. She had twenty-four hours to herself. Her tent mates and the other nurses were sympathetic.

She saw Doodles in the compound and thanked him for his help. She also went to see Father McCauley. She knocked on the door of his tent and stuck her head in, "Father, are you busy? Can we talk?"

"Of course, Lieutenant come in and sit please," he answered.

McCauley was a soft spoken Irish Catholic priest from Boston. He was gentle in manner and dedicated himself to the wounded that passed through the unit. "I heard about your friend. I'm so sorry. I pray he will be taken care of. We must never give up our hope," McCauley said.

"Father, why did God allow us to become friends?"

We were so happy together. I feel as if God has played a cruel trick on us.

For the short time, we had we were lovers. We were sinners. Is God punishing us for what we did?" Hope asked.

"No, of course not. You must not feel that way. God has a plan for us all. We may not always live up to his expectations and we may never fulfill the plan he has in mind for us. But he would never punish us directly for those things we may do that he disagrees with. It's up to each of us to live our lives within his light. We may stray from time to time but he always wants us to come back to him. He has a plan for you and your friend. Try to take comfort in the fact that no matter what has happened he is always looking out for both of you," McCauley answered.

Then she asked if McCauley would hear her confession. He agreed and they spoke for another hour.

CHAPTER 14

GRATIFICATION & SORROW

It had been two weeks since the news about Captain Randall. His status changed from MIA. He and what was left of his company had been found. His unit was brought to the rear and replacements were coming in every day. Hope was relieved he was still alive. Her mood picked up with the news and everyone was happy for her. Hope received a letter from Jack a few days later. He mentioned in his letter that his company was getting back to normal strength. He also noted that he had sent photographs of them together in Tokyo, home to his parents. She thought about their relationship. She knew she cared for him but she was still not sure if she was actually in love. His letter indicated it was written to someone he cared for deeply. He signed it, 'Always Jack'. With the news, he had been found and the letter he wrote Hope was feeling better. She was surprised however that a few days after hearing from Jack she received a letter from his mother. It was very informal and friendly. She hoped that Hope would write her back. She decided she would.

Colonel Jessup made plans for a medical team to visit the refugee camp outside Mubong-Ri. With new hostilities in the area more and more local people were being pushed out of their homes. The team would consist of a doctor, a nurse and a medic. One other man would make the trip as security and the driver. He notified Major Todd he would need a nurse. Todd felt that although Hope had performed her work shifts without fault a little change of pace might help her along with whatever residual effects she was feeling. Jessup approved and the team would start out the next morning early. The jeep was loaded down with medical supplies and some food. Captain Patrick Welsh would be the doctor. Staff Sergeant Colon would drive the jeep and provide security. PFC Oshinski would be the medic. The drive would take about thirty minutes into the village and the refugee camp on the eastern side. It was a bright sunny summer morning. Hostilities in the last couple of days had calmed down.

Hope and Oshinski sat on the top of the overloaded jeep in back. With the sun and wind in her face Hope was enjoying the ride. They arrived on schedule and set up to tend to the people in the camp. Most of the people had sores on their feet from the long walk to the camp. Some of the infants were malnourished but for the most part there were no major problems. They gave out what food they had and dispensed medicine to those people who would need it. Sgt. Colon spoke some Korean so language was not a problem. They spent the better part of the day in the camp and started back in mid-afternoon. Hope had enjoyed herself in spite of the work and the poverty of the people she saw. She especially enjoyed helping the children. It was horrible what these poor little people had endured.

Although they had dispensed all the supplies Hope sat on top of the spare tire mounted to the back of the jeep. PFC Oshinski sat on the rear seat sideways. There was plenty of room in back of the jeep with the supplies gone. Hope removed her soft hat and released the pony tail letting her hair loose. The ride back to the camp was pleasant. She was enjoying the sun in her face and the wind in her hair when they started over the hill. Climbing the hill, they entered thick forest. It was much cooler on the road now as the high trees with their thick canopy covered the road. The road ran over the top side of the hill and started its slow decent on the western side. Reaching the bottom of the hill they came out of the forest as if they were coming out of a tunnel. Once at the bottom of the hill and out of the woods Sgt. Colon jammed on the brakes suddenly.

There were two North Korean soldiers on the road. There were also two others one on the southern side of the road. The patrol leader was on the north side of the road. Hope was thrown off the spare and she hit the top of the windshield hard. Oshinski was thrown sideways getting pinned between the bench seat in the back and the front seats in front. As the jeep ground to a halt the North Korean on the northern side of the road fired his Tokarev SVT40 rifle at Captain Welsh in the passenger seat. He fired all ten shots from the magazine killing the doctor and PFC Oshinski. Hope was thrown backward and fell into the spare tire cracking a rib bone on her left side. She fell out of the jeep landing in a sitting position with her back against the driver's side rear tire. Sergeant Colon grabbed the Thompson from its scabbard on the driver's side of the jeep and fired three quick bursts over the windshield at the two soldiers on the road and the North Korean on the north side of the road as he reloaded his weapon. One of the soldiers on the southern side of the road fired his Soviet PPSH-41 sub machine gun and killed Colon with a long burst. Colon now hung half out of the jeep his body riddled by bullets. Hope felt a sharp pain in her right side as she realized she was now alone. The last North Korean was walking towards her. The Thompson sat on the ground next to her. She grabbed the weapon and fired the last of the magazine at the approaching North Korean.

To her amazement bullets impacted into the ground all around the enemy soldier as he fell. She dropped the Thompson in her lap and felt the wound in her side with her hand. She looked at the blood covering her hand. It was thick and looked almost black. She said out loud to no one, "Oh no, I'm been shot." Her head was pounding from hitting the windshield. Her left side was throbbing from the cracked rib and she was losing blood from the bullet wound. She had no idea what had happened to the other enemy soldiers. She was losing consciousness. She could here footsteps approaching her from the back of the jeep. I'm going to die she thought.

The footsteps reached her and she looked up. He must be twenty feet tall she thought. He spoke but it sounded as if he were far away, "Corpsman up!"

Lance Corporal Frank Kepler and his five-man recon patrol were tracking a North Korean patrol of four men. They had been following them for about a mile as they headed north. They started over the crest of a ridge when they spotted the enemy patrol crossing a road as a US Army jeep came down a hill covered in forest. The jeep skidded to a stop and there was a brief but furious fire fight. Kepler and his men lined up on the ridge a fired on the last Korean soldier just as a burst of fire from a Thompson opened up. They slipped down the ridge onto the road and checked the dead Koreans. Two Go's in the jeep were also dead. The driver was half in and half out of the jeep. He too was dead. Kepler walked along the back of the jeep and saw a wounded nurse sitting on the driver's side. The still smoking Thompson was in her lap. She was looking up at him. "Corpsman up," he yelled. She passed out as he checked her wounds. "We got a live one Doc," he yelled.

The other Marines collected weapons from the North Koreans, and pulled the bodies off the road. The corpsman checked the nurse and told Kepler, "She's in bad shape Frank. Belly wound, looks like she caught one in the liver. There's a

MASH unit about three miles down the road. If we get her there she might make it." The Marines removed the bodies of Welsh, Colon and Oshinski from the jeep. They put the nurse in the back with the corpsman and Kepler started the jeep.

"You guys stay here with the bodies. Me and Doc will drive to the MASH unit. As soon as we deliver her we will be back. Keep your eyes open," Kepler ordered. Kepler started the jeep. One of the other Marines dropped the shattered and blood-spattered windshield so it would lie flat on the hood. Kepler put the jeep in gear and started down the road.

Colonel Jessup and Doodles were walking across the compound when Jessup heard the gun fire down the road. "Doodles, check with I Corps and see if there is any enemy activity near us. That gun fire is too close for my liking," Jessup said.

"Right away Colonel," Doodles responded running for his office. Jessup stood on the main road as Major Todd approached. "Sir, did you hear that gun fire?" She asked.

"I did Major. Doodles is checking with I Corps. In the meantime, let's get ready for possible casualties," Jessup answered.

Major Todd returned with Lieutenant Cantrell and Captain Selleck.

"Problem Colonel," Selleck asked. He set down his medical kit and a stretcher.

"We may see some wounded. Heard a short fire fight down the road. Say, when is that detail to the refugee camp due back?" Jessup stated.

Major Todd replied, "They should be back soon. They may be..."

She was interrupted by the sound of a jeep. As they looked down the road they could see a driver and another man in the back. The jeep roared into the compound and skidded to a stop. The Marine driving jumped out and yelled, "Wounded nurse here. Get a doctor."

Selleck helped the corpsman get the wounded nurse out of the jeep and unto the stretcher they had brought. "It's Hope Costigan," Selleck yelled.

Colonel Jessup looked at the blood stained and bullet pocked jeep and feared the worst. "Corporal, where there any other people with this vehicle?" Jessup asked.

Kepler replied, "Yes sir. Three other men were with the nurse. They are all KIA. They ran into a North Korean patrol we were tracking. She is the only survivor. She was firing a Thompson when we opened up and killed the last of the North Koreans. She's a fighter. It looks like she got three of the four before she was hit. I hope she makes it. We got here soon as we could. I have three men watching the rest of the detail sir."

"We need to get her into OR (Operating Room). She's lost a lot of blood, "Selleck stated.

"Cantrell and Todd carried Hope into the OR. Selleck started to prepare for surgery. Doodles returned to the scene and informed Jessup that there may be enemy recon patrols in the area. "Get a two-man detail and an ambulance and take the Lance Corporal here back to his men. Recover the bodies of Welsh, Colon and Oshinski," Jessup ordered.

"Yes sir," Doodles replied sadly, as he left.

"Corporal there's hot coffee in the mess tent for you and your men if you come back," Jessup said.

"Thank you, Colonel, but I have to get my guys back to our unit. I'm sorry about your people. I hope your nurse will be all right," Kepler replied. The ambulance pulled up and picked up the Marines. As it left the compound, Doodles stood by the Colonel.

"Inform I Corps that we are short a surgeon and a nurse. I'm going into OR to help Selleck. Inform Father McCauley," Jessup said going into the OR.

Jessup scrubbed and dressed for surgery. Once he was done he went into the OR. Todd and Cantrell were assisting Captain Selleck. "How's she doing?" Jessup asked.

"Right now, I'm stitching up what's left of her liver. She lost about forty percent of the organ. Some of the bullets went straight through."

"We found some bullet fragments and some additional bleeding in her abdomen. She's lost a lot of blood. She's getting whole blood now and she's stable. She just might pull through Colonel," Selleck said.

"Thank God, anything you need me to do?" Jessup replied.

"Nasty cut on her head. The bleeding has stopped but if you could close it up we can be done here soon," Selleck replied.

"All right, I can get started right away," Jessup said.

Major Todd added, "There is one other thing sir. She's about five weeks pregnant. No damage to the fetus, sir"

"Well she had a good time on her R&R. Let's see if we can't get her and her baby home," Jessup said.

The operation continued for another hour and when it was finished they moved her to post-op. Hope would survive the ordeal. Major Todd and the other nurse kept a close eye on her as she rested.

During Hopes operation, the ambulance returned with the bodies. Doodles had notified graves registration and they would be picked up soon. The camp was in a depressed state. A lot of wounded people came through this unit. Many of them died. This time it was some of their own.

The loss was hard to take. The sad task of collecting the personal belongings and getting them cataloged for shipment home was a bitter pill to swallow. The war however, continued. The fighting that started a few weeks ago, was intensifying again. The sadness they felt was buried by the constant work. Hope was in post op recovering from her wounds. The news of her pregnancy was kept secret. Known only to Jessup, Todd, Selleck and one other nurse. It was Jessup's decision to conceal the pregnancy. She was going home as a hero not a party girl. Based on the written reports from the Marines, Jessup had recommended her for the Silver Star for valor.

Doodles had already sent the paperwork to I Corps. The next morning Jessup and Todd showed up at her bed. Hope was awake but groggy from the operation. "You're lucky Lieutenant. You had a bullet wound in the liver. We patched you up, you are going to be ok. You're also about five weeks pregnant. The baby is all right. You should be able to carry to term without any issue's," Jessup informed her.

"You're R&R trip to Tokyo must likely," stated Todd. Oh, my God. They're going to throw me out of the Army. I'll go home a disgrace. And what about Jack?" Hope cried.

"Now hold on Lieutenant. Let's not put the saddle on the horse just yet. According to the Marines that found you, you were taking the fight to the enemy. I recommended you for a Silver Star. Now your wound can be written up so that you can be discharged medically. We are keeping you here because of an infection. All of your recovery time will be here. I'll do the discharge medical exam myself. When you leave here, you'll go to Seoul and then straight home," Jessup told her.

"Infection? What infection?" Hope asked.

"First, we have to know if it's a boy or a girl," Major Todd replied.

"I'm going to miss you Lieutenant. We all will. For now, get some rest. No one knows about your pregnancy. I expect you'll be on your way home in about two weeks or so," Colonel Jessup said.

Father McCauley came to her bedside as Jessup and Todd were leaving. "How are you feeling Hope?" He asked.

"Colonel Jessup said I'm going home. He is going to write the orders himself. I can't believe I made it Father. I feel so bad about the others.

Why did they die? Why am I the only survivor? It doesn't seem right. I have to talk to Jack. He should know..." she started and stopped.

"Know about what?" McCauley asked.

"That I'm...wounded and going home," she replied with hesitation.

"I'm sure that Jack has enough to worry about. His company was just overrun. He is also lucky to be alive. You can always write him a letter. I can help you if you'd like," McCauley offered.

"No...not right now Father. I'm a little tired. Maybe later, all right," Hope replied.

McCauley answered, "Of course, get some rest. I'll stop by again later in the afternoon."

McCauley left leaving Hope to her thoughts. Pregnant and with Jack's baby. How am I going to tell him? How am I going to tell my mother?

Jack Randall sat in his tent and wrote a letter to his mother;

Dear Mom,

So, happy to hear the pictures I sent you arrived in good shape. I'm in the rear now. My Company is getting new people every day now. We should be up to full strength by the end of the week.

I'm lucky that the First Sergeant I have is top notch. He served with Patton in Italy and Europe. He makes my job so much easier.

In your last letter, you mentioned that you had written to Hope. I'm sure she will write back to you. You can see by the pictures I sent how pretty she is. I think of her often and the wonderful time we had in Tokyo. To answer your last question, No I cannot visit with her here. Her outfit is about twenty miles or so west and south of where I am now. Once we are up to full strength my Company will rejoin the Division north of here. I am looking forward to getting home. I'm not sure where the next post will be after the war. Hope was looking to get assigned to Walter Reed. If I had an assignment in the Pentagon we could see each other. Tell Dad to work his magic.

By the way how is Dad? It's been a while since his last letter. I guess he is keeping busy at the courthouse. Is he still going to be a judge? Tell him to write soon or he will be out of order and I will hold him in contempt. Ha Ha!

I miss you both. I have to go. Morning formation, I'll write again soon.

Love, Jack

Leaving the tent, he saw his Company in formation. Three platoons of fresh replacements. Some of the men who had been with him when the Company was overrun were now Sergeants. He also had three brand new Second Lieutenants, fresh out of the Officers Candidate School (OCS) at Fort Benning. None of these men had ever experienced combat. That would soon change. The Division was pushing north and had the North Koreans on the run. Standing now in front of his Company, he looked at the faces of very young men. How many would grow old is a question only time would answer.

After formation, the Company was dismissed for chow. A corporal from Battalion headquarters informed Jack to report to Colonel Kuebler at HQ.

When he arrived, the Colonel was talking to a new officer. He saluted the Colonel and reported in.

"Good morning Jack. I want you to meet 1st Lieutenant Robert Wagner. He will be taking command of your Company," the Colonel said.

"A pleasure Lieutenant, welcome to the outfit," Jack responded shaking the new man's hand.

Then the Colonel handed Jack something from his pocket. "Here Jack, pin these on. As of now you are my exec. (Battalion Executive Officer) Looking in his hand Jack saw the gold oak leaves of a Major. He was now the second in command of the Battalion. He lost the Company to a younger man and gained six more. "Wagner is a Point man, class of 49."

"Get him squared away and then come back here with your gear. We can have a long talk over lunch. Congratulations Major, you earned it," the Colonel said.

"Thank you, sir. Follow me, Wagner," Jack stated saluting his commander as he left.

As they walked past the tents that housed the battalion Jack informed the new officer, "You're getting an outstanding First Sergeant. He really runs the Company. If I gave you any advice at all it would be this. Listen to First Sergeant Howard, especially in combat. You have 90-day wonders for platoon leaders. There're fresh out of OCS. All of the Non-Coms (Non-Commissioned Officers or Sergeants) are all veterans. Good men and combat experienced. The rest of the Company are as green as grass." They arrived at Jacks tent and he started to gather his gear. The last thing he did was to pin the new oak leaves on his collar. Then Jack took Wagner to the Company HQ tent. When he entered First Sergeant Howard yelled, "Attenhut."

All the men in the tent stood at attention until Jack said, "As you were."

"Congratulations Major. I see my charm, good looks and expert tutelage has paid off," Howard said.

"Howard, you are neither charming or good looking. This is your new CO. (Commanding Officer) 1st Lieutenant Robert Wagner."

"Try not too corrupt his morals," Jack said shaking Howards hand. Jack then shook the hands of his Company Clerk and one of his platoon sergeants. "Good luck fella's, see you the trenches," Jack stated leaving the tent.

He found his bunk in the battalion HQ area and unpacked his gear. He did not have much. Everything he had was in a duffel bag. He changed into a cleaner uniform and pinned on the new oak leaves. Jack had also been to West Point. He was class of 43. After graduation, he was assigned to the 101st Airborne Division and had been at Bastogne during the Battle of the Bulge. He arrived as a green 2nd Lieutenant and was promoted twice, leaving Europe at the end of the war as a Captain. After an assignment to a training command at Fort Benning, he was now with the 2nd Infantry Division as second in command of his Battalion.

Jack met with his commander and learned the battalion was moving up in three days to join the rest of the division. Jacks job was to get the battalion ready to move. The Colonel would be at division HQ reviewing the planned operation they would all be involved in. They were heading north to the 38th Parallel. Jacks battalion would join other elements of the 2nd Infantry Division and the 36th ROK (Republic of Korea) Regiment along a ridge line that would later be named 'Bloody Ridge'. After three weeks of fighting the North Koreans would retreat to a new line of ridges just 1500 meters away. Another battle would begin along that seven-mile ridge line and would later be named, 'Heartbreak Ridge'.

Hope laid there in bed thinking. I'll be home in two or three weeks. I need to tell my mother when I get home. I also have to face the rest of my family. There would not be any way to inform Jack except by letter. What would he think. Is it even fair for me to tell him?

A Company Commander had great responsibilities. Is it even fair to burden him with this news? Jack is very close to his mother. What will she think? What is she going to think of me? How could I have been so careless? Despite her anxiety, she soon fell asleep. She was restless all night. In the morning, Mary checked in on her. She made notes on the chart and left her to her thoughts. Major Todd stopped to see her and Doodles showed up with the mail. She had three letters. The envelope on top had a Media Pa. postmark. It was no doubt another letter from Jacks mother

CHAPTER 15
COMING & GOING

Caroline had tired of the Washington DC environment. She wanted a new posting. Everyone in the District seemed to be self-centered. It was all about me and who I know. Everyone she met wanted to help her career along and always with a hand where it should not be. She was not interested in sleeping her way up the ladder. Senators and Congressman were the worst. It was almost as if they believed they were entitled to her charms by their position. It was time for a change.

She was also bored with her work. A lot of activity on the French desk dealt with a far off Asian country called Vietnam. The former French colony had declared its independence from France. The French were now engaged in a war with the northern part of the country in full revolt. French troops supported by the US seemed to have lost control of the country side, but maintained a strong position in the cities of the south. Saigon was the principal city in the southern part of the country. The US had a consulate there and Caroline applied for a transfer. She had been an analyst with the new agency and a transfer would require additional field training. She was good shape but she knew she would have to exercise more.

In a few weeks, she got her orders and reported back to Area F. Ninety days of enhanced field training in Bethesda Maryland turned her from a desk jockey to an operator. The specifics of her training include firearms, hand to hand combat and the customs of the Vietnamese people. She was not going to be a field officer. Her analytical talents would keep her desk bound in the consulate. The work that would cross her desk would come in from case officers assigned in the field and the assets they had recruited. The agency spent a good deal of training time teaching what was expected of her as a US citizen and as an employee of the Agency. Sexual relationships with Vietnamese and French nationals was forbidden. Her conduct had to be beyond reproach, otherwise foreign agents would use any scandal on her part as a way to gather intelligence through blackmail. She found the counter-intelligence side of her training fascinating.

She had leave time coming to her. She decided to allow the leave time alone. While living in Arlington she was able to go home any weekend she wanted. Finishing her training she had five days at home before leaving for Saigon. She was home alone thinking about lunch when the taxicab stopped in the street. All she could see was a female Army officer with an array of ribbons on her uniform blouse. Her heart sank and the feeling in her stomach brought bile to her throat. She went outside and saw the officer about to step unto the steps of her neighbor's home. It was Hope. "Oh, my goodness, Hope it's you. You frightened me. I thought the Army sent… You're not expected home for at least a year," Caroline said.

"Yes, well here I am. I'm out now, the Army discharged me. I wanted to surprise everyone."

Caroline noticed the ribbon for the Purple Heart. An award bestowed for wounds received in combat. Saying nothing the two women embraced.

"Welcome home, Hope. Your mother will be so surprised," Caroline told her.

"So why are you home? Still working in DC?" Hope asked.

"On my way to a foreign posting in Saigon, Vietnam. I leave on Monday. Let's go inside and surprise your Aunt Maggie and Dorothy," Caroline suggested.

Entering the home of her Aunt Maggie, Hope heard Dorothy and her Aunt back in the kitchen. It was common place for neighbors and friends to just enter a home on the street. People came and went all the time. Not alarmed at the sound of the door opening Dorothy and her mother continued with their lunch preparation. "Hello, anyone home? What's a girl have to do to get some lunch around here?" Hope called out. Both women got up from the table and upon seeing Hope, screamed and ran to her. Caught completely off guard the surprise Hope wanted was a success. Maggie and Dorothy fired questions at her not waiting for any answers. Dorothy also noticed the purple ribbon and knew what it was. Her brother Dylan had one. She looked Hope over touching and testing her. "Your mother is going to be so happy you are home. I can't believe your actually here. Are you hungry? We were about to have lunch. Join us Caroline we have plenty," Maggie said.

The four women sat at the kitchen table and prepared sandwiches. More and more questions were asked and Hope finally said, "I really would like to do this just once. So please let me wait for my mother. I'll answer all of your questions then. Just know that I am fine and happy to be home. Now I have lots of questions for you. Hope had read the letters about the upcoming wedding of Steve and Dorothy. She was happy for her. She knew about the attack and had left shortly after. Dorothy assured her she was fine. The physical wounds had all healed. She was still dealing with the emotional wounds. Her assailant had never been

173

caught. In fact, they learned that all of the attacks had stopped. The latest news from the police is that the man responsible had moved on and they had no idea where. Dorothy told Hope that Steve had been by her side through it all. "He was wonderful. He doted on her. I've never seen someone so devoted to another person," Maggie told them.

"He always did have a crush on you. I'm happy for you both," Hope said.

"Wait, how about you? I saw the pictures of that dashing officer you met in Japan. He looks like quite a catch. Are you still in touch with him?" Maggie asked Hope. Her eyes went sad for a second as she thought about Jack, and her last letter to him before she left Korea.

Dear Jack,

Your mother wrote another letter to me. She seems so nice. I hope I can meet her someday. This letter has some news I must share with you. First, I'm going home. There was an incident outside of camp last week. I'm all right so don't worry. I was wounded, but the surgeons here patched me up. I had a nasty bump on the head and I was shot in the stomach. The wound to my stomach damaged part of my liver so the Army is discharging me and sending me home. I'm fine and the doctors tell me I will live a normal life.

Second, and believe me when I tell you I wish I could tell you face to face.

I'm pregnant. I feel like I am trapping you telling you this way. I have no right to expect anything from you. The week we had in Tokyo is something I will always treasure. We shared so much. You have so much to worry about. The last thing you need is this kind of news. Please take care of yourself and your men. I cannot stress enough how important you are to me. When I learned, you were missing my heart broke. The thought of never

*seeing you again frightened me. At that time, I had no idea I was
carrying your child. I know you believe that it is your child.*

*Colonel Jessup arranged my discharge. He is such a wonder-
ful man. Everyone here at MASH 8044 has been just great. They
are my second family. I imagine by the time this letter reaches you
I will be on my way home. I really wanted to tell you all of this to
you in person. You deserve that. If you feel I have betrayed you, I
will understand. Again, you owe me nothing. You know how to
reach me at home. I hope to hear from you soon.*

In my heart, always,
Hope

"He is such a wonderful man. I wrote to him just before I left
Korea. I really hope to hear from him. I worry about him. He is
a Company Commander in the 2nd Division. I pray God will keep
him safe," Hope said.

The woman sat the rest of the afternoon chatting about wedding plans and Caroline's future job. Hope learned that after
the wedding Dorothy would return to Villanova and pursue a
graduate degree.

Colleen had made it a habit to have dinner each night with
Kevin and Maggie. The weather was pleasant today so she decided to walk home from City Hall. The Parkway was just starting to
bloom with a new spring. She had no idea why, but she felt happy
today. The late afternoon sun glistened off the Joan of Arc statue
that stood at the end of the Parkway.

She turned right and began to walk up 25th Street. Reaching
Maggie's house, she went in the front door. Standing in the liv-
ing room and the hall that led back to the kitchen was, Maggie,
Dorothy and Caroline. They were waiting for her and each had
a broad smile on their faces. Someone came up the hall behind
Maggie and Dorothy. When she saw who, it was she screamed

with happiness. Mother and daughter embraced tearfully. Caroline laughed with delight as Maggie and Dorothy hugged each other wiping tears from their own eyes. Minutes later Kevin came home. Another happy reunion. Questions, questions and more questions. Hope stated that after dinner she would explain it all. The women had prepared roast chicken for dinner. The Brogans sent Caroline home to invite her parents. Everyone enjoyed the meal. After clearing the dinner plates, they sat around the table drinking coffee. Then Hope clinked her cup with her spoon to get everyone's attention. "All right everyone, before you start asking questions I will tell you everything. Hopefully there will be no need for follow up questions. As you all know, I met a wonderful young man, in Japan. He is still in Korea, serving with the 2nd Division. He is a Captain. We had a wonderful time and have stayed in touch. I have also received letters from his mother. They all live in Media." Caroline and Dorothy interrupted with ewes and awes. Hope ignored them and continued, "After returning to Korea, I learned that Jack was listed as missing in action."

"Needless to say, I was very upset. My fellow officers and friends in my unit went out of their way to find out what happened. Thankfully we learned that Jacks company had been overrun defending a hill but that he was located and not hurt. Since then his company has been refitted and joined the Division just as I was leaving. A few weeks later I was on a humanitarian mission to a refugee camp. There were four of us. Myself a doctor a medic and a driver. We passed out food, medical supplies and treated the people in the camp as best we could. On the way, back to our unit we encountered a North Korean Patrol." Hope stopped a second, tears filling her eyes. Everyone sat still hanging on each word. "they opened fire on us. Doctor Welsh and Private Oshinski were killed. Sergeant Colon fought back but he was also killed. I was thrown from the jeep. I hit my head on the windshield and now have a small permanent part for my hair. I cracked a rib and fell beside the jeep. An enemy soldier saw me and fired at me hitting me here in side. I thought I was going to die. What I did not know was there was also a Marine patrol tracking these North Koreans. They killed the last man and took me to my unit. The doctors there saved my life. I lost part of my liver but the doctors tell me I need not worry. I am fine and will have no repercussions from my wounds. The Army gave me a medical discharge and well, here I am." Hope wiped away her tears and looked at her family. Colleen took a deep breath and replied, "Dear God, I never thought I could hold my breath so long." There was nervous laughter around the table. "I'm sorry I put everyone off until now. It was just something I wanted to do once. I think of the people who died that day. It breaks my heart. I often wonder why them and not me. They were such wonderful people. The numerous lives they saved just doing their duty. It seems so wrong that they should lose their own lives." Kevin added, "Thank God that you are home and safe now." Colleen looked at her daughter. Their eyes locked and she grasped her hand. There was something else. Looking into Hope's eyes she knew there was something else.

After dinner was over Colleen and Hope walked home. They spoke a little about Dorothy's recovery. Hope mentioned that she was looking forward to seeing her Uncle Mike and Aunt Susan. Arriving at their home on Ogden Street they went inside and found Hope's luggage that she had dropped off before going to Maggie's house. Colleen helped her daughter carry the suitcase and duffle bag upstairs.

Hope sat on the bed while her mother began to unpack. She waited patiently, knowing that Hope was working up the courage. "Mom there is one other little thing I need to tell you," Hope said quietly. Her mother sat next to her and put her arm around her. "I know, it' all right you can tell me," Colleen replied.

177

"Remember when you told me about the first time you had been with Daddy. You said that you knew it was wrong but that you wanted the first time to be with him no matter what. You thought it would be possible that he would be killed in France. I felt the same way in Korea. I was a virgin. Some of the doctors and other men in the camp dated some of the nurses. A lot of these men were married. I never did anything with any of those men in my unit. When I got to Tokyo and met Jack, I felt different. I knew that it was possible that I might be killed. I did not want to die a virgin. Jack was so sweet, gentle and kind. I thought he might be killed also. We really did connect with each other. We had a wonderful week together. I found that I could no longer restrain myself. The first time we made love I could not believe how wonderful it was. We spent that week together as if we were lovers and there was no war. It was just the two of us in this very romantic setting. It was just perfect," Hope said.

"It's all right honey. It sounds as if your first time with a man was like a fairy tale. In those circumstances, I don't think I could have done anything different. Every girl dreams about her first time. Just like she dreams of her wedding day. I'm happy for you. There's nothing to be ashamed of," Colleen told her.

"Mom, I'm pregnant," Hope declared.

Colleen sat there, for a moment taking in what had just been revealed.

"How did… never mind I know how. Is that why the Army discharged you?"

"No, Colonel Jessup did the exit medical exam himself. My pregnancy is not in my records. I was really discharged due to my wounds," Hope answered.

"Does Jack know about this?" Colleen asked.

"I wrote him a letter just before I left Korea. I wanted to tell him in person but I just could not get to him. I imagine by now he knows. I feel so terrible for him."

"Are you…in love with him?" Colleen inquired.

Hope sighed, "I don't know. I have very strong feelings for him. Maybe when he comes home we could pick up where we left off. With a baby, it might not ever happen. I can't decide if I love him or I'm in love with the idea of him. Was it just that one magical week or is this something that would be forever. It all depends on how he reacts to the news. I can't say I would blame him if he detached himself from it all."

"All right, what's your gut say to you? Let's say that Jack writes and tells you he wants nothing to do with you or the baby. What do you do now, and how do you feel?" Colleen asked.

Hopes lip began to quiver, "I guess the baby and I will go on together without him. I love the time we had together. I will always be in love with him even if it was just for that one week. My child will never know their father. Just like me." Hope broke down and her mother held her. The two women letting their own grief flow together with their tears.

Sitting on top of the command bunker Jack sat watching the sunset. His battalion had joined the rest of the Division. Tomorrow they would be moving up the line on a series of ridges. The mission was to push the North Koreans off the ridge line. For now, his thoughts were on the letter he was writing home. He broke the news to his mother and father. He had been promoted too Major and now was the second in command of his battalion. He expected with this new position that he would have enough points to come home in about a year. He kept the letter short. Sunlight was fading and he wanted to write Hope as well.

Dear Hope,

We will be moving out in the morning so I wanted to drop in a line before the sun sets. I have great news! I am now a Major and the exec of my battalion. You're going to have to work extra hard and make Captain before you go home.

My dad is going to be a county judge. He has some very influential friends. I'm hoping I can get a DC post when I leave Korea. If you want I can let him know about your desire to be posted to Walter Reed.

I think about you often. I really do miss you. We had a great time in Tokyo. I like to think we could pick up where we left off. I would like nothing more.

Listen to me, I sound like a love stricken teenager. We did have a magical time together. Please write to me soon.

Always Yours,
Jack

He went back into the headquarters tent and mailed his letters. He checked his M1 carbine and .45 pistol. He made sure he had an extra first aid kit and then laid down on his cot. Tomorrow was going to be a big day. He was responsible not only for the men in his old company but the entire battalion. Men were going to die. He himself might die. It was a restless night. When the artillery started to fire, its preparation rounds that morning he got up. His CO was already up. "All right Jack, it's time to earn our paychecks. Have the troops mount up, it's going to be a long day," the Colonel told him.

"Yes sir."

Mike and his father left for Police Headquarters. His dad was respected and a regular visitor. He often had coffee with the Police Chief at the local coffee house in town. Today was no different. While his dad and the Chief had coffee Mike and Dave were tending to their paperwork. The desk Sergeant called Mike on the intercom. "Hey Mike, You and Dave need to go down to Cape May. They had a rape homicide over the weekend. CMPD is holding a briefing for other departments. The Chief wants you both there, briefing starts at eleven."

"All right, Sarge," Mike replied.

"Get your jacket partner. We are going to Cape May. We have to attend a briefing at eleven on a rape homicide case, Mike told Dave.

"No shit, a major case. Let's go," Dave replied with excitement.

Putting on their jackets the two detectives signed out one of two unmarked cars and drove south down Route 9. During the drive, Mike thought about his niece Dorothy. She had narrowly escaped being killed by a rapist. Dave was excited. In his entire time with the OCPD he had never seen a major felony case.

They arrived around 10:30 and were directed to a large conference room already crowded with other detectives. They saw representatives from Wildwood, Stone Harbor, Sea Isle City, Woodbine and the NJ State Police. The coffee was bad and the briefing started on time at eleven. Joe Cox knew them all and as the lead investigator started the briefing.

"Gentleman, thank you for coming. On Sunday evening while her husband was working a tour for the CMFD, twenty-five-year-old Mrs. Audrey Miller was attacked in her home on Sunset Lane. Entrance to the residence was made through an unlocked door leading into the kitchen. The victim was in the process of taking a bath. She was undressed at the time of the attack. Based on the physical evidence we found the victim was raped in the hallway outside of the bathroom. We have blood and semen samples collected from the hallway from the attacker and the victim. There was also evidence of a more substantial struggle in the bathroom. The victim showed physical signs that she was beaten and strangled but the official cause of death was drowning. After the attack, we have evidence the suspect drank a bottle of beer and smoked a cigarette.

Finger prints from the suspect were collected on the door leading into the kitchen, the bathroom door as well as the beer bottle. Her body was discovered in the bathtub the following Tuesday morning by her husband. The bathtub still had bath water in it. A long piece of hair was taken from the victim. Some sort of souvenir. CMPD conducted interviews of the neighbors, who affirm that they saw nor did they hear anything on Sunday night. I'll answer questions now."

Several detectives asked additional questions and took notes. They learned that CMPD was still waiting for the results of a finger print identification to be made by the FBI. That process would take about two weeks. The suspect was unknown. They had no idea about his physical characteristics either. He was a ghost for now. Hopefully the FBI would give them a name.

CHAPTER 16

LOYALTY LIFE & LOVE

Vang Bo arrived at the Continental Palace in Saigon. He went to the desk and checked in. The lobby was crowded with Vietnamese and westerners. The young man at the desk greeted him in French, "Bon jour monsieur l'apresmidi comment puis-je vous aider?" Bo's French was passable but he replied in Vietnamese. He told the clerk of his reservation. He would be there for three days. After his check in he and the bellman went upstairs to his room. He had made notice of the bar off the lobby. He tipped the bellman, then looked around the modestly furnished room. A few minutes later there was a knock on the door. He opened the door to see his old friend, Hung. "Welcome to Saigon old friend. I hope you had a pleasant trip," Hung said greeting him.

"Yes, the drive here was most pleasant," Bo replied.

"Good, please come with me. I have something I need to show you."

Bo's room was on the second floor. They walked to the elevator and waited. When the elevator car arrived, they went up to the fourth floor and entered a large suite. There was a small foyer that opened up to a large sitting area. The suite was lavishly furnished in western décor. Two women sat together on a sofa facing the door to the suite.

They were dressed elegantly in Vietnamese Traditional au Dai attire.

Bo could not believe his eyes. Despite the years of separation and the anxiety of never knowing their fate, his knees buckled and he steadied himself on the side wall. His eyes started to fill with tears. The two women also recognizing him rushed to him crying out loud, "Baba, Baba."

The three people fell into each other's arms. Hung sat on a chair in the small foyer pleased with himself and the scene before him. Vang Bo had been reunited with his twin daughters Mei and Meilin. The three of them crying, kissing and hugging each other. The reunion took a good ten minutes. Finally, they moved further into the suite and sat on the sofa together. Hung joined them sitting in a side chair smiling broadly. Wiping tears from his eyes Bo declared, "I will always be in your debt for this. I could never repay such a kindness. How… where…I am so happy. Words cannot help me." Bo took a deep breath and holding the hands of his daughters was emotionally overcome. Likewise, his daughters cried and praised Hung for the gift of their father. Once everyone calmed down they looked at each other laughing nervously. Hung broke the silence, "My heart soars for your happiness. There is much suffering in my country. It is a joy to see such love long torn apart back together again. At my request, a friend found Mei and Meilin together in Changchun. He had them brought here, for me. They survived the Japanese and the war. Now just as you, they are Chinese Nationals living and working in Vietnam. You are a school teacher in a trade school in Dinh Quan. Your daughters are going to work in their own shop here in Saigon. Embroidery and seamstress work will be their profession as it was in Changchun. You can visit and see each other whenever you wish. I ask for no reward. Only your loyalty and friendship."

"Yesterday I would have given my life for you, old friend. You saved my life long ago and gave me a purpose for my life. Today is no different. I will always be grateful" Bo declared.

Mike and Dave drove back up Route 9 to Ocean City. Dave was reviewing the notes he had made during the briefing. "What's up old man? Your awful quiet. Something eating you?" Dave asked.

"This case. I can't put my finger on it. It just bugs me. My gut says this is the same guy that attacked Dorothy. Call it a hunch," Mike replied.

Most times a cop's hunch led nowhere. Sometimes though a cop followed a hunch right to the closing of a case. "C'mon there's no way. This case is more than a hundred miles away from Dorothy's. In Dorothy's case, all the other attacks were outside. Hers was outside and always around trains or trolley's. This one is a burglary. There's nothing in common here," Dave replied.

"I know, but there is something about it." Mike said, and going over the details of the Cape May attack in his head as he drove.

Arriving back at Police headquarters Mike got a message from the desk Sergeant. "Hey Mike, your old lady called. She wants you to call her."

"All right Sarge, thanks."

Mike went to his desk and called home. Susan answered on the second ring. "Hi baby, what's up?" Mike asked.

"Guess who surprised everyone and came home?" Susan asked excited.

Mike thought quickly and decided on Michael, Jimmy's older brother. Hope was in Korea and Dylan was in Manila. "Michael?"

"NO silly, Hope is home. She is all right, but Maggie told me she was wounded and the Army sent her home. She's even been discharged."

"Wounded, is she, all, right?" Mike asked concerned.

"I just said that. You don't listen. She's fine. Kevin and Maggie want us to come up this weekend."

"All right we can do that. Does Dad know?" Mike asked.

"Yes, he's here and very excited. We'll talk more tonight, love you," Susan, said hanging up the phone.

Mike put the receiver down as Dave asked, "Everything all, right?"

"Yea, Hope's home from Korea," Mike replied deep in thought.

Heavy explosive and White Phosphorus rounds were impacting along the top of the ridge. Jacks Battalion was moving slowly up the ridge line on the right flank. Baker Company was reporting heavy resistance. The North Koreans were dug in and had fortified their positions with bunkers. Heavy machine gun fire from the Koreans had wiped out a platoon from Able Company. Easy Company was on the far right of the entire attack by the Division. They had lost visual and physical contact with Baker Company. They were not responding to radio calls. Jack ordered Baker Company to send a squad east along the front to try and establish contact with Easy Company. The fighting started when the 36th ROK Division pushed the North Koreans and the Chinese off the ridge line. A counter attack by the North Koreans resulting in the recapture of the mountains. There fighting was fierce and there was hand to hand fighting. The 2nd Division sent in the 9th regiment which was successful in retaking the objective after ten days of heavy fighting. The weather turned foul and after heavy rains additional attacks and resupply became impossible due to the mud and the slippery slopes. Once the weather cleared, Jacks 23rd Infantry Regiment was added to the fight.

Easy Company lost contact with the rest of the Battalion. North Koreans had slipped in between Baker and Easy Company's and were causing havoc. The squad from Baker Company that was sent to re-establish contact with Easy was ambushed and shot to pieces by the Koreans infiltrating the American lines. Baker reported back to Battalion that the squad was now lost as well. "Jack, take a platoon from the reserve company and see if you can't plug up that hole in our lines," the Battalion Commander ordered.

"Yes sir," Jack replied grabbing his gear. He ran back to the rear of the forward battalion position and found 1st Lieutenant Wagner the new CO of Lima Company and 1st Sergeant Howard.

"Lieutenant, I need one platoon to come with me", he stated.

First platoon is your best bet," Howard informed Wagner. "All right, first platoon it is," Wagner replied.

"Permission to go along sir," Howard asked his CO.

"Permission denied sergeant. You stay with your company," Jack interrupted. As much as he would have liked Howard along for this mission, Wagner would need his expertise more.

He searched out first platoon and found LT. Honie with his old platoon Sergeant Hank Shockley. "Lieutenant you and I are going east up the line to establish contact with Easy Company. Have Hank get the platoon ready to move out in five," Jack ordered.

Honie looking startled stammered, "All right...Major."

Hank Shockley was already moving gathering up first platoon. Twenty-four men all green replacements followed Shockley and hooked up with Jack and Honie. In addition, they had a radioman from battalion and a medic.

Moving east behind the line established by Baker Company they came up on the far-right flank. Baker's third platoon was fighting their way north up the hill while trying to protect the eastern flank exposed by the loss of contact with easy Company. Jack and his platoon from Lima Company took over protecting the eastern flank. Moving east they came upon fox holes that had been dug by Easy Company. The North Koreans were now in these holes cutting up Baker's third platoon. Jack needed to get the enemy out of those holes so he could move east towards Easy. Machine gun and rifle fire had his men pinned down along the slope approaching those holes. A North Korean machine gun had an obstructed line of fire towards the east and south and one of the green replacements tried to throw a grenade uphill into the hole with the machine gun. The grenade went too far up the hill and exploded harmlessly. Broken trees and rough terrain blocked the view of the young private.

He tried another grenade him, this time holding it for a second and threw it high into the air. The grenade exploded in the air right over the enemy machine gun killing the crew. Lt. Honie got up and rushed the position yelling, "Follow me men."

"Get down Lieutenant," Shockley yelled.

He jumped over a fallen tree trunk and pulling his own grenade tried to lob it into the machine gun position with the already dead crew. The grenade lofted in the air as Honie curled up under the fallen tree. It came down outside the enemy hole and bounced back towards Honie. It hit him in the head and as he looked up it went off.

"Aw for Christ sake," Shockley complained. They continued fighting their way east and sent the enemy retreating back up the hill. By the end of the afternoon they had established a link with Easy Company.

The radio for Easy Company was shot up. That explained why they were not responding to radio calls. They also had their hands full. The terrain in front of them almost leveled off but at the same time curved around their position. To continue attacking north up the hill they had to maneuver into a dip in the terrain that formed a C shaped cup. The enemy had crossing fields of fire. Easy started out with 110 men. They had 13 killed and 39 wounded. Jack reinforced them with 28 men, with four wounded. Lt. Honie was the only man killed fighting their way to Easy Company. He used the radio to inform the battalion commander. The mission was a success but night was coming so they would stay until the next day.

The men dug holes and they settled in for the night. Low clouds and not much of a moon made it black as coal. Without the flares, continuously be fired overhead you could not see the hand in front of your face. Shadows moved among the fallen trees and the bushes playing tricks on your eyes. Grenades were thrown by both sides at moving shadows. Sleep came to the weary despite the terror.

At dawn, the artillery started up again. The orders were to push up the hill and take the ridge. The slope up hill was still slippery in spots from the rain days ago, and the terrain was pocked with holes and broken trees. The enemy fire was murderous and took its toll all along the line. Air support would decide the battle. US Air Force and US Navy planes would drop heavy explosives and strafe enemy positions with .50 Caliber and 20mm cannon fire. It was too much for the enemy defenders. Late in the day Jack, along with the platoon from Lima Company and the remnants of Easy Company took the top of the ridge. Now they occupied the bunkers and trenches the enemy had retreated from. The toll for the success was paid in blood. Easy Company lost 7 more killed and 6 wounded. Jack's platoon from Lima Company lost 8 men with 4 wounded.

The men were exhausted. They were covered in dirt, mud and blood. They were spent. It was almost dark when they heard the bugles. The enemy was coming back.

Mike hugged Hope so hard she cried out. "Let go, let go, I can't breathe."

"I'm just so happy to see you," Mike said.

Hope also welcomed Mike's father and Susan. Cupcake got most of her attention. They had arrived late in the morning and Colleen prepared lunch. Sitting around the dining room table they spent the afternoon talking. Hope answered all the questions and everyone was relieved she was going to be all right. Her pregnancy was still a secret only she and her mother shared. It would remain that way. Hope had discussed with Colleen how to approach the subject with Jack's family. Now that she was home she felt there would be an expectation to visit with his parents. They had decided to wait for Jack's response to her letter. Hope was checking the mail in anticipation every day.

Hope had been home for a week and thought that Jack would have received her letter by now. Assuming he responded right away his response would arrive sometime in the next week. Mike and Susan had returned to New Jersey after spending the weekend. Now just like the Army, it was hurry up and wait. She was starting to show a baby bump. That meant that everyone would have to be told soon. Hope wanted to wait until she had heard from Jack before announcing the news to the rest of her family. The waiting for Jacks letter and her hormones kept her on edge. There was also something else. She was having trouble sleeping and often had nightmares. She found that she was most comfortable after her mother left for work and she was alone in the house. Her anxiety was getting the best of her and each day when the mail came with no letter from Jack it increased. Colleen noticed the change in her daughter and assumed it was the pregnancy. Time would reveal it was something else.

Bugles blared all up and down the line piercing the late afternoon as the enemy launched a counter attack. Coming back up the back of the ridge lines the men of the 2nd Division had just fought so hard for the North Koreans had retreated, regrouped and challenged the Americans for ownership of the mountain range. As the sun set lower and lower on the horizon the enemy attacked in waves at the men of the 2nd Division. Easy Company and the rest of 1st Platoon of Lima Company had just gotten into the trench lines that connected the old Korean fighting positions. The bodies of North Korean soldiers were littered throughout the hilltop. Some of the bodies were booby trapped. The men had no time to clean up the dead bodies. The counter attack was starting and the men took up positions to repel the attack. Jack spread his men out along the lines but kept his four operating .30 caliber air cooled machine guns away from the old Korean machine gun positions.

When the attack was at its peak some of the North Korean dead came back to life. They threw grenades and charged up and down the trench lines shooting the fighting GI's in the back. When they ran out of ammo they attacked the GI's with bayonets. Fighting in the trenches was hand to hand. The four machine gun positions kept up a murderous rate of fire at the attacking waves of the enemy. The barrels of the guns overheated from the rate of fire and assistant gunners poured water from their canteens on the barrels to cool them down. One of the gunners was yelling for ammo. Jack grabbed a can of .30 calibers with 1000 rounds. Running through the trench he came upon two enemy soldiers. The encounter happened so fast Jack was not able to bring up his M1 carbine to shoot them. Using his left hand, he swung the can of ammo at the first soldier hitting him alongside his face. Teeth and blood spayed from his head as the edge of the heavy metal box cut into his mouth. The second Korean lunged at Jack with his bayonet and caught him under his arm on the left side. The momentum of swinging the ammo can and the piercing lunge of the Koreans bayonet had Jack falling face down in the trench. A burst from a Thompson close by had the second soldier falling on top of him. Sgt. Shockley pulled the dead Korean off of Jack. "Major, you ok?"

Jack stumbled to his knees, the rifle and bayonet still buried in his side. The weight of the rifle pulled out the bayonet as he tried to stand and Jack howled in pain, "Augh, Jesus Christ." The first Korean laying on his back was raising a pistol. Jack fired three rounds from his M1 killing him, but he managed to get off one shot that hit Shockley in the back. Shockley fell into him as they both struggled to stand. "Ammo, ammo," the gun crew called out. Jack moved down the trench line to the gun crew. He was having trouble getting his breath. Falling into the gun position the a-gunner grabbed the ammo can and attached the new belt of rounds to the last of the ammo belt feeding the gun. The enemy was concentrating their attack on his one very effective gun crew. The bodies of attacking enemy dead was stacked up like cord wood in front of the gun. Some of the victims lay just five feet away.

Sgt. Shockley stood up and made his way to the gun crew position. Standing next to the gun he fired his .45 caliber Thompson into the attacking enemy soldiers. Jack fired his M1 and emptied his magazine. His left arm and hand felt funny.

He tried to move them but the movement was not the way he wanted it. He had little control. His breathing was labored. He was coughing up blood. The noise of the machine gun shattered his hearing. A burst of automatic fire hit Shockley square in the chest. The force of the rounds pushing him back as he fell dead. The assistant gunner was engaged with an enemy soldier beating the Korean with his helmet. The gun kept firing never stopping and taking a toll on the enemy. Something hit Jack on the side of the head. It fell in front of him. Jack saw the grenade as another two fell into the hole. He tried to move his left hand and arm. He wanted to pick them up and throw them out of the hole. His hand would not obey the commands of his brain. Dropping his M1 from his right hand he grabbed the back of the shirt of the machine gunner pulling him towards the back of the hole, "GRENADE"

Unknown to him the enemy attack had been repulsed. Jack woke, looking up at the morning sky. Dirt covered his face. He tried to sit up. The machine gunner lay over his legs. His right hand still holding on to the man's shirt. The gunner's legs had been blown off by the grenades. A large pool of muddy blood collected where the man had bled out. Shockley's body lay next to him. Jack was the only survivor. His head burned. His helmet was missing. A piece of his scalp and his left ear had been torn from his head. Shrapnel from the grenades. There was no sign of the a-gunner or the Korean he had been fighting with. Jack fought to get to his feet. Coughing up blood he made it to the edge of the trench. Looking out over the edge he saw the .30 caliber laying in the dirt in front of the position. Korean bodies lay everywhere. The stench was incredible. When he exhaled a fine mist of blood came from his nose and mouth. He sat back down. I'm just so tired, so cold he thought.

CHAPTER 17

CRUEL TWIST OF FATE

Incoming wounded! The announcement made its way throughout the 8044th compound. Helicopters and ambulances arrived filled with wounded. Stretchers were stacked three high on either side of the ambulance Jack was in. In between the stacks sitting wounded occupied the floor. Jack was on the middle stretcher on the driver's side. The man lying on the stretcher above him had been shot through the neck and chest. He was already dead having bled out. His blood now covered Jack. Medics and nurses helped the sitting wounded out of the ambulance and then dealt with the men on the stretchers. As they moved the man above Jack they saw he was already dead. He was set aside for the graves registration unit. Doctor Selleck checked Jacks head wound and looked for a source of the blood he was covered in. "The man above him bled out Doctor, that's most likely not his blood he is covered in," LT. Mary Cantrell said.

"OK, head trauma on this one, set him up for OR. I don't like his color and his breathing is labored," Sellick ordered.

Jacks stretcher was set down in the OR staging area. The most critically wounded were already being set up on the operating

194

tables. Other members of the MASH collected items found on the wounded. Wallets, watches, rings and other personal items were placed in bags along with dog tags and other items. Patient identification cards listed rank, name, religious preference, blood type and serial numbers taken from the dog tag of each soldier. None of the wounded had any weapons. Jack regained consciousness. He was looking up at the sky. It was so blue.

The clouds by contrast were so white. He heard activity around him. He had no idea where he was. Then he was moving. Someone was taking him inside. The area was brightly lit. Strange people gathered around him. Everyone had a mask. They were all dressed in white. Then something covered his face. "Patients under Colonel, BP is dropping, breathing is very shallow."

Colonel Jessup lifted Jacks left arm and saw the bayonet wound. "Bayonet wound here in the left side." Jessup declared.

"He's not breathing; BP is still dropping!"

As company clerk, it was part of Doodles job to record the information of each patient going through the unit. He was writing the information on a form he had attached to a clip board. A new man Corporal Dickinson read out the information of each patient as he listed the personal effects from the heavy cotton bag. "One Hamilton watch silver with leather band, two incoming letters unopened, one wallet black leather, $13.25 in MPC (Military Payment Script) one picture man and woman both officers, one picture older woman, one picture older man, one picture younger woman, not bad nice tits, one army issued fountain pen, one army issue compass. All of this shit belongs to a Major Michael J. Randall, 86387946."

"Wait, what was the name and serial number again?" Doodles asked.

"Major Michael J. Randall, 86387946," Dickinson replied.

"Let me see those pictures," Doodles demanded. He looked at the photograph of Jack and Hope in Tokyo. "HOLY MACKERAL, give me the bag and the contents," Doodles said and then left for the Colonels office.

Dickinson shouted after him, "Hey, where are you going?"

Colonel Jessup sat at his desk. Major Todd and Father McCauley were with him. They were drinking coffee. Post-op was full of patients from the previous day's surgery. The had been in the OR for seventeen straight hours. Doodles burst into the office and dumped the contents of the bag he had on the Colonels desk. "What in blue blazes are you doing?" Jessup demanded.

"Sorry Colonel, but you should see this," Doodles answered handing him the photograph of Jack and Hope.

"Oh my," Jessup said.

"What is it Colonel?" McCauley asked.

Jessup handed the photograph to Major Todd.

Jessup asked, "Where is he Doodles?"

"Graves registration sir."

"I'll take care of this. Go back to work, Corporal," Jessup ordered.

"Yes sir," Doodles replied leaving the office.

Todd picked up one of the letters. "This is the letter I helped her write. He never opened it," Todd said sadly.

McCauley asked, "Will someone please tell me what and who we are talking about?"

"I'm sorry, Padre. It was my decision. You remember when LT. Costigan was so upset about her friend in Tokyo. These are his personal effects. There is something else as well. Costigan did not have an infection. When she was wounded, we discovered that she was five weeks pregnant. Her R&R to Tokyo where she met this young man. I wanted her to go home honorably. I'm going to ask you to keep that part of this on the QT. No one knows about the pregnancy," Jessup said.

"Oh, dear Lord. That's why she was so concerned about telling this young man she was going home," McCauley answered.

Todd replied, "This is the letter she wrote before she went home. She was letting him know that she was pregnant with his child."

"Oh my. Colonel, I think I should write to her and give her the news. The Army won't tell her. It would be better coming from us. I don't think it would be a good idea to send his personal effects home with her letter to this young man's family either," McCauley offered.

"I agree. You write her a letter and let her know the bad news. Send her letter and this picture later. The rest of the effects should be returned to his family. I've been at this since World War One. It has never been easy. I just want to go home and play with my grandchildren," Jessup said.

Three weeks passed. Hope had received a letter from Jack, about a week after she returned home. It had been forwarded from her MASH unit in Korea. His unit was moving out and he had been promoted too Major. Apparently, he had not received her letter letting him know she was going home and admitting to her pregnancy when he wrote it. Frustrated she sat alone at home day after day and drank coffee. It was usually spiked with whiskey. She was drinking every day. It helped her to nap in the afternoon. She was not sleeping well at night. She cried often. Wondering why she was at home. Her colleagues were dead. I should do something. I've been spared to do what she thought. Sit here waiting for a man to make a decision about their child. Maybe he does not want to respond. Ignore it. Why not, she said he owed her nothing.

She heard the mailman at the door. She got up and walked towards the door as the letters and other mail fell to the floor from the slot on the door. She picked up the stack and saw the usual bills. One envelope stood out. It had an APO postmark. She dropped the other items of mail and tore at the envelope to open it. Unfolding the letter, she found a single hand-written page.

My Dear Hope,

I hope this letter finds you well. Regretfully I have bad news. There was heavy fighting along the 38th Parallel. The 2nd Infantry Division was involved. I'm afraid your Jack was one of the wounded that was brought here to the 8044th. He died on the operating table, despite Colonel Jessup's best effort. He did not suffer.

We found your letter to him in his pack. It had never been opened. He never got the chance to read it. I'm so sorry for both of you. I had to send his personal effects to his parents. I left out your letter and a photograph he kept of the two of you in Tokyo. I'll send it off too you, along with your citations and medals that came here from I Corps.

I'm so sorry you have to learn of his passing this way. I don't know if his parents are still in contact with you. Colonel Jessup and I discussed this at length. The Army was certainly not going to notify you. We decided it would be best coming from your family here at the 8044th.

If there is anything you need or want us to do please be assured, we will do everything we can. God may have seen fit to take Jack away from you to be in heaven, but he left you something to cherish in his absence. The child you carry is one conceived in love.

I hope someday we will meet again.

The Lord be with you and your child,

Francis X. McCauley
Chaplain US Army
MASH 8044

Dead. Jack was dead. Oh, my God. What am I going to do? She thought. Then the tears came. Holding her stomach, she let the letter fall and cried. Her anguish taking over. She and her baby would be alone. She would be branded as an unwed mother.

Hope spent the rest of the afternoon walking aimlessly around the house. The letter in her hand she had read it over and over. Her tears falling on the page smearing the ink in spots. Finally, she worked up the courage to call her mother at work. She begged her to come home. She did not want to have dinner at her Aunt Maggie's tonight. Colleen did not get any details from Hope when she called. But she knew whatever news she got must have been bad. She took a taxicab straight home. When she arrived, Hope was in the kitchen. The day's mail was on the floor. Colleen walked into the kitchen and saw the letter on the table. Hope just sat there, her eyes red and puffy from crying. She picked up the tear stained letter and read it. The great mystery was over. All of the pent-up anticipation and apprehension was over. In a way, Colleen was glad it was over. Her heart though was breaking as she saw the anguish in her daughter's eyes.

"Honey I am so sorry. Are you going to be all right?"

"Yeah, I don't really have much choice, do I? He never knew. I'll never know what he thought. All my hard work…all for nothing. My dreams destroyed. Daddy knew I was there but wanted nothing to do with me. Now my baby will never know it's daddy. It's daddy never knew about his baby." Hope then fell into her mother's arms and cried. Colleen held her knowing that there was still one more hurdle. Jack's family had a right a too know about his child.

Bo spent the next three days in Saigon with his daughters. Bo had been rounded up by the Japanese to be used as slave labor. His wife protesting his arrest was shot and killed. He never heard of his girl's fate until they were reunited in Saigon. He learned that the girls were very gifted in the art of embroidery. It was a skill they were learning from their mother when she was killed by the Japanese. It was the one thing that sustained them. They had lived on the street begging for food and sleeping in alleyways when they lost their parents and home.

A neighbor that knew the girls found them on the street. She was an older woman who found a job cleaning the house for the wife of a high ranking Japanese officer. The girls had worked on the dress uniform of the officer.

Their work impressed him and he allowed them to stay. His wife also appreciated their talents and had the girls embroider silk scarfs.

The terrible fate of servicing Japanese soldiers was never realized. Major Sasaki had lied to him. He learned that Hung had arranged for them to have a small shop with an apartment overhead around the corner on Le Loi Street. An older Vietnamese woman known as Madame Lam would teach them Vietnamese and act as an interpreter for customers coming into the shop. Madame Lam was also an agent of the NLF. (National Liberation Front)

Over the past three days' father and daughters got reacquainted. Madame Lam followed them everywhere. Madam Lam was fluent in Chinese. She explained everything to the girls in Vietnamese and Chinese. They had an opportunity to visit the shop and the apartment. The apartment was small and modest and had two bedrooms. Madame Lam would use the smallest bedroom facing Le Loi Street. The girls would share the largest bedroom at the back of the apartment.

The girls told their father they had a shop in Changchun. The Japanese had lost the war and left China. Communism was overtaking China. Business was bad and the girls barely survived. A few weeks ago, agents from the CCID (Chinese Central

Investigation Department) showed up at the shop. They were both taken away and placed in a house in Shanghai. They were never told why. They were treated well, given medical attention and fed every day. Three days later a man came to see them.

He never gave his name but Madame Lam was with him. All of their personal and work items had been brought to them. Mei told the man they were both frightened. They had done nothing wrong. She wanted to know why they had been brought to this house. She told him that they wanted to go home. The man assured them they were in no danger. They were told they would travel by boat to Saigon in Vietnam. He said they would have a shop and a place to live. They would be given money. He did not explain why it was all going to happen. He only stated that this was happening because the Chinese government ordered it. This mystified the young women. Madame Lam was very polite and nice to the girls. She explained that she would be their teacher. She would tell them everything they would need to know about Vietnam. She began to teach them the language from the first meeting. At first Mei and Meilin thought they were to become prostitutes. Both girls were very pretty. Madame Lam assured them that this would never happen. She reaffirmed to the girls they were in no danger and would not be compelled to do anything they were not comfortable with. They would have a shop where they would continue the embroidery business they had in Changchun. When asked why, Madame Lam had no answer for them. She did not know. She found out about their father on the day he walked into the hotel room with Hung.

On the first night while the girls slept in the hotel, Hung, Bo and Madame Lam talked. Hung reminded Lam that her orders were to oversee the safety of the two young women and to assist them with their customers and others until they were comfortable with the language. Bo was told that he could visit with his daughters whenever he wanted. He would continue teaching at the school in Dinh Quan. If there were to be any changes he would let them know. Then he said goodbye and left Saigon.

The next day Bo, and his daughters spent the morning talking. Mei and Meilin learned about their fathers' time with the Americans in Shanghai and his ordeal with the Japanese. He explained how the resistance fighters in North Vietnam had found him after he escaped. They had given him food, shelter and taken good care of him. Bo explained that Hung had helped him become a teacher in the village of Dinh Quan. Mei was curious about all of this. "Father, why does this man do this. He says he wants only our friendship and loyalty. He has a purpose. Meilin and I are here because the Chinese government ordered this. Why are you here in Vietnam? Do you work for Chinese Government? Are you CCID?"

"What is CCID? I have nothing to do with communist in China. I am a school teacher here," Bo answered surprised at the question.

"Who is Hung working for? Does Madame Lam work for him? I am happy to be with you again. I wish we could all just go home. Why are we here father?" Mei asked with insistence.

Bo sat and looked at his daughters. He knew why he was in Vietnam. He knew why he was in Dinh Quan. He knows he is an agent of the NLF.

He is happy to do the work for Hung and Vietnam. Madame Lam was given orders by Hung. Protect his daughters and teach them the customs and language of Vietnam. Are they to become agents of the NLF too? He had to craft his answer carefully. He held each of his daughter's hands and told them, "Hung and I are like brothers. He saved my life. If not for him, we would not be together. He demands nothing of me. I teach young people to be a machinist like I was in China. Vietnam is now my home and yours. How Hung was able to arrange us to be a family again I do not know and I do not care. But if all he asks is friendship and loyalty then I will give him both happily. We are safe. We are together. That is all that matters to me." For Meilin this was enough. For her sister, Mei, the questions now unanswered only created more questions.

CHAPTER 18
MISTAKES & TRUTH

Music from the pier as well as the amusement rides and the crowd above stifled her screams. He was lurking under the pier when she surprised him and ran past. Barefoot and wearing a white dress she was laughing as she ran. The impulse was instinctive to him. Like the predator, he was he started after her. She was almost at the surf line when he caught her. She squealed with delight. Pinning her to the sand he was now on top. Her laughing changed to screams of fright. This was not Tommy. She saw the big knife in his hand as he pulled up her dress. The knife made quick work of her panties and he cut her. She cried out in pain. Then he slapped her, hard. The left side of her face felt like it was on fire. His hand clamped around her throat.

Sixteen-year-old, Tommy Pyle ran between the pier pilings searching. Where the heck did she go, he thought. He saw a flash of white at the surf line. It was dark but he saw that someone was wrestling with Rebecca. She screamed. Tommy took off running. He was a star player for his high school football team. He zeroed in on Rebecca's attacker like a linebacker going for a running back. He hit him with his right shoulder along the attacker's right side. The blow knocked the man into the surf. Both of them fell and tumbled into the water. Just as the man stood Tommy punched him in the face. The man staggered and swung low with his left hand. Tommy never saw the knife. The blade caught him high on his left hip and ripped across his lower abdomen. He cried out in pain. Rebecca watching saw the blood gush into Tommy's khaki pants. "TOMMY."

Tommy slipped to his knees in the surf line as Rebecca got up to help him. The man that had attacked her ran off down the beach. Rebecca was also bleeding as blood ran down her leg and soaked her dress. "HELP, SOMEBODY PLEASE, HELP US," she cried.

Breathing was hard. His right side hurt like hell. His nose was gushing blood. He made it back to his motorcycle and doubled over in pain as he kick started the only means of escape. The engine caught and he streaked down the side street. He drove out of town turned south and found a closed gas station on Route 9. Pulling in behind the building he cut the engine. He slipped along the side of the building hoping that the rest room door had been left unlocked. He was in luck. Closing the door, he felt along his right side. It was tender to the touch. Then he washed his face. The bleeding had finally stopped. His nose hurt and his eyes watered. Remembering the last time, he was cleaning up in a public restroom he hurried and returned to his motorcycle. Starting the engine hurt again. He drove south, every bump in the road reminding him with more pain in his side. A long hour later he was back in Wildwood. Ocean City had not worked out like he planned. He took a bath washing away his blood from his hands and face. The hot water felt good on his side. He dried off and laid down in bed with some effort. His nose was swollen and his side still hurt. It was a restless night. In the morning, he had a black eye and his side had a huge bruise. He could breathe through his mouth. The ribs were not broken. His face was a mess.

Dave knocked and let himself in to his partner's house. Mike and Susan played cards at the kitchen table. Cupcake demanded that his friend say hello to him. Dave rubbed his head and told Mike, "Let's go. A high school girl and her boyfriend were attacked on the beach about an hour ago."

"Oh, my goodness," Susan replied.

"Are the kids all, right?" Mike asked.

"Yup, both are in Shore Memorial. He has a stab wound in the abdomen and she was cut on the hip," Dave answered.

Mike strapped on the big .45 getting ready to leave. His father Joe had been reading the paper. "Be careful son," he said as Mike left with Dave.

Shore Memorial Hospital was just outside of town in Somers Point. They arrived in a few minutes and went to the ER. Tommy and Rebecca had been separated by hospital staff. Rebecca required stitches and Tommy was being prepared for surgery. By the time, Dave and Mike arrived, Tommy was already upstairs where surgeons were repairing the wound he had. Rebecca was still in the ER. Doctors had stitched her wound and her parents were with her. They identified themselves and asked Rebecca's parents to wait in the hall. They protested but Dave gently steered them outside assuring them she was safe and everything would be all right. "Hello Rebecca, I'm Detective McMullen. Can you tell me what happened tonight?

"Tommy and I were on the beach around the pier. We were... kissing and I ran away. You know like a game. Tommy chased after me. When I was down by the water, a man attacked me. He had this big knife. He pulled up my dress and he..." Rebecca started crying. Mike waited letting the girl gets her emotions under control. "What happened then, Rebecca?"

"Tommy punched the man. Then the man stabbed him. There was so much blood. I tried to help Tommy."

"Where did the man go?"

"He ran away."

"Did you see his face?"

"He was bleeding...Tommy punched him in the nose."

"Do you know who the man is?"

"No, I never saw him before...it all happened so fast."

"Can you describe him for me?"

Rebecca shook her head, and started to cry again.

"It's all right your safe now. How about what he was wearing? Do you remember anything?"

"He had a motorcycle jacket on. You know the kind with no sleeves."

"A denim jacket?"

"Yes...I think so."

"Any kind of buttons or patches on the jacket?"

"I don't know...I'm sorry. It was just so fast."

"That's all right. You did just fine. Try to get some rest. If you remember anything tell your Mom and Dad, then call me," Mike said handing her a business card. He went into the hall, and told her parents they could go back into the room. "Whatcha got, anything useful?" Dave asked.

"No real description. Just a guy wearing a sleeveless denim motorcycle jacket. The boyfriend clocked him pretty good. She remembered the suspect had a bloody nose. The guy was armed with a large knife. Maybe the boyfriend will be more helpful."

"He's in surgery. Deep and long flesh wound. They should finish sewing him up soon, but we won't be able to talk with him until the morning. You have to wonder, what the hell is going on in this crazy world," Dave replied.

"Got me partner. I just want to get this son of a bitch," Mike said.

They left the hospital and filed their reports. Then Dave took Mike home.

It was late and everyone was asleep. Cupcake looked at Mike as he entered the door then laid back down to go back to sleep.

Mike and Dave were briefing the Chief of Police when an officer knocked and pocked his head in the door. "Somers Point PD is reporting that an Esso station that was closed last night out on Route 9 called in, they found blood in the bathroom."

"Follow up with that. Might be our man stopped there last night," the Chief ordered. Mike and Dave left the office and drove out to the gas station. The responding officer was still there. He was told to wait for the two detectives from OCPD. "Nice set of bloody prints on the door knob and the sink. Heard you guys had an attack on the beach. Think this could be your man?" The officer asked.

"Could be. Our guy left the scene with a bloody nose. Mike and Dave took pictures and pulled the bloody prints. It was a stretch but sometimes you get lucky. All of it would go into the case file. When they finished, they drove to the hospital to talk with the boyfriend.

Tommy Pyle was awake, and alone in his hospital room. Mike and Dave introduced themselves and began to question him. "Tell us what happened last night Tommy," Dave asked.

"I was on the beach with Rebecca. We weren't really doing anything. We got separated. Then I saw this guy on top of her by the water. She was screaming. I tackled the guy and punched him in the face. Then he stabbed me...here." Tommy pulled the sheet down to show them where he had been stabbed.

"What did he look like? Describe him for us." Mike asked.

"A little taller than me. Skinny. Dark Greasy hair."

"How tall are you?"

"I'm five eleven."

"What was he wearing?"

"I think he was one of those biker guys. He had a sleeveless jacket on."

"Anything special about the jacket, buttons, patches?"

"I don't know. I don't remember."

"Did he say anything?"

"No...I don't think so. He just ran away."

"Which way did he go? South down the beach or north up the beach."

"South."

"Do you remember anything else about the man, white guy, negro?"

"No, he was white. I hit him pretty good. He had a bloody nose."

"All right kid. If you remember anything else tell your parents and then call us," Mike said handing him a card.

Outside the room, they discussed all the information. "Well, it seems our boy is a white man, six feet or taller. He's skinny maybe 150 to 175 pounds or so given the height. Has dark greasy hair and a new nose job. He used a large knife and he might be on a motorcycle. Not much to go on," Dave said.

"It's a start." Mike answered.

Grant stayed in his room Saturday and Sunday. His eye had gotten better the bruising was almost gone. His nose still hurt but the swelling had gone down. He still had a bad bruise on his side but he could tell the ribs were not broken. He debated on Monday morning on whether or not to go to work. He needed the money, so he went. Before he left he saw the motorcycle needed to be cleaned. There was dried blood on the handle bars and the fuel tank. He cleaned the Indian Scout and left for work. Comments were made about his eye but no one took special notice or even cared. He finished the day and went back to his apartment. He made some eggs for his dinner and sat and drank coffee. He went to the step that led to the bathroom and pulled out the toe plate on the step. He pulled out the metal box, opened it and picked up the S&W Model 10.

He pushed the button on the left side and opened the cylinder. There were five rounds in the gun. It held six. For some reason, the cop who carried it kept the empty chamber under the hammer.

He tilted the revolver and the five rounds dropped out of the cylinder. Closing the cylinder, he pointed the gun and pulled the trigger. It made a loud click as the hammer fell. He pulled the hammer back and pulled the trigger again. Another loud click. He reloaded the revolver and carefully turned the cylinder so the hammer sat over the empty chamber. He knew he needed the knife to cut away clothing. He also used it to cut their hair. He kept it sharp as a razor. From now on he would take the gun as well.

Colleen and Hope were sitting in the front of the trolley as it left the Providence Road Station and began its journey down State Street in Media. The trolley travelled right down the center of the street. A few blocks later the operator announced Jackson Street. The two women got off the trolley and walked two blocks north to Jacks home. It sat on the north-west corner of Jackson Street and 2nd Street. It was a nice two-story home with a brick wall in the front yard and a wraparound porch. They climbed up the three steps that lead into the front courtyard. Looking up at the porch they knew they had arrived at the right house. A small red banner with a white box had a gold star in the center. They summoned up their courage and walked up to the porch and rang the bell. Hope had called Jacks home two days after she learned of Jacks death. She spoke to his sister Joyce. Joyce was familiar as to who she was and gave her directions and the address. Joyce had told her that her parents had taken the news hard but were surrounded by family and friends. That was Monday, they agreed to come by for a visit the following Sunday. Today was the day. It would be another two weeks before Jacks remains would be returned to the family. He would be buried in Arlington National Cemetery. Colleen had worn a modest black dress; Hope was in her uniform. Judge John Andrew Randall answered the door.

"Good morning ladies or is it afternoon. Welcome please come in. You must be Hope, how nice to for you to come." He had a very deep voice.

"Yes sir, this is my mother Colleen Costigan," Hope said nervously introducing her mother.

"How do you do, Mrs. Costigan," the Judge said holding out his hand. Colleen took his hand and shook it. The home was a center stair home and the stairs faced the vestibule. Joyce and her mother came down the stairs to greet their guests. Introductions were made and the Judge invited them into the parlor to the left of the front door. Hope and Colleen sat on the sofa. The Judge sat in what was obviously his chair. Kay, Jacks mother sat between the two guests' while Joyce brought in a tray of club sandwiches and drinks. She sat on the arm of her father's chair. "Hope I am so glad you came to visit," Mrs. Randall said.

"Yes Ma'am, I'm happy to have come," Hope said nervously.

"Now then let's get one thing clear and out of the way. You can call me Kay. I'm not a missus or a ma'am. I want you both to feel at home," breaking the tension a little.

"Yes Ma'am...Kay, I mean."

"I was just delighted when Joyce informed you had called. I just wish you're coming to meet us would not have to be on such sad circumstances. Jack spoke very highly of you in his letters. I believe he was quite taken by you. Colleen you must be so proud of her," Kay told them.

"Oh, yes very much so."

"Joyce is two years older than Jack. She is a school teacher here in town at the elementary school." Kay continued.

"Oh, how nice." Colleen replied.

"My cousin…we are more like sisters is going to be a school teacher. She will finish her post-graduate work at Villanova this summer," Hope added.

Colleen and Hope had not touched the food or the drinks and seemed to be very nervous. "I'm so sorry for the loss of your son. Please don't hesitate to ask if we can be of help in any way," Colleen said.

Kay spoke to Hope, "I was just shocked from the news of your last letter that you had been wounded. How terrible for you. I see you are wearing your Purple Heart ribbon. I'm not familiar with the green and white one. What is it?"

"Oh, that's the new Army Commendation Medal. Colonel Jessup my CO recommended me for a Silver Star. The Army knocked it down to this. I guess combat awards for women is not comfortable for the Army," Hope replied. After answering the question Hope fidgeted in her seat. Then there was an awkward silence.

The judge sat quietly his head cocked to one side. He was in deep thought. Something is not right with these two. They seem to be waiting for something. They're nervous. Why?

His wife Kay had picked up on it too. "Something is troubling you honey what is it?" Kay asked Hope.

Hope cleared her throat and moved in her seat again and took a deep breath. "Well, the last letter I wrote to Jack I was still recuperating. I wanted to tell him I was coming home. I really wanted to see him in person, but there was no way possible for him to come to me. Obviously, I could not go to him. Jack received the letter but I saw he never had a chance to read it. When he came through the 8044th it was with his personal effects. The Chaplain there, Captain McCauley notified me about…Jacks death and returned it to me." She reached into her purse and produced the letter. "As you can see, it is still sealed." She held up the letter. Kay reached for the envelope and asked, "May I." Taking the letter Kay watched Hope intently and then asked, "Would you like me to open and read this?"

"Yes, of course please do," Hope said getting visibly upset.

Kay reached and opened a drawer in the coffee table. She removed a letter opener and slid the blade across the top of the envelope. The cutting sound seemed to be as loud as a sheet being ripped. The judge sat up in his chair sitting on the edge.

Kay removed the letter and began to read. Colleen held her breath. She had no idea what the letter said, but she did know that Hope had told Jack about the baby. She was on edge. Poor Hope must be dying inside she thought. Kay finished reading the letter and had done so not showing any reaction. She calmly folded the letter and placed it back into the envelope. She turned to Hope and said, "This letter…"

"Wait please!" Hope took a deep breath. "This is something I should say. I should take full responsibility. I'm pregnant with Jacks child," she stated with confidence.

"WHAT! How dare…" the judge stood as he spoke.

"John sit down," Kay commanded.

Hope and Colleen were startled. The judge's outburst taking them by surprise. Kay took Hopes hand and asked, "What do you want dear?"

Hope looked into Kay's eyes. "Nothing." Hope replied. "My child, will be born never to know it's father. My father died shortly after I was born. I never knew him. I know of him because of my mother and her parents. I want my child to know its father through me…and all of you. That's all. This is Jack's child, as much as mine. This baby belongs to all of us. I don't know if Jack and I would have ever had a life together. He is gone, but he left us with a very precious part of him. I don't know what else to say…"

Kay's eyes started to fill. "I see, a very strong young woman. It must have been terrifying for you and your Mother to come here. Especially at a time like this. You deserved that Silver Star. I would be very proud to have the opportunity to call you my daughter in law. But you're right. That's something we will never know. What I do know, and I speak for all of us," Kay, looked sternly at the judge. "We would be proud as punch to welcome this baby as our grandchild."

Hope and Colleen let out a collective sigh of relief. Joyce stood and with delight announced, "I'm going to be an aunt, and you are going to be a grandpa, daddy!"

CHAPTER 19

OLD LIVES BURIED, NEW LIVES BEGIN

Major Michael J. Randall was carried by six members of the 'Old Guard' as he left the Old Post Chapel at Fort Meyer Virginia. They lifted the flag draped coffin unto to the caisson that would carry him to his final resting place in Arlington National Cemetery. The procession from the chapel included a Color Guard, The Chaplain, a single horse from the Caisson Platoon in full saddle and dress with boots in the stirrups facing backwards, a horse drawn caisson, the honors firing squad, and an escort platoon. The family followed by car into the cemetery. The military members of the procession marched to the steady tap on the rim of a single drum.

At the grave site, just south of the infamous Tomb of the Unknown the family sat facing the grave. Kay sat in the center. Her husband and daughter sat to her right. On her left was Hope and Colleen. The rest of Jacks family and friends were behind them. The chaplain conducted his grave site service, noting Jacks dedication to his country and the men of his unit. When he concluded his service, the entourage was asked to stand during the presentation of military honors. The Sergeant in charge of the honors firing team called out his commands.

"Firing Team Attention." The team had been a short distance away from the burial site on the other side of the coffin away from the family.

"Half right face." Turning to the right half way they were now facing to the right of the casket.

"Prepare to fire." The team simultaneously lifted their rifles tucking the butt of the weapon under their right arm pit and using the left hand loaded a blank cartridge into rifle. The rifles now pointing over the burial site.

"Fire."

BANG

"Prepare to fire."

The seven-man team again using the left hand loaded a cartridge. The slapping sound of the movements of moving the action of the rifle and returning their left hand to the rifle seemed to echo across the cemetery.

"Fire."

BANG

"Prepare to fire "

The seven-man team again using the left hand loaded a cartridge.

"Fire."

BANG

The family still standing startled at the sound of the seven rifles firing as they fired all three volleys.

"Half left face."

The team turned to the left now facing the casket.

"Present Arms"

Each man of the seven-man team moved together in the position to salute the casket. The rest of the military escort all saluted. The escort platoon all came to the position of present arms with their rifles. The slapping sound of the movements echoing across the side of the hill.

"Bugler"

From off in the distance a bugler lifted his bugle and played Taps.

Many of the family members and others moved by the mournful sound wiped tears from their eyes. When he finished, he tucked his bugle under his left arm and saluted.

"Order Arms."

The Sergeant issuing the commands saluted the officer in charge. He now approached the casket. The Chaplain standing nearby said, "Please be seated." The family all sat and waited.

The casket team had been holding the flag over Jacks coffin. There was a light breeze today but the flag never moved. The way it was held so taught would give the impression it could hold the weight of anything.

Then the officer gave his command; "Fold the colors."

Working as a well-choreographed machine each member made his movements with precision and care. As each man finished his task he brought both of his white gloved hands up to his chest before slowly moving them back to his sides. The last man of the team to have the flag held it with reverence. He gently pulled and tucked at each part of the triangle it formed until the four stars were perfectly aligned. Then he took it to the officer in charge. The officer facing the flag saluted it. Then as he took it, the man from the casket team saluted the flag. Then he walked up to Kay came to attention, extending the flag to her as he bowed at the waist said these words;

"On behalf of the President of the United States, I present to you this flag, in recognition of your loved ones faithful and courageous service to our country."

Then he handed the flag to Kay, stood up straight and saluted as he marched away. All that was left was for family and friends to walk past Jacks coffin and place a single rose over it as they said their final goodbye.

The immediate family were the last. Colleen led Hope up to the casket. She placed her rose across with the others. Then Hope placed her rose kissed her hand and touched the cold silver casket. Joyce preceded her mother still clutching the flag. His father would be the last. With tears filling his eyes he placed his rose and touched the casket. "Farewell son, no father could be prouder. I shall miss you."

Major Michael J. Randall was laid to rest after the family left the burial site. The ground crew reverently lowered the casket in the grave, filled the void and laid a green grave blanket over the fresh earth. Some days later the crew would return level the mound of dirt and lay new sod over the grave. A stone would also be mounted to identify the occupant. Jack was now a memory and a member of hallowed souls in what the soldiers of the 1st Battalion 3rd Infantry Regiment known as the 'Old Guard' called the 'Garden'.

The case files Mike brought to Philly were each filled with papers. The copies of the Cape May attack still haunted him. They did catch a bit of a break on their own case. The finger prints at the gas station matched the ones from the Cape May case. It was the same guy. They still knew very little about their suspect. They had come up from the shore for the rehearsal dinner for Steve and Dorothy's wedding. Letting his hunch get the best of him he told Susan he was taking a drive.

He took his case files and started out for Radnor Township. It was mid-morning and traffic was light. He arrived just before lunch and identified himself to the desk sergeant at the front desk of Radnor PD.

"I need to speak to the detectives who worked the Red Arrow case," he declared."

The desk sergeant picked up the phone and talked with Detective Doyle.

Doyle listened and then called across the squad room, "Hey Mike, you worked the Red Arrow case, right?"

"Yea, what's up?"

"There's a guy downstairs at the desk. He's from Ocean City PD in Jersey. He wants to talk with you."

"All right send him up."

Detective Mike Meziaz walked to the stairway. Ocean City PD, why does that stick with this case. He thought. He saw Mike at the bottom of the stairs. He had two large manila envelopes under his arm. He looked familiar. "I'm Detective Mike Meziaz. Have we met? You look familiar."

"Detective Mike McMullen. We met at a hospital. One of your guys was hurt and I had a niece that had been attacked."

"Oh right. I remember you now. What can I do for you?"

Mike filled him in on the Cape May and the Ocean City attacks. Going over the case files they found that the blood type on their suspect was the same. Better yet, they also found out the finger prints on all three cases were also a match.

Mike concluded with, "We have his prints but the FBI says he is not in the system."

"He may not be in the system but this is now an interstate issue. The FBI will be helping us along with all of their resources." Bill Breker came to his desk across from Meziaz. "We caught a big break on the Red Arrow guy. Seems he's in Jersey. This is Detective McMullen from Ocean City PD. We have blood type and finger print matches from our cases and his," Meziaz updated his partner.

"No kidding. How about the hair trophies?" Breker asked.

"Oh right. We never released this information to the public. The suspect cut off pieces of the victim's hair. I guess he wanted them as trophies."

"Your niece was his last attack here. He dropped off the face of the earth after that. We had him you know," Meziaz said.

"You had him here in custody. What happened?" Mike asked.

"That cop who had the fractured skull, he was our jailer. Marking his last couple of weeks before he retired. He was supposed to bring him to interrogation, but the guy made a break for it. He also took Merv Boyd's gun. Another detail we did not release. He was picked up shortly after your niece was attacked cleaning up in a bathroom at a pizza shop nearby," Meziaz responded.

"Was he logged in? Mike asked.

"Nope, he had just come in. We had no idea who he was. All we have is a physical description," Breker answered.

"Caucasian male, tall and thin, six feet 160 pounds, dark brown hair heavy on the Brylcreem. We took blood samples from the towels in that bathroom. Same blood type," Meziaz stated.

"We had a task force set up in here in Delaware County. We shared all the information with the other departments but the guy just disappeared. Now he's in Jersey," Breker said.

"Looks like it's your case now. You had the last attack. Building your case is going to be a paperwork nightmare. You'll have case files from at least ten different departments here in PA alone. Once you have all the information then you can go to the FBI. Eleven attacks here and now two in Jersey, you got an interstate serial killer and rapist. I'll notify all the departments here. You'll have case files coming out of your ears in next couple of weeks. Good luck Detective. I hope you can catch the bastard. Remember, he's got Merv's gun, an S&W Model 10. Be careful," Meziaz told Mike.

"Yea, thanks," Mike said.

Mike left and began the drive down Route 30 back to Philly. He had been right about his hunch. He had also opened a can of worms.

He would have to make a case file for the FBI tying all of the attacks to one man in two states. Meziaz was right. It would be a paperwork nightmare.

Landing in Philadelphia from his connecting flight in Chicago, Dylan Brogan was happy to be home. His sister was getting married. As a case officer for the CIA stationed in Manila he had been gone for the more than a year. A lot had happened in that time frame. Shortly after arriving in Manila he was notified his sister was beaten and raped. He also learned of his grandmother's death in a terrible accident. Recently he found out that Hope had been wounded in Korea. He was coming home to a bundle of changes. At the rehearsal dinner to be held that evening he would find out that Caroline was in Saigon.

His taxicab pulled up to his childhood home on Olive Street just as his Uncle Mike was entering the home. He was happy that his uncle was the first one he would reunite with. The two men hugged each other on the sidewalk. "You're getting a little on the chubby side Uncle Mike. It's great to see you though," Dylan said.

"Your Aunt Susan feeds me too much. Let's go inside, I'm sure everyone will be happy to see you. You're still walking around with that damn stick I see."

Going inside the first one to greet them at the door was Cupcake. Then Maggie saw her son and ran to him. His sister joined in the hugging fest. He greeted his dad and his Aunt Susan and his Aunt Colleen. Then he saw Hope. She was beginning to show her pregnancy moving along well. "Hi cousin, how are you?" Dylan asked surprised.

"It's a very long story, we'll talk later. Welcome home," Hope replied.

She led him to a small group of people in the dining room. "There are people here I want you to meet."

"Dylan this is Judge John Randall, his wife Kay and their daughter Joyce. This is my cousin Dylan, Dorothy's brother." Dylan shook hands with everyone. The Randall's greeted him warmly. "So where is the groom?" Dylan asked.

"He'll be along shortly," Hope answered. His Uncle Mike came into the dining room with a cigar and a glass of beer for Dylan. "Care to join us, your honor?" Mike asked.

"Thanks Mike, I'll just take the beer. I have my pipe with me," Judge Randall replied.

The three men left the dining room leaving Hope with Kay and Joyce. "That was the young man you said was coming in from the Philippines?" Kay asked.

"Yes, he was also there as a Marine during the war." Hope replied.

"What does he do there now. Is he still in the Marines?" Joyce asked.

Hope lowered her voice to a whisper and leaned in towards the women. "He works for the CIA."

"A spy." Kay replied surprised.

"Shhh, keep your voice down, but yes. Everyone here knows of course. But there will be other people at the wedding that have no idea." Hope told them.

"How mysterious," Joyce said.

"You'll also meet the Grindell's from next door at the wedding. Their daughter Caroline also works for the CIA. She is in Saigon and will not be attending. Their other daughter Charolette works for the State Department," Hope informed them.

"You have a fascinating family dear," Kay said.

In the backyard, Mike and Dylan lit their cigars and the Judge prepared his pipe. Kevin joined them a few minutes later. "Good to see you again son. I see the stick is still with you."

"Yes, I still have it. Don't really need it as much. I guess it's more of an emotional crutch." Dylan replied.

"Why do you have it, might I ask? The Judge asked.

Dylan gave the judge the short version of the story. "Dear God, that must have been an awful experience. I would think you would like nothing to do with that country. What do you do there?" The Judge asked.

"I work for the Department of Agriculture, at the embassy in Manila." Dylan replied.

Kevin and Mike looked at each other. "Department of Agriculture you say. I am well acquainted with Senator Martin. We play golf together every month. Maybe you would like to be in DC?" The judge offered.

"Thank you, but I am very happy with my work in Manila," Dylan said. The conversation soon turned to sports and the weather. His years of experience as an attorney and now a member of the bench told the judge that Dylan had lied to him and no more worked for the DOA any more than he did.

The groom arrived shortly thereafter and everyone walked the short distance to the church of Saint Francis Xavier. The reception would be held in the school's gymnasium. Father Terry would officiate at the wedding. There were refreshments after the rehearsal. Joyce Randall was invited to be one of the bridesmaids. Caroline Grindell would not be available. Joyce was more than happy to stand in. The Randall's were getting used to being part of a new family group. Maggie and Kay became instant friends. Joyce and Dorothy also shared a passion for teaching. The two-family groups had a lot in common.

The wedding was held on a beautiful spring afternoon. Steve had chosen a high school friend and co-worker to be his best man. Dorothy had chosen Hope to be her maid of honor. The mass to administer the Sacrament of Matrimony lasted just over an hour. The reception started at five that evening. The bridal party had pictures taken along the Benjamin Franklin Parkway in one of the many gardens there.

The reception went well and after the father and daughter dance, cutting the cake and the tossing of the garter and bouquet the newlyweds were off to the train station for the honeymoon in Niagara Falls New York.

On the drive, back to the shore the next day, Mike told Susan and his Dad about his meeting with the Radnor Police. After Mike told them the news, Joe sitting in the back read the case files from Wildwood and Ocean City. He memorized the physical description of the suspect.

CHAPTER 20

A SMALL WORLD

Saigon was fascinating. Caroline was in love with the city and the country. Her first impressions were different. Stepping off the Pan Am Clipper that first afternoon she was greeted by the heat and humidity.

It was overpowering. She also noticed the peculiar smell as she walked down the portable stairs that had been brought out to the aircraft. She collected her bags and took a taxi to the Continental Palace. The agency had contracted for a small suite for her to live in until she found a suitable apartment approved by the consulate. The suite was small and comfortable. The décor was western. She decided not to unpack but instead went back downstairs to the lobby bar. Sitting alone at the bar she ordered a Singapore Sling in French. Looking around she saw people mostly that were western. She could hear bits of French and English as well as some Vietnamese. She was excited to begin a new phase of her career.

A year had passed since that first day. She had her own apartment and had settled into life in Vietnam. The country was in a state of hostility. The French Government with support from the US was desperately trying to hold Vietnam as a colonial possession. French Far East Expeditionary Corps (FFEEC) troops had established military bases around the country in an attempt to keep control. The National Liberation Front or NLF had a military arm known as the Viet-Minh. They would attack French convoys and bases around the country. The goal was eliminating French control and seizing independence for the country that had been given to them by the departing Japanese after WWll. Viet-Minh forces had also pushed into the country of Laos, a French ally.

In the southern part of the country, Saigon was relatively peaceful. An occasional attack near or in the city or an act of sabotage would occur. With French, western influence, social events were held on a regular basis around the city. As an executive secretary working for the Department of Commerce, Caroline attended many of these functions. Her real employment was known only to a few people in the Consulate. Travel within the city was unrestricted. Travel into the surrounding Providences or further into the countryside was risky.

Especially for westerners. Caroline was not a field agent or case officer. Her analytical skills were put to use reviewing reports by these types of people and their assets. She was privy to a lot of sensitive material. As such travel by her outside the main business district of the city was frowned upon. She was also required to notify security where she was going and when she expected to return. No matter where she traveled she always had a Smith & Wesson Model 36 snub nosed revolver.

Shopping on any one of her rare her days off was always a treat. She loved to go to the market place downtown and sample the many regional delicacies she found there. She especially loved the beautiful hand woven silk scarves she often found. Returning to one of her favorite shops she saw a powder blue silk scarf with the image of a multi-colored dragon on it. The image had been embroidered. The work was meticulous and very exquisite. Understandably so the price for this particular scarf was far above what she normally paid. She bought it anyway. She never inquired as too who had done the work. She walked to the Continental Palace Hotel and entered the bar. Instead of sitting at the bar she sat in a more comfortable chair with a small cocktail table. The bar tender delivered her drink and she relaxed admiring her new purchase. "Hello good looking!" Not at all interested in a pickup line she looked up annoyed. "Oh, my goodness, Dylan what are you doing here?"

"Came in this morning for a meeting. Now I'm killing time until my transport takes me back to Manila. May I," he gestured to the second chair at her table.

"Of course," she signaled to the bar tender who took Dylan's drink order. When it arrived, he lit a cigar and sat back in his chair. "You've been shopping I see," he said pointing to the newly purchased scarf.

"Yes, look at the delicacy of this embroidery." She said handing him the scarf. He took the scarf and examined it. She was right. The work was exceptional. "It's very nice. Whoever did this is very talented. This was done by hand. Where did you get it?"

"From a shop on the market place I go to frequently. Tell me about your family, how is everyone?"

"Last I heard everyone was doing well. Hope had her baby. A little boy she named Jack. Her mom retired. Dorothy is teaching first graders in Germantown. My mom and dad are considering selling their house to Steve and Dorothy. They may relocate to one of the new apartment buildings up on Pennsylvania Avenue near the Parkway. That's really about it. How's your mom and dad?"

"They're all right. Charolette is in Washington. I'm here. This country is really something. I love the city. The Providence's outside of Saigon is still dangerous though. How long before your flight leaves?"

6

The gasoline station attendant had filled Joe McMullen's tank and was wiping his windshield when the motorcycle pulled in. Joe stood in front of his car looking into the open hood. The attendant had checked the oil but Joe liked to check the hoses and belts for signs of wear. The young man riding the cycle got off after setting his kick stand. The cycle was dark gray. It was devoid of any chrome or other attachments that were common. It was almost as if it was invisible. He noted the make as a late year Indian Scout. The rider reached out and took a rag from the dispenser and opened the fuel cap on top of the tank. It was common for cyclist to pump their own gas. They did not trust the attendants. Spilling gas over a tank would bring out the worst response from the owner, so attendants let them get their own gas. When he was finished, he replaced the fuel cap and wiped the tank down even though he had not spilled a drop. He was tall, a good six feet or better. One hundred and seventy pounds. He had dark greasy hair, the remains of a bruise on his left eye. Engineer boots, dungarees and a white tee shirt. The dungaree jacket had no buttons or patches like most cyclist had. It had no sleeves either. Joe's heart began to race. He looked around hoping to spot a radio car. He was out on Route 9 in Rio Grande, just outside of Wildwood. Never a cop around when you want one, he thought. The young man paid the attendant and rode off heading into Wildwood. Joe let him get about a quarter mile away and closed the hood and got into his car. He gave the attendant three, one-dollar bills and told him to, "Keep it."

He headed into Wildwood. The man on the cycle was now almost a half mile away and just about to cross the draw bridge. If he got into town, Joe might lose him. He cycled through the gears on the column and had the car up to sixty quickly. He lost sight of him as he went down the far side of the bridge. As Joe crested the top of the draw bridge he saw his man turn left on Atlantic Avenue.

Please be heading to where you live, Joe thought. The young man continued north on Atlantic Avenue until he reached Baker Street turning east towards the ocean. Damn Joe thought, he's heading for the boardwalk. Joe reached Baker Street and after turning looked around. The guy was gone. The cycle was nowhere to be seen. Then he saw him as he entered a door on top of a stairway on the second floor of a corner building down the next block off the boardwalk. Joe parked and walked up to the boardwalk and approached the building from the front. It was a salt water taffy store. He crossed the boards and sat on a bench with his back to the ocean. He lit a cigar and watched. A few minutes later the young man appeared in a window facing the ocean. He raised the shade and opened the window. He was not wearing his jacket. He was home Joe thought. He got up and walked west on Montgomery. As he reached the back of the building he saw the motorcycle parked under the wooden stairs leading up to the door the man had entered. Joe memorized the license plate. Baker was an east bound only street. Montgomery was a west bound street. Joe walked up to Atlantic Avenue stopped and turned to look back at the stairway and the door. Returning to his car on Baker he wrote down the plate number. Joe was confident this was a solid lead.

There was just one more thing to do before he took the information to Mike.

The next day Joe went to the desk sergeant at OCPD headquarters. He had already had morning coffee with the chief. "Morning Sarge, do me a favor. Run this plate for me. Chief mentioned it this morning at the coffee shop. There's no hurry, I'll get the information tomorrow. Keep this on the QT, for now."

"All right, Joe. Hey, I got a new rod. Want to go surf fishing this week?"

"Yeah, sounds great. See you in the morning."

Joe left headquarters and drove to Wildwood. He parked his car on Baker Street and walked to the boardwalk and headed south. Reaching Montgomery Street, he left the boards and walked west. Passing the stairway, he saw that the motorcycle was gone. It was just past eleven in the morning. He returned to the boardwalk and began to stroll up and down occasionally stopping in a shop. He stopped at Mack's Pizza had had a slice with a coke. By three in the afternoon he stopped outside the salt water taffy shop and lit a cigar. Just past four he heard the motorcycle. A few minutes later he saw his suspect raise the shade and open the window. Joe left and returned to his car and drove back to Ocean City. He would have to get up early in the morning. The man most likely started work at seven or eight. Joe intended to follow him. He wanted to know everything he could before he gave it all to Mike.

He was up at five in the morning. Quietly as he could he left the house and drove to Wildwood. Parking today on Montgomery Street he waited. At six-forty-five the man he was stalking left the place where he lived. Joe sat low in the seat of his car as the motorcycle passed him and took a right on Atlantic. He drove north up Atlantic Avenue and made a left on Magnolia Avenue. Going west all the way to Lake Avenue he stopped and parked. A house on the corner was under construction. He watched from down the street as the man made his way to the roof. He and the other workers were setting the rafters of the new home. Confident that the work day had just started Joe drove back to Montgomery Avenue.

Climbing the stairs Joe removed a small leather case from his pocket. Just to be sure he knocked at the door. No one answered and as he checked the street and alley he saw no one watching him. Opening the case exposed several metal picks. He worked the lock careful not to leave any scratch marks. It took him longer than he wanted a s sweat broke out on his brow. Finally, the lock turned and Joe stepped inside softly closing the door. He stood there, listening.

He was alone. He looked over the apartment. In front of him and on the left wall was a kitchen, with a small table. To his right was an easy chair with a table and lamp. Two windows overlooked the boardwalk. A doorway in the middle of the wall on the right stepped up into the bathroom. A single bed was just to his right with a night stand and lamp. The place was clean and neat. He decided to start in the kitchen and opened the drawers and the cabinet doors. Everything he saw was stored neatly. Precisely was a better description. The top drawer held two sets of cutleries. Two knives, forks and spoons set in the drawer all lined up. Soup cans in the cabinets were all evenly spaced and lined up. The towel hanging on the door of the range oven was neatly folded. The ice box was on his left as he faced the kitchen followed by a cabinet, sink, cabinet and the last on the right was the range. The counter tops were empty except for a single empty glass placed in the very center of the twenty-four-inch square space. The circular table had a napkin holder with a salt and pepper shaker placed in the center. Moving into the living area he checked the drawer on the side table. Inside the drawer, he found two perfectly placed and sharpened pencils. A writing pad with no notes, but it did have pages missing. He found nothing under the chair or the cushion. He looked at the bed. It had been made. It reminded him of the cots when he was in the Army. It was perfectly made. The top blanket was tight. The folded white sheet on the top was perfectly aligned. The pillow right in the center. The guy was neat freak. He found nothing in the night stand or under the bed. He went through all the dresser drawers and found nothing but neatly folded clothes. The last place to check was the bathroom. It was spotless. Looking in the medicine cabinet he found nothing out of the ordinary. Everything was lined up just so and evenly spaced. He stood on the step leading to the bathroom and looked the place over. It was clean and as neat as a pin.

It was almost as if the young man was mocking him. There was nothing here.

He looked in the ice box and saw nothing but neatly lined up food items. Even the apples in the drawer were set just so. Joe's mouth was dry. He was sweating. He took out a handkerchief and wiped his brow. He ran the tap water until it felt cool. Then he filled glass on the counter top and he drank it down. He placed the glass back on the counter and went to the door. Looking outside he did not see anyone. He stepped out and closed the door. Descending the steps, he went up the street to his car. Sitting in the car he lit a cigar. Nothing. He thought. The place was spotless. He was hoping to find a knife, or the gun. The locks of hair. Crap, there was nothing. Feeling dejected he drove back to Ocean City.

It had been warm that day. Working on the roof in the hot sun, he and his fellow workers completed the job with the rafters. Driving to his apartment the cool air covered him as he rode down Atlantic Avenue. He needed a nice cool bath and a cold beer. He parked his cycle and went up the steps. Placing the key in the lock, it turned and he stepped inside his apartment and froze. Someone had been here. He listened. Not a sound. Then he walked over to the sink. Looking at the ceramic coated sink he saw droplets of water. It should have been dry as a bone. The glass on the counter top was not in its place. It had been moved and someone drank from it. He checked the rest of his apartment. It all looked normal. Then he went to the step to the bathroom. Removing the riser, he found the metal box. Opening it everything was still there. The locks of hair tied with ribbon and the knife and gun. Who was here and why. The only thing that had been moved was the glass. Someone is watching me? Cops? He went downstairs to the taffy shop. The owner was there and Grant asked him, "Has anyone been here to-day looking for me?"

"No, what's wrong Grant you look upset?"

Grant was upset. Someone had been upstairs. Someone, but who?

"Was any work done upstairs today?"

"No. Why are you asking? Is there a problem? The owner asked.

"It's nothing, don't worry, I'm all right," Grant said.

"Hey, look if something is not working you tell me. I'll have it fixed right away. I'll keep an eye on the place. I was here all day, working. No one has been in to see you and I never saw anyone upstairs. You in some kind of trouble kid?" The owner asked.

"Naw. I'm good. Just a long hot day in the sun. Cool bath and a cold beer I'll be fine. Thanks, Angelo. I'm going to take a few samples," Grant said grabbing some freshly wrapped salt water taffy.

"Sure kid, help yourself," Angelo said retuning to the front of his store.

Grant returned to his apartment. Someone was here. Why? He thought.

One of assets working for Bruce Parker the CIA Station Chief reported that a high level NLF Intelligence figure was coming into Saigon under an alias. Caroline had the initial report and made copies and sent them off to Washington in the diplomatic pouch. The man's name was Duy Minh. His movements in Saigon would be monitored by American field agents. Minh had been a member of the resistance forces during the Japanese occupation. After the war, he dropped out of sight presumed to have been killed. Recent pictures taken of Ho Chi Minh and General Giap with Chinese and Russian officials revealed that Duy was very much alive. His image also turned up in a routine photograph taken during the opening of a new Provincial Government Office in the village of Dinh Quan. Vietnamese agents loyal to the American government were now passively watching Duy. Most of the activity was in the small hamlet of Xa Phu Lam. It was learned that Duy lived in the hamlet with a younger woman. Her name was Huyen Trang. He spent most of his time at a small tea house. He did not work, nor did he farm. He had no known source of income, and locals claimed not to know of him.

He travelled very little always staying in the hamlet. He did take some trips to Dinh Quan, and to Saigon. His identity papers were all in order. He was suspected to be the Communist Commissar for Long Khanh Province. The woman he lived with also seemed to have no source of income. She was also not a farmer but travelled into the surrounding fields daily. For the American's this was big news. The information was secluded from the French. The CIA hoped to monitor this man's activity's and possibly turn him. There was a concern about the woman's activity during the day. She was rarely home and when she went into the fields during the early morning hours she sometimes did not return until late that night or the next day. When soft inquiries were made by the agents with the locals, they all claimed not to know of her.

Huyen Trang dressed and prepared for her trip into the jungle. The old woman next door had told her about the strangers asking about her. She and Minh had decided to abandon their small house in the hamlet. He would travel to Saigon and stay at an NLF safe house. She would rendezvous with the local cadre of the NLF and be escorted to a small village across the Cambodian border, near Tay Ninh. She had two large baskets that she would suspend from a long pole across her shoulders. One contained a back pack with her clothes. The other had ammunition and extra magazines for the US .30 caliber M2 Carbine with a folding stock. Minh had left yesterday in the afternoon. The sun was just coming up as she left the house and walked into the fields were other farmers were beginning their day. Once she crossed the fields she made her way unto a path used by the farming workers that led to an area used to relieve themselves. Out of sight in the jungle she put on her pack and loaded the M2. She took the extra magazines that were stored in an old bandolier and put it on over her shoulder. She found the path that she knew would be there and headed west. She had only been on the path a short time when she heard movement behind her.

Still a long way to the rendezvous point she walked a few meters south into the jungle and hid. She saw a Vietnamese woman in her early twenties walking in the same direction on the trail. She was holding a French 8mm Lebel Revolver. She was not travelling or out for a walk, she was tracking Trang. Trang knew that the trail travelled west and then turned south by a small creek. If she cut across through the jungle she could reach the creek before her tracker. The trail would turn west again and there should be a trap there she could activate. Moving quickly, she found her way to the creek. The trap was still there. All she had to do was to pull the long branch back to point where it connected to a trip wire on the trail. Once it was activated she moved into the jungle a few meters on the north side of the trail and waited. Within a few minutes the woman was coming down the trail. She tripped the wire activating the trap. She turned quickly towards the noise of the branch whipping towards her. It was too late. The two-foot-long punji stakes wired to the branch caught her low in the stomach. The branch was large enough that it pushed her off her feet. Traveling the whipping distance, it returned with the young woman still impaled. It was now bouncing with her body until it stopped. The stakes had gone all the way through her. They had been barbed so that once impaled the victim could not remove the stakes. They would have to be pushed all the way through. The woman never cried out but was clearly in agonizing pain. She moaned and watched helplessly as Trang came from out of the jungle. The pistol lay on the ground just a few feet away. No matter she would never be able to reach it holding on to the branch and dancing on her toes. Trang looked at her with indifference. The woman tears falling down her face pleaded, "Please, help me."

"I think not, who are you?"

"My name is Lan, please...I beg you."

Trang bent down picking up the revolver. "Why are you following me?"

The woman looked at the revolver. It was hopeless. Impaled on the branch she was helpless. There was no point in lying.

"The Americans paid me to follow you."

"Why?" Trang asked.

"I don't know. They pay me to follow you, that s all. I tell them...where you go. Please...I beg...you help...me." The woman was dying.

"Did they give you this?" Trang asked holding up the revolver.

"No. It was my...fathers. I brought...it for protect..."

Trang looked at the massive pool of blood on the jungle floor as the woman bled out. Her body collapsed and weighed down the branch. She could no longer stand on her toes. On her knees and bent over backwards her body was released by the branch spraying blood and pieces of her intestines in front of her. Trang still standing to the side of her watched as she took her last breath. The Americans, she thought. Why are they interested in me?

She searched the young woman and found nothing of interest other than a few spare rounds for the handgun. Leaving the body on the trail she headed back down the path. Someone might come looking for the girl. She came across two more traps and set them both. If anyone else were following her these would be the first indications if they were tripped. Both were simple grenade traps. All she needed to do was to pull the pins on the grenades and insert them into the old soup cans attached to trees on the side of the trail. Anyone tripping the wire would release the grenade from the can. Without their pins, the spoons would be released activating the grenades. She did not see or hear from anyone while she travelled. Getting late in the afternoon she was approaching her rendezvous point. The trail climbed a small hill, she would make her first contact at its base. Standing on the trail she called out her own name, "Huyen Trang." There was a rustle of leaves and then she saw a young boy emerge from a spider hole by the side of the trail. "Welcome comrade Trang, you are behind schedule. My name is Phan Duong. I will take you to our camp."

The young boy led the way up the trail to the top of the small hill. He pointed out several booby traps along the way. She was taken to the camps man in charge, Phan Tuan. The first part of her journey was over.

CHAPTER 21

LIFE GOES ON

Colleen and Kay drank their coffee. The two women spent a lot of time together as the proud grandmothers of little Jack. He was napping. The little man had just turned two. He was a challenge for both of them. His energy never seemed to cease. From the time, he was awake until he slept the little boy was moving all the time. He especially loved to be outside. As soon as his little feet hit the ground he was off and running. Followed by someone calling, "Jack...Jack, slow down."

Both women were retired. All of the time they had was spent watching their grandson. Hope had found a job at the new Veterans Hospital in Philadelphia. She was a nurse in the Psychiatry Ward. She continued to read as many psychology books and papers she could get her hands on. She also noticed that the same symptoms the men she cared for had were the same as those that she and Dorothy shared. She had frequent nightmares. She also felt an overwhelming guilt about her survival. She also noticed at times that memories intruded into her thoughts suddenly. Sometimes these thoughts should be triggered by a smell or sound.

Whatever this ailment was she and the men she cared for had it. Dorothy confided that she felt some of the same symptoms. She also had nightmares. Her guilty feeling was not being the kind of wife that she wanted to be. She avoided sex with Steve. She also noticed that no matter where she was she was always on alert. She had intrusive memories just like Hope. Both of them drank more than they should. For Dorothy, it affected her relationship with her husband. For Hope, she had no interest in any relationship. Neither of the two women thought that there was much of a future.

Colleen and Kay noticed the problems and shared their thoughts with Maggie. She remembered all too well the problems Dylan had when he returned from the war. Colleen was able to share that she saw the same problems with her husband Jimmy. Kay remembered the change in her son when he returned from Europe. It seemed as if the family was cursed.

Maggie also knew and had shared the news that the man who attacked Dorothy was close to being arrested. Mike told her they had a suspect and that they were getting close. This news made Dorothy tenser.

She would have to relive her experience again once the man was caught. She may even have to testify in court. This terrified her and put her on edge. She drank more and slept less. Fortunately, it was summer and school had already been closed for several weeks.

Kay came into the city several days a week to visit with Jack and Colleen. That morning they had taken Jack to the park and let him run around the gardens on the back side of the Art Museum. They had brought him home, fed him his lunch and put him down for a nap. The one benefit of his energy was it tired him out. Drinking their coffee, they talked about what was happening at the shore. Mike was close to an arrest. The story shocked

Kay, and she hoped it would all end soon. Then perhaps Dorothy could find some peace.

Joe McMullen spent his mornings at police headquarters and continued to have breakfast with the Police Chief each day. The two men had become close friends. Joe had assembled a file of men who owned motorcycles. Whenever he saw a man fitting the description of the man police were looking for he logged the information. He had addresses, employers and other information on the men he tracked. He kept all of his information to himself. Retired and alone it gave him a purpose in life. He felt he was making a contribution. He had files on seven different men. He knew what make and model motorcycle they rode. Only one had a criminal background. He had been arrested for being drunk and disorderly in Sea Isle City. The latest attack occurred in Sea Isle City last week.

After his breakfast with the Chief, Joe stopped by Mikes desk. He and Dave were discussing a stakeout on the beach where people liked to walk in the evening. The area was remote and had dunes close to the water.

"Any new leads on our rapist," Joe asked.

"A witness reported seeing a dark gray or black motorcycle leaving the area of the attack last week," Dave offered.

"How about the suspect?"

"Nothing, just the cycle. Not much of a lead," Mike said.

"Wait here, I have something to show you," Joe instructed.

Dave asked Mike, "What does he mean by our rapist?"

"Beats me," Mike replied.

Joe returned with a file folder. Inside was all the information he had on a man named Grant Williams.

Joe handed the folder to Mike. "Where did you get this Pop?"

"I've been running a little investigation myself. This guy owns a motorcycle like your witness described. He's also a neat freak. Keeps to himself, doesn't go out much. This could be our guy."

"This guy lives down in Wildwood. Have you been following him? What are you doing Pop?"

"Look, I got files on six other guys that fit the description. This is the only one with a dark grey motorcycle. He was the first one I saw. Call it a hunch, but I think he could be the guy."

"Six other files. Pop you're not a cop anymore. You're retired. This could be dangerous."

"You listen to me boy, I walked a beat when you were crapping in your pants. Once a cop, always a cop. I think this guy could be the one we are looking for. You should see his apartment. Neat as pin. Really weird..."

"You have been in this guy's apartment?" How did you get in?" Dave asked.

"I picked the lock..."

"Holy cow Pop, that's burglary."

"No kidding. If you have better information to go on, then forget it. I'm just trying to help. Do whatever you want with the file," Joe said leaving the office.

"I think you hurt his feelings," Dave offered.

"Yea, well that's better than having him arrested, or worse. I guess it would not hurt to run this guy through the system. Who knows maybe the old man got lucky," Mike replied.

Joe returned home feeling hurt and rejected. A good cop always follows his gut he thought. Arriving at the house Susan was sitting at the table reading the paper. "Hi, Dad. How was breakfast?"

"All right, nothing special. I'm gonna go lay down," Joe replied.

"Are you feeling all right?"

"I'm fine honey just tired today."

Once inside his room Joe took the locker he had under the bed and took out an item wrapped in an old towel. It was an old nickel plated .45 S&W Schofield Revolver with a seven-inch barrel. Opening the top loading breech, he filled the cylinder with cartridges from a box. Later that night Mike returned home from work. "Pop, I owe you an apology. I'm sorry I said what I did. Turns out you may be right. Dave and I ran the guy in your file. He is originally from Baltimore. Raised in orphanages, he's been in and out of reform schools. Got a summons for feeling a girl up at a dance. Never showed up in court. He shows up again as a suspect in a burglary in Colwyn, Delaware County PA. Shop owner reported it the day after Dorothy's attack. No sign of breaking and entering, but an employee who had a key and rented a room in the same building went missing. It was Grant Williams. He works as a carpenter for a local builder in Wildwood."

"You lock him up?"

"No, not yet. We have to build up our case. Right now, we don't have anything."

"What about his fingerprints?"

"Nothing on file in Baltimore or Pennsylvania."

"Right and as an employee of the shop his prints would be everywhere anyway," Joe said thinking.

"We need to get him with the cop's gun and the locks of hair from his victims. You were in the apartment where he lives. Did you find anything?"

"Nothing. Like I was trying to tell you. The place was squeaky clean. Too clean. Everything he had was all lined up. It was like he was expecting an inspection. You know like the Army. It was strange," Joe said.

"Dave and I have a meeting with Wildwood PD tomorrow. I don't want you involved with this guy in any way. If he's the one, Dave and I will get him. Promise me, Pop."

Joe nodded already in deep thought.

Waking at the crack of dawn, Trang walked to the latrine to relieve herself. The camp was small. It had one small hut that served as a meeting and eating area. The camp itself was remote. Sitting atop a small hill in the middle of the jungle, you could walk past it without knowing it was there. It was occupied by one man and a small girl. The camp was located ten miles east of the next leg of her trip to the Dong Nai River. From there she would go by boat across the Ho Tri An Lake which feed back into the Dong Nai into Bien Hoa. She would be met in Bien Hoa and travel by truck north to Tay Ninh.

A young girl was preparing tea. She offered some to Trang. The man in charge joined her. He had been a local farmer when Moroccan troops came to his village. Brought to Vietnam by the French, they were especially brutal. Fighting broke out and man's wife and son were beaten. He was branded by the French as a member of the Viet-Minh. He had been living here since that day over a year ago. He was not much of a communist, but he hated the French and the Moroccans'. Someday he hoped to be able to return to his village. His son came to the camp often. He was fourteen. It was the young boy that had met Trang on the trail. Phan Duong appeared with fish from a local stream. They had already been cleaned. He handed them to the young girl and she started to cook them on the fire. She said nothing. Putting down the heavy M1 Garand rifle Duong said, "She does not speak. I believe she can, but I think she chooses not to. We do not know her name. We call her Thu. She cooks and cleans, that is all."

Trang said, "She works hard."

"She is a child. Maybe ten years old. She appeared in our camp one morning. Cold, hungry and very afraid. We have no idea where she is from," Phan Tuan told her.

Trang drank her tea. Looking at Duong she asked, "That is a heavy rifle for a young boy. Do you know how it works?"

"Yes, my father showed me. We have only five bullets for it. Do you have bullets for it?"

"No. I do have a pistol you can have. I will not need it. A young man with a handgun he can hide is not as suspicious as one with a rifle. You should leave the rifle here. I will stay just one more day before we leave for the, river Trang told him. She sized him up. He was not tall just average height but stocky. He seemed eager to do his task and please his father. The camp was a rendezvous point for travelling Viet-Minh. Trang remembered she was just about his age when she stared with the Viet-Minh. It had been a long ten years since those days. Duy Minh had schooled her about the use of weapons and tactics. They were never romantically involved. The truth was he never saw him in that way. She had met a young boy just a year older than she. They were lovers. He died from malaria. She vowed to herself never to become a lover again. She thought despite herself that this young boy was quite handsome. He would be her escort to the river.

The camp was supplied with rice, beans, medical supplies and ammunition. Every month or so a small contingent of soldiers from the north would come with the supplies. Locals loyal to the NLF that lived in the surrounding Provinces would come to get resupplied. Farmers by day, they would attack convoys and French detachments at night. These guerilla tactics were only employed in the south as they were needed. Still, troops had to be fed as well as their weapons. The camp was just twenty miles or so from the river to the east. To the west another twenty miles was QL20. A major road that intersected with QL1 the main highway running north and south through the country. A major resupply route. It was remote enough not to draw attention from locals or even the French. Logging trails and paths well worn by use crisscrossed the area. Supplies were transported by loading them on bikes or livestock.

During her last day in the camp Trang showed Duong how the French pistol worked. Using a thin vine, she demonstrated how he could carry the revolver under his shirt. The vine attached to the lanyard ring on the butt of the pistol. Pulling on the pistol would break the vine when it was needed. He was attentive and asked her many questions. She learned that the Moroccans beat him and his mother. He had no knowledge of politics. All he wanted from life was to live peacefully in his village. Working alongside his father tending their crops and honoring the ancestors who had lived and worked there for generations. She explained to him that westerners colonialized their country taking its resources for their own profit. The Japanese granted Vietnam its independence at the end of the great war fought by the western nations. The French seized control again with the help of their western allies. This is why she was fighting, so that the Vietnamese people would control their own country and destiny.

Both women collapsed on the couch. They had just taken young Jack up for his nap. The tiny ball of boundless energy took his toll on them both. "Someday I think that boy will be the death of us," Kay said to Colleen.

"He is just like my Maggie's boy Dylan he was bouncing off the walls as a toddler too."

"Has Maggie had any news from him?" Kay asked.

"She gets a letter every other week or so. He seems to be spending some time in Saigon. The neighbor's girl Caroline is working there. They were a bit of an item before the war. Those two are a pair. Funny how they both wound up working with the CIA. I think he is coming home next year."

Hope and Dorothy returned from the Penn Fruit Grocery store. Each of them held two bags of groceries.

The store was located some blocks away at 19th and Market Street. Colleen and Hope had saved their money and purchased a used 1951 Mercury Monterey coupe. After unloading the rest of the groceries Colleen drove Kay out to the 69th Street Terminal. From there Kay would take the trolley back to Media. It was now part of the routine. Several days a week Colleen would pick up Kay in the early morning and return her to the terminal in the afternoon. The system worked well. Kay had the opportunity to see her grandson on a regular basis. Now that he was walking and talking Colleen needed the extra help. Living on the edge of Fairmount Park, Poplar Drive was just across the train tracks from Ogden Street. Colleen and Kay often took Jack to the park to let him run. Today had been no different.

Hope and Dorothy sat and drank coffee at the kitchen table. Hope was concerned for her lifelong friend. Dorothy had not been sleeping well. She had heard from her Uncle Mike that the man who attacked her may have been found. The thought of the possibility of testifying in court terrified her. The memories came back and her nightmares increased. "How are you and Steve doing?" Hope asked.

"God, I feel so guilty. He wants to start a family. I have no desires for sex. As soon as he touches me I freeze up. I want to scream and run away. He has been so patient. I feel awful about it. Why he stays with me I'll never know."

"He stays because he loves you. Hopefully this nightmare will soon be over, and you can get on with your life."

Dorothy looked up at Hope, "Look who's talking. You should get on with your life too. Go out and meet someone. Your too pretty to be single."

"I know, my mom is after me all the time. What man in his right mind wants to date a woman with a child? Especially a toddler. Hi, my name is Hope. I live at home with my mother and my little boy. Want to go to a movie?"

Dorothy responded, "You sound so pathetic."

"Well I am pathetic. I mean I can get by telling a man, my son's father was killed in Korea. It's just so unethical. Once he finds out that the truth has been stretched and we were never married, I'm just another easy woman."

Dorothy laughed, "You were easy. You spent a whole week with Jack. Granted the circumstances were difficult, but from what you told me, you did manage to keep your virginity for a whole day, before you threw yourself at him."

"Listen to us. Two beautiful young women in their prime and we can't get our lives together. We're both pathetic," Hope declared.

"You need to have sex with a man and won't, I have a man and won't. Maybe I should send Steve to you. That would solve two out of three problems," Dorothy said mischievously.

"I'll think about it and let you know," Hope replied. Both women laughed. The thump, thump, thumping noise coming from upstairs alerted them that Jack was now awake. He liked to hold unto the side of his crib and jump up and down. Getting up from the table Hope said, "I swear one day that boy will jump right out of that crib."

CHAPTER 22

HUNTING FOR DANGER

Wildwood PD had Williams under surveillance. One man was detailed to sit on the boardwalk and notify his headquarters when Williams left on his motorcycle. Then detectives in an unmarked unit would follow him. Once he drove out to Route 9 they would break off the tail and turn it over to OCPD who was also notified of movement by Williams. Dave and Mike were on twenty-four-hour call. On this Sunday evening Williams was on his way to Sea Isle City. Mike got the call at home and notified Dave. They headed south on Route 9. Passing Williams going north at Stone Harbor they let him get well beyond them before turning around. Unknown to them Joe had also left the house. Susan was taking a bath. Joe had a portable radio he had gotten from the desk sergeant. He could hear all of Mike and Dave's communication's. He also had a newspaper that concealed the big Schofield revolver. He saw Williams turn on the road leading into Sea Isle City. He followed him into town and turned south a block beyond where the motorcycle turned south. He heard the radio traffic notify Sea Isle PD of the presence of Mike and Dave. SIPD would keep their distance.

Grant found the parking spot along the beach with some pines to help conceal his motorcycle. He had no idea he was being followed. Walking along the dunes he looked for the spot he had searched out before. The sun was starting to set. He knew the young girl would be coming north up the beach soon. He waited an hour then spotted her down the beach about a half-mile away. Perfect he thought. By the time, she reached him she would be tired and less likely to fight him. He had his knife and the .38.

He was ready. He was a few blocks south of the nearest homes on the far southern edge of the city. No one would hear her screams.

Mike and Dave knew where he was going. Mike took a position south of Williams and Dave took a spot north of him on the beach. Both men stayed in the dunes. Mike saw the young girl running on the beach. The hairs on the back of his neck prickled. This was it he thought. We're going to get this bastard and catch him in the act. A solid case.

Joe parked his car on Central Avenue between them. He sat and waited. The radio was quiet. He poured a cup of coffee from the thermos. He was proud of himself. It was his long hard work that led his son to the killer. He was a cop again. His instincts were solid, but he also had a bad feeling about this night. Something was troubling him. Even though this could be the night.

Helen Pierce was nearing the end of her run. It was getting dark. Her parent's home was six blocks away. She had been training for her high school cross-country team. As she approached the spot where the run would end she saw the man coming at her from the dunes.

Grant saw her start to slow her pace. He charged out of the dunes. His knife was in his left hand. He was only twenty-five yards away. The sand here was soft and deep. She was on the edge of the surf. As he hit the harder sand he tackled her. She screamed. He slapped her hard across the face. Holding the knife against her throat he leaned in and told her to be quiet. Using the knife, he cut the sweatshirt up the front of her. Then he cut the bra away exposing her breasts. "NO Stop." She pleaded. He slapped her again as she tried to fight him off.

Mike saw the attack and left his hiding spot and ran at the girl and her attacker. The soft sand slowing him down. The big .45 from the war was in his hand. Getting closer he saw the knife flashing in the bright light of the rising moon. "Police, drop the knife," he yelled.

Startled Grant looked up and saw the big man coming at him. He dropped the knife and pulled out the .38 from his pants.

Firing blindly, the shot went wide. Mike stopped and dropped to his knees. He could not return fire the attacker was too close to the girl.

Dave could not see the girl or the attack but he heard the shot. Running from his hiding spot in the dunes he ran down the beach. He saw the girl sitting on the edge of the surf. Mike was with her. The man they had been hunting was running back towards the street, and was almost into the dunes. Dave went after him. "Police, stay where you are," he yelled. The man turned towards Dave and fired his revolver. The shot went well wide of Dave. Dave took aim with his S&W Model 36 and fired back. He missed and the man continued to run towards the dunes.

Joe sitting in the car heard Grant's first shot. He jumped out of the car and ran north up Central Avenue. Taking the big Schofield from the newspaper he headed for the dunes. Now he could hear men screaming. Two more-gun shots broke the silence of the evening. He turned east on the street leading to the beach. He was out of breath. His age and inactivity taking its toll. He saw a man with a gun break away from the dunes. The man stopped and turned towards the beach. Then he saw Mike come out of the dunes. Grant aimed his gun and fired.

The shot hit Mike just above his knee. He fell on his face yelling out in pain, and lost his big colt as he fell. He knew he had been hit. The colt was just five feet away in the sand. Looking up he saw Williams coming back towards him. He was leveling his gun getting ready to fire again. Mike realized he could not make it to the colt in time. Then the night lit up from a muzzle blast and he heard the boom of a large caliber weapon. Mike fell over backwards the image of his attacker's head exploding. Something heavy was on his chest. He could not get his breath. Then everything went black.

Dave came over the top of the dunes. He saw Grant fire at Mike as he broke away from the dunes. Mike fell and howled in pain. Dave aimed his short barreled .38 and fired again at the attacker. The man ignored Dave as he aimed his gun at Mike. Standing a few feet from Mike, Williams fired at Mike. There was another gun shot from the street. This shot was different. The muzzle blast lit up the dunes and the report of the big Scofield was louder than the .38's being fired. Williams was hit. The big .45 Long Colt round hit him in the head. Dave saw his head burst open from the shot. Williams was knocked down by the bullet that tore into his head. Dave turned and saw Joe standing on the street, smoke coming from the barrel of a huge revolver. Mike lay on his back on the sand. He was not moving.

Joe saw the man level his gun at Mike. He took a deep breath and aimed the big Scofield squeezing the trigger. The big gun bucked in his hand. Then he saw the attacker blasted off his feet as he fell. There was also another shot. The attacker still managed to get off the shot he was aiming at Mike. Then he saw Dave run out from the dunes. He went straight to Mike. He was lying in the sand. Dave tore open his coat. His shirt was soaked with a large red pool of blood covering his chest.

Helen Pierce sat on the edge of the surf. Pulling her cut sweat-shirt around her she was crying. The policeman told her to stay put. He left her and she watched as he pursued her attacker on the other side of the dunes. She heard all of the gun shots. Dave ran back over the dune. He saw the girl still sitting on the beach. He hit the talk button on the portable radio. "10-13, 10-13, shots fired officer down. Location beach and 63rd Street." Dave using the NYPD code for assist officer was not used in southern New Jersey. The dispatcher called back, "Unit identify yourself." Dave gathered his wits and pressed the talk button, "Car 1D, OCPD. Officer needs ambulance, beach at 63rd Street." Joe walked up too Mike. Knelling next to his son he cradled him in his arms. "Michael, Michael, look at me boy. Say something." Mike did not respond. The only sound Joe could hear was his son wheezing fighting for air. Dave looked at Joe holding his son, "Joe, stay with Mike, I'll be right back. Dave could hear the radio come alive as units started responding. Sirens could be heard in the distance. Dave ran towards Helen. She back tracked in fear. "It's all right I'm a policeman. Are you hurt?" The girl shook her head. "Good, come with me. What's your name honey?"

"He...Helen."

"Your safe now, come along." Dave led her back towards the dunes.

The first car on the scene was from Sea Isle PD. Officer Dennis Wood was an army medic during the Battle of the Bulge. He looked at Mike and checked his wound. He reached into his pocket and took out a pack of Lucky Strikes. Removing the cellophane wrapper from the pack of cigarettes he used his finger to push the wrapper into the bullet hole in Mike's chest. Mike's breathing improved. Taking a handkerchief from his pocket he placed it over the wound and told Joe, "Keep pressure on this. Ambulance is on its way." He looked at the body of Grant Williams. Nothing was going to help him.

In the next few minutes the scene came to life as police cars filled the street. Mike was put on a stretcher and put into an ambulance. It left with its siren blaring. Joe rode in the ambulance with his son. He was still breathing heavily. "Stay with me Michael, stay with me," he told him.

The jungle was dense. The heat and humidity was taking its toll. They stopped for a rest. Sitting by a small creek they ate some fish and rice. Duong watched Trang as she ate. His father had taught him to eat his food slowly and to chew it well. Trang wolfed her food down. He was not sure she even chewed it. She had learned to do everything quickly. Living in the jungle was a challenge. Having finished eating they started out heading northwest. They came out of the jungle unto a well-traveled trail. Using the trail would be faster but it was also more dangerous. Booby traps were always a risk on the trails. This area was not controlled by the French. Trang was not sure of any Viet-Minh units in this part of Long Khanh Province. They took the trail with Trang leading. She knew the signs that would warn her about any traps. Encountering no traps, they made good time. They should be able to reach the river in another day. The trail led up to a small hill.

Trang decided to move back into the jungle and take up a night time position on top of the hill. It would be chilly here during the night. She cleared an area for them both to sleep. Unpacking her back pack, she had a hammock that she tied between two trees. She built a small fire.

Without any inhibitions, Trang took off her sweat soaked pajama top and pants. Using a small branch, she spread her cloths over the branch and fire to dry them. Standing there naked, Duong watched her. He had never seen a woman naked before. She knew he was looking at her. "You will have to take off your clothes," she told him. He sat there not sure of what he should do. Using the branch, she moved her clothes over the fire. Duong took off his shirt, but hesitated taking off his pants. It was clear to her he had an erection. "Have you ever been with a woman before?" She asked him. Embarrassed at his condition he replied, "No."

"I understand. There is nothing to be embarrassed about. It is natural for a young man. We have to dry our clothing. The smoke from the fire will hide our scent from the animals that live here." Finished with her top and pants she hung them on a branch. She showed him how to dry his cloths. Then she climbed into the hammock and watched him. He used the branch as she had showed him. He was clearly uncomfortable. When he finished, she told him to hang his cloths as she had done.

Then she invited him to the hammock.

Standing by the hammock he climbed in with her. The warmth of her skin against his excited him further. She was tired and needed to sleep but she knew he would not rest. Reaching down she closed her hand on his erection and a few seconds later he ejaculated unable to control himself. "Now we should sleep," she told him. Huddled together in the hammock and exhausted they slept.

The next morning, she woke early. Climbing out of the hammock she went a few steps into the jungle to relieve herself. He sat up in the hammock and watched as she returned. She dressed quickly after she inspected her clothes and took out some rice to cook. He got out of the hammock and began dressing himself. "You should look them over first, make sure nothing has found a new place to live." He was not sure what she meant but as he looked at his shirt he found a centipede. Now he understood. Eating the rice, she cooked she told him, "We should reach the river in another day. You should come with me when we reach it."

"What about my father? He will expect me to come back."

"Do you think you could find your way back to him? It will be very dangerous. It is a long way back to the camp. You don't know how to survive in the jungle. There is much I need to teach you. There is no time for that now," she said.

"Will I ever see him again?"

"Someday perhaps. For now, our struggle against the French is more important. You realize we fight for our country. You are a soldier now. We must all sacrifice for the freedom of Vietnam."

"Why are the French here?"

"Western people think we are primitive. We live a simple life, like your father. We farm, raise livestock for no other purpose but to survive and provide for our families. We honor our ancestors that did the same thing in the same place. This is life. We wish to be free, too live this life. For us it is all we need. Westerners come here and take what they want. They treat our people as if we are beneath them. Vietnam wants to be left alone. First it is the French, then the Japanese. Now the French again. It is time for them to leave us."

"Do you think we will win?"

"Yes. The French are a foolish people. They are not very good fighters. When the Japanese came, they bowed to them. They were defeated quickly. We formed the Viet-Minh to resist the Japanese. When they were defeated by the Americans the Japanese gave Vietnam its independence. Their French lackeys stole it back. Now we will push the French from our country. We should start moving, pack your things."

She moved about the small site where they had camped. Duong watched her as she checked the camp site. When she had finished, he looked again and was surprised to see there was no evidence of them spending the night there. Even the embers from the fire had been swept away. They walked down the hill to the tail and headed northwest. By the end of the day they would reach the Dung Nai river. She selected a spot about one hundred yards from the river to spend the night. Duong had much to learn. The prospect of seeing her naked again excited him.

After setting up the camp she took him to the river as the sun started to set. She told him to leave his weapon and stripped. Taking her clothing with her she stepped into the river squatted and washed herself. Then she rinsed her clothing. He did the same as she instructed him. Finished she took their clothing and spread it on some bushes. Sitting on the bank with his knees tucked under his chin he watched her. She glanced at him and saw he had an erection. He was staring at her breasts. She told him to go back into the river and wash himself. Returning Duong was embarrassed. "I do not want you to get the wrong idea. We are not nor will we ever be lovers. I did what I did last night so that we could sleep. From now on you will take care of your own needs. There will be no fire tonight. We are too close to the river. Our cloths will dry during the night. One of us needs to be awake. We will not share the hammock tonight. Come, we should return to the camp."

Duong was confused hurt and embarrassed. Returning to the camp he had nothing to say. Their clothing was still damp and she spread them over some small branches. They ate some dried fish and chicken. Then she said, "Remember when I told you to listen to the jungle? Do that tonight while I sleep. If something sounds out of place or the creatures that live here are silent you must wake me. Don't do anything unless you wake me. See the moon there in the sky?" When it is over the trees on the river side of the camp wake me. Then you can sleep. Do not fall asleep. If you start to drift off stand up. There is always movement on the river at night. It could be French or Viet-Minh. Understand?"

He nodded that he understood. She climbed into the hammock and was asleep in seconds, leaving him to his thoughts. He wore only the pistol attached to the vine around his neck. Her M2 carbine was against the tree. He listened to the jungle. He could barely make out her form in the hammock. Lying on her back he could see the nipples of her breasts. Pushing out the thoughts Duong listened to the jungle. At night, it seemed to come alive. He found that if he closed his eyes for a few seconds when he opened them again he could see better. She had taught him this. She had told him to do this by alternating between his left and right eye. Looking down at the jungle floor he could see things that seemed to glow in the darkness. It was spotted all around by things that turned luminous in the moon light that filtered through the canopy. He heard something move a few feet away. It was not crawling or walking. It seemed to brush against the jungle floor as it moved. A snake perhaps. It moved away from him. He heard birds in the trees above him. Off in the distance he heard splashing in the river. Sound seemed to travel so well at night. Then he heard voices.

Brushing her hair on the bed, Susan heard the phone ring. She found she was alone when she got out of the tub. Mike had called out that he was going to work. She wondered why Joe had gone with him. The phone rang and she went into the living room to answer. "Hello."

The voice on the other end was known to her. It was the Chief of Police. He was at Shore Memorial Hospital. He was sending a car for her. She dropped the phone and ran to the bedroom. She started to dress. She heard the siren off in the distance. It was getting closer. She fixed her hair into a pony tail as the siren and the car pulled into her driveway. She ran out the door before the officer driving the car could even get all the way out of the car. She got into the passenger side. The young officer driving told her that he had no information. The Chief had told him to get her and return to the hospital, code 3. She feared the worst. The car sped through the streets of the city with its siren blaring. There was very little traffic and they reached the hospital quickly. Arriving at the hospital the young officer took her to the third-floor surgical waiting room. The hallway was filled with policemen. The Chief spotted her and he walked up to her and announced, "Susan, Michael has been shot. He is in surgery. We are all waiting and praying. Joe is here too." He took her arm leading her over to where Joe was sitting. He looked ashen and had been crying. They embraced. The Chief sat with them and Susan asked, "Where was he shot?"

The Chief relied, "It was during a stakeout in Sea Isle..."

"NO, where on his body?" She demanded.

"He took a bullet in the chest and the leg." The Chief replied.

Joe whispered, "Sucking chest wound, the officer said. He was an army medic."

Susan took a deep breath. A sucking chest wound was serious. It meant that one of his lungs had collapsed. Mike trying to breath was taking air into his chest cavity collapsing his lung. The fact that he was in surgery so quickly was a good sign, but she knew this was a life-threatening wound. Susan looked at Joe. He was not well. His breathing seemed labored and his color was bad. She spotted a nurse walking past with a stethoscope around her neck. "Nurse, I'm an RN can I borrow your scope please?" The nurse was startled by the request but handed over the instrument to Susan. Following Susan to Joe she noted his appearance. Susan was listening to Joe's chest instructing him to take deep breaths. The nurse was already looking and checking his pulse. Both women knew that Joe was on the verge or already in the throughs of a heart attack. "I'll get a gurney and a doctor," the nurse said. She ran down the hall pushing policemen out of her way. She returned with the gurney as policemen moved out of her way. They helped Joe unto the gurney and pushed him towards the elevators to get to the ER. "Pop, look at me. You stay with me. Everything is going to be fine," Susan told Joe.

Finishing their dinner Vang Bo sat at the table. His daughters were doing well with the new business. Mei was cleaning the dishes. Meilin sat with her father. "You two are doing well in your business. Your Vietnamese is coming along as well."

"Yes, Baba. The French soldiers like their fancy uniforms. Our embroidery work is much desired."

Mei returned from the kitchen. "Baba, how long will you be staying in Saigon?"

"I am going to stay here for a short time. There are some business matters I must attend to. Things are happening up north. The French are getting ready for a big operation."

"Madame Lam has told us she may be leaving us. Most day's she is not here. She is spending more time away from us."

"Do you know where she goes?" He asked.

"She does not share with us where she is going. I thought you would know," Mei said.

"No, I have no information about her. She has been good for you both.

Maybe she is preparing to leave you both on your own. Time will reveal her purpose soon enough. Tomorrow we should have dinner together at the restaurant I told you about."

"That would be nice. We could close the shop early," Meilin said.

"If the French Colonel picks up his uniform we can close after that. It is the only order that is due," Mei added.

"That man is awful. The way he looks at us. He makes me feel uncomfortable. He only behaves when Madam Lam is with us," Meilin told them.

"The French treat all Asian people the same. They believe they are better than us. The Chinese have a long history of greatness. We invented gun powder and built the Great Wall," Bo told them.

The door to the shop downstairs had a bell. It clinked when Madame Lam entered the closed store. Coming upstairs she noted Bo's presence.

"It is good to see you once again Comrade. It is also good you are here. I will be leaving tonight. Your daughters are ready to be a part of Vietnamese society. They have learned all that I can teach them. The business is very successful," Lam told Bo.

"Where will you be going?" Mei asked.

"It is better that you do not know. Your father is familiar with such matters. I must pack my things. Please excuse me," Madame Lam said.

She left them at the table and went into her room. They heard her opening and closing the drawers. "Where will she go Baba?" Meilin asked.

"I'm afraid I do not know. She must be needed somewhere else. Perhaps someday you will see her again."

Madame Lam came out of the bedroom holding a sack with her belongings. She hugged and kissed both the girls. "Someday soon, French soldiers will come and ask for me. Tell them nothing. I left some useless things in my room. Tell them you have no idea when I left or where I was going. Remember you are Chinese. Remember that I taught you that you came to Vietnam to be free. I will pray for you both. Until we meet again Comrades," Madame Lam said as she left.

Both of Bo's daughters were upset and surprised. They both knew that they would miss her. Bo assured them that she was leaving because it was no longer safe for her here in Saigon. "Go about your normal routine. Open your shop on time. I will be back tomorrow. We will have a nice dinner." Bo got up to leave and said goodnight. Going down the steps he let himself out. Looking both ways up and down the street he noted there was no sign of Madame Lam. He turned and walked back to his hotel.

Reaching the hotel, he passed through a small park. He spotted Hung sitting alone on a bench. As he approached Hung ignored him as if he were a stranger. As he passed Hung Bo heard him say in a low voice, "Remember who you are Vang Bo." He walked across the street and entered the hotel. Checking in at the desk he was greeted by two Frenchmen in business suits. They flashed credentials in his face and told him that they were with the SDECE. (Foreign Documentation and Counter-Espionage Service) Bo knew what to do. His American friends had taught him how to use a poker face. "You are Vang Bo, a Chinese national?"

"Yes, I am Vang Bo. What do you want with me?"

"Perhaps we should speak upstairs in your room."

"As you wish. What is this about?"

The three men walked to the elevator. Bo noticed that there were French soldiers in the lobby and the hall upstairs. He did not have to unlock his door. Another Frenchman was already in his room looking through his things. "There is nothing here," he reported as they all entered the room.

"I have done nothing wrong. Why is this man in my room? What do you want"? Bo demanded.

"Tell us about Madame Lam," one of the men said.

CHAPTER 23

THE PRICE OF PEACE

It was a long night. The sun was coming up over the ocean. Susan walked slowly towards the house. Cupcake was at the door and ran past her as she opened it. Running to the end of the driveway she watched him relieve himself. He had been inside all night. Finishing he raced up to her, happy to see her. Something was wrong. He sensed it. She walked slowly and sat down at the kitchen table. Then she cried. It was a cry produced by great sadness. Cupcake laid at her feet. He waited for her to finish and say something, but she just sat there and cried. Then he sat up and bumped his head against her leg. She looked down at him tears filled her eyes. "He's not coming home, sweetheart. He's gone," and then the tears returned. Sadness and grief aside she had to return to the hospital. She changed her clothes and called headquarters. She informed the desk sergeant she was ready to be picked up. He expressed his condolences and told her a patrol car would be dispatched right away. A few minutes later the police car pulled into the drive. The two officers extended their sympathies and asked if they could help in any way. "Please stop later and let the dog out," she said.

His entire body tingled. Clutching the French revolver in his hand gave him some reassurance. Then she startled him by whispering, "Get dressed." She was already awake and dressed. "Who is it?" Duong asked. "They are Viet-Minh, French and Vietnamese soldiers do not travel at night," she replied.

"Do they know we are here?" He asked as he dressed.

"I think not. Something is happening. I am supposed to meet a boat on the river. I can't imagine why they are here," she replied.

"What do we do now?"

"We wait. The sun will be up soon. Then we will see. Until then be quiet and still. Put the gun away, it will not be needed." They sat together in the fading black of night. The jungle resumed its night noises. Duong noticed that she had her weapon in hand. At the same time, she seemed to be calm. The sky above the trees turned from black to grey. As the sun rose higher in the sky it turned blue. The light in the jungle was still a soft grey. She stood put on her pack and told him to follow and stay close. She walked calmly towards the river. She cradled her weapon in her left arm across her chest. After walking about a hundred yards the sunlight filtered down to the jungle floor. The various shades of green and brown could now be distinguished from each other. She walked slowly. She knew eyes were watching her. She noted a man to her left, hiding in the brush. She kept walking. As she passed a tree with a large trunk a man hiding behind it asked in a calm voice, "Are you here to fish?"

Turning towards him she saw movement to her left. Another man was crouching in the brush. "I am here with my brother to travel on the river, Comrade."

Duong could not see the man behind the tree. He could see the other man crouching in the brush, he watched him stand. Then he felt or sensed the presence of another man behind him. Both men had rifles. They wore bandoliers with extra ammunition.

"The river is dangerous these days. All travel has been cancelled. Identify yourself, Comrade." The man said.

He was asking for the code name she had picked so many years before. "I am Antoinette, identify yourself, who are you?" She replied and asked.

"I am Pagoda." I am in command of this patrol. We have been sent to find you by Bishop," he replied.

The man said he was Pagoda, which meant nothing to her. But the fact that he was sent by Bishop, which was Minh's code name, let her know she was among friends. This is Duong. He is my companion. He is still a young boy. Trang's description of Duong meant he was not a soldier. Pagoda introduced his two companions. The man behind Duong was Nguyen. The other man's name was Xuan. Then he gave his own name, Chi. "There has been much activity up north. The French have shut down all of the river traffic. Travel on the roads is also heavily restricted.

Large units of French soldiers and supplies are being moved north. Bishop sent us to find you and take you to a safe place in the jungle. He told me to tell you not to travel to Tay Ninh."

"Where did you see him?" Trang asked.

"I saw him in Saigon. He is safe there. You cannot return to Dinh Quan or Xa Phu Lam. The French SDECE is looking for you. Osprey was captured and tortured. He revealed you and Minh. He also told them about a man known to us as Gayal. They have no idea who he is, only that he exists. My orders are to escort you to a safe camp. Once there you will receive new orders. We should start moving."

"All right. Which way?" Trang asked.

"We will be travelling west along the river until we reach the Ho Tri An Lake. The camp is just south of the lake. There is one more thing, Trang."

"What?"

no apo

"I want the boys pistol. We cannot make any enemy contact. He can have it back when we reach the camp."

"Give Chi, the gun." Trang told Duong. He was surprised and a little hurt, but he gave up the revolver. Then they travelled along the southern side of the river. Xuan was the point man, followed by Chi. Trang and Duong were behind Chi. Nguyen was the last man. He kept in site of Trang and Duong but was always far away. His job was to detect any movement to their rear. They travelled all morning and stopped just past noon. Moving south further into the jungle they set up a defensive perimeter. They ate some balls of rice wrapped in cabbage. They remained there all afternoon waiting for the sun to get low in the sky. Then they moved north west until they saw the river again and continued west. The broke through the jungle but made no noise as they travelled. As it got darker and the jungle lost the light of the sun they set up an overnight camp. It would be another day's travel before they reached the safe camp somewhere in the jungle.

The patrol car dropped Susan off at the hospital. She took the elevator upstairs. Standing outside his room she looked in and saw he was sleeping. The surgery he had under gone had saved his life. His father would never know. Joe McMullen suffered a massive heart attack before reaching the emergency room. The running the shooting and Mike being so badly wounded was too much. She sat in the chair by his bed, after reading his chart. His vitals were good. He was going to make it. Later that morning Dave his partner showed up. "How's he doing?"

"I think he's going to be all right. Hopefully he will wake up soon. How are you doing?"

"Me, I'm all right. I just came back from Wildwood. I stopped here on the way home. I just need some sleep. Call me when he wakes up, OK."

"I will. Go home and get some rest."

Dave left the room and thought through the events of the previous night. The chief wanted his written report. They had solved one hell of a case.

Susan sat in the chair and dozed off. The nurse had come into the room on a regular basis checking Mike and making notes in his chart. A few hours later he woke. Looking up at the ceiling he could see the overhead light. It had been turned off. Daylight from the afternoon sun came in through the window. There was an IV bag hanging on a post. Picking his head up he saw Susan in the chair by his bedside. She was sleeping. Then he felt the pressure and pain in his shoulder and chest. He was wearing a mask giving him oxygen. He blinked to clear the blurry vision. The nurse arrived and smiled. "Hello, there handsome. How do you feel?"

He made an attempt to speak but his mouth and lips were dry. "I know we can fix that." Susan woke and came to his side. Tears filled her eyes. The nurse moved his mask and using a swab began coating his lips and the inside of his mouth. It tasted like lemons. "Does that feel better?" She asked. He nodded and turned to Susan. "Hi. How long have I been here?"

"Since last night. You had surgery. That bastard shot you in the chest. Doctor says you should be all right. You are going to retire Mike McMullen. I cannot go through this again. I thought I lost you..." She began to cry. "Hey. Don't cry. Everything will be all right."

The nurse returned and began the routine of checking his vitals and the IV bag. She made the notes in the chart. Susan sat and composed herself. She knew he would be asking questions. She had no idea that Mike did not know that his father was there at the shooting. The nurse left. Susan got up from the chair and stood by his side. "Did Dave get the guy? Is he...all, right? Tell me what happened."

"Yes. Dave is fine and the man is dead." Susan stopped. There was no point in telling him that his father was gone. Not now.

"You should rest. I'm sure the doctor will be in to see you soon. It was close Mike. Very close. I could have lost you." The tears returned as she held his hand.

"I know. I'm sorry." Mike took a deep breath and closed his eyes. His body demanded sleep. He was in no position to argue.

He slept the rest of night. Susan had notified the family in Philadelphia. She stayed by his bedside. The doctor and the nurses had been in and out of his room checking on his progress. The next morning Dave came in to see him. Susan talked with him before he went into the room. "He has no idea Joe was there. He doesn't know that his father is dead. I will tell him later."

"All right Susan, whatever you want, "Dave replied.

Dave went into Mikes room. It looked as if he were sleeping, but Mike turned his head hearing Dave approaching. "Hey there partner. How are you feeling?" Dave asked.

"Still a little sore. What happened out there?"

"Well, let's see. Williams is responsible for all of those rape murders in Pennsylvania. We found the hair cuttings he took from each of his victims. The gun he had was a department issue .38 from Radnor PD. We have blood and hair matching samples from his crimes here in NJ, not to mention his fingerprints. Blood on the knife up under the hilt matches the blood type from the stabbing victim on our beach. We got a good solid case. We busted it partner. Me and you are like legends now."

"Don't forget it was my dad that broke this case. He deserves some credit."

"Eh, yeah sure. He did…all the ground work," Dave said with hesitation.

"What? What is it Dave? Your holding something back."

"Me, naw we got the guy. A solid case."

"Dave, we have been partners for too long. I know you, what is it?"

Dave swallowed hard. He was in a corner. "Susan should be back soon, I wonder where she got to?"

"Tell me." Mike was looking at his partner with determination. Dave realized he was not able to hold back the information.

"Maybe we should wait for Susan."

"Why?"

"Susan should be here."

"I am here. How do you feel?" Susan said entering the room.

"I feel like you two are holding something back." Somebody talk to me. What happened out there?"

Dave looked at Susan, then turned to Mike, "Joe was there. He must have followed us. It was Joe that shot and killed Williams. He stayed with you all the way to the hospital."

"Was my dad shot?"

Susan took his hand and said, "No. He was really upset about you. Mike, Dad had a heart attack. He died the night you were in surgery."

Mike looked back and forth at both Dave and Susan. Then he turned his head to the side and began to cry. Dave said softly, "It was your dad, Mike. He broke the whole case. He and Williams fired at the same time. He probably saved your life."

Mike cried softly. Then Dave said, "I have to get back to the job. The chief is screaming for my report. I'm sorry Mike. Joe was a hell of a cop. Take care."

Dave left the room feeling bad. He had a long day of paperwork in front of him.

Standing in his hotel room, Bo turned to answer the man's question. "Madame Lam is a teacher I hired to assist my daughters with their business and teach them Vietnamese."

"How did you meet her?"

"Through an employment agency."

"Ah yes, the one on Pasteur Street. It is no longer conducting business. It was a front for the NLF. Do you know about this?"

"No. I have no knowledge about rebels. I am a teacher myself."

"Yes. We know. Tell me, as a Chinese National how did you come to live and work here in Vietnam?"

"I came after the war. The Japanese opened the borders. I left China. Vietnam was free. My wife was killed by the Japanese and I had no idea where my daughters were. After I found them I had them come here."

"Where is Madame Lam now?"

"She was at my daughter's place of business earlier. She left to visit a friend."

"Do you know who this friend is?"

"I have no idea. We do not pry into Madame Lams personal life. She comes and goes as she pleases. I demand to know why you are asking me these questions. I have done nothing wrong."

"This is a matter of national security. One final question… Who is Gayal?"

Bo kept his poker face but was shocked by the question. He answered, "I have no idea. I do not know anyone by that name."

"Very well, I apologize for any inconvenience. If Madame Lam should return, please notify us immediately." The man handed Bo a business card.

"What do you mean, if she should return? We expect her to open the shop in the morning," Bo replied.

The man smiled and said, "Yes, of course." Then he left with the other agents and the soldiers. Bo sat on the bed. What is happening he thought. He went into the bathroom and washed his face with cold water. When he came out of the bathroom Hung was sitting in the chair in the corner of the room. Startled Bo asked, "What is going on? The French SDECE was just here. They know about Madame Lam. They asked me who Gayal was."

"I see you did not tell them. Otherwise you would be in prison. The French are worried. Their position here is grave. There is a battle up north at Dien Ben Phu. Our army has the French surrounded. Victory is within our grasp. The French will be

269

defeated by the end of the month. Vietnam will be a free and independent country."

"Are my daughter's safe?"

"Of course, the SDECE has known or suspected Madame Lam for years. They even arrested her once in Hanoi. Do not be concerned. This will all be over soon."

"They asked me how I came to Vietnam."

"This is of no concern. Many Chinese are in Vietnam. The Chinese replaced the Japanese up north. The British took control of the south and turned everything over back to the French. The French have been up north since the Chinese left. Soon they will be leaving."

"What has happened to Minh and Trang?"

"Minh is here in Saigon. Trang is in a safe camp northeast of here."

"How long will you stay here in Saigon?"

"A few days. Then I will meet with Trang at her camp. Enjoy the days with your daughters. Then return to Dinh Quan and the school. All of your students are real. None of them are working for us. Once the French are defeated I will see you there."

"You sound very convinced of victory."

"It is inevitable. They are surrounded and cannot resupply. General Giap has them clenched in his fist. Be well my friend, I will see you in the coming weeks." Hung left the room leaving Bo to his own thoughts. He spent the next few days in Saigon with Mei and Meilin. He noticed that wherever they went they were followed.

A few days later he left for Dinh Quan. Once gain he was followed. Within a week of returning home and work he noted he was no longer followed. News from up north was being discussed everywhere. The end of the month came and the French were still holding on. Another week passed and it was all over. The French had suffered their defeat and surrendered.

CHAPTER 24

TWIST OF FATE

Vietnam had its victory. As the peace treaties were being signed western influence would still maintain control over the destiny of the newly independent nation. In Geneva, it was decided to split the country in two along the 17th Parallel. The communist would maintain control of the north and the newly independent Republic of Vietnam would be in control of the south. The south was rich in resources. Much of the world's rice came from the Delta Region. Rubber plantations were also plentiful. Western business interests would prevail, but would set the stage for more war. The NLF, and the new communist government would form the People's Army of Vietnam or PAVN. Prisoners on both sides were exchanged. Ho Chi Minh was not discouraged. His dream of a united, and independent Vietnam was still very much alive. It would be achieved twenty years later, after another bloody war.

Duong returned from another training patrol in the jungle. He was learning how to survive in one of the harshest environments on earth. The camp seemed to more alive on this morning.

A man had arrived in camp while he was gone. Duong learned that this man was one of the original members of the Viet-Minh.

He and others fought the Japanese during the World War. He brought exciting news with him. The French had been defeated a few weeks ago. The war he was preparing to fight was over. He could go home. He hoped to be reunited with his father. In the center of the camp there was an open-air hooch. Four posts from trees that had been cut down supported a roof of jungle that had overgrown the structure. It was here he found Trang sitting with this man. She introduced him and told him the news.

The man was legendary in the Viet-Minh. Many of the other fighters who were training him, spoke about this man. Duong was surprised to see that he was so short and thin. Hung spoke to him in a soft voice, "It is my pleasure to meet you Duong. Trang has told me how you helped her reach this camp. I am grateful. You will be welcomed back in your village as a hero of the people."

"It is really true. I can go home. I will see my father again. How soon can I leave?"

Trang answered, "We will all leave this camp tomorrow. Comrade Hung has brought money with him. You will get enough to make your way home."

"Where will you be going Trang?" Duong asked.

"I will return to the north with Hung and some of the others. Everyone else will be going their own way."

Then Hung told them, "We will spend the rest of the day preparing for our own journeys."

Hung added, "Tonight we will all celebrate General Giap's great victory."

Unknown to those in the jungle camps western countries had already been deciding their fates. Although the French were no longer in power the Provincial Army forces and police units of South Vietnam were still in power. Many of the returning Viet-Minh in the south were arrested, tortured or shot on site. By the time the Geneva Accords were in place a new government was taking charge in South Vietnam. Bao Dai who had been appointed Emperor by western powers in Geneva had been displaced in a rigged plebiscite backed by the US. Prime Minister Ngo Dinh Diem backed by the United States and their French allies would take over as President and form a new government. France would have no control but would still have a strong influence on South Vietnamese society. South Vietnam had become westernized quickly but only in the major cities. The country side villages and hamlets continued with their simple lives. A new western power was injecting its influence on the country. Provincial forces would be integrated into the Army of the Republic of Vietnam or ARVN with the promise of support and military aid from the US. The US was already providing military equipment and training to the new ARVN. President Diem was a devoted Catholic and discriminated openly with Buddhist's in his country. The United States tried in desperation to have President Diem tour the country to gain the support of the people. Instead he confiscated land owned by Buddhists. Civil unrest in the cities saw students marching in protest. The Diem government would be riddled with corruption and nepotism. The stage was set for more war in Vietnam.

Trang along with Hung and a few others travelled north along known routes in Cambodia. After travelling for weeks, they turned east towards Khe Sanh. It was there that they learned of the Geneva proceedings. Contacting Hanoi, Hung learned that all Viet-Minh forces were to remain in place in their jungle bases. Before becoming President, Diem acting as Prime Minister urged all Catholics in the north to flee south. At the same time, Buddhists were fleeing to the north. Hung learned of the arrests and the executions of Viet-Minh comrades who had returned home to their villages. He had seven men with him and he ordered them to return to a base in Cambodia. He and Trang would stay in a safe house in Khe Sanh.

"Once again the west interferes. When will they learn. Vietnam is destined to be one country, independent and free. Now we have a new puppet to contend with. The Japanese propped up the cowardly French. Now it seems the great United States will prop up this Diem fellow. I'm confident that Uncle Ho and General Giap will crush them as well," Hung declared to Trang clearly angry.

"I believe it too, but the US is not like the French. It will take us many years to defeat them."

"We are a strong people. Those that defend their homeland cannot be fully conquered. We will prevail," Hung offered.

A small crowd had gathered at the front door of the hospital to welcome a hero going home. Mike was embarrassed by all the attention.

He had done his job. His father helped and was now gone. A good cop up until the end. The hospital insisted on him leaving in a wheel chair. His chest wound healed nicely as well as the one on his leg. The knee still bothered him. He waved and shook hands with his family and friends. It was time to go home. Arriving at the beach house he was happy. Stepping out of Kevin's car the first one to greet him was Cupcake. The big overweight bulldog jumped up and banged into his leg sending spasms of pain through his knee. Mike did not care. He was pleased to see his buddy. Most of his family and friends came home with him. Beer was packed into an ice cooler and the kitchen table was filled with food. Mike sat in his chair and thanked everyone. Susan was just pleased as he could be that he was home. Colleen had come with Hope and she brought little Jack with her. Mike had not seen much of the boy but they became buddies quickly. Playing with Jack reminded Mike how he used to play with Dylan. Adding Cupcake into the mix just made it more fun for them both.

Once things settled down Dorothy sat next to her uncle and told him, "Thank you. I'm glad your all right. I'm glad that Grandpa killed that son of a bitch. I wish he were here so I could thank him too." Mike took her hand and replied, "He is. Just like your Grandma they are always with us, right here." Mike held his hand on his heart and Dorothy gave him a hug.

"Everyone tells me the nightmare is finally over. It's not Uncle Mike. I still live with it every day. It just won't go away."

"You can have your life back now," Mike replied.

"That's what everyone tells me. When I heard that you were getting close to catching that bastard...I thought, Oh God. Now I have to face him in court. I was going to have to relive the entire thing all over again. I could not sleep for days. The nightmares. Every time Steve tried to hold me I pushed him away. Now this. You were almost killed and now Grandpa is gone...all because of him. God forgive me...I am so happy he's dead. I only wish he would have suffered." She was crying now and Mike held her. Don't cry sweetheart. It is over. He can't hurt you anymore. You have to find your life again. You have a good husband. Your parents are the best. You can take it all back and put Williams out of your life. Plus, you have the handsomeness uncle in the world."

Dorothy laughed and wiped the tears from her eyes. "I'll try...I promise."

" Good girl now go over there and give your husband a hug and tell him, you love him."

Dorothy smiled and crossed the room to Stevie. She hugged him and whispered, "I love you."

I know, I love you too," Stevie replied. The marriage had been rocky. The news about her attacker about to be caught really affected her more than usual. Stevie had been thinking about a divorce. He still loved her, but he knew that living with her was going to be hard. Maybe too hard. Time would tell.

The little beach house was crowded. Even Michael Costigan had come down from New York. He was sitting with Colleen at the kitchen table. "We have not seen you for some time. How have you been?" Colleen asked.

"Good. I have a nice quiet life in Manhattan. The only thing I regret is the cold weather. I think I got accustomed to warm weather. Winters in New York are no fun. Tom say's I should go back to Havana. I'm giving it some thought."

"Really, and is he going with you?" Colleen asked.

"Yes, he is very enthused with the idea. Havana is really getting to be a big tourist attraction. The hotels and casinos are always crowded. That might be too much hustle and bustle for me. I think about a little cottage somewhere near the city on the beach," Michael replied.

"I don't know. The politics on that island are troublesome," Colleen said.

"Well, like I said. The hotels and casinos are booming. That means lots of jobs. Of course, that also means property values are going higher. I wish I still had my old place in the city. A nice apartment with its own private parking just two blocks from the beach. I made a good profit when I let it go…but now I bet I could get twice what I got."

"To bad we all don't have a crystal ball," Colleen answered.

Little Jack interrupted them, "Gammie, I want a cookie."

"What do you say?" Colleen replied.

"Peeze give me cookie."

"Here you go sport, have two cookies," Michael laughed.

"Ohhh," Jack said smiling and walking away.

"I suppose things have been tough for Hope. I mean a single mother with no husband. Our society is not very tolerant of these things," Michael inquired.

"Yeah, but Kevin had her named changed to Randall. That way if anyone asks she can claim Jacks father was killed in Korea.

Which is true. Most people just assume she is a widow whose husband was killed in the war."

"She works for the Department of Veterans Affairs, right?"

"Yes, she is an administrative manager in the nut department. She complains about the paperwork. She tells me that someday, someone is going to complain about all the trees that have to be cut down just to keep the paperwork flowing."

Michael chuckled, "Our tax dollars at work. Has she been seeing anyone?"

"She has had a few dates here and there. Most men run away when they know a child is part of the equation."

"How about the father's family? How did they take the news about a grandson?"

"Oh, my God. I went with her when she told them. Don't get me wrong, they are wonderful people. But you could cut the tension in the room with a feather. Jack's Grandmother, Kay is such a strong and kind-hearted woman. She was delighted. Her husband, got his dander up a little, but she straightened him out pretty fast."

"Sounds as if you are all one big happy family?"

"Yes. You could say that. Kay and I share babysitting with Jack. We get along great. We have a lot in common. Her husbands a Judge in Delaware County."

"Really, that's impressive." Michael added.

"He's turned out to be a nice man. He loves little Jack. So, I guess everything worked out for the better."

"He is a cute kid. I wonder where he gets all that energy?" Michael asked.

"I don't know. Do me a favor if you find the source, destroy it...JACK NO NO honey don't pull the dogs ears!"

Colleen got up to pull Jack away from Cupcake.

Tension in the city was as thick as the surrounding jungles. Saigon had become a hot bed of protests. Caroline was ordered to take her revolver whenever she left the new Embassy building. She could not understand how her government could support Diem. The man was a pig in her opinion. He held lavish parties at the Presidential Palace. The only good thing he accomplished was the crackdown on the Binh Xuyen crime enterprise while he was the Prime Minister. They had full control of opium dens, prostitution and gambling in the hotel casino's. He had appointed his younger brother Ngo Dinh Nhu to be his chief advisor. He would later take control of the South Vietnamese State Police. Intel reports crossed her desk every day. She had a clear understanding of what was happening in the country outside the city. Diem confiscated land from Buddhists and gave the land to his Catholic supporters. His army along with the various police units were sweeping the villages and hamlets searching for and arresting suspected Viet-Minh suspects. Many were shot while 'attempting to escape.'

Those who had returned to their villages found themselves returning to the safety of the jungle. The Viet-Minh recognizing the threat began to restock and fortify its jungle camps.

Duong returned to his hamlet of Phu Loc. It was located where Tai Lai Road that intersected with HL120. Once there he learned that his father had been arrested by the ARVN. No one knew where he had been taken, but he was told that he was near beaten to death. The ARVN were also looking for him. He would not be able to stay. Sadly, he was told that his mother had died from a snake bite while working in the fields. With a heavy heart, he left his hamlet travelling south down Tai Lai Road. Once he was out of sight of his hamlet and there was no traffic to be seen in either direction he turned west into the jungle. The only place he thought he could go was to the camp where he taken Trang. He reached the camp by nightfall. He had a sack with some clothes, food and Trang's old M2 carbine. He still had the old French revolver as well. The jungle had started to reclaim the camp site so he knew that he had work to keep him busy starting the next day. That night alone in the jungle he mourned the loss of his mother. Based on what some friends had told him he believed his father was dead as well. At dawn, he woke and looked around the camp. His training by the Viet-Minh told him the first thing he needed to tend too were the traps that were placed around the approaches to the camp. Having set them with his father he knew their locations. He made repairs and replaced the camouflage, then returned to the main camp area.

It was then that the thought struck him. Where was the girl? He had not seen her when he went home and she was not here. No one had been here for some time. The thought troubled him. He began his work.

Clearing the camp area was hard work. He had a good pile of leaves and branches. Some would be used for kindling and firewood. The greener and fresher waste would have to be scattered around the jungle. Piles of dead vegetation were indicators a camp was nearby. It was when he was getting rid of some of this that he saw the small mound covered by an old log and some stones. He had found the girl, but had no idea of how she perished. The discovery made him sad again as he thought about his own family. Nearby he also found another mound that had been camouflaged. It was not a grave. He cleared away the dead brush and dug into the earth. He cleared a small hole about a foot deep when he exposed a heavy canvas. Digging deeper and making the hole larger he found a wooden crate wrapped in the heavy canvas tarp. Working the rest of the day he was able to get the crate out of the ground. The tarp would be useful for shelter. Inside the crate, he found six AK-47 rifles.

Each had been wrapped in a heavy paper packed with cosmoline. At the bottom, he found bandoliers of ammunition and magazines for the rifles. He removed a bandolier containing ninety rounds and three magazines. He took one rifle and returned to the camp. It was getting dark. Tomorrow he would rebury the other rifles and place new camouflage. This camp was used to resupply travelling Viet-Minh. The discovery of the rifles led him to believe there would be other caches of supplies around the camp.

He spent two weeks alone in the jungle. He made sure to patrol the area surrounding his little camp. He did find more supplies. He had no food nor did he find any. He was living off the land. Beside his own clothes, he found more. He found a shirt and a pair of pants that fit him among some clothes he found in a nearby cave. It was a uniform. A soft jungle hat also fit him. Had he a mirror he would see that he looked just like some of the men who had trained him. Thinking about the fate of his family, he decided to become a freedom fighter that Hung had talked about. He had no idea where they would be. One thing he did know, this camp was set up as a resupply point. Sooner or later they would come. He had a purpose in life now. He would either run this camp like his father or go off with the first group that showed.

CHAPTER 25

SECRETS

S ummer at the Jersey Shore was to be a new experience for little Jack. Sun, sand and the ocean were all new wonders. The best part was chasing sea gulls with Cupcake. Mike was fond of the little boy. It reminded him of those days that he played with Dylan. He was getting old. Colleen decided to stay a few weeks with Jack. Mike was recovered from his wounds but the leg still bothered him. Susan had convinced him to retire. The beach patrol jeep went by every morning and Jack and Cupcake chased it. Mike did not miss the job. He had had enough. Ocean City was no comparison to New York but enough was enough. He spent his mornings after breakfast watching Jack and the dog play on the beach at the surf line. Susan and Colleen sometimes joined them but for the most part mornings on the beach was guy time. Dave also retired a few weeks after Mike. They saw each other on a regular basis. Mike found that spending his mornings on the beach tired him out. After lunch with the girls, the three boys would take their afternoon naps. Mike missed his father. Reflecting, he knew that time he had with his dad was invaluable. He thought about Jack who would never know his father, except from stories he would here from his mother and grandparents.

The Randall's came to the shore that summer for a week. They stayed in a boarding house not far from Mike and Susan. Mike liked them. He took notice that Kay and Colleen seemed to be close. He got along with John Randall. They both had things in common. The judge was aware of the attack on Dorothy. "I would have sent the son of a bitch to old sparky so, fast," he would often claim. Mike's first summer after the shooting would be time of new adjustment. The quiet and lonely winter months to come would start to change him. Idle hands were the devils workshop. Idle minds would bring memories long ago buried.

Mike enjoyed the summer months. During the spring and fall the weather was tolerable but these were times little Jack would be home with his mother. He found that he missed not having him around. The boy kept him busy. They played in the sand, walked on the beach and Mike started teaching him to surf fish. Jack was a smart kid. He learned quickly. He looked forward to his summers at the shore with his Aunt Susan and Uncle Mike. Grandpa and Nanna also spent a week or two at the shore during the summer. His Aunt Joyce would come on the weekends sometimes. For a little boy life was perfect with one exception. He had no father. He knew that his father had been killed during the Korean War. He was a war hero in World War II as well. The closest person that would fit for him, or as he saw it was his Uncle Mike. He talked with his uncle as they walked the beach together. He was a war hero too. He had also been a policeman.

Much to Hope and his other Grandmother Colleen's dismay he had an obsession with the police and the military. It was not a life either of them wanted for him. They tried to expose him as much as they could to his Uncle Kevin. He loved his Uncle Kevin. He saw him as a successful lawyer like his Grandpa, but that held no interest for the boy. Uncle Mike also told him the stories about his Uncle Dylan during World War ll. He was still overseas in the Philippines. There was something mysterious about him. They had only met twice. He worked for the government but Jack was never told exactly what he did.

As a young boy, Jack read a lot. He brought home books from the library about the Secret Service, the FBI and the US Marshall's. He read books about the world wars. The first real book he ever read was an English assignment in school. It was titled 'Hot Rod'. He did a book report and received an A. He was ahead of his classmates when it came to reading. One day at the library he wanted to check out a book by Leon Uris. The title was 'Battle Cry'.

The work fascinated him. He liked one of the characters whose name was Marion. It was the same name of one his favorite movie stars, John Wayne. He saw all of his movies at the theater with his friends. Uncle Mike had given him a 'Mattie Mattel' gun set for Christmas. It had a Thompson machine gun and a Colt .45 with a holster. Uncle Mike had a real .45, and showed it to him one summer. He was looking forward to this summer because Uncle Mike was going to take him shooting. It was a secret between the two because his mother hated guns. The school year ended and plans for Jack to go to the shore had been made. He was ready.

Dorothy lay in bed staring at the ceiling. Steve had already gotten up preparing for work. Their relationship was cordial. They did not argue or fight. At the same time, they were not happy. Steve wanted to start a family. Dorothy would like that as well but that would mean they would have to be sexually active with each other. She loved him. There was no doubt about that. The one person that was with her during her recovery that never wavered was Steve. Before they were married he was so kind, gentle and patient. She thought she might have a chance of a normal life. But the creature in her life came back. Her Uncle Mike and her grandfather had found the man that changed her life. Thoughts

283

of testifying in court frightened her. Reliving the nightmare and seeing him again was unbearable. The nightmares returned. Any attempts of intimacy by Steve was rejected. Sometimes angrily. Eventually he stopped all together. She needed to do something. Today she would see a therapist. She had made the appointment without anyone knowing. Maybe she would find the answer to help her to be happy again. If not, she dreaded the possibility that Steve might divorce her. She was getting desperate.

Her appointment was for 10AM. She was early and waited in the outer office of Doctor Kevin Laughlin. At the top of the hour Doctor Laughlin opened his office door and invited her into the office. "Good morning, Dorothy how can I help you?"

"I not sure where to begin. I'm here because my husband and I are having some trouble."

"I see, what kind of trouble?"

"Well, we seem to be getting further apart."

"Does your husband know you're here?"

"No"

"What's your husband's name?"

"Stevie, Steven."

"All right."

There was a brief moment of silence. Doctor Laughlin waited patiently. Dorothy fidgeted in her seat. Then Laughlin asked, "Are you still in love with him?"

"Oh, yes. Very much so." Then she began telling him the story about how they came to be married. Before she knew it, the hour was up. Laughlin listened intently and made notes as she spoke. "I think I can help you. I will have to see you again. This is a healing process for you. We will have to get into your feelings about what is bothering you. One of the things I want you to think about is what happened to you. You never said why you were hospitalized. Let's explore that next week when I see you again. Is the same day and time next week good for you?"

"Yes, that would be fine."

"Good. In the meantime, you have my number. If you feel you need to speak with me, please call me at any time."

The session ended and Dorothy left the office. She knew that she needed to relive the horror of her attack again.

But, Dorothy was committed to getting better. She liked the doctor. She felt like there was hope for her and her marriage.

She returned home and sat with her mother. She confided with her about her doctor's appointment. Maggie was supportive and promised to keep their talk between them. Maggie was confident that the doctor would be able to help. She also expressed her happiness that Dorothy was finally going to face her demons.

Finished with his daily patrol of the camps perimeter, Duong was looking forward to lunch. He had been surviving on fish and plants. Today he had been lucky. He came across a pheasant and was able to shoot it. Cleaning the insides and getting the feathers off was a task he learned years ago, with chickens. Returning to the camp he prepared a small fire. What he really wanted was some rice for a perfect meal. This would do very well today and he expected to have enough meat for his dinner as well. That night with a full belly he heard men in the jungle. They were getting closer. He took his AK47 and left the camp. He would need to know who these men were. They had been travelling along the river and getting close to the camp. He made contact with the point man of a small unit carrying supplies. Keeping his AK ready he called out, "Welcome comrades, I am Duong."

The point man was startled at the sound of his voice. Some of the other men in the small patrol were surprised as well. One of the men answered him by saying, "I am Wong comrade. We were told no one would be at the supply camp."

"My father used to take care of the camp. He was arrested by the ARVN."

"Lucky for you then, we are not ARVN. We have been sent to add supplies to the camp. We have food and medicine. How long have you been here?"

"Several weeks."

"I knew your father. Phan Tuan was a good man. I'm sorry he has been arrested. The last time I saw him I brought him news of our great victory. He should not have gone home. Uncle Ho has ordered all southern born Viet-Minh to go north."

"I have had no contact with anyone since leaving the camp south of the lake. I went home and was told of my father's arrest. I learned that the ARVN were also looking for me. I returned here. I had nowhere else to go. I knew someone would return to the camp sooner or later."

"The camp will receive supplies on a regular schedule. More Viet-Minh will also be coming. Let us go back into the camp. We will talk more in the morning," Wong stated.

Duong led the men back to the camp. Putting down their heavy packs they went to sleep. Duong stayed awake for some time. He was not sure what his future had in store for him. His path in life had been chosen by things he knew very little about.

The next morning everyone was awake at dawn. Wong was the first to rise and was making tea. Duong sat with him by the fire and asked, "What will happen now?"

"Those two will remain here for a short time. You and I will find a new camp location closer to the river. Your father's arrest means the ARVN will learn about this camp. We will have to move all of the supplies to the new camp."

"My father would never tell them about this camp. He is a brave man," Duong said.

"Your father will be tortured. Everyman reveals all that he knows. This changes my mission. I have no choice."

"What mission?"

"My mission was to re-supply this camp. Then take your father to the headquarters of my unit. From there I imagine they would have sent him north. Once there he would be assigned to a unit and receive training."

"I would rather stay here," Duong answered.

"Duong, you are a soldier now. Soldiers follow orders. There is nothing for you to do here. You have done a fine job repairing the camp. I will make note of this in my report. There is no choice in the matter. You said yourself you cannot return home. The ARVN are looking for you."

"Maybe I could go to another village."

"Even if you stay here in the south they will arrest you. The ARVN will torture you. This camp and whatever else you know will be at risk. Do you understand?"

"Yes," Duong answered feeling hopeless.

"Good, have some tea and rice. You and I will leave within the hour."

Wong then went over to the two men that came with him. They had a short conversation. Both nodded their heads. Duong thought about his father. Tortured. The seeds of avenging his father's fate had been planted in a young man. Wong was right. He was a soldier now.

Leaving the house early, Jack and his Uncle Mike drove to Woodbine NJ. The drive took about thirty minutes. Mike gave verbal instructions to the boy along the way. Their destination was a range used by local shooters. Mike brought three pistols with him. The old Colt .45 he had brought back from France and his father's old Schofield. Both of those were too much for the young boy to handle. A few weeks ago, he purchased a Colt Peacemaker in .22 caliber. Jack had no idea Mike had made the purchase for him.

Arriving at the range Mike made Jack repeat the rules they discussed on the way. "Always point the gun in a safe direction. Always assume a gun is loaded. Never point a gun at anyone," Jack recited.

"Very good. Mike unpacked the two big pistols from the canvas bag he carried. He set them both down on the wooden bench. Then he took out the box containing the new revolver. "This is yours. Call it an early Christmas present."

Jack looked at the box. COLT was in big letters above a picture of a cowboy gun. "Wow, this is really neat, Uncle Mike. Thank you!" Jack was excited beyond words. Opening the box, he broke the first rule. Taking the gun out of the box he turned it over and over in his hand looking at it. "Hey, remember the rules buddy!"

"Oh, sorry." Jack's smile beamed across his face.

Mike showed Jack how to load the revolver, taught him about sight alignment and how to hold the gun. Soon they were shooting and to Mikes surprise Jack was a natural. At ten, twenty, thirty-five and fifty feet Jacks shot groups were all in the 9 point or 10-point bulls eye rings. Mike tried the new revolver and matched Jacks performance until he got beyond the twenty-foot range. He was still on the target but the groups were much wider. Beyond twenty feet the target was just a blur. Jack was thrilled to be shooting and enjoyed the competition. Beating his uncle on the long range targets the first day was a memory he would keep forever. Once they finished Mike showed Jack how to disassemble and clean and reassemble all three pistols. The range had a snack bar and they had hot dogs for lunch.

"Just so you understand the Colt stays here locked in the toolbox, OK," Mike told the boy.

"I know, and don't tell my Mom," Jack smiled.

"Right."

"Suppose a burglar breaks into the house. Should I defend Aunt Susan?"

"No. Aunt Susan can take care of herself. She's tougher than both of us."

"Uncle Mike, when I get older do you think I should go in the Army like you, or the Marine Corps like Uncle Dylan?"

"I thought you wanted to be an FBI agent."

"Nope, changed my mind. Besides when I join I'll be eighteen. After twenty-years I'll be thirty-eight. That's not old like you. Maybe I can still be an FBI agent. Or maybe I can do the Army and the Marines. Can you do that? Wait maybe… I can be an undercover guy in the FBI investigating the Army for a while."

"All of that is a long way off buddy. Right now, you just concentrate on your school work. You can't do any of that stuff if you're not smart. Keep up your grades and you can be whatever you want."

"Mom wants me to be a lawyer or a doctor. Boring! I want to be like John Wayne or Aldo Ray. Did I tell you they made 'Battle Cry' into a movie? I saw it at the Fox theatre down town at Easter time. It was just like the book. This is my rifle, this is my…"

"Hey enough of that. Your mom doesn't like it."

"But it's funny!"

"All right, it's funny but your mom doesn't think so. Look kid real life is a lot different than what you read in books and see in the movies. There are a lot of bad people out there. The only way to stay ahead of them is to be smart. Fighting with guns is never fun. It's nothing like the movies or TV. Remember that."

"I know stay in school, get all A's."

"Nothing wrong with getting all A's."

"School is so boring."

"Your Mom was a good student. She was a nurse in the Army, and she is a war hero too."

"Mom, a war hero. I don't think so. My dad was a war hero"

Then Mike told Jack the story of how his mother was wounded and fought back and killed a North Korean soldier. He also told him about how the Army gave her a medal for getting wounded. "Wow, that's so neat. How come she never told me?" Jack asked.

"Because your mom and grandmother Colleen don't want you to go into the military or be a policeman. Women worry about these things, Jack.

They're always crying about how we can get hurt and stuff. It's just the way they are. So now you know about your mom but let's keep it as our secret."

"We have a lot of secrets Uncle Mike. I might need to make a list."

"No list. You start righting this stuff down and someone could find it. Then it's not a secret anymore. Memorize. That way no one can know."

"You don't want to get in trouble, huh?"

"WE get in trouble. WE! Not just me. Besides, us guys gotta stick together. Right?"

"Yup, I got it."

CHAPTER 26
GETTING BETTER MOVING ON

Doctor Laughlin sat in his chair waiting for Dorothy to answer the question. She had been fighting with this all week. She knew if she were ever to get better and save her marriage she had to face the events that had changed her life. She told him about the attack. She talked about her physical injuries. Then she told him how it all came to an end. Her grandfather dying from heart failure and her uncle almost being killed in the gun battle that ended it all. In each part of the story she went into great depth and detail. When she was through she found herself with tears in her eyes and a feeling of exhaustion. Like she had been running. She was breathing heavily. Laughlin sat through it all taking notes. "How do you feel now?" He asked Dorothy.

"What? I don't understand."

"How do you feel? Right now, this very minute."

"I feel so tired. I'm out of breath." She took a deep breath. "I don't know...relief? Like maybe I finally...got it all out...I'm not sure."

"You went on a bit of a tangent. You described everything in vivid detail. "I saw and heard anger, fear, and disgust. But there was also love, tenderness and appreciation. You went through an entire range of emotions. Our session is almost over..."

"What, how can that be. What time is it?"

"You spoke for nearly forty-five minutes non-stop. Do you remember everything you said?"

"No, well, yes I suppose."

Dorothy looked at the legal pad Doctor Laughlin used during her session. He had several pages of notes he had taken. "I want you to come back next week. Same day and time every week. Is that all right?"

"Yes, I can arrange that."

"During this week, I want you to focus on just the initial attack. This is where the anger, fear and disgust came from you today. Try to remember everything you said. Try to focus on the emotions you experienced as you remember todays conversation. Can you do that?"

"Yes… I think so. I'll try."

"Very good, then I will see you in a week. You have my number if anything happens."

"Thank you, Doctor." Dorothy left the office and walked home. She tried to go over everything that she said as she walked. I must have really rambled on she thought.

Arriving at her mother's house she sat and had coffee with her. Maggie was very happy today. A letter from Dylan had arrived, he was coming home for a few weeks. He was scheduled to arrive the following week.

"How was your session with the doctor?"

"All right, I suppose. We talked about the attack. Actually, I talked about the attack, my injuries and the aftermath. He did not say much, but I see him again next week."

"Are you going to tell Steve you have been seeing him?"

"Not just yet."

"I know he loves you, honey. He was always there for you. He will be now. Try to remember that."

"I will. It's just so hard to talk with him about it all. I really opened up today. I imagine that talking to a stranger helps some. There's no judgement there. He just listens. Maybe that's what I needed. Just to be able to speak about it all without having to worry about any opinions one way or the other."

"Well, one thing is you are talking about it. You can only get better from here. Maybe seeing your brother is going to help too. Having the family around for support goes a long way."

Dorothy spent the rest of the day thinking. Soon Steve would be home from work. She left her mothers, went home and prepared dinner. She decided to fix his favorite, fried chicken.

Another supply camp site was located by Wong. It was closer to the river and it was 1000 meters away from the original site. Located along an L shaped ridge with steep inclines and thick jungle on the river side the inside of the ridge faced an open area filled with high grass and small trees. Defensively it was perfect. Anyone approaching from the north alongside the river would have to navigate steep inclines to reach the top on the ridge. Forces approaching from the south would have to cross open ground with intersecting fields of fire from the top of the ridge. Getting the supplies from the old camp to the new site took three days. The four men were exhausted once they finished. Wong and Duong would leave the new camp after a full day's rest. Wong left the other two men to build defensive bunker positions and secure the camp. He and Duong travelled for four days before reaching a very large base camp. Duong was amazed at the size of this camp. Tunnels had been dug and Wong explained that all of the tunnels reached out from the main tunnel complex to all of the fighting positions surrounding the camp. Inside the main complex there were several hooch's. Under this area was a series of rooms that had been dug out. Wong reported to the camp commander. He was Colonel in the NVA. The camp held over 300 men. He informed him about what had happened to Duong's father and the location of the new camp. The Colonel ordered thirty men to go to the new supply location. Their orders were to build up the camp and relieve the two men left by Wong. The Colonel thanked Duong for his work. He also learned he would be going north.

Two days later he saw another 100 men arrive in camp. They all carried supplies. Some would stay here and others would return north. The men returning north carried their own personal supplies and mail. Duong learned that the trip north would take about two months. He said goodbye to Wong and left with four other men. They were all experienced fighters and had made the trip back and forth several times over the last ten years. Duong was amazed at the dedication of these men.

Although he was an outsider they welcomed him and treated him well. He learned a lot of things during the trip.

Travelling the first week they informed him he was in Cambodia. Here they could relax. The paths they were taking today would one day become the infamous 'Ho Chi Minh Trail.' They travelled more than 700 miles north into Laos. Then they turned east to a base in the town of Ky Son. Arriving in North Vietnam they came out of the jungle unto a road. Hitching a ride on a military truck was easy. They had been walking ten to fifteen miles per day. Along the way other Viet-Minh units were moving south. The base was the home of a battalion of the 33rd NVA Regiment. It would be Duong's new home. He would not fight with the Viet-Minh. He was now an enlisted man of the North Vietnamese Army. He would be here for two years. He impressed his cadre trainers with his knowledge of the jungle and how to live off the land. He excelled in camouflage and setting booby traps. He was also knowledgeable on the AK-47 assault rifle. The time he spent with his father, Trang and the others at the camp where he met Hung had paid off. He quickly attained the position of squad leader despite his age. None of the men in his squad had seen combat. They all respected Duong for his knowledge. The only thing he did not enjoy during his time with the regiment was the political classes he and the others were required to attend. He had no concept of democracy. Communism was all he knew. It's not that he disagreed with the political concept, he just found it all so boring. The soldier's life is where he found a home.

Dinner was ready when Steve came home from work. The smell of fried chicken greeted him as he came in the door. "Oh boy, chicken. What's the occasion?" He asked.

"No special occasion. I just wanted to please you. I talked with my mother today and I have been thinking about what we discussed."

"Oh."

"Steve, I have been seeing someone."

The look on his face surprised her. He looked as if all the life had been sucked out of him. Then she realized what she had just said.

"No no not that. I'm seeing a therapist. You know about what happened to me and how all of it has affected us."

"Christ Dorothy!" He replied.

"I'm sorry, I should have phrased that better."

"I should say so. Jesus! So, who is this therapist, and how long have you been seeing him?"

"His name is Doctor Laughlin. He's very nice. I've been to two sessions with him and he has given me a lot to think about. I want you to know I'm trying. I really feel like I can get better. I want our marriage to work. I know this has been especially hard on you. I am sorry, but I will need a little time. I hope you understand."

Steve hugged her. "You're right it has been hard. This whole thing has not only affected you but me too."

"Let's eat before it gets cold."

They sat and ate the dinner. When it was finished, they did the dishes and sat in the living room having coffee. They talked well into the night.

When they went to bed Steve laid there next to her. His mind was racing. Part of him wanted to stay married. He knew it was possible that they could make it work. Another part of him was thinking about the meeting he had just that day with the attorney. His heart told him to stay, his mind told him to go. He did not know it then but it would be a conflict within himself that would last for some time.

A week went by and Dylan returned from the Philippines. He would be home for three weeks and then take on a new position in Saigon. He spent a few days at home with Kevin and Maggie and then drove to the shore to see his Uncle Mike and Aunt Susan. He was able to get a car from the navy yard in Philadelphia. Arriving at the shore home in Ocean City the first one to see him was Jack. Jack had been sitting outside playing with Cupcake. When Dylan pulled into the driveway the first thing jack noticed was the government plates and the star on the side of the grey government sedan. Dylan got out of the car and was greeted by Cupcake. "Hey there Jack. Man, you're really getting taller." Jack had herd that his Uncle Dylan was coming for a visit. "Hi Uncle Dylan."

Mike heard the car and came outside. "Hey there squirt." He called out.

"Uncle Mike, good to see you. How are you?"

"Living the life here at the beach."

"Where is Aunt Susan?"

"At the store. She should be back any minute."

"Uncle Dylan, you want to go surf fishing tonight?"

"You bet, buddy sounds like a plan. What grade are you in now?"

"I'm going into the sixth grade. Uncle Mike and I went shooting..."

"Hey, that's supposed to be a secret remember," Mike interrupted.

"No problem, I can keep a secret. That's my job remember," Dylan said.

"What is your job, Uncle Dylan?"

"I work for the government. Keeping secrets is what we do. I work for the CIA, but don't tell anyone, it's a secret ok."

"Wow, really. Are you a spy like James Bond?"

"Well not exactly. What do you know about James Bond?"

"I read one of the books."

"He reads a lot of books, Mike offered."

"Really, I read a lot too.

Susan pulled into the driveway, and greeted her nephew. Then they went inside for lunch. Jack rambled on about all the books he had read.

Dylan was impressed. Learning about Jack's desire to go into the military reminded him of his days as a boy. "So how does your mom fell about that?" Dylan asked the boy.

"She wants me to be a lawyer or a doctor."

"I don't see anything wrong with either of those two vocations. In fact, a lot of the people I work with are lawyers. A law degree goes a long way," Dylan said.

"Are you a lawyer, Uncle Dylan?"

"No, I'm what you call a case officer. Which reminds me. When I go back to work I'll be posted in Saigon."

"Oh, will you be working with Caroline? She's in Saigon," Susan asked.

"Yea, I have seen her a few times. Part of my transition work has already been in there."

"Where is Saigon?" Jack asked.

"A little country called Vietnam. It's in Asia. The big boys screwed that one up too. Just like Korea," Mike answered.

"Don't get started. He thinks our next war is going to be there," Susan scolded.

"Hey, we already have troops there as advisors. It won't be much longer before we have troops operating on the ground," Mike defended himself.

"All right, enough talk of wars. Let's have a nice lunch," Susan said.

They finished lunch and Mike, Dylan and Jack all went to the beach.

Jack played in the surf under the watchful eyes of his Uncle Mike and the two men talked about world affairs. "So, what's your take on Vietnam?" Mike asked.

"I think you're right. I don't think the Diem government can get the job done on its own. Diem's policies are not popular with the people. The level of nepotism and corruption are mind boggling. The military is very weak. The Viet-Minh or as they're identified now as the Viet Cong still have the support of the people around the country. The Viet Cong are very influential and capable of causing a variety of security issues. I see reports that some of the Provincial forces around the country have been infiltrated by the Viet Cong. Even in the general population young men of military age are farmers by day and Cong at night. The South Vietnamese Army or ARVN are just not motivated enough to defend the country."

Mike added, "I think dividing the country in two was a big mistake. I don't see a permanent DMZ like we have in Korea. The Soviets and the Chinese are very much involved with supporting North Vietnam. They are spending a lot of money in the process, and we are ramping up our own financial support."

"Many people are unaware that American pilots were flying missions at Dien Ben Phu. The CIA is adding more people and we conduct a lot of operations in the country already. The new administration is going to have its hands full."

"That will most likely be Nixon." Mike declared.

"Could be. I can't think of any Democrat that could beat him."

"I just hope it's all over before he gets to be military age. His mother and grandmother would have a fit if he had to serve in a war," Mike offered.

"Knowing what life is like after serving in a war, I can't say I blame them. How have you been? Getting shot at again must have brought back some pleasant memories."

"Christ, I can't sleep. When I do, I dream about that asshole holding that gun. Funny thing is he's a German. Then I see the muzzle blast and wake up."

Dylan replied, "Still haunted by France, and now being shot as a cop. Combining the two must mean something. We should get you a room at Byberry."

"That nut house, no thanks. I know I can be goofy as hell, but anyone coming out of that place is one sick puppy."

Jack came out of the water and joined his uncles.

"Uncle Dylan, do you know 'Wild Bill Donavon'?"

"Donavon, how do you know about him? No let me guess, you read a book."

"Yea, it was about the OSS in World War ll. I read 'Guadalcanal Diary' too. Did you go to Guadalcanal? You were in the Pacific, right? What islands did you go to?"

"Whoa, slow down boot. No, I never met Donavon. I was in China and then the Philippines. Why not read something else like some of the classics, Moby Dick or Treasure Island."

"That stuffs for kids. Hey look Aunt Susan is waving. I bet dinners ready, I'm starving, race ya!"

Jack took off before either of the two men could react. He reached the house in a flash. "We better hurry, that kid eats like a bear coming out of hibernation," Mike said.

"Hey Aunt Susan, guess what? Uncle Dylan called me boot!"

"Of course, he did," Susan replied shaking her head.

Mike and Dylan came into the house. Burgers and hot dogs with potato salad and fresh Jersey tomatoes were on the menu. Much to the dismay of Mike, Jack had already consumed a hot dog. "Hey save some for the rest of us."

"If your fast, you fast," Jack chuckled back.

Susan added, "He's a growing boy, you just a fat old man, getting fatter."

"Hey, I still turn heads on the beach."

"Yea, they all turn away," Jack laughed already wolfing down a burger.

"Don't talk with your mouth full, and you talk more so your mouth is not as full," Susan corrected.

"Man, you really are taking some abuse," Dylan said.

"It's the price I have to pay. You know when you're this good looking other people just naturally get jealous," Mike replied proudly.

"Ha, who's the best-looking guy in the house, Aunt Susan?" Jack asked.

"You are sweetheart. How about another hot dog?'"

"Hey, slow down," Mike hollered.

CHAPTER 27

A TASTE FOR BLOOD

Havana had changed. New high-rise hotels and casinos were part of the city's new skyline. Downtown was a bee hive of activity. Tourists flocked to the island nation like never before. Prices for homes on or near the beach were very high. They decided to look for a place outside the capital on the eastern end of the island. They found a nice home on top of a mountain overlooking Playa Del Mar Verde on the southern end of the island just west of Santiago de Cuba. The view was stunning. Overlooking the Caribbean Sea, they were treated with both sunrise and sunsets. Michael was thrilled and bought the home paying cash. Back in New York, Michael and Tom were forced to keep their lives hidden.

Here in a beautiful home, secluded from anyone they could be free. Once a week they drove to the city for supplies. They purchased an old 1956 Ford Pickup to get back and forth. The home was isolated on the mountain. The nearest neighbors were on the beach along Route 20 which was nothing more than a dirt road. Tom spent most of the day drawing and painting. Michael liked to hike the mountain trails. It was peaceful and quiet. Michael and Tom were very happy. The next few years they would live the perfect life.

Cuba however, was facing a problem. It was not lost on Tom and Michael. But they had confidence that whatever happened on the tiny island their lives would not be affected. Politically the Batista government was as corrupt as one could imagine. A man named Fidel Castro was beloved by the people of Cuba. He and his group of revolutionaries were based in the mountains somewhere around Santiago but they had never been seen or heard from by the two of them. Tom continued to paint and draw and was able to sell some of his work to tourists in the city. Michael took care of chores around the house. One day some men with guns came down one of the trails Michael was walking on. He was able to speak to them in Spanish. His years of living there had perfected his language skills. They showed no sign of being a threat, but the guns they carried was a concern. They were just passing through and were carrying sacks of supplies. They gave him no information as to who they were or where they were going. The encounter still worried Michael.

That night over dinner Michael told Tom of his meeting on the trail. Tom asked, "What did they want?"

"Nothing."

"I wonder where they were going?"

"I have no idea, and they never told me."

"I don't like it. I mean we knew they were around here somewhere. Do you think they know where we live?"

"I'm sure they do. Men like that know these things. We are no threat to them. I don't think they are a threat to us. We are not involved in politics and we live a secluded life here.

We have no contact with the government. Why should they be concerned? Look whatever happens we are just two guys that live here."

"Yes, isolated and alone. Do you think they may want to rob us?" Tom asked concerned.

"And steal what? We only have what we need to live and your paintings. We have no guns. There's no money here. Supposedly they are doing what they do for the people. We are part of the people. There has never been an incident where they attacked anyone."

"Still, I think we need to be cautious. The next thing you know, government soldiers will be here."

Tom was not far from the truth. That spring government soldiers did come into the area. Batista was adamant about finding and destroying the revolutionaries and eliminating them.

During the time of Batista's campaign to defeat the rebels there were several battles that were waged around the mountains surrounding Santiago. Government soldiers were never able to find the camps were the rebels hid. Michael and Tom could hear the gunfire far off in the distance. They decided to go into town to stock up on supplies of their own. In town, they learned that Batista's forces had been defeated and that the town would soon come under control of the rebels. It was the Christmas season and any further military action seemed to be doubtful. Not concerned they stocked up on supplies and returned to their home on the mountain.

A few days later, Tom was working on his paintings. Michael packed a lunch and walked into the jungle west along the trails he was familiar with. He cut fresh flowers and herbs he found along the way. He had walked about three miles when he came across a rebel patrol of ten men and two women. Speaking with the leader of the group in English he learned that Fidel Castro had taken control of Santiago. Batista's forces had been turned back and were in full retreat back to Havana. Both of the women were suspicious of him and their hostility was not lost on Michael. Speaking in Spanish they seemed to be convinced Michael was a spy working for Batista.

They had no idea Michael could speak Spanish fluidly. The two women argued with the leader of the patrol when they were approached by five other men who were also rebels. One of these men was clearly in charge. The two women made their arguments to him about Michael. He had not seen any of these rebels before. Then listening to them discuss the issue the man in charge tired of the conversation ordered them all to proceed north. They had orders to rendezvous with the main rebel unit. Michael heard them mention they needed to meet up with Che Guevara. The women asked what they should do with Michael. The new leader of the group just shrugged his shoulders. Before Michael could say anything one of the women drew a pistol and shot him in the back. Standing on the trail next to ravine Michael fell into the jungle and down the into the ravine. He heard the men shouting at the woman who shot him. Lying in the jungle he stayed still. Recognizing the new leaders voice he heard him say in Spanish, "Enough, the gringo is dead. Leave him and start moving". Then Michael passed out.

An hour later he became conscious again and was in terrible pain. He was lying on his stomach with his head facing the bottom of the ravine. He could feel that his shirt was slick with his blood. He had been bleeding quite a lot. The jungle floor around his face was soaked with his blood. Then he realized he could not feel his legs. The more he tried to move them but the more he tried the more pain he felt, except he could not feel his legs. Now he panicked. Using his arms, he tried to lift himself. The pain was unbearable. He lost consciousness again.

Back at the house Tom worked on his paintings. It was getting later into the afternoon. Michael had been gone all day. He was usually back by late afternoon. He started to worry. As darkness finally came Michael had still not returned. Hiking the trails at night was fraught with danger. Feral cats roomed the jungle at night and were most active after sunset. There was also the danger of roaming too far into the jungle and getting lost. Looking for Michael now was out of the question. He turned all the lights on at the house. He stayed up all night to insure the generator they had kept running. When dawn came, Tom thought the worst. He imagined that Michael had fallen and had hurt himself. He took the large first aid kit they had and left the house. Travelling the trails west of the house he saw little sign of his partner.

He called out his name and listened and never heard a response. By midday Tom knew he needed help. He returned to the house hoping Michael was there, but the house was just as he left it. He wrote a quick note to say he was going into town for help. Starting the pickup, he made the drive into the city.

Arriving in the town he noticed the population in a state of celebration.

Fidel Castro had left the city, but that was not the reason. The revolution had started and was spreading west to Havana. He went to the police station and expressed his concerns about Michael to deaf ears. Instead he was arrested. Tom spoke a little Spanish. Just enough to get by. He learned he was to be jailed as an informant for the Batista government. He protested the charges and was beaten. Then they hauled him off to jail. He spent the next couple of days in his cell alone. Then he was taken to a judge who charged him with being part of the American Mafia. He was sentenced to prison. He demanded to speak to someone at the American Consul in the city. Through bits and pieces and without an interrupter he learned the Americano's had left Cuba. He was all alone, his fate unknown. His only hope was that Michael would find him.

Training was completed and the men of the 3rd Battalion of the 33rd NVA Regiment settled in to garrison life. Now to supplement their initial training they conducted mock patrols, ambushes and built defensive and supply bases in the jungle surrounding the garrison. The soldier's life had taken over Duong. Despite his youth his skills that he had learned impressed his commanders enough that he was placed in command of a squad of men. The primary mission for his squad was the initiation of ambushes. New recruits from another battalion were used as guinea pigs. Duong's men learned the art of patience, concealment and inter-crossing fields of fire. The new recruits learned what not to do. They had all gone through the same training cycle. At one-time Duong and his squad were the victims of ambushes set by those who trained before them. Rifle and pistol practice was conducted as well as mine and booby trap setting. Duong and his men would spend another year here in Ky Son. Then they were informed that the battalion would join other units of the regiment as they marched south.

Duong had made the same trip on the same trails coming north. He was amazed that some of the trails were now roads with bivouac and supplies points along the way. The goal was to move at least ten miles per day. The entire trip would take just over two months. They learned weeks later as they neared their destination, where they were going. It was a large NVA base in South Vietnam. Located in a group of mountains known as the Chu Pong Massif it sat on the western side of the Ia Drang Valley near the village of Plei Me.

The overall NVA strategy was to set up large bases along the Laotian and Cambodian borders. The trails and roads that ran north and south through Laos and Cambodia would be used to keep supply lines open. The central point of command and control was set up in the jungle on the Mimot Rubber Plantation along the Cambodian border north of Tay Ninh, in an area later known as the 'Fish Hook'. NVA units established in their bases would attack eastward towards major towns and villages driving to the coastal cities. Finally turning south to the capital of

Saigon. Their Viet Cong counterparts had set up their bases in the southern most point in the country in the Mekong Delta region. They would simultaneously push north to the capital. The plan was that the weak ARVN army would not be able to sustain a massive and complete assault and would fold up quickly. Not part of the overall plane was US intervention. When Duong and his squad arrived at the Chu Pong Massif, US military advisors numbered over 12,000 and the US would be in the process of building up and expanding the air bases in Bien Hoa and Da Nang.

Duong and his men spent their days digging. Fighting positions were dug at the base of the mountain and the along trails. Tunnels were also dug. Under the mountain entire rooms had been dug out that would be used for communications, supplies and a hospital. In the local Provinces, the Viet Cong had their own network of bases. These were the bases that ARVN units would encounter. Operations along the borders of Laos and Cambodia were rare, ARVN forces were not inclined to mix it up with the NVA.

Patrols were an everyday duty. Squad size elements were sent into the valley. Duong and his men walked northeast on a trail by the Ia Drang river. The area was high grass and small trees and brush. The trail turned east forming an L shape. Duong ordered his men to set up an ambush.

He was not suspecting any enemy so he thought this would be good training. His instructions were that no one would fire until he did. Setting himself were the trail made its turn he realized this was a perfect site. Walking out on the trail he inspected each man's position instructing them about their individual fields of fire and camouflage.

Satisfied by his squad's performance they settled in as if was the real thing. An hour later they heard voices. An ARVN patrol of seven men were coming down the trail. Duong whispered orders to his men to wait for him to open fire. The ARVN patrol was sighted by Duong, he saw they were relaxed. They were talking loudly, sometimes laughing. The point man had his M1 Garand over his shoulder like a he was carrying a pole. The others were at sling arms or held their weapons in one hand. Sitting in silence they waited. The first three men of the seven-man patrol passed Duong. He was aiming at the fourth man that carried a radio. When he reached the bend in the trail Duong squeezed the trigger. The other members of his squad all opened up with their AK-47's killing the rest of the patrol instantly. In total, they killed five more of the ARVN. The last man turned and ran away down the trail. He had dropped his weapon. Duong fired some rounds at him but he cut into the high grass and was gone. Coming out of their positions his squad was ecstatic. In their first combat involvement, they killed six of the enemy who never fired a shot. They gathered up the ammo, the radio and weapons and made their way back to the base camp. Along the way, they encountered another NVA patrol of a full platoon. They had been sent to investigate the gunfire. Duong reported to the platoon leader who was an officer what they had just done. Pleased with their accomplishment the platoon leader ordered them all back to the base camp. The platoon left Duong and his men and proceeded towards the ambush site.

Along the way back Duong thought about what had just occurred. He had killed a man. He was also responsible for the deaths of four other men. Their deaths did not bother him. He had avenged his father whose fate was still unknown to him. What bothered him more was the conduct of the enemy soldiers. They seemed to be undisciplined. He had no idea why they were there. Was this a chance encounter or were these men part of a larger ARVN force. Reaching the base camp, he reported to his platoon leader. Giving him all the details he was congratulated by the officer. The officer took him to the headquarters area. They entered a cave that opened up to a large room that had been dug out. His battalion commander was there. This man was a Colonel.

The officer reported what Duong and his men had done. The Colonel praised him and thanked him for his courage and leadership.

Returning to his squad Duong joined with his squad as they were explaining to their comrades what they had done. Showing off the weapons they captured the men were laughing and celebrating their victory. Duong was already respected by everyone in his platoon, now he had become legendary. He knew now that the war would end soon. The enemy was no match for them. But years later in this same valley he would learn the war would go on for some time when the Americans arrived.

Intelligence reports that came across Caroline's desk indicated that large units of NVA were infiltrating the country along the Laotian and Cambodian borders. The ARVN had yet to engage the enemy in any kind of large-scale battle. Most of the fighting that did occur was in the Mekong Delta region were ARVN units engaged units of the VC in a series of small scale skirmishes. The US was providing training and advisors. Units of the US Army Special Forces were setting up defensive bases with local Montagnard and ARVN Special Forces units north of Saigon in the Central Highlands. They trained these units in all types of tactics and weapon use. The strategy was to patrol the countryside from these bases and deny the enemy any movement in the region. In the Mekong Delta VC forces seized land from property owners and redistributed those lands to the people. Support for the VC from the local population was growing. From her reports to MAAG (Military Assistance Advisory group) it was looking as if the Mekong Delta region was all but lost to the enemy. The first major battle between ARVN forces and the VC would occur years later in January of 1963. The ARVN would suffer their first major defeat. It set the stage for increased US involvement in the war. Despite the demoralizing news, Caroline still loved the country and its people.

Caroline left the office for the day. As per regulations she carried her S&W Model 36 revolver. Student protests in support of the Buddhist monks erupted on a regular basis. Today it was quiet. She left the new embassy and walked to her favorite shops. Shopping in town was always a pleasure for her.

Arriving at the embroidery shop she wanted a new scarf. The older woman who worked there was no longer around and had been gone for some time. Still she became friendly with the two women that owned the shop. "Good afternoon Meilin, how are you?" She asked in Vietnamese.

Her Vietnamese was getting better, but she still preferred French. "Ah, Miss Caroline. So, nice to see you again. I have been fine. Looking for something special today?"

"A new scarf, I think. My mother's birthday is coming. Something with flowers on it."

"Oh, how nice. I have a piece she might like. It is purple with white lotus flowers."

Meilin went to a drawer and took out the scarf. Laying it on the counter she displayed the intricate embroidery work. "My sister finish this just yesterday. She works on this scarf for over a week."

"Oh my, that is really beautiful. Maybe it is too expensive." Caroline knew from experience that all Orientals loved to haggle. Still she knew this piece was going to cost her some money. "For you I make a special price. You are a good customer." A man entered the shop. He was in a heavily starched fatigue uniform. Meilin tensed immediately. The man was an ARVN officer. A major from the ARVN Ranger Regiment. "Is my order ready today?" He demanded ignoring Caroline.

"Yes, Major it is in the back. I will go for it now," Meilin answered nervously. Meilin left the Major and Caroline at the counter.

"That was rather rude Major, what makes you think you are more important than me?"

"I am a busy man. You Americans think you are so special. Are you special, Miss?" The major moved closer to Caroline looking her up and down and putting his arm around her waist.

"Oh, I'm very special Major." Caroline drew her revolver from her pocket and pressed it against his groin. The Major looked down at the gun pressed against his groin and smiled lewdly.

"I see. Let me guess, CIA?" You know that these women here are suspected of being communist sympathizers.

Pressing the revolver more forcefully Caroline answered, "Are you here to arrest anyone, or will you leave that to your wife Major Dinh?"

"You know who I am. So, you are CIA. We are allies, yes?"

"Maybe so, what makes you think these women are with the enemy? How do you know I'm not an enemy?" Caroline asked provocatively.

"Ha, you have a sense of humor, I like that in a woman."

"That's not surprising. I bet Mrs. Dinh never laughs unless she sees you naked." Caroline pressed the revolver even harder.

Major Dinh's face grew hard. He was being insulted.

Meilin returned with a dress uniform blouse with embroidered epaulets and ribbons. Looking at the scene before her she was shocked to see Caroline with a gun pressed against the Majors groin. The three-people stood there in awkward silence, then the Major spoke, "Put the charges on my account. I will pay you later." Turning away from Caroline he took the blouse from Meilin roughly and left the shop.

"I do not like that man. He is rude. He has the hands of an octopus."

"He is what we call in America, an asshole."

Meilin smiled, "I must remember the phrase. He treats my sister and I like we are whores."

"He claims you are both VC."

"No, we are not VC. We are Chinese. My mother killed by Japanese in the war. My father was taken from us. He was brought here by Japanese. He escaped and started a new life here. A few years ago, we were united again by a good Vietnamese man. The older woman who used to be here, I think she was VC. She is gone. She not come back. My father worked with Marines in China. He good man. We wish only to live in peace. Vietnam is nice, but too much war."

"That's very sad Meilin. I'm happy you and your father are together again."

Caroline put the gun away and turned her attention back to the scarf.

"Now then. How much for this beautiful scarf?"

"For you I make special price. Ten Piaster."

"Sold. Do you have a box?"

"Of course, thank you so much, I hope your mother enjoys such a nice gift."

Caroline paid for the scarf and went right back to the office. She needed to look into the history of the Vang sister's.

CHAPTER 28

PRELUDE TO WAR

Summer at the Jersey shore was just what Dylan needed. Long mornings on the beach with Mike and Jack were relaxing. Dylan was surprised at the never-ending questions from his young nephew. The kid knew things from the books he read that most boys his age were unaware of. He was a smart kid. Dylan thought he had a bright future.

He also loved discussing world affairs with Mike. Getting the opinion of the so-called man on the street was interesting to him. Their conversations seemed to always fall on Vietnam. "When Nixon gets in do you think he will expand US efforts?" Mike asked.

"You seem convinced Nixon will win."

"Well, I can't imagine who the Democrats will nominate. Some pansy ass, I'm sure."

"Assuming Nixon is the next President, I would say the US involvement will increase. If US troops become involved, we will most likely defeat the communist in short order. There is however, the possibility of Chinese or Soviet intervention. Then things could get dicey," Dylan answered.

"Sounds like a repeat of the Korean screw up. Maybe we should just push the commies back up north of the 17th Parallel."

"Well, for now all we have is some advisors and military support. The air bases in Bien Hoa and Da Nang are getting built up."

Dylan continued, "To me it seems that any US intervention will be with air power and support. The ARVN worry me though. It looks like they just don't have the stomach for a fight. There is just too much corruption in the government."

Mike added, "One thing we must learn is to stop meddling in other countries affairs. We've already been suckered into two World Wars. Maybe Patton was right. If we had kicked the Russians asses back to their own country maybe we would not be getting into this shit."

"Dicklamats will tell you that negotiations and diplomacy prevent wars."

Mike laughed, "Did you just say dicklamats?"

"I did."

"Aren't you a dicklamat?"

"Hell no, I'm a spy. I gather information. I keep dicklamats in the dark and feed them nothing but horseshit."

Mike replied, "Sounds like a vicious circle of bullshit."

"Ah, yes, it is the American way. Inject ourselves into exotic foreign lands, cram our way of life down their throats, and kill them if they don't behave."

"It seems we have to have a war every couple of years. Our history is filled with it. I don't want that for him." Mike gestured towards Jack playing in the surf with the dog. "It has screwed up my life, your life, shit the whole family has been affected."

"I know. This stick has been with me since the war. My limp is not as bad. I don't really need it, but something just won't let me let it go."

Mike sighed and added, "Susan says I'm drinking too much. I snap at her all the time. In the summer, it's not so bad. Once winter sets in, I go from Jekyll to Hide." Mike lit a cigar. "Funny, every time I light one of these I think about my buddy Jimmy. There was a really nice guy. Damn war turned him into a raving asshole."

"I know my mother told me the stories."

Susan came out and joined them on the beach. "Have you two solved the world's problems yet?"

Mike answered, "Hell no, we're trying our best to create some."

"Have fun, I'm going down to the water with Jack," Susan replied.

Dylan spent a week at the shore with Mike and Susan. Jack would stay with them the rest of the summer. He liked being home but his work was something he missed. Aside from the interest in his work there was also the charms of one Caroline Grindell. In another week, he would leave and return to his new duties in Vietnam. Conversations with his parents and Aunts Colleen and Hope were far different than those with Mike. Jack had impressed him. They spoke at length about communist aggression in the world. Jack was all for putting on a uniform and defeating them like his father in Korea. He knew his father's history as a war hero in Europe beating the Nazi's and again fighting and dying for the liberty of oppressed people in Korea. If he did not know better, he could make the claim the young boy he played on the beach with had been fully indoctrinated.

On the day, he arrived home, his Aunt's Colleen and Hope stayed for dinner. When the meal was finished he and his father lit their cigars and had brandy while the women drank coffee. Sitting at the table the conversation quickly went to Vietnam. "Honey, just what exactly is going on over there?" Maggie asked.

"Mom, the Geneva Convention cut the country in two. The North is communist, and the South is supposed to be a republic. The communist in the north want a unified and independent country."

"So, what's wrong with that? Why can't we leave these poor people alone? It's their country, let them do whatever they want," Maggie replied.

"The problem is the north is communist and the south is a republic," Dylan repeated again.

Colleen then interjected, "So, what. Let the country be united and independent. If they want to be communists then so be it, who cares?

Or if they want they can be a republic they can be a republic. Either way how does it affect us?"

Kevin answered, "A lot of the world's rice supply comes from Vietnam. The country has a lot of rubber plantations as well. The country is rich in timber too. Remember the French developed much of the countries natural resources."

Colleen replied, "OK, there it is the French. We have ties to the French, so we are protecting their interest. They do still have interests in the country, right Dylan?"

"Actually, in the south the French are very much instilled in the social and economic activities. French influence is very much a part of who South Vietnam is," Dylan replied.

Hope now said, "So there you have it. Vietnam our ally in World War II is now split in two because they wanted to be a free and independent nation. Just like us. As a French colony, Paris said no. So, the Vietnamese kicked the French out of their country and western powers via the Geneva Convention splits the country in two so the west in particular the French can still have its stuff."

Dylan replied somewhat taken aback, "Wow. I guess that pretty much sums it up."

Maggie added, "I don't think people in this country care one way or the other about Vietnam. I know I don't. If they want to have a war and kill each, then I say let them have at it. Screw the French. Let them fix it."

"Mom, they can't. The Vietnamese kicked their butts at Dien Ben Phu."

"Right, and again I don't care."

Kevin added, "One thing for sure, Ike has sent in military advisors. Maybe the next administration will see the folly of getting involved and just pull out."

"All I know is, that I do not want my grandson, who is in love with all this military crap to be sent over there to fight their war," Colleen complained.

Dylan lied as he replied, "I don't see that happening. Advisors are one thing, but actual troops in country conducting combat operations are another."

With his leave over Dylan took the train from 30th Street Station to Washington DC. He would be here for eight more weeks before going back to Vietnam. During this time, he went through additional training and a familiarization of Vietnamese culture and customs. Once he left a train took him to Los Angeles. From there he had a flight to Hawaii. He stayed on the island for a day and left Henderson field on a military transport to Guam. One final leg from Guam to Bien Hoa and he was back in Vietnam. The air base at Bien Hoa was under expansion. He was amazed at its transformation in the four weeks since he left.

He bummed a ride with a US Air Force Police jeep going into Saigon. They dropped him at his apartment and he unpacked. He would report back to work in the morning. Now he called the embassy looking for Caroline. She answered on the second ring. "Caroline Grindell, how can I help you?"

"It's me. I'm back. Can you leave early? We can have dinner?"

"Sounds great. The Majestic all, right?"

"Sure say, 1600?"

"All right. I have something interesting to show you."

"Yum, I can't wait."

"Not that dopey. A little project of my own."

317

"Work related?"

"Yes, and it involves you. I'll see you at four, gotta go, bye."

He hung up the phone and thought about what she said. Wonder what she has he thought as he stripped to take a shower.

School was back in session. The sixth grade was no challenge for Jack. The nun who taught him was impressed at how well he was doing. Sister Joan told the class in the beginning of the year that two book reports were required to pass her English class. One was due before the Christmas break and the other before Easter. They were allowed to pick whatever book they wanted as long as it was more than 100 pages in length. Jack had handed her two separate reports before Thanksgiving. The first report was on the 'Ugly American' and the second was a new book published that year entitled, 'Street Without Joy', both books dealt with western involvement in South East Asia. In geography, they were studying South America. Jack had hoped it would be about Asia. He earned all A's in math, spelling and history. He was so far ahead of his class by the Christmas break Sister Joan talked with the principal about moving Jack up a grade. Sending Jack to the seventh grade in mid-term was a gamble. Sister Joan along with the principal had a meeting with Jack and his mother before the holiday break. Sister Carmella who would possibly become Jack's new teacher sat in as well.

It was decided that the best interest of the boy would be served leaving him in the sixth grade. Sister Joan would continue her curriculum. Jack would be allowed to do some extra credit work from Sister Carmella. If he were successful in that consideration would be made at the end of the year to promote him to the eighth grade. The extra work from Sister Carmella would weigh him down, but he finished it all. He told his mother he wanted to stay in his normal grade. He figured out on his own that he would start high school two years younger than most of his freshman class. He had already started grade school early. Hope agreed but was excited none the less for her son's academic future. Instead of Roman High School he could possibly go to St. Joseph's Preparatory High School. That would mean a good college. Hope discussed it all with Kay and they both agreed that would be the goal. Kay's husband had gone to Princeton. Getting him into an Ivy League School was a possibility.

The dining room of the Majestic Hotel was not crowded when Caroline arrived. She had a manila envelope with her. She spotted Dylan sitting at a table in the back of the room. Of course, she thought where else would he be. Smiling she approached the table as he stood to greet her. "Hi, nice to see you. How is everyone back home?"

"They'll all good. I had a week at the shore with Mike and Susan. You would not believe how big Jack is getting."

"Believe me I know. Hope sends me pictures all the time." The waiter came over and they ordered drinks. After looking over the menu they decided on dinner. The waiter returned with the cocktails and took the food order. Once he left Dylan's curiosity was getting the best of him. "So, what is this project you have been working on?"

"Wow. You want to go there right away, huh. Not even small talk about family, friends or maybe even, Honey I missed you so much. I can't wait until we are naked and sweaty," she teased.

"We can talk about family anytime. The naked and sweaty, I'd really like to do right here and now. I don't think that would be appropriate so let's talk about your project."

"All right. There is this little embroidery shop I go to. It's where I buy all those pretty scarfs and my fancy silk pajamas. Which reminds me, I forgot my pajamas," she teased. She waited for him to respond but he was intent on learning what she was about to tell him. He sat there waiting.

"Any...way, there are two women that own the shop. At one time when they started out an older woman was there. Her name was Madame Lam. She is Vietnamese. The two women that own the place are Chinese." The waiter brought the food interrupting her. They started to eat. Dylan was still not sure where this information was going. "Okay, so the woman's a Viet and the two girls are Chinese," he said between bites.

"Yes. Madame Lam has a company (CIA) file. The SDECE has a file on her, as well as a white mouse (South Vietnamese State Police) file. She is suspected of being with the NLF. She has been known to travel throughout the VC controlled Mekong like a butterfly. Her current whereabouts are unknown. Now here is the real interesting part. The mice are really hot and heavy to find this NLF agent known only as 'Gayal'. No one knows who he is. We don't have a file on him. Anyway, this Madame Lam is supposed to know his identity. She was living at the shop with these two Chinese women for just over two years. She taught them to speak Vietnamese. Last year the mice where on her ass when she gave them the slip. She hasn't been back or seen since except here and there in the Mekong."

"So, the Chinese girls are NLF and they might know who this 'Gayal' guy is?" Dylan asked impatiently.

"No, I don't think these women are NLF or anything. They are just what they appear to be, Chinese. They did come here oddly enough with the blessing of the Chinese government. They were given visa's, work papers and identity cards all issued on the same day. Their father has been in Vietnam since the end of World War II. He was listed as a prisoner of the Japanese, who brought him to Hanoi. The Japs have no further records.

"What military records they have only indicated he was missing presumed dead."

Dylan sat having finished his food. He was thinking all of this over.

"To bundle all this up, we have an NLF guy known only as 'Gayal' that the mice are hot for. No one knows his identity. WE...have no info at all on this guy. This Madame Lam is a known NLF agent, last seen in the Delta. Just prior to arrest she slips the mice, from where she was living with these two innocent Chinese women who have suspicious documents. Their daddy was a Jap prisoner brought to Hanoi who is listed as missing presumed dead. My guess or suspicion would be that 'Gayal' is the daddy."

"That the same conclusion I came too." Caroline said proudly.

"Do we have an ID on daddy?"

"Yes. He is a teacher at a machinist school in Dinh Quan."

"That's the village with all the big boulders up in Long Khanh Province?"

"Yes, it is. It turns out the Corps has a file on this guy," Caroline said grinning broadly.

"Our Corps? The US Marines?"

"Yes, submitted by Sergeant Dylan Brogan, USMC, while assigned to Naval Intel in Shanghai China."

"What, holy smoke who is this guy?" Dylan asked shocked at the information.

Caroline smiling broadly answered, "The girls are Vang Mei and Meilin Their father is Vang Bo."

"Oh, my God." Dylan was stunned. He remembered the man. "Waiter."

"Are you that excited for me?" Caroline asked a mischievous smile on her face.

"Forget that, we are going to Dinh Quan."

"Are you nuts? We can't go to Dinh Quan now. Case you haven't noticed it's dark outside. Travel outside of the city is out of the question."

Dylan paid the check and was already heading to the door. "Dylan wait," Caroline said chasing after him. Reaching the street, he was walking fast towards the embassy.

South Vietnamese Army vehicles were racing around the city. Jeeps and APC's (Armored Personnel Carriers) or tracks filled with troops were moving at high speed. Dylan stopped on the corner as Caroline caught up to him. "Somethings happening. We need to get back to the embassy fast," he said.

"What. Where are all these troops going in such a rush," she replied worried.

"My guess is that either the VC are about to attack the city or…A coup is under way."

"Diem has been preparing for this. He surrounds himself with loyalist. If this is a coup we need to notify Washington," she said.

The embassy was only five blocks away. They walked quickly but did not run. Reaching the embassy, they learned that a coup to overthrow Diem was underway.

A new administration would be taking over the White House. The handsome young Senator from Massachusetts had won the election.

Susan was pleased, and Mike was apprehensive. With the winter months setting in Mike became more anxious. Adding to the negative mood, Cupcake was getting old. He was not eating much and his back legs bothered him. Mike knew it was time to put him down and relieve his suffering. Susan avoided the conversation. It made Mike angry. The issue was settled one night when Susan let the dog outside before going to bed. Waiting at the door she noticed the dog walked to the edge of the dunes and laid down. The weather was clear but was chilly. No matter what she did she could not coax him back inside. "Mike, Cupcake won't come in. I'm worried."

"All right, I'll go get him." Mike walked outside and kneeled down next to the dog. Petting his head, he spoke softly to him, "C'mon buddy time for bed." Cupcake laid there with his head down.

Mike made an attempt to pick the dog up, but he just whimpered and refused to let Mike get him. Mike got the message. He wanted to stay outside. Returning to the house Susan said to him, "What are you doing? Why won't he come in?"

"I guess he just wants to stay outside. It would not be the first time he was out all night."

"But it's cold out, it's not summer time."

"Let's go to bed. If he wants to come in, he'll let us know." Getting into bed Susan cuddled up to Mike. "I'm really worried, Mike. He seems so lethargic anymore. I don't want to see anything happen to him." She was crying softly. "We'll see how he is in the morning," Mike comforted her.

The next morning, Mike got up and saw the dog was in the same spot. He went outside and kneeled next to his old pal. Cupcake had passed during the night. Kneeling next to him he cried over his loss. Then he gently picked him up and took him inside. Susan was awake but still in bed. Mike put the dog down next to her. Susan held him and cried.

After a few minutes, Mike went outside to the spot at the top of the dunes where Cupcake liked to lie. He dug a deep hole in the sand. This would-be Cupcakes' final resting spot. Later that morning with tears streaming down their faces, they buried Cupcake.

Susan was sad for a few days. It would take her some time to accept the loss. Mike, however took the death of his dog very hard. He was agitated easily. He often snapped at Susan for no reason. The nightmares of war and his encounter with the rapist plagued him more often. He spent much of his time walking on the beach alone. When he came back to the house he drank more than usual. The loss of the dog brought back long buried demons.

CHAPTER 29

AWARENESS & IDEOLOGY

Diem had survived the attempted coup. Saigon however became a hot bed of anti Diem protests. Buddhist monks were setting themselves on fire. The grisly scene taped and broadcasted to the world by news agencies. Students in the city were demonstrating. Travel by Americans outside the city was restricted. The VC had control of much of the southern Provinces. The Mekong Delta Provinces were entirely controlled by a massive VC build up. ARVN forces were defeated numerous times in that area of the country. Bombings in the city by the VC increased. It looked as if the new republic was on its last legs.

Dylan wanted to get to the village of Dinh Quan. Restrictions on travel outside the city prevented him from getting there. The only thing he was able to do was to visit the shop owned by his daughters. Caroline went with him one morning shortly after the attempted coup failed. "Good morning Meilin. So, nice to see you again. This is an associate of mine; his name is Dylan Brogan."

"Good morning. It is very nice to meet you. How may I help you today?"

Meilin replied smiling.

Dylan, ignoring all formalities was direct with his questions, Caroline tells me you came to Vietnam from China. I'm curious about how your travel here was accomplished. I'm also curious about your relationship with Madame Lam."

Meilin was shocked by the directness of Dylan's inquiry. "Why do you ask me these questions? My sister and I have not broken any laws. Ever since Madame Lam left the government seems to think we are not as we appear. The police have questioned us many times. We have never been arrested."

"Meilin please understand, your father and Mr. Brogan knew each other in China. He would like to see your father again," Caroline interrupted.

Meilin looked at Dylan and replied to Caroline, "Your friend is rude. It seems you and he are with American Police. You are same, same as Vietnamese Police."

Mei entered the store from the rear. She had heard the exchange with Meilin. "No sister. They are not police. They are with American CIA. They lurk in shadows. Why else should they ask these questions. Is there a gun in your purse today Miss Caroline? Mr. Brogan has a gun under his shirt. You claim to know my father. He is like we are. Chinese. We are not involved in Vietnamese affairs. We live here for a better life. We escape the communist in China to be free. Nothing more, nothing less. You should leave now. Do not return. Take your...business someplace else."

Pulling on Dylan's arm, Caroline turned to leave. Once outside she complained, "Thanks a lot. Now I've been banned from one of my favorite shopping spots."

"What did I do? I just asked the questions that needed to be asked."

"Sure, like a dime store novel detective. Meilin was right. You were rude. Damn it, wait here." Caroline left him on the sidewalk and went back to the store. Entering the shop, she saw Mei comforting Meilin who was crying.

"Mei, Meilin. Please I am so sorry. It was not my intent to hurt either of you. You are right, Mr. Brogan was rude."

Mei answered, "Why do you lie to us. We thought you were nice lady. You were a good customer. Now we know you just spy on us."

"That's not true. I have never spied on you or gave any information about you to the Vietnamese. Yes, I admit Mr. Brogan and I are with the CIA. We are here to help the Vietnamese people. I have only been coming here just as a customer. Mr. Brogan was in the Marines in Shanghai during the war. He mentioned your father's name to me in conversation. I told him about you. He just wants to see your father, they were good friends in China."

There was a long pause while Mei thought about what Caroline had just said. Thinking that there was no more to say or do, Caroline turned to leave. As she opened the door Mei said, "My father is in Saigon for a visit. He is in the Hotel Majestic. He leaves for a business trip today."

Caroline found Dylan standing on the corner. "I think I may have repaired the damage you caused," she said to him.

"What damage, I was honest and straight forward," Dylan replied.

"Come with me, your friend is at the Hotel Majestic."

They walked to the hotel and entered the lobby. Dylan went to the front desk and asked for Vang Bo. "I am so sorry sir, Mr. Vang has checked out. He left just a few minutes ago," the desk clerk informed him. Dylan swept the lobby with his eyes. He saw Caroline standing at the front door of the hotel talking with a man. As he approached Caroline gestured towards Dylan. The man turned and introduced himself. "Hello, my name is Nguyen Hung. You are looking for my friend Vang Bo?"

"Yes, is he here?"

"I am sorry to say he has left for Bangkok. A business trip. Your lovely friend tells me you are old friends from China," Hung said.

"Yeah, how do you know Bo?" Dylan asked.

"Dylan, you're being rude again," Caroline noted.

"Mr. Vang and I are old friends.," Hung offered.

Dylan noted the evasive answer, but did not press any further. "Thanks for your help," Dylan told Hung, then waved for a cab. Getting into the cab he told the driver to go to the airport. Caroline was angry. "How do you get by in this country? You have no manners at all."

"Ah huh, just how did you come to meet Mr. Hung?"

"That's Mr. Nguyen, not Hung. He was standing there at the entrance to the lobby. I asked him if he saw a Chinese man leave. He asked if I was looking for Vang Bo. I said that…I…was…oh shit."

"See that's why you're an analyst, not a field agent."

The cab arrived at the airport and Dylan checked the flight status board. There was one flight to Bangkok and it left an hour ago, at 11:30AM. He spotted an American Air Force Security Policeman and showed him his credentials. Together they went to the Pan American desk and asked for the flight manifest. Vang Bo was not on the list.

Exiting the bus, Dorothy walked to Broad Street just south of city hall. Entering the office building she went to the eleventh floor to Dr. Laughlin's office. The session started on time and Dorothy reported that things between she and her husband had improved. "It's almost like before we were married. Steve is very attentive and patient. We are even talking about starting a family. I think Steve has wanted that for a long time."

Dr. Laughlin responded, "Well that's very good. It sounds as if you ready to get on with your life."

"I am. My sessions with you have been helpful. I know those things that bring on the anxiety. I 've learned to confront those. Sometimes it's hard but I find if I put my mind too it I can get through it. I'm still very sad about losing my grandfather." Then of course we have the situation with my attacker and my Uncle Mike."

"Do you see your uncle often?"

"He was just here a few weeks ago, for a visit."

"We were talking about the mess the world has become. He is convinced that we about to get into another war. His wife Susan has told me that he is having more nightmares. He keeps to himself. He can go off the handle at the most trivial thing. I see in him the same things I have been dealing with."

"Sounds as if he is suffering from depression."

"I would not be surprised. He has been through an awful lot in his life."

"You might want to discuss with him that he should see someone."

"His wife Susan has been after him for some time. I suppose things have to get so bad that he realizes he needs help."

"Isn't that what happened with you?"

"Yes, precisely. Susan will win him over."

Dr. Laughlin changed the subject. "We talked about having sessions with both you and Steve together. I think maybe we are ready to take that next step."

"I have not mentioned it to Steve. I think maybe he would be receptive, but then again he may not."

"Will he be able to take time off from work during the day, or do you think we should do evening settings."

"I'm not sure, like I said we have not discussed it."

"Well, let's work on that for next week. How have you been otherwise? Are you still having nightmares? Are you getting enough sleep? How has your mood been?"

"Sometimes I still have nightmares. Other than that, I sleep all right. My mood has been ok."

"Tell me about the nightmares. Do you see yourself in these dreams outside of yourself or are you an active participant?"

"Both. Sometimes I have the same dream. It's dark and dusty. I'm having a hard time breathing. I'm also in a lot of pain. I'm by myself. Then I wake up to a loud noise and a bright light."

"Your brain is trying to resolve your experience. Remember when you regained consciousness you crawled unto the train tracks. The light and the loud noise is the train."

"Why do you think the rapist is not in my dream?"

"I think your subconscious is still dealing with the attacker. He resurfaced when your uncle found him. He is responsible for your pain and the loss of your grandfather. Add to that he shot and almost killed your uncle. Until you resolve those things he will most likely not be in the dream. When he reappears, you may be getting close to resolving the trauma you went through."

"Gee, I thought we were getting to the point that we would be finished. I mean I know that Steve still has to come in…I guess I'm still going to have to too do a lot more work."

"Indeed. Well I need you to get Steve in here and then we can proceed. Call me and make an appointment when he is ready."

"I will." Dorothy left the office. She was going to speak to Steve that night over dinner. She was confident that he would see Dr. Laughlin.

The door opened and Mike came into the little bungalow. "Mike, we need to talk."

"Great here we go again."

"Look, I've seen this before. You know I've had experience with this sort of thing. Dorothy was having trouble. She has been seeing someone. She's getting better. It's not like you have to have surgery," Susan said.

"I'm not crazy."

"Neither is Dorothy or for that matter Hope. The three of you have been in some pretty traumatic situations. Hope has been studying this. She feels that trauma, from an attack or a shooting or even war is the root cause of these things."

"And just what things are we talking about, goddamn it," Mike responded angrily.

"That for one. You lose your temper at the smallest things. You isolate yourself. You would rather spend your time alone than with me or anyone else for that matter."

"That's bullshit."

"Is it? Really. Ever since Cupcake died it has gotten worse. You need to see someone."

Mike went to the counter and grabbed a bottle of Jack Daniels.

"And that is not going to help. You drink too much."

"It helps me sleep."

"Sure, drink yourself into a stupor. Then the nightmares come."

"They don't happen that often." Mike poured a glass of the bourbon.

"How about every night. I sleep next to you. Sometimes you cry in your sleep." Mike took a long drink from the glass. "Sometimes I have to make you turn over or wake you." Mike sat down thinking. He knew that Susan was telling him the truth. Despite that he emptied the glass got up and poured another. "Maybe we should go up to the city for a visit. You can talk with Dorothy. At least consider that, please, Susan said."

"Fine. We can go anytime. I don't exactly have a full schedule."

"Thank you." Susan replied. She got up and went to bed. Mike finished his glass of bourbon, and poured another and finally went to bed. Later that night he had another nightmare.

The next morning Mike woke first. He made breakfast for the two of them. Sitting at the table Susan told him about the night before. "I had to wake you again last night. Do you remember what you were dreaming about?"

"France. I was back in France. I guess something like that never leaves you."

"How could it. Remember Pearl. You thought I was killed during the attack. I know what I went through at the hospital will never leave me.

All those wounded Sailors and Marines. It was terrible."

"So how come you don't have any problems?"

"I have bad dreams too. Sometimes I would like to be alone. What you went through in France was terrible. I guess maybe the shooting is bringing it all back. Losing your father and then Cupcake." Susan began to cry. Mike thought about what she said. They had been through some tough times. Maybe she is right he thought.

Sitting at the kitchen table Kay and Maggie were having coffee. Jack was having trouble in school. His grades had not been affected but he became more rebellious. He was getting into fights. It all started after the additional school work had been completed. Coming back from the shore he had changed. For some reason, he became more aware of world affairs. He was staunchly anti-communist. The growing turmoil in Vietnam and the new crisis in Cuba consumed him. He liked the new President.

Jack had for some reason become very 'hawkish' about the naval blockade. It was very real, and was on TV every night and the President had addressed the nation last night. The possibility of a nuclear war kept the nation and Jack on edge. In school, they practiced air raid drills. They would crawl up under their desks in school waiting for the all clear. As if this would supposedly insure their survival in a nuclear blast. At noon on Wednesday's the air raid sirens would be tested. The world was holding its breath as US Naval Forces challenged all ships bound for Cuba.

"I'm really worried about Jack," Maggie said to Kay. He reads the newspaper and all kind of military books. The news programs on TV really have his attention."

"I know he feels our involvement in Vietnam is worthwhile. This Cuba mess has everyone on edge."

"I know, I'm scared to death. I just hope Mr. Kennedy keeps his wits about him. Hope is really concerned too. You know Jack has all of these pamphlets about the Marines and the Army Green Berets. I feel like I'm reliving this all over again. Dylan did the same thing aa a young boy.

Mike and Susan are coming up for a visit. I hope Mike can talk some sense into him."

Kay asked, "How are Mike and Susan?"

"I guess everything is fine. Jack really looks up to his Uncle Mike. He has been the closest thing to a father for the boy."

"Oh, how I wish my Jack was still here. The boy would have loved him.

He was such a good man," Kay said sadly.

Maggie replied, "I'm sure. But Jack does idolize his father's memory. I remember when Dylan went into the Marines how we fought over it. When it comes down to it there is nothing I could have said or done to change his mind."

"Hopefully this Cuban thing will be resolved. You still have not had any word about what happened to Michael Costigan."

"No. We tried writing letters. Sometimes they just come back as undeliverable. He has not called or written either. I just hope he is all right. Kevin seems to think as an American he may have been put in jail. That would be just terrible."

"Well the President addressed the nation last night. Maybe he will announce soon that Americans still in Cuba will be released."

"I really hope so. Michael was such a nice man. I can't imagine what Krushev was thinking starting all this uproar."

"You think Krushev would know better than to start all this. God only knows what he was thinking."

Jack came home and put his book bag down. He kissed his grandmothers and opened the icebox.

"Don't go filling up on anything, we will be having dinner soon. Oh, by the way your Uncle Mike and Aunt Susan are coming up from the shore."

"Ok, that's boss. When are, they arriving?"

"They will be here for dinner. I think they are going to stay for the weekend."

"Are you going to stay for dinner?" Jack asked Kay.

"No, your grandfather is going to pick me up anytime now. We have tickets to a show at the Pitman theater in Jersey. We will be seeing Red Skeleton."

"That guy is funny. I saw him on Ed Sullivan."

Maggie added, "Don't forget the Globe Trotters are on TV tomorrow."

"I know. Can't wait."

"Do you have homework for the weekend."

"Nope." Jack grabbed a coke and picked up his book bag and took it to his room.

The judge arrived a few minutes later. "Jack, your grandfather is here. Come down and say goodbye," Maggie called up the steps.

Jack came running down hugged and kissed his grandparents as they prepared to leave. Maggie said, "I really wish you could stay for dinner."

"That sounds lovely, but we will be dining at the Pub, before the show," Kay replied.

"I love that place," Maggie replied.

"Enjoy your dinner, Maggie. I will see you again next week," Kay said.

Mike and Susan arrived and Jack was thrilled to see them. When Kevin arrived home from work he greeted Mike and Susan. He made drinks for everyone and then Dorothy arrived with Steve. Everyone sat down to a dinner of pot roast. During dinner Dorothy discussed her sessions with Doctor Laughlin. Mike was attentive and learned that Dorothy was getting much better. Susan said, "See, it's not that bad. All you have to do is talk."

"All right, but I'm not driving all the way up here to see this guy."

"Of course, not silly. We can find someone local."

"Uncle Mike, why are you seeing a nut doctor?"

"Because your Aunt Susan is convinced I'm crazy."

Susan replied, "You're not crazy. Look if this has worked for Dorothy least you can do is try."

Steve added, "Dorothy is really doing much better. I'm going to go with her next week to see Laughlin."

"Aunt Susan, I don't understand. If Uncle Mike is not crazy what's wrong with him."

Maggie replied, "Gee, where do we start. I can give you a list a mile long.

"Ha ha, very funny." Mike said.

"We should compare our lists. I have one too," Susan laughed.

"Go ahead, gang up on me. Have your fun. Don't you worry Jack. By the time, I get done with seeing whoever it is, he'll declare me a genius." Mike said.

Mike and Susan stayed for two days and left to go back home. Mike talked more with Dorothy and found that she was having the same issues he was. Maybe seeing someone was not such a bad idea.

A week later the Cuban missile crisis was over. The Soviets would remove all offensive nuclear weapons from Cuba. As part of the deal the US would remove missiles from Turkey. That part of the deal was kept secret. There was no announcement about the fate of any Americans still in Cuba. The fate of Michael Costigan and Tom Brady was still unknown.

Sitting alone in his cell, Tom Brady heard the guards coming. He had been in prison in Santiago for three long years. Life in the Cuban prison was hard on him. He had been kept in isolation most of the time.

He lost a lot of weight. Down to 112 pounds he was malnourished and sick. He scratched several drawings with a small nail he found on the walls of his cell when he first arrived. It was the only thing that helped to keep his sanity. He was given just two meals a day. A small cup of rice with beans and on occasion some chicken or beef. Whenever he was allowed out in the yard or other places where prisoners gathered he searched for Michael. He was never there, and when he asked, no one had seen him or knew him. The door to his cell was unlocked and two guards motioned for him to come out. He was taken to the showers where he was told to strip and wash himself thoroughly. When he finished, he was given a haircut and a shave.

They gave him a pair of sandals, khaki slacks and white shirt. Then the guards took him to an office where he was met by a Cuban prison official.

Speaking in Spanish the man told Tom he was to be released. Stunned at the news Tom was excited. He was given no specific reason for his release. A few minutes later a man entered the office exchanged pleasantries with the Cuban official and was introduced to Tom. The man's name was Robert LePiere and he told Tom he was with the Canadian consulate. He would be released to his custody. Leaving the prison with LePiere Tom had a multitude of questions. He asked, "Why have I been released?"

LePiere answered, "The US and the Cuban government have made an agreement to release any Americans held in Cuban

Prisons. I will be taking you back to Havana. A doctor will check you over at the consulate and once you are well enough to travel you will be flown to Miami. Your State Department will provide you with clothing and money so you can go home."

"I can't leave Cuba. My home is just outside the city here. I want to go there first. I lived with another man and he was missing when I was arrested. He may still be there."

"How far is your home?"

"Go east on Route 20, the drive is only about twenty minutes."

"All right, we can go that way, but understand I have orders to take you to Havana." They drove along Route 20, Tom told LePiere about Michaels disappearance, and how he had come to be in prison. Then they came to the road that went up to Tom and Michaels mountain top home. Arriving at the house Tom was heartbroken. Vandals had taken everything and the home had suffered extensive fire damage. There was of course no sign of Michael. Falling to his knees after getting out of the Range Rover Tom wept. LePiere could only stand and watch. He felt sorry for the American. Everything he owned had been destroyed. It was obvious no one had been there for quite some time. The fate of his friend was unknown. Consoling Tom, LePiere got him back into the Range Rover and drove back to Havana. They arrived in Havana late that afternoon.

Tom was given a full physical and was told he would stay in the consulate for a few days.

He was told the Canadians would keep him and take care of him. During his time at the consulate he asked repeatedly about Michael. He was informed that the Cuban government was not holding Michael. There were no records of his arrest or that he was even still on the island. Tom's only hope was that his friend had somehow made it back to the US. After a week, he was taken to the airport and put on a plane bound for Miami. The flight arrived and he was met by US State Department officials. He was issued a new passport, $500 and new clothes. He was also given a ticket from Miami to New York, his last home of record. Once he arrived in New York he took a cab to his parent's home in Queens. They had been notified by the government of his pending return. The reunion was emotional. Happy to be home finally he would begin his quest to find Michael.

Another hot and steamy day was just getting started. Duong and his men dug fighting positions and tunnels. Then after lunch in the late afternoon they went on another patrol. For the most part, the patrols were quiet. It was rarity that South Vietnamese soldiers came this far into the territory they controlled. The only real concern was the Montagnard tribesman made up of the Jarai ethnic group that also lived in the area. These people lived a very primitive life living off the land. They were despised by the Vietnamese. The people in the village of Plei Me were always friendly when they came. That would soon change. The new President in the US had approved more advisors and sent the Army Special Forces to Vietnam. The elite force of soldiers commonly known as 'Green Berets' would be setting up camps around the country to help cut off supply lines to the VC and NVA or PAVN. In addition, they would make attempts to win over the local populations. Duong and his men learned from the local villagers that these soldiers had come to Plei Me for just that purpose. This was useful information and Duong reported it to his command operations center dug deep into the mountain base.

Living on the mountain was a rough life. He and his men not only had to be concerned with potential combat but dysentery, malaria and infections that almost always came with any kind of open wound. Poisonous snakes and insects were a constant threat. The base they had established was one of the largest PAVN (People's Army of Vietnam) in South Vietnam. There was a constant supply of food, medicine, clothes and ammunition. All of it stock piled in rooms deep inside the mountain. Duong had been suffering from his latest bout with malaria. The doctors however had plenty of quinine to battle the disease. Once his symptoms improved he preferred to be outside. The fresh air and sunshine helped with his recovery. Once he had fully recovered it was back to the laborious task of digging and patrols. The patrols he did not mind, he hated the digging.

Inside the command center there were maps of every trail marked with every booby trap. In addition, every fighting position, tunnel entrance and small caches of ammunition were plotted, on the mountain and in the valley below. Each man of the 4200 men under General Chu Huy Man's command knew the area as if he had lived there all his life.

They had been there for years. Strategically they were the finest light infantry in the world.

After several months, helicopter landings had been made on a small hilltop just east of Plei Me and twenty miles from the Cambodian border. Heavy equipment was flown in and cleared the hilltop of trees and brush. A defensive perimeter had been set up with barriers made from tree trunks, barbed wire and claymore mines. The camp itself was shaped like a triangle. It was one of many camps set up by the Green Berets in the Central Highlands. Heavy machine gun emplacements on the corners provided interlocking fields of fire. The ten Green Berets assigned to Plei Me also recruited hundreds of the Montagnard living in the area and trained and equipped them with the weapons of modern warfare. The only South Vietnamese soldiers in the camp were fourteen members of the South Vietnamese Special Forces. General Man's objective was to attack and secure the city of Pleiku and control Highway 19 just twenty-five miles to the north. Before he could do this, he was tasked with destroying the

Green Berets camps in the area. All of this was plotted on maps under the watchful eyes of the local VC and the PAVN.

Landing by helicopter at the Plei Me camp, Dylan and officers of the II Corps Command Post would assess the camp and its operations. Patrols by the US advisors and their Montagnard or CIDG (Civilian Irregular Defensive Forces) units in and around the camp had encountered both VC and PAVN units in small skirmishes. Many of the Montagnard had family members living in and around the camp. Listening and observation posts outside the camp had been set up to monitor movements of the enemy forces in the area. Dylan was there to see the effectiveness of the CIDG. Another operation was taking shape.

The CIA would use the best soldiers comprised of the CIDG for Operation Phoenix. These units would be used to infiltrate VC units. The main purpose was to assassinate local VC cadre, political and operation officials. Later during the war US troops would encounter these units and engage them. They would later come under the command of MACV SOG. (Military Assistance Command Vietnam Special Operations Group)

Dylan was impressed with the dedication and skills of the CIDG. He would report back to Saigon that the Phoenix program would be a go. Out in the field Dylan wore civilian clothes but was armed with a .45 pistol and a Thompson. He toured the camp with one of the Green Berets who also took him out to the various listening and observation posts. His escort spoke both Vietnamese and the Jarai Montagnard dialect. He was skilled with explosives, small arms and hand to hand combat. He was also cross trained as a medic. Approaching one of the observation posts he was amazed at the way the CIDG men conducted themselves. He came into the position without even knowing it was there. The soldiers of the CIDG would be an effective fighting force.

The helicopter that would take him back to Saigon lifted off the pad and travelled west. Below him was the Chu Pong Massif a perfect base camp area for PAVN. In just two more years it would be the site of a massive battle between Duong's men and the 1st Cavalry. The stage was set for the battle of the Ia Drang. But first Plei Me would come under attack.

CHAPTER 30

FALLEN LEADERS

Saigon was in turmoil. The latest coup attempt against President Diem had been successful. Assurances by South Vietnamese military leaders that Diem would be allowed to leave Vietnam failed when news agencies around the world broadcast the pictures of Diem and his brother who was his chief advisor had been murdered. The coup was led by General Dương Văn 'Big' Minh. President Kennedy was shocked by the death of the Diem and his brother. Various factions in Saigon would blame each other for the death of Diem. Events in Saigon continued to be in a state of upheaval as another coup led by General Nguyễn Khánh would succeed. General Dương Văn 'Big' Minh would be exiled to Bangkok in Thailand. The successful takeover of the Saigon government would lead the way for a new President Nguyen Van Thieu. With all the turmoil in Vietnam, US involvement in the country came under scrutiny.

Jack was in class discussing his history lesson on the causes of the American Civil War. Sister Carmella was emphasizing slavery as the chief cause, while Jack argued his points about States' rights. The PA system was activated all over the school when the principal made the following announcement; "Attention all teachers and students. We have just learned that during his visit to Dallas Texas, President Kennedy has been shot. We do not have any details; more information will be broadcast as updated news arrives."

Teachers and students were shocked. Everyone was talking and some of the students were crying. Sister Carmella announced to the class, "All right everyone let's calm down. We will continue our discussion about the Civil War tomorrow." Sister Carmella told her class to take out they're rosary beads so they could pray for the safety of the President. The class began praying and had reached the Apostles Creed when the PA was activated again. The principal made the following announcement while choking back her tears; "Attention all…teachers and students. We will be dismissing…classes early today at 3PM. We have received con-formation…that President Kennedy was shot…and…killed in Dallas. I have…no other information at this time. All extra-cur-ricular school activities are cancelled."

On his way home from school Jack thought about what all this would mean. He was convinced this had been done by the Cubans with help from the Russians. Arriving at his house he turned on the TV. Every station was broadcasting the current events live on TV. This was unprecedented. Broadcasters like Walter Cronkite were fighting back their own emotions as they broadcasted the news. Video tape of the motorcade in Dallas was shown. Then there was a breaking announcement that Dallas Police Office J. D. Tippit had been shot and killed. Cronkite and others were shocked, to report the death of the officer and that at that time they were not sure if this was all part of the assassina-tion of the President. Later they would announce that an arrest had been made in Officer Tippit's shooting.

Hope returned home from work early and found Jack in front of the TV. He hugged his mother and his motions caught up with him. He began to cry. Hope cried with him. They sat and watched the events unfold before them on the television. Then the announcement came that a man named Lee Harvey Oswald had been arrested for shooting Officer Tippit. Pictures of the man were shown and later it was announced that Oswald was also the suspected assassin.

The live news broadcasts on all three networks continued into the night that Friday and would be the only thing on TV all weekend. President Johnson had been sworn in and pictures of the event were shown.

The Presidents body was returned to Washington and pictures of Jackie Kennedy in her blood stained pink suit shocked the world. Refusing to change her clothes the now former First Lady wanted the world to see what they had done to her Jack.

On Sunday morning, everyone was at Maggie's house for breakfast. No one wanted to go to church. The entire world was glued to the television broadcasts coming from America. Reaction to the assassination saddened the entire planet. In Berlin, a make shift shrine with flowers was made at the site where President Kennedy had spoken and declared to all world, "Ich bein ein Berliner."

Then it was announced that the suspected assassin would be moved from Police Headquarters to the Dallas County Jail. Everyone watched as Oswald was led out of the elevator. "Someone is going to shoot him," Jack said.

"Jack, why would you say such a thing?" Hope asked as the world watched and heard, "OSWALD." BANG.

Stunned they watched Oswald clutch his stomach as his assassin fired a single shot into his abdomen. "OSWALD HAS BEEN SHOT, OSWALD HAS BEEN SHOT!" Was announced from the screen.

"Dear God in heaven, what is happening," Maggie cried out.

Stunned they were all talking, amazed at what they and the rest of the world witnessed. Kevin asked, "My God, Jack. How did you know?"

"I don't know. It was just a feeling," he replied.

The following day the world watched and listened to the sound of drums that echoed across Washington. Little 'John John' saluted his father's casket as it passed him. The fallen President beloved by the country was laid to rest at Arlington National Cemetery. The same day without any fan fair Lee Harvey Oswald was buried. A group of news reporters would be needed to carry his casket to a lonely gravesite. Lee Harvey Oswald, would take the truth with him, into his grave.

The assassination of President Kennedy held Jack's focus and interest. He read all of the newspaper articles. Somewhere deep inside he felt that there was more to this historical event than was reported. Questions were raised, and the conspiracy ideas were born. Jack was unsure of Oswald's involvement. The young boy growing into a man would always believe there was something more. President Johnson appointed the Warren Commission to investigate the assassination.

His Uncle Mike shared his skepticism. Whenever they were together they discussed the Presidents death, the timing of the Diem coup, and other conspiracy themes. Mike had been seeing a doctor about his own problems. He and Susan had found a doctor in Atlantic City. At first Mike went once a week. He was now scheduled on a monthly basis with Doctor Leo Lewis. They discussed all of his symptoms. Based on the traumas he had been through the doctor concluded Mike suffered from deep depression that was driven by guilt, related to his father's death. The incidents in France had long been buried but resurfaced in their sessions. Mike also had guilt feelings about the loss of Tommy O'Brian in France, and then there was the death of Jimmy. He felt he should have done more to help his friends. He also had to deal with his feelings for Colleen. Mike discovered he had been in love with her all these years and had felt a sense of betrayal towards Jimmy. Doctor Lewis conclude that his marriage to Susan was brought on as a substitute for Colleen. In order to get better he would need to confront and acknowledge his feelings. That meant talking with Susan. He had no doubt he loved her. But he also had buried his feelings for Colleen. Doctor Lewis told him that he needed to be honest with Susan and Colleen. Once the so-called cat was out of the bag, he could concentrate on his guilty feelings. He knew the doctor was right, but he was apprehensive about discussing it all with Susan. The last thing he wanted to do was hurt her. She had always been there for him. During the time that he avoided getting involved in a relationship with a woman, he knew he had avoided it, not because he was as screwed up as Jimmy. But because he was in love with his best friend's childhood sweetheart. Driving back to his home, his mind was in turmoil.

Sitting on the beach the next morning drinking coffee, he lit a cigar to help him relax. "So, how did your session with Doctor Lewis go yesterday?" Susan asked.

Mike sat there in silence, trying to formulate his thoughts. She could tell that something was bothering him. Susan sat patiently waiting for him to begin. Several minutes went by. Finally, he spoke, "We discussed the reason about why I never got involved with a woman. I never really had any real girlfriends. I dated, but I never let anyone get real close to me."

"You said that you never wanted anyone to go through what Jimmy had put Colleen through," Susan replied.

"Yeah, well that's the thing."

"What thing?"

"You know that I love you."

"Of course, I don't doubt that for a second. I love you too."

Mike sat for another few minutes, Susan knowing to be patient remained silent waiting for him to begin again. "The real reason is…I was in love with Colleen."

Susan sat there thinking. She knew he had always been attracted to her.

There was always a special kind of closeness. She was not jealous of Colleen. They were good friends. "Are you still in love with her?"

The cat was out of the bag. Mike knew he had to be forthright and honest. Tears came to his eyes as he replied. "Yes."

Susan felt betrayed. How am I supposed to deal with this, she thought?

"So, all these years we have been together...you were still in love with Collen?"

"I love you, Susan. I don't know how I could have lived without you. You're the best thing in my life. Because of you, I became a better man. I shudder to think what kind of man I would have been without you."

"That does not answer my question. All this time you have still been in love with Colleen, right?"

"Yes."

"So, that night when you got into her bed, you really wanted to make love to her?"

"I wanted to make love to both of you. Christ, how fucked up am I?"

"Really Mike. How am I supposed to deal with this shit?"

"Actually, Lewis wants both of us to go see him, next time. I have all these guilty feelings about you and Colleen, and the war. Then there's the loss of my father."

"I don't know how to deal with this. I really don't. To think that...that night in your head..." Susan began to cry.

"Please don't cry. I never intended to hurt you."

"How am I supposed to feel." Susan got up to go back to the house. "Stay here, please...I need some time to be by myself."

Susan left Mike on the beach returning to the house. She went inside and laid on her bed crying. She thought about the night she and Colleen had played their joke on him. To her and

Colleen it was just a prank. They had always played on his feelings. The flirting between the two of them. Then she felt guilty. She also knew it would change the relationship with her close friend and her husband. Then she wondered if Colleen knew the truth.

Mike sat on the beach and thought about what had just happened.

Now what? Christ, what a fucked-up life I have. Maybe it would have been better to have died that night on the beach when Williams shot me. Or for that matter in France. It seemed to him that that dying would have been a blessing. Great, now I'm suicidal. The cigar had burnt down and burned his fingers. He put the cigar into the sand to put it out. He sat there for another hour. A storm was brewing. But it wasn't just the weather. He felt his entire life was about to change.

Hope was worried. Jack had become more rebellious. The Kennedy assassination made him skeptical of the government. The war in Vietnam was a deep concern for her. Jack spoke of the need to defeat communism around the world. His interest in the military increased. She knew that as head strong as he was he needed some type of male influence in his life. The fact he had never really had a father to talk to as he grew older was an influence in his thinking.

He loved his Uncle Kevin, but he adored his Uncle Mike more. Perhaps she should reach out to Mike. He would be able to talk some sense into the boy. She knew that Mike had been seeing someone to deal with his own problems. The last time she spoke to Susan, she informed her that Mike was seeing a doctor on a monthly basis and was showing signs of improvement. Dorothy was also doing better. Maybe Jack needed some professional help as well. Jack was still doing well in school. But as a teenager she felt he was confused. Maybe a weekend at the shore would give Jack some time to talk with Mike. She decided on a weekend in August. She would call Susan later to discuss the idea. She had no idea that Mike and Susan were dealing with a bigger issue.

She called Susan, but Mike answered the call. Hope discussed her concerns and her plan for Mike to talk with Jack. Mike was receptive, but Hope felt he was somewhat disturbed. She put it out of her mind and looked forward to the weekend at the shore.

Dylan was going over the plan the CIA had for an operation to attack a gun boat base of the 135th Torpedo Squadron in North Vietnam. The operation called for South Vietnamese Special Forces organized by SOG (Special Operations Group) to attack the base the next night at Hòn Mê Island. Commandos would be air dropped into North Vietnam and would conduct the attack on the base. Four SOG vessels would shell the base from off shore in support of the commando raid. The USS Maddox an American destroyer would be operating in international waters near the base. The Maddox was not part of the operation. Everything was in place and the operation was a go.

Dylan finished his work and walked to the Majestic for a drink. The bar was crowded. He ordered a Jack on the rocks and sat at a small table and lit a cigar. Two high ranking MACV officers in civilian clothes that he recognized were sitting at a nearby table. He overheard bits and pieces of their conversation.

"Johnson will have what he needs..."

The noise in the bar diluted the rest of the statements. "Another forty-eight hours..."

"I have all my investments..."

"Washington...or the whole thing..."

"Don't worry...Congress...before the weeks over."

Dylan sat and tried to get more of the conversation. Then he was approached by an Air Force pilot he knew. "Hey buddy, how you been? Where's that pretty lady of yours?"

"Home, more than likely. I had to work late. I figured to stop here and get a quick drink."

"How about another? I'm buying."

"Sure, why not."

The officer raised his hand getting the attention of a waitress. He ordered the drinks and sat down with Dylan. "Still flying C-130's?" Dylan asked.

"Yup, daily flights from Guam into Bein Hoa. Bringing in a shit load of supplies. I think the powers that be plan on a long haul here. But, I think you would know more about that than me."

"Even if I knew, I could neither confirm or deny," Dylan replied.

"I know, you spooks are all the same. Been out to Indian country lately?"

"Been up to Plei Me and Pleiku."

"Those are the badlands. Me, I'm happy with my work. No boonies for this stick jockey. I'm going home in another two months. I'm too short for your kind of shit. The wife wants me to put in for a stateside posting."

"Any idea of where you might end up?" Dylan asked.

"Hopefully, MacDill in Florida. Housing off the base is real affordable. Saved up some of my money looking to get one of those new Mustangs. I'm thinking a convertible."

"Does Ford make those in a rag top?"

"I think so. When do you go back?'

"I'll be here for a while. Nothing at home to tie me down. Besides, I have everything I need here."

The two of them finished their drinks and said good night. Dylan was thinking about his overheard conversations by the two officers. What did they know, he wondered?

The next night he was in the command center. Dylan would monitor the attack on the North Vietnamese base from MACV headquarters in Saigon. The South Vietnamese commandos were air dropped into North Vietnam with no complications and the four SOG gunboats arrived near the base for fire support. North Vietnamese radar detected the boats before the attack was implemented. Responding to the radar images the commander of the base sent his own boats out to meet the attacking vessels. While responding to the radar images the commandos initiated their own ground attacks. They inflicted casualties and damaged several buildings but the boats that were the primary targets were not there. The mission was deemed a success. The North Vietnamese also declared a victory.

The following night, the USS Maddox was operating closer to the shore. The large destroyers radar image left no doubt that an attack was emanate in the base commanders' mind. Once again, the commander of the base dispatched his boats to meet the attack he expected. The Maddox came under attack and it set the stage for the Tonkin Gulf incident that would propel the increase of US military involvement in Vietnam.

Caroline finished preparing dinner when Dylan arrived at her apartment. He was deep in thought. "You seem distracted. Something on your mind?" Caroline asked as she poured him a glass of wine.

"Something about this Gulf of Tonkin resolution passed by Congress stinks to high heaven. I feel like the whole thing was some kind of setup."

"A setup. Why would you think that? And, set up by who?" Caroline asked.

"I don't know. I will say this. I don't trust McNamara and his whole crowd of idiots. I think this whole thing was organized to get us into a war here."

"We're pretty much are involved in the war as it is. We have base's and troops here already."

"No, I mean fully involved. I heard today that the 1st Cavalry Division will be coming soon."

"Where did you hear that?"

"The rumor mill at MACV. If we bring in the Cav, we are getting ourselves into a mess here. The country is so unstable."

"Well, it is just a rumor. Let's eat and forget work."

Arriving at Mike and Susan's, Hope and Jack were greeted by Susan. Mike was sitting on the beach. He spent a lot of time there, since he talked with Susan. The impending visit by Jack and Hope made him uncomfortable. They had had more discussions about their own relationship. Susan had been more standoffish. Mike sensed that she was uncomfortable around him. She never joined him on the beach and if she were on the beach before him she left when he arrived. He was worried about their future.

Hope had told him about Jack, his arrival would complicate the weekend even more. Mike had talked with a recruiter in town about the Special Forces. Knowing the time and training Jack would need he hoped to talk him out of it. The training just for the Green Berets would take a year. Before that could even happen, he would have to be appointed for the training. It would be a long haul and take at least a six-year commitment on his part.

He heard the car pull up and he knew they had arrived, but he stayed where he was. Then he saw Jack coming towards him. That meant Hope and Susan were alone together. Great he thought, just what I need, a cat fight.

"Hey, Uncle Mike. How you doing? You heard about the Maddox. I guess Johnson's looking to kick some commie ass, huh?"

"Good to see you kid. You know what, let's take a walk. I need to stretch my legs."

"Ok."

They started walking south along the beach. Mike was concerned about Hope and Susan but realized he could do nothing about it. "Your mom tells me that you want to finish school and then join the Marines or the Army."

"Yea. If I join the Army I want to be a Green Beret. But, then again, I might go into the Marines like Dylan. I'll be old enough to join when I'm seventeen."

"Green Berets. That's tough to get into. You'll need at least a three-year enlistment. You have to be Airborne qualified and go through Infantry school first."

"I know. I'm also looking into going to Ranger school first. A lot of those guys get picked for Special Forces. When I talked to the Sergeant at 401 North Broad he said I'll do eight weeks of basic followed by eight weeks of AIT. (Advanced Individual Training) Once that's done I'll have three to four weeks of jump school. Then I can go to Ranger training for six months. That's almost a whole year before I can even go to Special Forces. That training is a full year at Fort Bragg."

"Sounds like you have it all planned out, kid."

"Yup."

"You know, with what's happening in Vietnam you might be assigned to a unit and be deployed there. You may never get to Fort Bragg."

"I know, but with combat experience, Special Forces School could be a lock."

"Look kid, all of that is a long way off. A lot of things can change."

"You sound like my mom."

"I'm just looking out for you Jack. I could put in a word here for the Police Department."

"Nah, besides you have to be twenty-one for the Police."

"So. In the meantime, you could go to college. You have great grades..."

"My mom, put you up to this, didn't she?" Jack interrupted.

"I won't lie to you. Yes, she did. She's worried about your future. So am I. This thing in Vietnam is just getting started. The last thing she wants is for you to get hurt."

"I can take care of myself."

"I bet you can. Look Jack, war is no picnic. For that matter neither is being a cop. Things happen that affect your whole life. Trust me, I know."

They walked in silence, both thinking about what had been said. Jack was more determined than ever. Reaching the down town area, they turned back for the house.

"Uncle Mike. Mom told me about the doctor you are seeing. What's wrong?"

"I got problems buddy. I never knew how bad I was. It all started years ago, after France and being a cop. Things are complicated. Think long and hard before you decide what you are going to do with your life. Decisions you make today have a lifetime of affect."

Sitting at the kitchen table drinking coffee, Hope sensed that something was wrong. Susan seemed distant. Hope wondered if she and Mike were having problems. "Susan, are you all, right? You seem as if something is bothering you. The last time we talked you told me Mike was making improvements since he started seeing Dr. Lewis. Is everything ok?"

"We both have to see him next week." Susan replied flatly.

"Really, both of you. Are you and Mike having problems?"

Susan hesitated, then she spoke. "Recently...that is to say... Christ."

"Susan what is it?" I've known Mike a long time. We have always been very close."

"That's just it...isn't it? Your mother has always had a very special relationship with my husband." Susan replied looking Hope in the eye.

Hope sat back. It was the way she said husband, not Mike. Her thoughts were turning over in her head like balls in a drum going around and around at such a pace, she could not pin one down.

Then Susan continued, "I should really talk with him about this later. Tonight, after dinner. I think it would be best for the two of us to clear the air. I think there are some things that need to be said before Mike and I go see Doctor Lewis." Then Susan got up and went outside, leaving Hope to her thoughts. She walked to the beach saw Mike and Jack coming home. She walked away from them wanting to be alone.

Hope was confused. What in the world just happened? Clearly something was driving a wedge between Mike and Susan. That wedge was my mother she thought. But, how and why? They only see each other a couple of times a year. Was Susan jealous of her for some unexplained reason? Then Mike and Jack came into the house. "You're just not going to let it go, are you?" Jack said defiantly.

Great just what I need she thought.

The tension in the house was obvious. Jack knew something was up. His suspicions were confirmed when Mike gave him some money to go to the boardwalk. Leaving the house Jack thought the three adults were going to discuss his plans for the military. The news of Vietnam convinced him that he would be needed to enlist. He felt that war was coming. His father was a veteran of two wars. His Uncle Mike served in France during WW1. His own mother served in Korea. This was going to be his time. Reaching the boardwalk, he turned his attention to the rides and games offered. He wanted a soda. Stopping at a pizza stand he ordered a coke. Turning away after getting his soda he bumped into a girl. She was pretty. Dressed in a blouse and jeans she smiled at him. "Sorry, I mean excuse me," he said.

"That's all right, I wanted a coke too."

Jack ordered another coke and paid for it. "Thank you, but that really wasn't necessary."

"I don't mind...my name is Jack," he stammered.

"Eilis McDevitt," she told him.

"Eilis, that's really unusual."

"Both my parents are very Irish. My great grandmothers, and my grandmothers name was Eilis and so is my mothers. It's kind of a family tradition to name the firstborn girl after them."

"Wow, that's kinda cool. I have two Uncle's named Michael. Do you live here?"

"No, we live here in the summer. I live in Media Pennsylvania"

"No kidding. My grandparents live in Media. Maybe you know them. My grandfather is a judge, his name is Randall."

"Randall what?"

"Oh no, I mean John Randall. My grandmother is Kay Randall."

"Sorry, I don't think I know them. How about you do you live here?'

"No. I live in Philly. My Uncle Mike and Aunt Susan live here. My mom and I are here for the weekend."

"Where's your father? He didn't come down with you?"

"No. He was killed in Korea," Jack said sadly.

"Oh, I'm sorry, I didn't know."

"It's ok. He was in WWII too. He was an officer in the Army."

Jack looked at the pretty girl in front of him. She had long reddish blond hair tied back in a ponytail and freckles. Not a lot of freckles. She had blue captivating eyes. He guessed she was about his age.

They walked the boardwalk together and played some of the games. Jack was pleased he was able to win her a teddy bear. Before the night was over they were holding hands. The Army and the war in Vietnam was quickly forgotten. They made a date to meet on the beach the next morning. When Jack left her, and went back to his Aunt Susan's she was all he could think about.

Uncle Mike was sitting on the beach. He was smoking a cigar. A six pack of Ortliebs beer on the sand next to him. "Hey, it's illegal to drink on the beach. Ocean City is a dry town. Wanna get yourself locked up?" He greeted his uncle.

"That would be a blessing."

"Something wrong?"

"Here kid have a beer."

"Really!"

"Sure, why not. I'm already in deep shit. Just don't tell your mother or Aunt Susan."

Jack used the opener and opened the can. Mimicking his uncle, he opened one side all the way and just popped the other side. Taking a drink, he took a mouthful. The beer was cold and he liked it. "Got another cigar?"

"Yes, and no you can't have one."

"Just thought I'd ask. What's bugging you? My mom pushing you about the Army?"

"I wish. That I can handle. How was the boardwalk?"

"Great, I met a girl. Her name is Eilis."

"A what?"

"Eilis. E I L I S, he spelled. Its Irish."

"Irish huh? Irish women are a curse kiddo. Watch yourself."

"So why are you in deep shit? Does it have something to do with two Irish women we both know?"

"You could say that. Look kid...aw never mind. Let's just say it was a rough night."

"Ok. Eilis is really pretty. We're meeting on the beach tomorrow. I really like her."

"That's how it starts. First you like em then you love em. Then your whole world explodes, Burgh," Mike made an exploding sound.

Jack drank more beer wondering what had happened.

The next morning Jack was up early. He took a shower combed his hair and put on his bathing suit. He made some breakfast and prepared to leave the house. Mike woke up and came into the kitchen and made a pot of coffee. "Where you off to so early?" He asked Jack.

"The beach, I told you last night I met a girl. I'm going to meet her."

"Oh yeah, I remember now. Have fun kid."

Jack put on a shirt grabbed a large beach towel and left.

Hope was up next. She sat at the kitchen table waiting for the coffee to perk. "How did you sleep?" She asked Mike.

"There was supposed to be sleep?"

"Uncle Mike, I could not help but notice some tension between you and Aunt Susan. Is everything all, right?"

Susan walked into the kitchen. "Tell her Mike. Tell her what you told Lewis. Tell her what you told me."

"I don't think that would be a good idea," Mike replied sheepishly.

"Why not? You said yourself that Doctor Lewis advised that you should admit your feelings," Susan said defiantly.

"Don't take this out on Hope. She has nothing to do with this."

Hope interrupted, "But my mother does, right?"

Susan and Mike both looked at Hope.

"Whoa, who…what makes you say that?" Mike asked.

Hope looked at Susan, "You told me yesterday. Remember? You said that my mother always had a special relationship with Mike."

"Yes, I did. I'm sorry. I spoke out of turn. Damn you Michael McMullen. I really wish you had kept all of this to yourself."

"Look, you're the one that said I needed to talk to a shrink. I'm just doing what I'm told," Mike answered.

Hope interrupted, "So, how does all of this involve my mother. I mean I don't get it. How many times do we really see each other. A few times a year. Please tell me that you're not saying that my mother and Mike are having an affair. I would know if that were true."

Mike poured coffee for the two women and himself. "We are not and have never had an affair. That's not it."

"Then what is it, Uncle Mike? Tell me," Hope said.

"Cats out of the bag now, tell her," Susan said.

"During one of my sessions with Doctor Lewis…I came to the realization about…then…no I can't do it. This is not right. I'm not going to stand here and talk about Colleen behind her back. It's not right," Mike said.

"Oh, aren't we the chivalrous one?" Susan said.

"Damn it, Susan. How many times do I have to say it. We have everything, or at least I thought so. This has never ever been something that ever affected our marriage. Lewis said to be honest with you. No secrets. No hidden agendas. If you're feeling insecure and betrayed it's all on you, I shared, I admitted it. You're the one with the problem," Mike replied angrily.

Hope interrupted, "Stop it, my God, what are you two doing to each other. I don't know what's causing this and right now I don't want to know. I love you both, and to see the two of you like this hurts me. So just stop, please."

Susan broke a brief silence, "Your right, honey. I'm sorry. Maybe I have been overreacting."

"Ya think!" Mike said.

"Stop it, sit there and behave yourself," Hope demanded.

"Please Susan what were you going to say?" Hope asked.

"What I was going to say is…when you first told me what you and Doctor Lewis discussed I was angry. I felt betrayed. I felt like the last kid to be picked for the team because I wasn't good enough. It hurt me Mike, it really hurt me," Susan said beginning to cry.

"I'm sorry. How many times do I have to say it," Mike told Susan.

Mike and Susan embraced. Whatever demon had made itself known it appeared to Hope it have be vanquished. But there was still the nagging thought for her, what and how was her mother involved.

Jack was early. He waited on the beach at the place where they agreed to meet. Then he saw her coming down the steps from the boardwalk.

The morning sun on his back made her squint behind her sun glasses. She had a large beach bag over her shoulder. She hoped the new bikini she wore was not too revealing. A part of her did not care. Jack Randall was the one. She knew it the first time she looked into his eyes. "Good morning," she said to him.

CHAPTER 31
BLOOD & FIRE

The camp at Plei Me was on high alert. Observation and listening posts around the camp were reporting movement. Lots of movement. The base commander recalled them all back inside the wire. Even the Jarai family members of the Montagnard living outside the wire were brought inside. Dogs belonging to the Montagnard families barked constantly. One of the observation posts southwest of the camp came under attack. The assault on the camp was about to begin. General Man deployed the 33rd Regiment of his PAVN forces to attack the camp. He held his 32nd Regiment in reserve to ambush any of the newly arrived 1st Calvary troopers of the American Army, when they would attempt to relieve and reinforce the camp. The attack on the camp itself started on the North, east and west.

Duong and the members of his company set up their jump off position on the north side of the compound. RPG (Rocket Propelled Grenades) crews were tasked with taking out the corner observation towers. The towers were fortified with heavy timbers and sand bags. Two machine gun crews manned by the Montagnard would need to be eliminated. To the southwest of the camp Duong heard the small arms fire as a company of his comrades overran an outpost of Montagnard as they retreated back to the camp. The siege of Plei Me had begun. Crawling through the grass that surrounded the camp he and his squad moved closer to the wire. The RPG crews fired their rockets taking out the tower closest to Duong and his men. As the attack began heavy fire from the defenders erupted.

Red tracers streamed through the night like a constant flow of death. Duong and his men charged the wire firing their AK-47 assault rifles. The green tracers from their weapons poured into the defenders' positions in the wire. The sound of the battle was overwhelming. Duong shouted to his men to keep assaulting the defenders. Moving within a few feet of the wire they began cutting a path for the rest of his company to attack and occupy the trenches of the defending Montagnard. Fighting in the trenches became hand to hand. His magazine empty Duong came upon a wounded Montagnard still firing at his attackers. He lunged and stabbed the man in the chest with his bayonet killing him. Reloading he ordered his men to continue to fire inside the camp. They now occupied the defenders trench line. Flares lit up the dark night sky. Shadows from the flares danced across the compound as red and green tracer fire crisscrossed the compound. The plan General Man had conceived was working. The plan was to draw out reinforcements from Pleiku. Artillery fire and air strikes around the camp had a devastating effect on the attacking PAVN. For those fighting from the trench line this overwhelming fire had no effect. Their fighting was too personal. Montagnard fighters tried to counter attack and regain the trench line, but the PAVN forces were determined to hold. Fighting continued all night, and as dawn approached, Duong and his men pulled back to the jungle. US Army Major Charles Beckwith was air dropped by helicopters with a 175-man ARVN Ranger force five kilometers' northeast of the camp. Fighting his way to the camp he encountered Duongs company and more fighting erupted.

Fighting his way to the base Beckwith took command and made attempts to pursue the attackers. Driven back by heavy contacts he made his way back into to the base to await more reinforcements and resupply. The PAVN forces regrouping in the jungle also were resupplied with ammo and water. Wounded and dead comrades were taken back to the Chu Pong Massif.

Duong praised his men. They had fought bravely and with honor. They were dirty and bloodied. Duong had suffered a shrapnel wound in his side but refused to leave his men. His ten-man squad was now down to just six men. They had a variety of minor wounds but pledged to stay and fight. They would not be disappointed. Beckwiths pursuit of the attacking PAVN forces failed.

The men of General Man's command were committed to the fight. The men of his 32nd regiment were already preparing to ambush the reinforcements being sent from Pleiku. A 1,400-man armored Task Force, led by Lieutenant Colonel Nguyễn Trọng Luật, moved out to Phú Mỹ, 20 kilometers south of Pleiku.

Ordered to linger in the area around Phú Mỹ, Lieutenant Colonel Nguyễn Trọng Luật slowly continued pressing towards the besieged camp. The 32nd regiment did its job when the convoy was ambushed at 1730 Hours inflicting heavy casualties at the front and rear of the convoy. Limping into the Plei Me camp the convoy had reached its objective. The camp was resupplied by air lifts and patrols in the area continued to meet fierce fighting as the two regiments regrouped and made their way back to the Chu Pong Massif stronghold.

Duong and his men were fed and resupplied on the mountain base. The wounds they had were treated and although the cost of the siege was heavy they were proud of their mission. In the next few weeks US, and ARVN forces were subjected to heavy contacts with the enemy. The troopers of the 1st Calvary Division were preparing their own operation. Air attacks and artillery barrages continued in the area and took a heavy toll on the forces of General Man. Duong and his men learned that soon they would be sent against the American forces and they prepared themselves for the bloodiest battle of the new war.

In Saigon, Dylan was being briefed on the siege at Plei Me. He learned that Lt. Colonel Hal Moore and his 1st Battalion 7th Calvary Regiment would make a helicopter assault on a landing zone at the base of the Chu Pong Massif. The landing zone was designated LZ X-ray. Finishing work, he met Caroline at her apartment. The events around Plei Me and the upcoming operation troubled him. "I guess you heard about the recent events and the new operation?" He asked her.

"Yes, it turns out you were right. We are getting ourselves more involved.

This situation is going to be far worse than we had hoped."

"I have to wonder, why we are pushing this. It's almost as if war has been our overall strategy. Why? The South Vietnamese should be fighting this war. We are expanding our role of support into a full-fledged US war."

"You sound like you don't agree with this."

"I don't. We have boots on the ground now. I'm not sure the people back home are going to accept this. What happened in Plei Me is just the start. We are looking at a long and bloody campaign. The North Vietnamese are committed to uniting the country."

"You don't think the South Vietnamese are committed to their own cause?" Caroline asked.

"No. Look at this country, it's in turmoil. The level of corruption and ineptitude of the leadership is in total disarray. The VC control all of the Delta. The NVA and VC occupy most of the Central Highlands. I'm not so sure we can win the war that's coming."

"Really. We have the air power. We have tanks and artillery. Plei Me showed us that the North cannot sustain the casualties we can inflict. How can they sustain the fight? Even if we just use our power in support of the ARVN, the commies cannot endure the cost of their mission."

"I don't think so. This upcoming operation will reveal what the future will be. I think we are headed into a bee hive. We know we inflicted heavy casualties on the PAVN forces. Our air strikes and artillery barrages decimated the PAVN. But these little bastards just kept coming. The ARVN are just not up for this. If we take over the fight, I think Marvin the ARVN will sit back and let us do their dirty work."

"Ha ha, you sound like Benjamin Spock."

"Maybe so. But he could be right. I'm sure he and his looney liberal group will be screaming their heads off in the next couple of weeks. The only thing we can hope for is that this operation by the Cav is decisive enough to keep the North Vietnamese from expanding the coming war. Don't forget the NLF is supported by the Soviets and the Chinese. Remember what happened in Korea. If the Cav kicks Charlies ass will they send in their own troops. We already have reports of Soviet advisors working with PAVN."

"There is one other consideration." Caroline offered.

"Yea, what's that?"

"The unit that's going against the PAVN in this operation is the same unit commanded by General Custer."

"Great just what we need another massacre at the Little Big Horn."

The morning sun rose and the wide-open area east of the Chu Pong Massif got warmer. Two men of the 32rd PAVN Regiment looked up into the blinding sunlight. The open area in front of them consisted of high grass, termite mounds and small trees. Then they heard the screams of artillery rounds fired by the 105mm guns at nearby LZ Falcon. High explosive rounds impacted around the open area. Hot shrapnel from the exploding rounds danced in the air and bounced along the ground. The barrage lasted for a half hour and was supplemented by aerial rocket and machine gun fire from helicopter gunships. An eerie quiet came over the landing zone and then the steady whoop whoop of helicopter blades cutting the air to the east could be heard. Appearing in the morning sky there were eight birds each loaded with troopers of the 1st Air Calvary Divisions, 1st Battalion 7th Calvary. Before either of the two men could react, the choppers landed in the open space and troopers of the 7th Cav jumped out and began dispersing around the LZ. An entire platoon of men approached them. It would be another thirty minutes before the next sortie would arrive. One of the men panicked and was chased by the Americans.

The other made a futile attempt to hide and was discovered quickly. An ARVN Ranger with the group of Americans began to interrogate him. The Americans learned that the mountain was the base of a PAVN Division, more than 4500 men, and they wanted very much to fight the Americans. By the time all of the sorties arrived the 7th Calvary would air lift 450 men unto the field of battle. The group of Americans that chased his comrade would find themselves cut-off from the main battle group and would sustain heavy casualties as they ran right into the charging elements of the PAVN soldiers. Before all of the men of the 7th would arrive the LZ was declared 'HOT.' New sorties of arriving troopers would find themselves jumping from the choppers before they landed so the birds could get off the LZ as quickly as possible. Lt. Colonel Hal Moore in command of the group found himself at the beginning of the bloodiest battle of the new emerging Vietnam War.

Dylan monitored the progress of the airborne assault on LZ X-ray at MACV headquarters. He was not part of the planning for the operation, but he had the clearance to be there. The assault started around 10:30AM and two hours later the LZ was alive with small arms fire.

Radio traffic from the FO, (Forward Observer) and Lt. Colonel Moore could be heard in the command center. Moore was directing his troops as they landed. The FO was calling in the artillery and the FAC (Forward Air Control) officer coordinated air support. Their attacks around the base of the Chu Pong Massif kept the North Vietnamese from overrunning the LZ. Then the broadcast went out that 2nd Platoon of Bravo Company had been cut off from the rest of the battalion. Dylan recognized one of the officers from the hotel bar talking with another company man (CIA) that had arrived recently in Saigon. "Shit, the last thing we need is the massacre of an entire platoon." Fighting continued throughout the day and the last push to liberate the 2nd Platoon failed. The overnight hours were a test for the lost platoon that endured three more attacks during the night.

Duong' squad and the rest of his company were placed on the southern side of the Ia Drang river 2.5 kilometers north of LZ X-ray. The sound of the battle could be heard all day and into the night. Despite heavy losses endured by their comrades fighting on X-ray, Duong's company was told to stay where they were. Listening and observation posts were manned. Duong and his men knew every square inch of the area. Fighting positions and bunkers had been dug in the area. Occasionally artillery support from the American base at LZ Falcon fired rounds near Duong and his men. They suffered no casualties. The next day they were re-enforced with another company. The men soured at missing this important fight but followed their orders. Their chance would come three days later.

The battle on LZ X-ray lasted all afternoon and into the night. Artillery barrages continued into the late-night hours. The lost platoon would endure three probing attacks but managed

Creatures Born of War

to survive. Dylan was in the command center at MACV before dawn. It promised to be a long day. During the pre-dawn hours, the NVA moved into positions to close for the Americans to use their artillery and air support. Another attempt was launched to rejoin with 2nd platoon stranded from the day before. Then the NVA attacked in force all around the southern perimeter of LZ X-ray.

Fighting was intense and the southern perimeter had been breached. The 7th Calvary had a been pushed back and the NVA was in their perimeter.

The radios in the command center came alive with requests for artillery and air cover. Incoming choppers coming into the LZ with more troopers from Alpha Company 2nd Battalion of the 7th were taking heavy small arms fire as they began to land. To their amazement, the NVA troops firing at them where right in the LZ. Alpha Company troops jumping off the choppers found themselves in close quarter combat with the enemy. Assessing his position Lt. Colonel Moore instructed his radio operator to make the following call; 'Broken Arrow, Broken Arrow.' The command center at MACV was stunned. The call of 'Broken Arrow' meant that every combat aircraft in the skies over Vietnam were now directed to support the American troops being overrun. Dylan heard the CIA man who had arrived yesterday say, "Shit, there's no hiding this now." The press was not briefed about the situation in the Ia Drang valley. They knew an operation was under way but had no details. It was bad enough that 2nd Platoon had been cut off since the operation began, but now an entire unit of the 1st Calvary had been overrun, and in danger of being massacred. Adding to the problem was a friendly fire incident from supporting aircraft killed several troopers inside their own perimeter. This had become a public relations nightmare. Dylan realized that the first major engagement by US forces was about to become a defeat with horrific casualties. Somehow however

367

Lt. Colonel Moore managed to close the hole in his lines and keep the enemy from taking over the LZ.

Later in the day the men of 2nd Platoon were rescued and brought back to the LZ with their wounded and dead. Inbound choppers still taking small arms fire were able to resupply the weary men with water, medical supplies and ammunition. By the end of the day the NVA regrouped and began their own resupply efforts. Bodies of dead NVA littered the LZ. The NVA made four major attacks in the pre-dawn hours and were repelled by Bravo Company. The NVA retreated due to heavy and precision artillery fire on their lines. By mid-morning of the third day LZ X-ray was declared secure and Moore and his troopers were ordered out. Dylan had been in the command center all day and night. Exhausted he left the command center and got some much-needed sleep.

Duong and his men now reinforced by the 66th Regiment held their positions in an area that was designated by US forces as LZ Albany.

The men of 2nd Battalion 5th Calvary and 2nd Battalion 7th Calvary arrived at LZ X-ray and began their afternoon match to LZ Albany 2 clicks to the north. B52 air strikes on the Chu Pong Massif and LZ X-ray itself began on the afternoon of the 16th of November. The men of the 2nd Battalion 5th Calvary and 2nd Battalion 7th Calvary arriving at LZ Albany walked right into the headquarters position of the 66th Regiment. The NVA set up a brutal L shaped ambush and engaged the Calvary troopers. Dylan returned to the MACV command center and quickly learned that another battle had started. The NVA had not been defeated and the fresh but under strength men of the 33rd Regiment reinforced by General Mans 8th Battalion 66th Regiment were now engaged with men of the 2nd of the 5th. Heavy casualties were reported as the NVA overran the column of troopers.

Duong and his men lay in the tall grass, their scouts reporting the movement of the American column. The tired troopers were strung out in a line of march 550 yards long. Duong and his men had been sitting here during the battle at LZ X-ray and were anxious to get into the fight. The NVA launched their assault and overran the column of weary Americans. Duong fired his AK as he and his men charged and found themselves in close quarter combat and hand to hand fighting with the Americans. Bayonet and rifle butts came into play as Duong and his men swept through the line of resting and startled American soldiers. Coming out of the grass Duong fired his AK, emptying his magazine on a group of Calvary troopers. Using his bayonet Duong plunged it into an American locked in hand to hand combat with one of his men. Another American knocked him down and using his helmet hitting Duong on the head. He fell over bleeding from a wound on his scalp. Losing his weapon, he grabbed the American by the throat. Wrestling on the ground with him Duong gained the upper hand rolling on top of him, choking him with his left hand he punched the soldier several times before his comrade he had just rescue shot the man in the head. Splattered with the man's blood Duong grabbed his own weapon reloaded and began firing single shots at Americans around him. The field of battle was littered with dead and wounded American and NVA soldiers. Napalm bombs were dropped from aircraft and the heat of the napalm was overwhelming. Breathing heavily Duong was knocked down from the blast as he sucked the hot air into his lungs. Regaining his composure Duong walked among the wounded Americans killing four more. Regrouping his men, they continue their vicious assault killing more of the American troopers. Some of them clustered together forming small defensive positions but the overwhelming number of attackers wiped them out quickly. Throwing grenades and firing their weapons Duong and his men cut through the weak defenses. Exhausted Duong and his men regrouped and looked over the battle ground. Bodies of dead and dying soldiers littered the battlefield. That night Duong and his men along with other NVA troops from the 66th walked the battleground dispatching the wounded Americans. Moaning and crying troopers were bayonetted or shot. Some of the NVA laughed as they went about their grisly task. It was a long and lonely night for the Americans that hid in the high grass.

MACV headquarters was a bee hive of activity. The press had learned of Lt. Colonel Moore's attack and battle at X-ray. Now they also learned of the massacre at LZ Albany. Despite the heavy losses of the 1st Calvary troopers the press also learned of the massive losses the NVA had endured. The troopers of the 1st Calvary suffered 305 dead and 524 wounded. Battle reports estimated that the NVA suffered 3561 killed with more than 1000 wounded. Both sides claimed victory. The NVA learned that attacking the Americans had to be up close to minimize the effects of artillery and air support. The Americans learned that the enemy was determined and well equipped. A new battle plan emerged. Body count was now the objective. The US reported a ten to one ratio of battlefield deaths. The US strategy was that the NVA could not sustain the war with a kill ratio that high. The new strategy would continue for the next seven years. In the end, it would fail.

Duong and what was left of his platoon made their way back to the mountain they had called home for so long. Regrouped and resupplied he and his men made their way back into Cambodia. They were tired and bloodied. Moral however was very high. They had met the enemy and inflicted huge losses. They would rest and get new replacements.

Out of the fight for now they returned to the mundane life of surviving in the jungle. The 33rd Regiment had performed with courage and persistence. Before this long war was over the 33rd would develop its reputation as one of the most effective and battle-hardened units of the NVA.

CHAPTER 32

NEW LIVES & CHALLENGES

Vang Bo left the school in Dinh Quan. Hung had instructed him to relocate to Xuan Loc. He had taken a position with the same rubber plantation that Hung had used as a cover for years. He saw his daughters on a regular basis when they came to visit him. He was told to stay away from Saigon. Dylan Brogan had travelled to his old school looking for him. Bo wanted to see Dylan but his position as a CIA officer complicated the re-union. Learning about Dylan from his daughters he reported their last meeting with Dylan at the shop to Hung. Fearing the worst Hung intervened just in time at the hotel he was staying and sent the CIA officer on a false lead. Hung spoke with him at length about his involvement with Dylan. Hung learned from other NLF sources that Dylan Brogan suspected Bo of being an intelligence operative for the communist government in Hanoi. He lived in a modest home on the outside of the town and kept to himself. Hung minimized Bo's duties with the NLF and he was used to pass messages from the local VC cadre and Hanoi. The war in Vietnam was expanding as more and more US troops were deployed to bases around the country. The man known as Gayal had simply vanished and as the war continued he was forgotten about. Eventually Bo was relocated to a large base just inside the Cambodian border. The Americans designated the base as COSVN. (Central Office of South Vietnam) Located on the Mimot Plantation, its exact location was unknown to US forces. The base itself was huge and built into the forest north of Tay Ninh. Once again Bo found himself living in the jungle fighting mosquitos, snakes and living a primitive life. Occasionally he would travel to Phenom Penh, where he would be able to visit with his daughters.

Hope and Jack returned from the shore. Jack talked almost non-stop about the girl he met on the boardwalk. Hope was happy that Mike had spoken to the boy, but for now he was only interested in his new girlfriend. Learning that she lived in Media, Hope was hopeful that this new distraction would take over Jacks thoughts about his future. On the drive, back to Philly he never asked about Mike and Susan's troubles. That night after they arrived home she sat with her mother. "How was your trip?" Colleen asked.

"Not too bad, Mike talked with Jack. I don't know if it had any affect, but the new girlfriend has his interest for now."

"He seems quite taken by this girl."

"Yes, he does…Mom I have to ask. Was there ever anything between you and Mike?"

"What? Why would you ask me that, and what exactly do you mean?"

Hope waited a few seconds before she answered to form her thoughts.

"When I got there, Mike and Jack were on the beach. Susan and I had a chance to talk. She mentioned that they would be seeing Mikes therapist together. She said something that troubled me."

"What did she say?"

"She said that you and her husband…had always had a special relationship. She did not say Mike she said husband."

Colleen was surprised. Taken aback she had no idea what all of this meant. Finally, she spoke, "Mike and I would always flirt with each other. Even when your father was still alive we would carry on. Nothing ever happened, I was always faithful to your father. Your grandfather would laugh at us, the way we interacted. I mean for that matter your Aunt Susan and I would always flirt with him. I can't imagine what if anything could cause a problem. We acted this way for years." Colleen paused and then asked, "Is Susan mad at me?"

"No…I don't think so. She told Mike that whatever happened her feelings were hurt. It almost seemed as if she thought you two were having an affair."

"An affair! Me and Mike, that's ridiculous. I have always been honest with Susan. I love her like a sister. I should call her."

"I would wait until after she and Mike see the therapist," Hope replied.

"Why do you say that?"

"I just think they need to work out whatever problem they have before you say anything."

"All right, I'll wait. By the way Tom Brady is really in bad shape. He's using drugs."

"Oh, my God, that's awful. It's so sad. How did you find out?"

"I talked with his mother on Saturday. Your Uncle Michaels disappearance has really broken his heart. I can't imagine what he is going through. It's all just so mysterious, it's as if he just vanished."

"The Cubans say they released all the Americans in Cuba. Why would they keep him?" Hope asked.

"I have no idea. Tom said they were never involved in any politics. God only knows what happened. I fear the worst. We may never know."

"Poor Tom." Hope said.

Doctor Lewis sat across from Mike and Susan. He scribbled in his note pad as Susan explained how she felt about Mike's admission about Colleen. Mike sat in silence, clearly uncomfortable. "I mean, I always knew about how they flirted with each other. Hell, I even played along," she said finishing. "Do you feel as if this is something that can be mended?" Lewis asked.

"I suppose so. I mean I still love him...I always will. But this is just so hard to face. I don't know how I will react when we see Colleen again. She of course has no idea about all this. Her daughter, Hope visited with us last week. She knows something is happening but not the details. I'm sure she will say something to her mother." Colleen and I are very close. I feel hurt by her as well."

"But if she has no idea about what Mike revealed then your relationship with her has not changed. You have control over that. How you treat her when you see her is up to you. If you still value your relationship you with her you should remember that. She still values her relationship with you. If you come across to her that she betrayed you, she will obviously be hurt. Is that something you want to happen?"

"Oh, God no. I love her. I would never hurt her."

"Then that's how you need to approach this. Remember, she has no idea what Mike's true feelings are. Yes, there is a special bond between them, but that bond includes you," Lewis said.

Susan listened and took in what the doctor said. "Mike, do you have anything to say on the matter?" Lewis asked.

"I don't know what to say. I never wanted this to happen. I know I hurt Susan, and I'm very sorry. But, I don't want this to destroy Susan's friend ship with Colleen. I also don't want to hurt Colleen. What the hell am I supposed to say or do? You say this needs to be out in the open. That this is the only way for me to get some control back in my life. To me it seems I've lost all control over my life."

"But that is the point, Mike. You really have no control over your life. Things will happen that will affect you in a positive or a negative way. How you approach these things is the only place where you do have some control. Negative things can be treated with medications or other forms of therapy. Your friend Jimmy was told to take long hot baths. While that may be therapeutic it was only temporary. The under lying reason and effect of the negative experience he had in France during the war remains. The feelings you have for Colleen need to be explored. For example, you told me that Jimmy spoke about her all the time when you were together in France. The real question is, did you fall in love with her or your perception of her because of Jimmy's stories? Then meeting her for the first time she was a real person, not just a fantasy imagined by you. You became closer to her due to your continuous exposure. Then you had to deal with the idea of betraying your best friend. You admitted that you constructed a wall so that no one could ever get close to you. You kept everyone outside of that wall except for Colleen. In your mind, she deserved a place with you on your side of the wall. Understand?"

"So, what your saying is I'm really not in love with her, I just think I'm in love with her." Mike replied.

"Let me ask you this, and take a moment before you answer. Is the love you have for Susan on the same level as Colleen?" Lewis asked.

Mike thought about the question. Looking at Susan he knew that he still loved her. "I love Susan. I know that. My life would really be a mess if not for her. I can't imagine the life I would have had without her."

"And yet you have had a happy and successful relationship with another woman, and not Colleen. I believe your love for Colleen is still a fantasy you imagined since your time in France.

You do love Colleen, but not on the same level as Susan. The real person of Colleen you love but not the fantasy you developed is not the same. She is just a very special friend that shared a difficult part of your life." Lewis said.

"Wow, that's a lot to process," Mike replied.

"Indeed, but once we can get to a point that you are able to put this bag of bricks down and walk away from it, we can then explore some of the other things that have impacted your life." Lewis said.

Susan asked, "So, how do we treat Colleen going forward. She is bound to know that something in her relationship with Mike has impacted our marriage?"

"For you, there should be no change. Treat her as you have always treated her. Mike on the other hand must accept that the fantasy he created in his own mind is just that a fantasy. Mike needs to tell her how he felt about her and why."

Mike replied, "Oh, great. Just what I need."

"Ask yourself this, what am I willing to do to keep my marriage to Susan?" If the answer is you are willing to do whatever you have too, then all of this is just academic. Our session is ending, I want to see you both again next month. In the meantime, both of you should think about your relationship with Colleen, and how you want the relationship to continue."

Their session over, Mike and Susan left and had lunch. There was a lot to think about. That night over dinner they discussed how they would approach Colleen.

Tom still concerned about Michael had visited with his family in Philadelphia. They had not heard from Michael since Castro had taken control of Cuba. Diplomatic ties with the tiny island had been cut off. The US placed embargos against the island. With no news about Michaels fate the family along with Tom waited for news that never came.

Depression set in and Tom lived a life of anguish. Back in New York he stayed with his parents. He began to drink heavily and started using marijuana to numb the pain. Before long he started using heroin. He got involved with the growing anti-war movement. Attending anti-war protest in the city was a daily event. It was also where Tom purchased and expanded his drug use. His usual spot in Times Square to sell his drawings fell through. The popular tourist area was now changing. Porn theaters and adult book stores seemed to pop up overnight. At late afternoon and into the night prostitutes trolled the square. Young teenage boys as well as girls that had run away from home found a new life to live on the streets of mid-town Manhattan. The ant-war movement became a haven for drugs, alcohol and sex. Tom's drug use needed money and with no tourists to buy his drawings he soon gave up on his talent. Petty theft and panhandling became his new way of life. It was a new life, the old life he had, he was giving up on. He was arrested several times, issued a summons and released. He spent some time at Rikers Island. He found that life on Rikers was no different than street life and compared to the Cuban prison he spent years in Rikers was a cake walk.

When he first returned home he actively looked-for Michael. He went to the State Department in New York and Washington. No one there was able or even interested in helping him. The Cubans insisted that there were no Americans held against their will in Cuban Jails. If Michael was still alive he must surely be at their mountain top home. He could not travel to Cuba. He made an attempt to go back from Nassau in the Bahama's but was refused a visa by the Cuban Government. He wrote to Michael at the mountain top home but the letters went unanswered or were returned unopened and marked undeliverable. Their peaceful life of solitude was now a curse. There was no one he could contact for help.

Walking north on 5th Avenue, he reached 59th Street. He would spend another night in Central Park in some bushes by the Gapstow Bridge. Another protest was planned for the following day. He would be there to feed his new heroin addiction. The war was something he no longer cared about. But he played the role to get his drugs. Tom would panhandle outside the Plaza Hotel until either the police or the hotel doormen chased him off. On the day of the protest, police began to forcefully move the protesters out of the park. At thirty-five Tom, did not run as fast as the younger hippies and found himself in the back of an NYPD van. Arrested again he was taken to the Greenwich Village area of the city and dumped on the street. Everything he owned was in a bag hidden in the bushes where he slept. He had to walk back uptown to the park.

Getting off the bus, Colleen was met by Susan. They greeted each other and talked about the upcoming weekend. They had spoken on the phone to plan the trip and neither of them mentioned the under lying problem. Everything seemed normal. That night after dinner the three of them sat on the beach as the sun set. Mike smoked a cigar and drank his Jack Daniels. The women had made a pitcher of margaritas. Colleens plan was to say nothing. She noticed that Mike was on edge. Small talk about Steve and Dorothy was discussed and Colleen noted that their relationship had improved. This opened the door for Susan as she mentioned that she and Mike were also seeing a therapist. "Mike and I have been seeing his therapist together. Dr. Lewis has really been helping him. He has finally opened up about his life. You're doing much better now aren't you honey?"

"Yea, I suppose."

"You sound like you don't agree Mike. Are you getting better?" Colleen asked.

"Yea."

Susan added, "Mike we discussed this. Dr. Lewis said that you need to confront your feelings. You have to be honest, remember. Part of this is to be honest with Colleen."

"Me. What do you have to be honest with me about? Tell me please." Colleen inquired.

"All right here goes nothing. When I was in France with Jimmy and Tommy, you were all he talked about. Over a period of time I developed feelings for you. Not real feelings…just feelings." Mike said.

"What kind of feelings?" Colleen asked.

"I…that is to say…well I sort of fell in love with you. I guess it was more of a…dream. I wasn't really in love with you just the idea of you. Jimmy talked so much. Then when we got home, and I actually met you. I sort of brought home those feelings with me. Over time being around you, I felt that I really was in love with you."

Susan said, "But there was also an attraction. Mike's feelings became conflicted. Feeling the way, he did and being attracted to you made him feel bad, because he felt that he was betraying his friendship with Jimmy."

"So, when I had all my problems with Jimmy and I confided so much in you it just…I don't know sort of fed the way you felt," Colleen said.

"Yea." Mike said.

Colleen added, "I admit that there was a time I thought that we could have been together. Things with Jimmy were so bad. You told me that I would change one monster for another. I've come to grips with that. You were right. We could not ever be together. You would have felt so guilty being with me, even after Jimmy died. It would never have worked. When you met Susan, I saw how happy you were. I knew then that she was one woman that could bring you happiness."

Susan said, "The way you and I carried on with him was no help. You and I were complicit in our own way we treated him."

"So, did this create a problem for you two?" Colleen asked.

"I have to admit it did. I felt so betrayed by him…and you actually. But Mike and I have discussed this and we both feel that all of that was just a mistake. I know that you two will always be close. Our marriage has always been strong and we both love you. I can't see any reason that our relationship is any different. Mike needed to get this on the table so he can move forward with the issues he has from the war and being a policeman," Susan said.

Colleen sat and listened. They were all quiet for a few moments then Colleen stated, "Hope was here a few weeks ago, and told me that something was brewing. She never told me the specifics but that's why I'm here now. Mike, I love you, we have been through a lot together. But I hope you understand that whatever happened between us, I have moved on from that. I'm sorry that all these things happened. It was never my intention to come between you two, or to hurt either one of you."

Mike added, "It's not your fault, it's mine. I was just so…confused and I guess so lonely that my feelings for you were not real. I know that now.

Susan has been…the best thing in my life. I really just want to get on with our life and I hope that you're not hurt by any of this."

"Well, as far as I'm concerned nothing has changed. I always knew Mike had feelings but it makes sense now. I'm just glad things turned out the way they did, for both of you. I'm happy now. I hope you two continue to be happy."

"Well, I'm happy, the Jack is half gone and I feel pretty good," Mike said.

Susan announced, "Colleen, I'm going to make another pitcher. Anyone need anything?"

"I could use another cigar," Mike said.

"All right, but lay off the bourbon," Susan said leaving them to make more margaritas. Sitting on the beach alone together Mike and Colleen sat in silence until Colleen broke the silence, "If you ever do anything to hurt Susan I'm gonna kick your ass, you big dope."

"Ha ha ha. I just remembered the first time I saw Rose," Mike laughed.

"Oh God, I remember that. That was so funny."

"We have some stories to tell."

"Yes, we do. Not all of them good. Mike, I hope you get better. I only wish that Jimmy had available to him what you have today. You have seen and undergone so much tragedy in your life."

"Do you miss him?"

"Yes, every day. He really was my first and only love."

"Think you can ever find a man that could make you happy?"

"No. Like I said, I've moved on. The only man in my life now is Jack. God, I hope this stupid war would end. He is so head strong about serving."

"How are things going with him and his girlfriend?"

"She is a real sweet girl. Hopefully she can convince him to stay home and go to school. I know you spoke to him, how did your talk with him go?"

"I tried to convince him that the Green Berets would be very tough. I just hope he listened. It's his life though, all we can do is point him in the right direction."

Susan returned with a fresh pitcher and a cigar. "Are you two behaving yourselves?"

Mike answered, "Of course, were best buddies."

"Good, anyone want to go skinny dipping?"

"Ah, for Christ sake!" Mike exclaimed.

Then they laughed and talked late into the night.

Jack saw Eilis as often as he could. Travelling by public transportation he would walk to 30th Street Station and take the train to the 69th Street Terminal and get on a trolley that took him to

Media. Staying with his grandparents for the weekend allowed him to see her almost every Saturday and Sunday. He never learned about the tension between his Uncle Mike and Aunt Susan. The only two things he cared about was finishing high school and Eilis. He did well with his classes and participated on the cross-country team. They were two very young people very much in love with each other. Eilis had only one concern, Jacks obsession with the military and the Vietnam War. She had no real opinion of the war, but she knew that she did not want Jack to leave.

Leaving the movie theater that evening, they walked hand in hand back to her house. They had just seen Lee Marvin in the 'Dirty Dozen'. "That was a great movie," Jack said.

"I felt sorry for Jim Browns character," Eilis said.

"Yup, that was a shame. He was really a good guy. Maggot was a real creepy guy."

"Just goes to show that not everyone in a uniform is a hero."

"True."

"Jack, what are you going to do? You graduate this year. Tell me you will never leave me."

"I would never leave you. Eilis, I believe I have fallen in love with you."

He stopped with her at the corner and faced her. He kissed her and held her. "That's good because I feel the same way."

"Really, you love me too?"

"I love me too, silly."

"What?"

"Yes sweetheart, I do love you." Eilis laughed at her joke.

"You had me going there for a second." Jack replied happily.

"Do you think about our future?"

"All the time. I think about a life with you. How do you feel about being a military wife?"

"If this is a proposal, you're going to have to do better."

"What's better. We would be together, travelling the world, living in exotic places."

"Like Vietnam?"

"Well, maybe not at first. But I think if we can free those poor people from communism maybe someday we could live there."

"I don't know Jack. I'm not sure I could sit back watching you run off to war. We are still very young. Things could change. Have you really set your mind on this?"

Jack felt that he was now in a corner. Part of him wanted to full fill his dream. Another part of him wanted to be with her always. Joining the military and leaving her was hard to think about.

"Tell you what. Let's just see what happens. All I know now is that I love you and I want to be with you."

"Ok." They reached her home on West Franklin Street. They sat on the porch and talked me more. She was early, her parents told her to be home by eleven. Her parents liked Jack and felt comfortable with him. Her mother knew that Eilis had strong feelings for this young man. The relationship would strengthen over the next several months. Eilis wanted to go to college. Marriage was not part of her future plans, but as much as they liked Jack his plans for the military was a concern.

CHAPTER 33

BEGINNING OF THE END

The grey unmarked Huey made its landing on the landing zone at Dong Ha. Dylan stepped off the chopper and waited for the returning mission. One of the missions he was involved in planning was a success. Bob Tevenson a CIA operative was returning with an NLF political officer and a bunch of intelligence documents. He had formed a team of South Vietnamese Special Forces members and had infiltrated North Vietnam. Dressed as NVA soldiers they had kidnapped the NLF official in his home and was on their way back. Three Hueys appeared on the horizon and began their dissent to the LZ. Once the choppers landed Stevenson jumped off the helicopter with a man handcuffed to a chain around his waist. He had a hood on his head and needed help walking. He had been drugged. Another two Americans got off one of the other birds carrying a large bag filled with documents. Tevenson turned the prisoner over to two men that had made the trip with Dylan. "Hey, Brogan got some presents for you," Tevenson said. "I see that, good job."

The Americans turned over the bag and Tevenson introduced them. "This is Lieutenant Tom Combs and Staff Sergeant Les Stevens."

"Good to see you fella's, good job." Dylan told them.

The men all shook hands and then turned to leave. "See you guys later, thanks. We can go on another walk in a couple of day's Les," Tevenson said. Alone with Tevenson, Dylan asked, "You used US troops for this op?"

"No, that's against the rules. Those guys are from Grim Reaper Recon, 1st of the 11th. Paperwork shows that two of their teams were on their own routine operation close to us. They secured the LZ for us to get out and would have been used as a QRF (Quick Reaction Force) if we needed it."

"Bob, if you get caught doing this shit there will be hell to pay," Dylan said shaking his head.

"No sweat man, don't mean nothing. Besides, mission accomplished. I gotta get my NVA guys back to their base before the Marines here freak out. See ya in Saigon, you're buying."

Dylan watched as the US Army Huey took off filled with NVA soldiers. The sight was surreal, to say the least. Boarding his own chopper, they took off for the airbase at Quang Tri. A C-130 was waiting on the tarmac for them and would take them to Saigon. An Army medic was on board the C-130 to check the prisoner. "He seems all right to me Mr. Brogan the sedative he got is about to wear off."

"OK, no sweat. Let's get him strapped into the seat, I would not want him to fall out while we are in flight," Dylan said. The flight took just over an hour when they arrived in Bien Hoa Airbase. Once there the prisoner was transported to a remote area of the base. He would be interrogated there by the South Vietnamese. Interrogation techniques used by his allies were known to be brutal. The prisoner was stripped and was seated in a metal chair that had been bolted to the floor. Dylan had no desire to participate, he left with the bag of documents that would be analyzed by US personnel. He drove himself back to MACV headquarters and turned the bag of documents over to one of Caroline's assistants. Walking over to her desk he asked, "Leaving on time today?"

"I guess, we will want to get to those documents though. Did you look at any of it?"

"No, I just gave it to intake to be inventoried, that should take a while."

"Then I guess we can go to dinner. Where do you want to go?"

"How about your place. The city is getting ready for the new year, there's just too much hustle and bustle. A nice quiet dinner and then we can relax with a bottle of wine." Dylan responded.

"I'm not making anything fancy. I have some chicken and some rice."

"Sounds perfect."

"All right, just give me a few minutes to clean up some of these files and we can go."

Dylan walked downstairs to the command center. The new year celebration was about to begin. Both sides had agreed to a cease fire. The command center was quiet. It was Monday, not that it made any difference. War was conducted seven days a week. Ask any grunt in the bush. For them, Dylan knew they only counted days. Many of the commands had made plans to bring their troops in from the field for stand-down's. A chance to clean up, rest up and drink away the pallets of beer that had been shipped around the country in anticipation of the break from war operations. Leaving the command center, he met Caroline in the hallway and they walked back to her apartment together. The city was preparing. Fireworks and firecrackers were already being used, much to the dismay of US troops in the city. Packets of firecrackers going off sounded like automatic weapons fire. Dylan hated them, as did many of the soldiers who found themselves in Saigon.

Reaching her apartment Caroline made dinner and they sat and talked about the war. Caroline loved the country and thought that the mission the US was involved in was worthwhile. Dylan was the opposite. He saw an uglier side of it all. He felt that the level of corruption and the apathy of the population would be its downfall. "You know they stripped that prisoner and put him in a metal chair. I knew what was about to happen so I left. Not a big fan of torture," Dylan said.

"I can understand why, but that's a Vietnamese issue. I don't like it either. I think this war will be over soon. The country is becoming more secure. Even the Delta is back under our control. The North just can't sustain the number of casualties we are inflicting," Caroline said.

"Oh, by the way, did you know that Bob Tevenson was using US troops on this last operation?"

"No, but the brass has its suspicions. If he gets caught there gonna fry his ass. Why would he do it? Risk his career like that? Who did he have this time?"

"I think he told me they were from 1st of the 11th, Reaper something."

Caroline thought for a moment, "That would be the Recon Platoon in Quang Tri. They are part of the 5th Infantry Division. I get a lot of intel across my desk from those guys."

"There not Rangers or Redondo's?" Dylan asked.

"No, but they are one tough group. Like the Rangers they operate with five or six-man teams. Charlie has bounties out on them."

"Who is the Ranger Company up there?"

"I could be wrong but I think it's Papa Company, 75th."

"I'm supposed to see Tevenson tomorrow when he comes down from his little outpost near Dong Ha. I'll talk with him, but your right if something happens to some poor GI on one of his ops, the brass will crucify him. His Vietnamese guys were dressed as NVA. I'm surprised the Marines up there didn't light them all up."

They finished dinner and a second bottle of wine and went to bed. Fireworks were going off at a regular clip and intensified around midnight. Dylan was having a hard time sleeping. The next few hours things started to quiet down when Dylan was awakened by a large boom. Sitting up in bed there was another big boom. "Those aren't fireworks," he said out loud shaking Caroline. Caroline never had a problem sleeping. Waking from a sound sleep by Dylan she asked annoyed, "What, go back to sleep." Another large boom, followed by another. Then the small arms fire started. The cacophony of sound was deafening. More explosions were heard and as Dylan dressed looking out the window the night sky around the city was filled with smoke bright flashes from large explosions and tracer fire. "Get dressed now, we have to get to the command center."

"What...holy shit what's happening?" Caroline asked sitting up in bed.

"Get dressed lets, go." Dylan urged. Caroline jumped out of bed and dressed quickly. "Make sure you bring your sidearm and extra ammo," Dylan offered.

"Jesus, it looks like the whole city is on fire," Caroline said stunned.

Duong stood before his company. He was now a senior company sergeant. He was the highest ranking enlisted man in the unit. His men loved and respected him. Other members of his squad and platoon that had survived the battle of the Ia Drang had also been promoted. When that engagement was over the 33rd Regiment made their way back to a base in Laos. There they received medical care and a much-needed rest. New uniforms, weapons and foot wear came down from the north along with new recruits and some veterans of other units. Troops in his company had been issued AK-47 and SKS rifles. New canvas web gear was also provided. The company stood in formation waiting for the captain commanding the company who would inspect his troops. Duong was impressed with his new company as they stood at parade rest, dressed in their new khaki uniforms, pith helmets and gear. As Captain Vim Dong approached, Duong order the company to attention. They all came to attention in one movement and sound as the commander came to attention behind Duong. Turning about face to face his commander Duong saluted.

The commander announced the plans that had been modified by General Giap, the Supreme Commander of the North Vietnamese Army. They all learned that they would be moving south in the next few days now part of the 6th NVA Regiment. They were to travel by trucks that would take them further south into Laos. Their destination was still held as a secret but once they left their base they had been joined with other units of not only their own Regiment, but other Regiments within the Division. Something big was coming and Duong knew that the movement of this many troops meant a large offensive. There was excitement in the air. Once they boarded trucks and began the trip south, Duong knew his suspicions were correct. The road south that the trucks travelled had deep ruts in the road made by the tires of many vehicles.

Travelling for days Duong marveled at the effort being made to move so many troops. Workers along the road made quick repairs when the road was bombed or damaged by artillery fire. A good number of the workers were women that cooked meals for the troops as they stopped to bivouac overnight. Moral was high and the troops of his company were in good spirits. They finally arrived at their destination in the Xe Xap forest on the Laotian and Vietnamese borders. A large camp had been prepared and he and his men settled in for classes and training. During this time, they became familiar with B-40 rockets, RPD, RPK machine guns and new RPG launchers. They also had new radio's.

Their enemy still had the advantage of air power, but Duong learned that Soviet made M46, 130mm Field Guns were already hidden in the jungles in South Vietnam. After several weeks of additional training they began to move north towards the city of Hue. This was their objective.

Moving only in the late afternoon and early evening they began the 120km march to Hue City. Dense jungle and mountainous terrain made the two-week trek difficult and tiring. Duong and his men were careful and there was no enemy contact. They reached an area just south of QL49 and QL1A just west of the Perfume River. It was late January and the country was looking forward to an agreed cease fire during the New Year celebration. After just one day's rest they began their assault on Hue at 3:30 on the morning of January 31st. The assault started with mortar and rocket fire and two battalions of NVA headed towards the Citadel. This was the headquarters of the 1st ARVN Division. Most of the ARVN were home on holiday leave and the Citadel was poorly defended. The NVA also made an attempt to seize the local MACV headquarters but a rag tag team of 200 Americans held their ground. Duongs company was part of a 5000-man force.

The Citadel is an ancient fort built in the 19th Century. Large earthen walls and stone were surrounded by a moat. As dawn approached Duong and his men had breached the moat and had gained access inside the old fort. General NGO Quang Truong commanding the ARVN could not keep the NVA from taking the fort. Heavy fighting ensued all day throughout the city. VC units had infiltrated the city days before the assault.

Dressed in civilian clothing and hiding their weapons in trucks, on the night of the assault they changed back into their uniforms and wreaked havoc inside the city.

Unknown to Duong and his men, the NVA had launched a massive assault all over the country. Days before the NVA had begun an assault on Khe Sanh. US forces were deployed to meet the diversionary challenge at the large Marine Base. The strategy of the NVA appeared to be working. All over South Vietnam more than 80,000 NVA troops made assaults on 100 cities as Duong and his men fought for control of the Citadel.

Inside the walls of the Citadel there were gardens and elaborate pagodas. The fort itself had more than 150 buildings. As Duong and his men made their assault they had to clear each building room by room as they advanced. Sniper fire and machine guns from the ARVN made moving between buildings treacherous. Moving down hallways and throwing grenades into rooms cleared out ARVN resistance. ARVN troops fought the NVA off but the battle for the old fort see-sawed back and forth. The NVA eventually took over the fort but the ARVN continued to hold the Mang Ca Garrison on the northern side of the fort.

Duong and his men had breached and secured the western gate and by 8AM that morning the North Vietnam Flag had been raised at the Flag Tower on the southern side of the fort. Fighting near the Imperial Palace was heavy but eventually the ARVN withdrew. Duong took an advantage of a lull in the fighting to rest and regroup his men. The new weapons and radios had made a big difference. As his men, rested Duong looked about the old structure known as the Mieu. Damage to the building due to the fighting was extensive. This was a holy place with much history. To see it under these conditions saddened him. Another thought nagged at him. The Americans had not responded with the one advantage they had. Air power. There were no planes or helicopters attacking his men. He realized why as he looked at the ornate beauty around him. His commander Captain Vim ordered him to gather his men and to move to the north and cross a bridge into the city itself. The American MACV headquarters was under attack and Duongs company was to re-enforce the VC units fighting there.

Working their way to the bridge Duong made note of a field hospital station set up on the southern side of the fort near the flag tower. Protected by the walls of the fort doctors and medics treated the wounded. Urging his men forward they crossed the bridge into the eastern part of the city. Small arms fire and grenades could be heard down the street towards the MACV complex. Urban street fighting was part of the training they took while back at the base in North Vietnam. Now he knew why. Part of the overall plan was that the populous was supposed to join them in fighting the Americans and the South Vietnamese forces. This never happened.

Moving and making his way down the street, he saw bodies of dead VC and NVA. Collecting magazines and canteens of water from his dead comrades he continued leading his men towards the MACV compound. Duong then came across a cluster of bodies of young men all military age but dressed in civilian clothing. The way the bodies lay on the ground he could see they had been lined up and shot. He was standing in the spot the shooter used, spent brass cartridges at his feet. Passing a home, he heard movement inside. Gesturing to two of his men they made their way inside. The house had been ransacked. A photo of a South Vietnamese soldier in a frame hung on the wall. It was askew on the wall and the glass had been broken. Then he and his men heard voices from a room in the back. As they entered the room Duong saw a woman holding a baby. She was crying and trembling in terror. Sitting on the floor in a corner the baby sensing the fear from its mother was fidgeting. Duong knelt before her and asked, "Why do you cry mother, there is nothing to fear." Collecting herself the woman said, "VC come and take away my husband. They shot him and other men from his unit."

"We are not VC. We are soldiers of the People's Army. We are here to liberate you and your child. To defeat the Americans and send them away. Uncle Ho has promised freedom and peace to all Vietnamese."

The woman cried and finally spoke, "If Uncle Ho promises peace then why do Vietnamese fight each other. Kill each other. I have no husband. My baby has no father. He is dead at the hands of VC communists." Then she held her baby tighter as firing in the street increased. Duong and his men left the woman and her child where they found her.

Most of Duong's company had gotten closer to the Americans and had passed Duong and the two men with him. Moving down the street he could see the American compound. Inside the sand bagged and wire covered walls the Americans were putting up a fierce fight. Duong heard the steady chatter of the M-60 machine gun as red tracers and other rounds impacted in the street and walls around him and his two comrades. One of them fell after being shot multiple times as he made his way down the street. The other had been wounded in the legs and as Duong tried to pull him inside a building to get him out of the line of fire Duong was hit in the head. Looking down the street he saw the red tracer coming at him. It was surreal as if normal time had slowed down. Instinctively Duong tucked his head down into his shoulders as the bullet struck the top of his pith helmet. The round tore the pith helmet off his head and creased his scalp along the right side. The force of the impact lifted Duong off his feet and he landed on his back. More o hit the street as they danced towards the man he had been trying to help. The gunner walked his rounds into the man killing him. Duong lying on his back turned on his side and rolled into the doorway of the building. His vision was blurred and his head hurt. Blood was already soaking his uniform shirt and covered his face. Then he passed out.

Running down the street in Saigon to the MACV Command Center, Dylan and Caroline stopped close to an alley. Caroline was out of breath and needed to rest. Dylan held her hand and had been pulling her along. He had his Thompson and his 45.

Breathing heavily Caroline pointing towards the alley cried out. "Look!" Ten NVA soldiers running down the alley crossed the street and continued down the alley on the other side. Small arms fire and explosions could be heard all over the city. "Was that, were they what I think they were?" Caroline asked.

"Fuckin A, those were NVA. Come on we have to get to MACV. Running again they came up on the MACV Compounds main gate. A large group of Army MP's and other soldiers were at the gate. Dylan saw an officer he knew and called out, "Yo, Prawtoski, hold your fire I'm coming in."

"Who are you? Prawtoski replied.

"It's me Dylan Brogan."

"OK, come on in."

Dylan and Caroline ran towards the gate and made it inside the building.

Once inside they went to the Operation Command Center. By now the room was alive with activity. Radio transmissions from bases and cities all over the country were coming in indicating massive numbers of NVA and VC troops assaulting their positions. Khe Sanh which had been attacked several days before was still under siege and the base was under rocket and artillery fire. Dylan left Caroline sitting in a chair and found his friend Bob Tevenson. "Bob, what the fuck is going on?" Dylan asked.

"Oh, hey buddy where ya been? The shit is really hitting the fan. Charlie's got a major case of the ass. Little fucker is hitting everything from the DMZ to the Delta."

"I saw a whole squad of NVA in full gear running down an alley on the way here. How the hell did we miss this?" Dylan asked.

"Beats me, I guess old Charles held his cards real close. This is some bad ass shit. Embassy has been breached. Sappers got inside. Fuckin, MP's are 11 Bravo (infantry) now. Westy (Westmorland) has no clue. That dumb ass moved a whole bunch of people up to Khe Sanh couple of days ago. Most of them are stuck now.

Highways are clogged with refugees from Quang Tri, Hue, and Da Nang. Marvin sent most of his people home for the holiday. Our pilots are scattered from Bangkok to Vung Tau. We are officially in deep shit."

Looking at a map of the country mounted on a wall red magnetic arrows showed that the enemy had launched a large operation. Arrows indicated that all NVA units were moving east out of Laos and Cambodia. Quang Tri, Hue and Da Nang were under heavy attack. The enemy's objective was clear. Take control of the major cities and restrict movement on all the roads. From a military stand point the enemy was about to take control of the country. Every Province in the south had been overrun. The size and the magnitude of the operation was not known yet but the US and their South Vietnamese allies were dealing with more than 80,000 enemy troops that had joined with the already 300,000 estimated to be in country. Together they had simultaneously attacked eastward cutting the country into sections.

Dylan returned to where he had left Caroline. She was still sitting in the chair. She also saw the map. Looking up she said, "Maybe you're right. It was stupid to get involved. We may even lose."

"We haven't lost yet, but I think we are getting our ass kicked."

During the day, Dylan learned more about the situation. Every major city, provincial capital, and hamlet had come under attack. Addition reports came in about the mass executions of South Vietnamese government, military and police officials. Finishing the seventh cup of coffee Dylan needed something to eat. He found Caroline in an office sleeping on a sofa and decided to let her sleep. Making his way to the mess hall he saw no one was serving any food, but cases of C-rations were on a table. He opened a can of turkey loaf and devoured it. Then he found a larger can of beans and franks. Bob Tevenson came in and joined him. "If you heat that up it's not that bad." Tevenson offered. Taking a beer can opener from his pocket he started opening wholes around the used turkey loaf can. Then he took out a piece of what looked like putty placed it in the can and lit it with a match. The putty caught fire instantly. He placed Dylan's can on top and to his amazement it was getting hot quickly. "What was that, it burns super-hot?" Dylan asked.

"C-4." Bob replied.

"What, that stuff is explosive."

"No shit, just don't stomp on it to put it out."

"You carry high explosives around in your pocket?"

"You really are a desk jockey. Relax, no sweat. Grab your beans their hot." To Dylan's amazement the broth in the can was boiling. The clump of C-4 had almost burned away. Bob had been right the hot food did taste better. "What's the latest sit-rep?" Tevenson asked.

"US troops are already reacting. It seems as if the shock of the operation has worn off. Even a lot of the ARVN units are starting to move on the NVA. The VC, however are still causing havoc. Most government officials and their families have been murdered. If we don't contain this the Saigon government might collapse. We knew the NVA traffic on the trail had increased, that's why Westmoreland sent all those units towards the border. The ruse worked. US and ARVN units left the cities and provincial capitals vulnerable." Dylan replied.

Tevenson said with some concern, "I hope my guys are all right. Their a tight group and should be ok."

"Your guys probably got dressed in their NVA outfits and went to town with the NVA."

"Hey man, that's low. My guys are loyal. They hate the communist's"

"Sorry, I didn't mean they joined the NVA, I just meant they could have blended in."

"I trust those guys with my life. You could be right. They could blend in."

"Now the other group you work with, could never pull it off."

"The Reapers. I love those guys. Now there are some bad ass soldiers."

Caroline entered the mess hall looking groggy. "Any coffee or breakfast?"

Bob looked in the case of B1, C-rations and found a can of chopped Ham and Eggs. He opened the can and lit another piece of C-4. The food was hot in under a minute. "Is that one of those heat tabs things?" She asked.

"Nope C-4," Bob replied.

Caroline took the spoon and tried the food after blowing on it. "Oh my God, this is delicious."

Tevenson laughed heartily. "What's so funny?" Dylan asked.

"Do you have any idea what the grunts call those?"

"No."

"Ham and motherfuckers," Bob replied grinning.

"I think their great," Caroline said.

His head pounding Duong woke with his face covered in blood. Using a canteen, he splashed water into his hands and cleaned himself as best he could. The wound had stopped bleeding. Thick dried blood covered the top of his head. He could hear small arms fire outside. The battle for Hue city continued. He had no idea how long he had been unconscious. He looked outside and saw that the sun was getting low in the west. It was late afternoon. Knowing he was wounded and separated from his unit he tried to stand. Dizziness was now a concern. He took a minute to gain his composure and stepped outside. Walking back towards the bridge he came to the house with the mother and baby.

Going inside slowly his AK-47 at the ready he went to the back room where they had found them. They were gone. No one was in the home.

Then he remembered the aid station at the southern wall of the Citadel. He needed to make it back there. Moving slowly not because of the dizziness, but shooting could be heard nearby. He passed bodies in the streets. He saw that dead NVA soldiers had no weapons, ammo or water. He hoped his comrades had gotten them. Duong then came on some civilians. These were not the young men he had seen earlier. Older men, women and some children lay in the gutters. He knew that sometimes civilians get caught in the cross fire but this was different. He heard something behind him and turned weapon ready. One man was assisting another with a bad leg wound. "No no, Hold your fire comrade." One of the men said.

They were both NVA. "Let me see your wound, I am a medic."

The medic checked his head as they sat in the street. "You have a bad laceration. It will need stiches. Do you feel dizzy?"

"Yes, sometimes. Who are you what unit are you with?" Duong asked.

We are with 4th PAVN Regiment. I am medical specialist Ngo Tam, I am taking this man back to the aid station. Who are you?"

"Senior Sergeant Phan Duong."

"Come with us Sergeant Phan, we will help you to the aid station. The doctor needs to stich that wound."

"What is happening? Give me a situation report," Duong demanded.

"The Americans still hold their compound. That is where we are coming from. We have been successful in taking the Citadel. The puppets soldiers are holding their own garrison. The city is under our control. There have yet to be any counter-attacks. Many civilians are moving south. We have caught them at their weakest," Tam said putting a bandage on Duongs head.

Finishing with the bandage the three men made their way back across the bridge to the aid station.

Tam made his report to the doctor on duty and gathered his supplies. Before he left he stopped to say goodbye and wish Duong luck.

Duong thanked him and lay done on the ground. Dizziness came back as the sky seemed to swirl looking up. He closed his eyes and was soon asleep. The doctor woke him and helped him into a tent. He washed and cleaned his wound and stitched it. "I would not wear a helmet for a while. Do you have a soft cover?" Duong checked his side pants pocket.

The boonie hat was still there. "Keep that on your head comrade it will help to keep the wound clean. Stay here tonight and get some sleep. I will check you in the morning," the doctor told Duong.

"I must find my company." He said.

"We can deal with that in the morning, get some rest."

Duong left the tent and found a spot against the earthen wall of the ancient fort. Sporadic gun fire could be heard inside the fort and in the city. He settled down and soon fell asleep.

The next morning, he woke with a headache. There was also the funny sensation that the top of his head was pushed together. Looking up he saw that the flag of North Vietnam was still flying over the Citadel. He went to find the doctor but he was busy tending to a man that had a bad leg wound. He found a medic and asked for some aspirin. The medic gave him some pills and went back to help the doctor. Duong went into the Citadel at the Thuong Tu Gate. Fighting continued on the northern side of the Citadel. He came across some men from his 1st and 3rd Platoon. They were excited and happy to see him. He learned that Captain Vim and the other officers had been killed fighting at the MACV compound. Ten of the men had no wounds but the other twenty-three had a variety of wounds none of them serious. They had set up on their own defensive positions to protect the gate Duong had just entered. They knew that the enemy would soon gather and make assaults to take back the fort. That very morning heavy fighting could be heard southeast of them as US Marines started to move into the city. Duong had the ten men without wounds to go outside the walls and collect any weapons, ammo and water they could carry. He and another man went to the aid station to talk with the wounded that were still coming in. They learned that the Marines had entered the city. There was house to house fighting. The Marines had brought tanks, clearing buildings of NVA in fortified positions the urban battle had begun. The Americans had still not deployed any attack aircraft but smaller prop planes the Americans called 'bird dogs' flew over the city. Duong wondered how much longer the Americans would hold off using their air power. Catching the doctor between patients he said, "Sir, maybe you should move inside the fort, it would be safer there."

"Actually, comrade I have orders to move the wounded to the railroad bridge to the west. Tonight, trucks will transport the wounded back into the mountains."

"Are we retreating?" Duong asked.

"No, we just want to get the wounded out. This battle will continue for some time. Each night the medics will get the wounded into the mountains. A field hospital was set up in tunnels months ago. We can better treat them there. I see you have found your company."

"Yes sir, but regrettably I have lost my commander and sixty men."

"I know you will do the best you can. As more wounded come in I will have the medics leave as much ammo and water as they can, good luck."

The doctor left to treat another wounded man. The ten-man patrol Duong sent out returned with as much ammo and water as they could carry.

With heavy fighting, all over the city and the Citadel on the northern side he and his men built up their fortified positions to protect the gate.

By the end of the day US marines had fought their way to
the besieged MACV compound and set up and secured an LZ
nearby. Duong and his men settled in for a long night. He knew
the Marines would come in the morning. There were sporadic
fire fights all night as NVA sappers and snipers tormented the
Marines. With the sun rising the day started with heavy fighting
as the Marines made their way house by house, block by block
towards the ancient cities fort. On the northern side of the fort,
ARVN units attacked NVA positions. The Garrison at Mang Ca
was never taken. NVA units now found themselves in defensive
positions to keep the fort. The American's had still not used air
strikes or artillery fire on the city or fort. The Marines and the
ARVN did bring tanks. NVA forces did have anti-tank RPG and
B40 rockets.

Duong and what was left of his company had fortified their
positions inside the fort. Today they were firing their weapons at
US Marines foolish enough to show themselves on the other side
of the Perfume River.

As the Marines cleared streets along the bank of the river
they took fire not only from entrenched VC and NVA, but from
Duong and his men as well. He posted the only sniper he had
with a Soviet SVD-63 Sniper Rifle on top of the gate. A demolition team came through the gate late in the afternoon. They had
orders to blow the railroad bridge west of the gate Duong was defending. Before night fall the railroad, bridge blew and collapsed
into the river. Duong wondered why the other bridge with access
to the city was still standing.

That bridge would be used by the Marines to cross from the
city to the walls of the old fort. They brought tanks and heavy
trucks with Quad-50 Machine guns. The heavy firepower decimated the makeshift defensive positions in and around the
southern gate guarded by Duong and what was left of his company. Initially the Marines were held at bay but the heavy weapons

and assaults by the Marines pushed Duong and his men further into the fort. The destruction of the sacred buildings was shocking. Duong made contact with another platoon of NVA that had been guarding the western gate to the fort. They were facing several companies of Marines with armor support. One of the M48 Patton Tanks had been knocked out by a recoilless rifle. With very little food and water the battle was taking its toll on Duong and his men. Pushed away from the southern gate they were now looking to break out of the western gate that evening. Several of his men were wounded and the ARVN re-enforcements were now pressing their attack from the northern side. Duong kept up the fight and while moving between his spread-out position took a bullet in the left shoulder. The round turned him knocking him down but fortunately it had gone straight through. A medic was able to bandage the new wound and stop the bleeding by using the tip of a hot bayonet.

He knew that this was the beginning of the end. He and his men had been fighting the Marines for almost three weeks. He was covered in dirt and blood. His uniform was torn and ripped. He had not eaten in two days. The ARVN re-enforcements had closed off their resupply. They were also running low on ammo. Water was in short supply. They had given all that they had. With no source of resupply their fate was sealed. Fight to the death or slip out during the night and make their way back into the jungle and mountains to the west. Some of his men had serious wounds. They endured their pain and their fate. Unable to travel they would be here when the Marines made their final advance and recaptured the ancient fort. They would be the rear guard so that their comrades could escape. Duong looked over the entire group of what was once a fine company of light infantry. They looked as bad as he did.

But he knew in his heart they would fight. He went to each man that was to be left behind. He helped them lay out what was left of the magazines and grenades. He left a full canteen of water. As he went to each man he embraced each one. Tears of sorrow and pride streaked through the dried dirt and blood on his face. Duong was the last man out of the west gate. He turned to his comrades and called to them, "Crack the Sky".

He heard the weak response of "Shake the Earth" as he left.

Later that day the North Vietnamese Flag that flew since the first morning of the assault had been cut down and taken by the Marines. It was over, once the sun set they would leave. The Marines came at dawn.

The press was having a field day. With fighting in Saigon and the rest of the country, military and Defense Department people were being bombarded by questions about the surprise offensive. Even Walter Cronkite was now broadcasting that the war was not winnable. Pictures and video tape of events in the country shocked President Johnson and the public. Dylan and Bob Tevenson sat in the hotel bar at the Continental having drinks. It was a normal scene in the early evening in Saigon but today there was a difference. Dylan's Thompson was on the table and Bob had his Car-15. "So, where is that round-eyed honey you pal around with?" Tevenson asked.

"She went home. Some MP's took her to her apartment." Dylan replied.

"So, does she have a friend I could meet or do I go to one of the local house's?" Bob asked.

"Local...are you nuts? With your luck, you'll run into a couple of VC

Getting their rocks off."

"Hey, I've been in the bush for a while, a man has needs."

"Tell it to the Marines at Khe Sanh and Hue."

"They can handle it, their Marines. Besides, the city is pretty quiet now, most of the VC have been rounded up and the NVA have gone back to the boonie hotel."

"Still not a good idea. Although, Hue should be wrapped up in a day or two. Three weeks of fighting has destroyed the city. Ever been to Hue? I still say it's one the prettiest places I have ever seen."

"Yeah, how about Shanghai? You said you liked it there too. Which reminds me. Ever catch up to that coolie turned VC."

"Vang Bo. Nope, that guy has just vanished. His daughters go to Phnom Penh about every other month. Maybe they meet him there."

"You ever tail them…you know looking for the mysterious 'Gayal.'

"No. Langley is not interested. Even the local desk doesn't care. They have their own fish to fry."

"Well, I need some female companionship. So, intend to prowl the city in search of a young girl who wants to satisfy my warrior lust."

"Yea, well as long as you have enough money you can pretty much get whatever ya want. Another couple of years and we will be leaving here with our tail between our legs. So, you had better get what you want now."

"Dylan old pal, do mean to say we are going to lose this war?"

"Already have."

"You're kidding, right? Charlie just launched the largest surprise attack in military history. Every province was hit. A hundred cities hit. Most of the entire countries infrastructure destroyed and a majority of opposition government official's dead. And we still kicked his ass back into Cambodia and Laos. How the hell do you figure we lost already?"

"You just said it yourself. How the hell did we miss it. We were caught with our pants down. We knew about the increased troop movements along the borders. Look what they pulled off. We can never win, it's their country and they want it back. They'll never give up."

Dylan sat alone after Bob left to pursue his lustful indulgences. He ordered another drink and thought about the past three weeks. Saigon itself was hit the US embassy had been attacked. Fighting in the Cholon section of the city had been vicious. He was convinced the war could not be won. The only way the Republic could survive would be if the US kept a large military presence for many more years. Anti-war protests back home had increased after the TET offensive. The public was tired of coming home from work, eating their dinners while watching the war on TV. Finishing his drink, he shouldered the Thompson and started walking to Caroline's. There was still a heavy presence of ARMY MP's and ARVN units patrolling the streets. Saigon was slowly getting back to normal. Reaching his own apartment first he locked up the Thompson and took a shower. Changing his clothes, he decided to keep the 45. Then he stopped, bought a bottle of wine and went to Caroline's apartment. He met her on the street as the MP jeep pulled up in front of her place. "Thanks fella's, be safe out there," she told the MP's.

"Goodnight Miss Grindell," they said pulling away from the curb. "Out picking up lonely GI's?" Dylan mocked.

"Sure, why not. You however, have a bottle of wine, so I sent them away," she smiled.

"What's for dinner?"

"Me of course, then afterward maybe I'll cook you something," she laughed opening her door.

CHAPTER 34

WAR IN THE STREETS

Washington DC was a favorite anti-war protest site. They came by the thousands. After the Tet offensive and the casualty reports the general public's support for the war was waning. No one knew it at the time but America was facing its first defeat since its revolution. "Hell, no we won't go," was chanted by young college age men on every campus. Draft cards were burned and young men facing the draft left for Canada. Jack was furious. How could they. Desert your own country, and even refuse to serve. It was a sore subject and everyone who knew him avoided the conversion.

Strolling along the East River Drive Jack and Eilis talked about his upcoming graduation. She knew as head strong as he was he would enlist before the year was over. He wanted his mother to sign the papers that summer. He was seventeen and months away from turning eighteen and would no longer need mom's permission. It was Easter weekend and the spring flowers were starting to bloom. "Uncle Mike and Aunt Susan will be up this weekend. I guess he will attempt another heart to heart with me about enlisting," Jack said.

conversation?

"I like your Uncle Mike. I think he is so funny. Susan's really sweet too. You know how your mother feels. Just try not to be angry or mean. Be nice, Jack for my sake all, right?"

"Yea, yea, I know."

"Besides, next year might be different. Have some patience. I talked with my Dad, he wants me to go to a community college. Then find work after school. I still have not decided what I would like to do. I suppose I will figure all that out later. I'm in no rush, you see."

"Oh, I see what your about. Your taking your time, waiting for the groove to reach out and turn you on. I already know. I've known since I was a boy. I still do," Jack said defiantly.

"I know. Did you know your mother spoke to me too?"

"Can't say I'm surprised about that. If my mother could she would get an audience with the Pope. I'm just so tired of talking about it. It is my life,"

Jack said getting angry.

"Ok, I'll change the subject. What do you think about the new Beatles album?" Eilis asked.

"I'm not too excited about it. I still say the best was Sgt. Pepper," Jack said stopping to sit on a bench. "Look Eilis, if you want to go with someone else while I'm gone I'll understand. I know you don't like the idea either but this is something I must do."

"Jack Randall, I have never said anything on the subject. Why would you say such a thing? What will be will be. Your right I don't like the idea of you going off to that war, but I also don't appreciate you telling me this. I think your mother is right, you're just a damned dope."

"Sorry."

"Come then, it's getting late. We best not be late for dinner," Eilis said standing. She started to walk back to his house her arms crossed in front of her. Great Jack thought, now she's mad at me.

Once they made it back to the house, Eilis started helping his mother and grandmother with dinner. He went upstairs to wash up. Sitting in his room he thought about his future. Everything he imagined it to be was right there. The time was now. He had made this decision so long ago. There would be no regrets, other than leaving Eilis. He combed his hair and went down stairs. The table was set and Jack saw that Eilis sat in her usual seat next to him. She said grace and they started to eat. He had a feeling the train and trolley ride back to her house would be a long one.

With dinner over they started returning to her house. If they made their connections the trip would take about an hour. Eilis was quiet for most of the trip but Jack was able to make small talk with her. Reaching her home, they sat in the basement. Her parents had set up a play room for her and her older brother years ago. Sitting on the sofa Jack started kissing her. At first, she was non-responsive but soon gave in. They continued kissing and Jack put his hand up under her shirt. She gently pushed his hand away. Then Jack made an attempt to unbutton her shirt when she broke the embrace. "This afternoon you wanted to give me away. Do you think you can just feel me up now like a common whore?"

"No...I was just...I mean,"

"Just what do you mean Jack Randall? Do you want me with someone else? Is this your way of pushing me off?" She was angry and hurt. She crossed her legs and folded her arms. Jack knew that was it. She would not discuss it any further. As his Uncle Mike would warn him, "She had her Irish up." He tried to plead a case but it useless. "Look, I'm sorry. I never meant that. I mean, I just thought it might be hard for you, with me away and all."

She never looked at him but said with a scary confidence, "Go to your grandparents Jack. Go now, before I say things I'll regret."

Jack stood slowly, and went upstairs. He grabbed his over-night bag and said goodnight to her parents. Then he walked the few blocks to his grandparents where he would spend the night.

Eilis sat there until she heard the screen door on the porch open and close. Then she buried her hands in her face and sobbed. She loved him. She could not help it. Wiping her face, she went upstairs. She never said anything to her parents sitting in the living room. She went straight to her room lay on her bed and cried herself to sleep.

Jack sat on his grandparent's porch. Before long, his grandfather came outside. "Your home early Jack."

"Yes sir." Jack replied as if his grandfather were miles away.

"Oh, I see. I'm looking forward to your mother and Colleen coming for Easter dinner."

"Granddad, am I wrong about going into the service?"

"Wrong? There's nothing wrong with wanting to serve your country son. The real question to ask is why and how. You're under no obligation to follow in your father's footsteps or anyone else's. Civil service is just as valuable as military service. Everyone plays a part."

"Yeahhh."

"Did you have a misunderstanding with Eilis?"

"Yes sir. We were talking about my enlistment. I said if she wanted to go out with other people it would be all right with me."

"Ouch."

"I was just trying to be honest with her Granddad, that's all really."

"You have a lot to learn boy. First and foremost, never, ever try to tell a woman how she should feel. Whether or not she wanted to see someone else was always her decision, not yours. Remember, when and if you enlist, your decision affects everyone else in your life. You'll make your decision and they all have to live with it. How they chose to deal with it is up to them not you."

His grandfather went back inside letting him think about what he said. Jack sat there on the porch for a long time. Finally, the chill in the night air got to him. He got up and locked the door and went to bed. Sleep came hours later well into the early morning.

He woke around ten that Easter Saturday morning and went down stairs. His grandmother was cutting up vegetables for the big dinner the following day. "Good morning, Jack are you hungry? How about some eggs and scrapple?

"Ok Grandma, thank you."

"Do you feel all right? You look like a lost puppy," Kay said.

"Eilis and I had a fight."

"Yes, the Judge told me. Have some breakfast, clean yourself up and go see her. If she's willing bring her back here, so I can talk to her."

"Aw, I don't know Grandma, she was pretty mad."

"Nonsense. I'll bet she had a good cry and will see things differently today." Jack poured coffee from the percolator and waited for his breakfast. His Grandmother had it ready quickly and he was surprised how hungry he was. Washing his own dishes, he went upstairs took a bath and changed his clothes. He walked to Eilis's house and found her sitting on the front porch. As he came up the steps she smiled and said, "Hi."

Cold, he was so cold. He shivered constantly. The chills would pass followed by the sweats and the hot flashes. His muscles hurt, and he was lying in his own filth. Duong had lost thirty pounds. Between the infection of his shoulder wound and this latest bout of malaria he was a very sick man. Doctors and nurses in clean hospital gowns took care of him. Eating sickened him and he had no control over his bowels. He had no idea where he was. Am I a prisoner, he thought. This is a clean hospital. A real hospital. Where am I? How did I get here? A nurse came by changed his bedding and washed him. She gave him some water that was cold. "Where am... I, who... are... you?" He managed to stammer.

"Lay still. You are safe and at home. This is the Central Military Hospital in Hanoi. You are a very sick man. Your wound to your shoulder was infected. You also have malaria."

"Hanoi...how...I don't remember."

"Just rest. My name is Anh. I have other patients; the doctor will come by soon." Duong lay there on the cool sheets. His entire body hurt. The chills and the sweats came back to back on and off. Someone else came by and fed him some broth. It wasn't much but at least he kept it down. A man next to him on the right lay still. His head was bandaged, and Duong could see that his left leg had been amputated. Duong lifted his head looking for his feet but as he moved them they hurt, so he knew he still had them. His shoulder was heavily bandaged. He felt his head with his right hand. The wound had healed and he discovered all his hair was gone. They must have shaved me he thought. Exhausted he fell into a very deep sleep.

Sunshine on his face woke him. There was an IV in his arm. He wondered, "Was that there before." He turned his head to the right. The same wounded man was still there. Hanoi...she said this was Hanoi. A man appeared at his bedside. He wore a clean white coat and smiled at him. "Good morning. I am Doctor Cao. How do you feel today?" The doctor asked as he checked his heart and lungs with a stethoscope. "This is Hanoi?" Duong asked.

"Yes comrade, this is Hanoi. You are safe here. Looking at his chart at the foot of the bed the doctor said with pleasure, 'Excellent, I see your temperature is coming down. Are you hungry, comrade?"

"Yes, and very thirsty."

"Good we shall get you some water, and maybe some rice with chicken broth." The doctor spoke to someone in the ward and a few minutes later a young girl gave him water and a small cup of rice in chicken broth to eat. After the girl fed him she left and Duong was left to his own thoughts. He tried to remember what had happened.

He was the last to leave. Tears filled his eyes as he ran out the west gate. Duong had said goodbye to the men that would fight so that he and the others could escape. He ran towards the now destroyed railroad bridge. The others who had left before him were now engaged with ARVN units guarding the west end of the old fort. Duong ran to the river along the bank. He was about to join some other NVA when he slipped on the bank falling into the Perfume River. He drifted off to sleep.

The memory still in his mind he dreamed of being in the river. The water was filled with debris from the fighting, including bodies. The current was taking him south away from the city and the Citadel. He had managed to keep his AK-47. Holding it up with right hand he tried swimming with the current with his left hand. The pain was extreme. The fire fight he had heard was now off to the north. He reached a small flat area where he was able to get out of the river. He followed the river moving south. The sounds of battle for the Citadel behind him. He ran into thick jungle. He could hear the helicopters now. Lots of them.

He woke from the dream and saw the blades of a ceiling fan turning. The sight startled him and he sat up in bed. His shoulder screamed with pain in defiance. He lay back down. Watching the blades of the fan turn slowly he remembered.

Falling in the river separated him from other members of the NVA escaping from the fort. He was alone. Making his way southwest through the jungle he marched all day. He was exhausted. Finding an old dead tree trunk, he broke off some small branches and hid behind them and lay down next to the tree. He fell asleep there. When he woke the next day, he saw a tall burly negro soldier.

The patch on his sleeve had the white head of an eagle. The man was urinating just ten feet away. Duong lay very still. The man had belts of ammo across his chest. He never saw Duong. When he finished urinating he turned and spoke to other soldiers behind him. It was a company of US Army soldiers. They were noisy. Then he closed his eyes, the turning blades of the fan lulling him back to sleep.

He saw his father. He was cutting wood for the fire. The supply camp had a visitor. A young girl who would not speak. She was small and frail; her face was a skull.

Startled by the nightmare, Duong opened his eyes. A girl woke him and fed him rice and chicken broth. Anh came to his bed after he ate. She helped him sit up. The pain in his shoulder bothered him. Anh and another older woman changed the shoulder bandage. The process was painful. His fever was down, and he felt stronger. "Maybe tomorrow You can sit in the garden. Fresh air and sunshine will help you heal," she said. "How did I get here?" He asked.

"You came here on the trucks. You were very sick." Anh replied.

"How long have I been here?" Duong asked.

"It's been two weeks now. You are getting better." She replied. Doctor Cao came to his bed. "How are we feeling today?"

"My shoulder hurts."

"You had to have surgery. The wound was badly infected. It was gangrenous. The surgeons had to remove some of the deltoid muscle. I'm afraid you will have very limited use of your left arm. The scalp wound has healed but you will have a nasty scar. Maybe when your hair grows back it will be hidden. You're lucky to be alive. When you came in the malaria was very bad. But I see you are improving. Try to eat as much as you can. There is water on the tray. Be sure to drink it. You are very dehydrated. Do you remember anything?"

"Yes, I was at the Citadel in Hue. Somehow, I made it here. I left my men. They fought to the end." He began to cry. Remembering the souls, he had to abandon. "There now Sergeant. You all did your duty. It was a great victory. We are all very proud of you and the others. Get some rest, I will be by later to heck on you. Remember to drink all the water you can." Cao left him to his thoughts and the memories came to him.

He remembered the Americans finally left him. He got up from the tree trunk. His shoulder hurt so much. He was weak and hungry. He found the area where they had stopped. Trash and other debris left behind littered the jungle ground. He found empty cans of rations. He used his finger to pull what little morsels was left in the cans. The Americans had no respect for the land he thought. He could hear them off to the west. He stayed at that place until he could not hear them anymore. Then he marched again. Avoiding trails, he made his way as quietly as he could through the jungle brush. Travelling all day, he heard fire fights off to the north of him. When it started getting dark he lay down next to a large tree. Nestled in the roots he slept that night. Duong heard the helicopters again. He could not see them, but he knew that these were the guns ships the enemy used. Off to the north he could hear them fire their rockets and machine guns. He started moving again and came to a small creek. He drank the water. He was so hungry he remembered.

The young girl came back and fed him again. This time there were pieces of beef mixed with the rice. He emptied the bowl quickly. Anh came to his bed and began to change the sheets. He noticed the soldier with the amputated leg was not in the bed to his left. "Where is the man that was there? He asked.

"I am sorry to say he died. He had lost so much blood. You are getting better Sergeant. Get some sleep and I will see you tomorrow." The man next to him was awake. Looking over at Duong he said, "My name is Tranh."

"Duong. What unit were you with?

"I was with the 4th Regiment. I was a radio operator. We assaulted the base at Khe Sanh. I had a chest wound. What unit were you with?"

I was a Senior Sergeant with the 6th Regiment at Hue." As they talked more, Duong learned of the magnitude of the assault made by the NVA.

Tranh told him about the many battles at Quang Tri and Da Nang. He also learned about the fighting in Plei Ku, Xuan Loc, and Saigon. "Is the war over? Have we won the final victory?" He asked.

"No. Sadly, the war continues. But we have had a great victory. We inflicted many casualties on the Americans and their puppet soldiers of the south."

"How do you know this?"

"I told you I was a radio operator with the command center at Khe Sanh. I heard all the radio reports coming in. We lost many of our comrades, but we dealt the enemy a serious blow. We were very close to ending the war."

Duong drank some of the water at his bedside and lay back down. He fell asleep.

He was still alone. Moving through the never-ending jungle by himself he was confident he was going in the right direction. The sounds of helicopters and explosions made it had hard to move. As much as he tried it felt as if the vines of the jungle held him in place. But it wasn't the vines. Hands reaching up from the ground held him back. He smelled something bad. He knew it was scent of rotting bodies. He saw them and they saw him. Lined up side by side they lay there calling for him. The wounds of their deaths were horrific. "Save us comrade, help us to return home."

He woke from the nightmare. He was sweating. He remembered the scene of the eleven bodies he came across. His first clue was the expended brass on the ground from a multitude of weapons. The bodies lay side by side. Stripped of everything except their torn and bloodied uniforms. The smell was over powering. Side by side they lay. Some of them still had their eyes open. The expressions on their faces frozen when they died. Birds and other animals had been feeding on the corpses. One of them had the white eagle head patch on his chest. It was from the American unit responsible for their demise. There were signs of an intense fire fight in the area. He was saddened he could not take the time to bury them. He had nothing but his bare hands. He left them there, just as he had left his men in the Citadel. He wept silently. A sense of failure overwhelmed him.

The train known as the El, arrived at 30th Street Station. Jack and Eilis walked across the Parkway past the Art Museum on their way to his house. Mike and Susan would arrive that morning and would stay the weekend. Eilis was looking forward to their visit. Jack was apprehensive.

With just a few weeks of school left he knew he would be enlisting soon.

Jack and Eilis had mended their relationship. She told him to do whatever he felt he needed too. "What will be, will be." She told him. Walking hand in hand they turned off of 29th Street and walked the final block to his house. The brand new 1968 Chevy Impala was parked in front of the house. Burgundy with a white vinyl top and interior, Jack knew from the New Jersey plates that it belonged to his Uncle Mike. "Wow, check it out. That is one boss looking car."

"It is beautiful," Eilis added.

"Maybe my Uncle Mike will let us take a ride," Jack said with excitement.

They went inside and greeted the visiting couple. Despite her Irish heritage, Mike loved the young girl. He felt that she was a good influence on Jack. Hope loved her as well. She was hoping that Eilis would be a good reason for Jack to avoid the military.

He would be eighteen in a few months. The draft concerned her. The war in Vietnam trudged on and more and more young men were drafted into service. Jack mentioned the shiny new car out front and his Uncle Mike tossed him the keys. "Do not wreck my new baby," he told the two teenagers.

"Wow, this is so cool, thanks Uncle Mike," Jack said with anticipation.

"Be back by lunch time you two," Colleen called after them as they left.

Getting into the car they marveled at the white interior and all the amenities. Jack started the big V8 engine and let it idle. "Oh, this is so boss," he told Eilis. "Once up the East and West River Drives and then we come back for lunch," Eilis said.

"Ok, here we go." Jack put the car in drive and drove up the narrow street. The car felt big and powerful to him. Turning north on 29th Street he went up to Poplar Street made a left and drove into Fairmount Park.

CHAPTER 35

STRIKING A DEAL

They were gone for an hour. Instead of driving up and down the drives along the Schuylkill River they parked on Lemon Hill in the Park.

They were making out when Eilis broke it off. "I thought you were excited to drive the new car?"

"I am, I did. This even more fun. We're alone." Jack said still kissing he neck. "Jack…it's still day light. We are not alone. Look around there are people everywhere."

"I know, it's just that we don't get much time to ourselves. Someone is always around."

"What did you think we were going to do?"

"Ok, I know. No sex outside of marriage. We can do other stuff."

"Well, we won't be doing any other stuff here."

"I know…but it just that I love you so much and you're so beautiful, it just drives me crazy sometimes," Jack said reaching up under her sweater.

"Jack…stop there are people all around."

"I wish I had my own car. Then we could come up here at night," Jack said as he fondled her breast.

"You're impossible. Now stop your ~~messing up~~ my bra. Besides we should go back to the house."

"All right, but I bet I know what we will be talking about."

"Don't forget you will be eighteen soon. You can go without your mother's permission. You might also get drafted. I talked with my dad, he told me that if you do enlist you get to pick what you would do in the Army. If your drafted, you can almost bet on being sent to Vietnam."

Jack started the car and put it in gear. They drove back in silence Jack thinking about the argument he would make. Eilis and his Uncle Mike had the same idea. Enlist and pick your MOS. (military occupational specialty)

Jack parked the car and they went inside. "Your both just in time. washup and let's have lunch," Hope said as they came in. They washed their hands and sat at the table. There was a variety of cold cuts as well as potato and macaroni salad. Jack was hungry and piled ham, cheese, pickles and lettuce on one of the Kaiser rolls. Jack and Eilis had cokes while the adults had beer. When lunch finished, Eilis helped Colleen and Susan clean up. Once lunch was cleared away they all sat at the table. Mike knowing the purpose of the visit wanted to get to it.

"Jack, your mother is concerned now that you are going to be out of school. I can guess what the answer will be, but I'll ask anyway. When school is over what do you want to do?" Hope had promised not to be emotional or argumentative. She sat and waited for Jack to answer. Jack looked around the table. This is it he thought. "I think everyone here knows my answer. I have given this a lot of thought. In a few months, I will be eighteen and eligible for the draft. Getting drafted is not something I want to do. I lose any and all control over what the military will do with me. I could even be assigned to the Marines. That being said, my initial plan is to enlist in the Army and ask for Special Forces School. That process will take at least a year and a half. If I go to

Ranger school before Special Forces that will take up two years of my three-year enlistment. By then the war may be over."

"I wish this damned war were over now. How much longer it will last is anyone's guess," Colleen said.

Mike added, "You know as well as I do there are no guarantees that you can get into Special Forces. Jump school and Ranger training may not be a problem, but finishing that you will be sent to Vietnam. So, I have an idea you might want to consider. Join the Navy. You can sign up for UDT school. (underwater demolition training) Once you finish frog man school you can put in for SEAL school. SEALS are just like the Green Berets. As a frogman, even if they send you to Vietnam, you will be on a big ship off the coast. They don't need frogmen in the jungle. That will make your mother and grandmother happier."

"Please, Jack just think about it before you do anything. I will promise you this. If you want to join the Navy, I will sign the papers," Hope told him. Jack looked at his mother. Wow. He thought. That's a surprise. In fact, I think I'm being set up. "When did you all decide this?"

In Saigon, MACV was still recovering from Phase One of the Tet offensive. Now they were dealing with Phase Two of a three phase offensive. Dylan was more convinced that the war was lost. The NVA had besieged Khe Sanh for almost three months. They had finally withdrawn. The large Marine base all but destroyed. Finishing his work, he met Caroline at the bar in the Continental Hotel. She was at a table and had already ordered her drink. He waved at a waiter and ordered a beer. Sitting down he seemed to be frustrated. "Problems at the office?" Caroline asked. "I have an asset. His name is Nguyen Tam. Nice little guy. I trust him. He gets me good intel. Problem is his cousin is a big wig NLF intel guy. I keep getting telexes from Langley that the guy can't be trusted and I should drop him. Some desk jockey in finance keeps rejecting his pay vouchers."

"Is Langley convinced that the guy's cousin is really NLF? I mean, Nguyen is a very common Vietnamese name."

"I know. I asked for the file on the cousin, and can't get it. I'm here, in country and their telling me I'm not authorized."

"Maybe the cousin is an asset for us in another operation run out of Langley. Give me the info tomorrow and maybe I can turn some of the bureaucratic wheels."

Dylan thought about the offer but realized he could not do it. "I can't. I have to go upcountry for an operation. Tevenson is doing another snatch and grab tonight. I have to get a flight early in the morning."

"Is he still using US troops for his little parties?"

Dylan finished his beer and said, "He assured me that any of our troops are for LZ security or as a QRF." (Quick Reaction Force)

"Yeah sure, I've heard that before."

"I gotta go. Flight leaves at 0500. How about dinner tomorrow?"

"Like I said, I've heard that before."

"Ha, very funny. I should be back by 1300 or so. I'll see you in the office. Hopefully I'll be bringing back lots of work for your group."

"All right, but if you stand me up I'll have to jump someone else. Girl has to leave her options open."

"See you tomorrow." Dylan left the bar and headed to his apartment. Arriving there he took a shower, cleaned his Thompson and 45 and went to sleep.

Waking to his alarm, Dylan dressed and got his gear. Two MP's in a jeep were waiting for him downstairs. They drove him to Tan Son Nhut airbase and he boarded his C-130 that would take him to Quang Tri. Once he landed another jeep was waiting for him.

The driver introduced himself as Ernie Sanchez. He wore a 45 on a pistol belt and he had an M16 in a scabbard strapped next to him on the outside of the jeep. He wore camo fatigues and the tab over his 5th Infantry Division patch noted he was RECON 1st of the 11th. Dylan knew a driver was going to pick him up but the unit his driver was from made him worry. This was the same outfit Tevenson had used before.

The driver took him to Camp Red Devil. This was the main base for the 11th Infantry Regiment of the 5th Division. An empty chopper pad was where Ernie pulled up and parked. Another jeep was also there. Five men in camo fatigues loaded down with weapons and their rucksacks were waiting for their insertion chopper. Dylan looked at the men. They had no US patches or other identifiable insignia on their uniforms. The M16's all had silencers on them. One very tall man was looking over his XM21 sniper rifle and scope. The jeep was labeled under the windshield. "Grim Reapers." Looking at the bumper Dylan saw the jeep was originally assigned to the Battalion Chaplain. The painted letters had been scratched off but enough remained that Dylan could read them. He laughed to himself and shook his head. Ernie walked over and talked with the men. Overhearing their conversation Dylan learned that this was Team One getting ready to go out on a mission. A few minutes later two inbound Hueys came and landed on the chopper pad. One of the birds was empty. As Dylan watched the second bird landed just as Tevenson jumped out.

Team One geared up, mounted their bird and were off.

"Well where is the guest of honor?" Dylan asked as he watched four US troops with the same uniforms and gear as Team One get off of Tevenson's chopper. They jumped into the Reaper jeep and drove off. "Rat bastard got away. He got spooked by all the barking dogs in the village. Then the goddamn Ruff Puffs got nervous and almost engaged us."

"Where are your NVA guys?"

"They're back at their base."

"Those Reaper guys were part of your mission?"

"No, that's against regulations. Those guys had a legitimate mission by the village where our guy hides out. I went along to try and snatch him, by myself."

"You just said the Regional Provision forces almost engaged, *us*." Dylan was angry. Tevenson was told about this.

"Like I said, I went alone. Those guys sort of followed me."

"Goddamn it Bob, you can't pull this mickey mouse bullshit. We talked about this. If Langley or for that matter the Station Chief catches you, you're gonna be in deep shit. Those guys belong to the Army not the company."

"Yeah, I've heard it all before. Look that's my ass in the sling out there. I need to know the people with me are on the up and up."

"You have you're NVA guys, why didn't you use them?"

"Two of them are family members of people in the village. That's why. The families think they're dead. Before you ask, they wanted it that way to protect the families from any retaliation. Look as far as any Viets are concerned I was part of the RECON team."

"Ernie was standing next to his jeep smoking a cigarette listening to the two CIA guys arguing. He had to laugh. Why would anyone want to get involved with this shit? This is one fucked up war, he thought.

Not much was said on the ride to the 69th Street Terminal. Jacks Uncle Mike had offered to drive them back to Media but Jack insisted on their taking the trolley from the terminal. Eilis knew Jack was angry. She was sure to hear about it once they were alone. The 5:15 trolley sat in line as the next trolley car to leave for Media. Jack and Eilis said goodbye to Mike and boarded the trolley. Sitting in the back, Jack set his overnight bag on the floor beside his seat. Two other people were on board when the operator got on and closed the doors. Once the trolley left the terminal Jack spoke. "That was all planned. They're trying to push me into the Navy. It's my life. Why can't they just let me be who I want to be. Am I really wrong for wanting to do what my grandfather, mother and uncle did. I know everyone hates the war, but why is it such a bad thing to want to serve your country. Am I that out of touch with the rest of the world? Guys just like me are doing it every day. What makes me so special?"

Eilis took his hand and said, "They love you. I love you. No one wants to see you go away. Certainly no one wants to see you get yourself killed. Suppose I was the one going away? Would you be happy? If I was a nurse in the war would you worry for me? Try to see this from our perspective. We all know what's coming. You have this obsession with fighting in a war, like your granddad and mother. Why I don't know. Do you? But, whatever drives you to this desire it's not just you that's affected."

"I have to do this Eilis. I can't go to college and get a deferment. I could not live with myself to know that someone else went in my place. That I stayed home and they went instead. I have to go. It's my duty and desire. Why should I take the coward's way out and join the Navy?"

"That not fair Jack. My father was in the Navy in World War II. He was no coward. He was not on a big ship. He was on a PT boat like JFK. Don't ever think that men who serve in the Navy are cowards."

Jack looked at her. She was angry and hurt. "I'm sorry. I didn't really mean that. It just that they want to shield me from combat. I know why. I would worry for you if you were going. But this is something I feel compelled to do." Jack was thinking. He remembered the book he had read as a boy. He remembered, Pedro Rojas. Ok, he thought. That's how everyone will be happy. I can play games too.

The trolley pulled into the last stop in Media. Jack and Eilis walked to her house. Eilis noted that Jack had a little more bounce in his step. "You don't seem as angry anymore. Are you feeling better?"

"I'm fine. Just fine. I think I may have found a way to make everyone happy."

"Really, tell me please."

"Nope it's going to be a big surprise. It's not easy to fool old Jack Randall."

"You're not going to tell me, are you? Not even me?"

"It's going to be a big surprise. A very big surprise."

Once they arrived at her house Eilis learned her parents were going to the movies. They had ordered pizza and soda's. Jack was hungry and ate two slices before Eilis sat down with two glasses filled with ice and root beer. "Hey save some for me."

Jack his mouth filled with pizza answered, "There's plenty. Besides you're only going to eat one slice."

"A girl has to watch her figure."

"Tell you what. Eat a second slice and I would still watch you're figure."

"Never you mind. It's my figure, you can watch just no touching."

"We'll just see about that."

"Jack Randall sometimes you can be positively wicked," Eilis blushed. They finished eating and Eilis cleaned up. "Wanna listen to some records?" Jack asked.

"Yes, that sounds great. I bought that new album by Gary Puckett the other day. Let's listen to that."

Eilis went upstairs to her room and Jack took the stairs to the basement. Finding the new album, he set the record player up for 33RPM. Opening the album, he placed the record on the player and started reading the back cover. Eilis came down the stairs wearing her jeans and an oversized tee shirt. They sat together on the overstuffed old sofa, listening to the music. Before long they were kissing and petting while the music played. Eilis had read the song list when she purchased the album and paced herself to the music. When the last song on the first side was playing, she began to slow Jack down. When the music stopped, she broke his embrace to turn the record over. Jack protested but it did him no good.

Returning to the couch he could see the nipples of her breasts pushing against the thin fabric of the tee shirt. She sat on his lap facing him as the music started to play again. They continued kissing, Jack reached up the front of her shirt touching her breasts. "Let me see," he whispered.

"No"

"C'mon please. You let me touch them, let me see them."

She stopped kissing him and smiled mischievously. "Tell me the big surprise...and maybe just maybe I'll let you see them."

"Ok, you first, take the shirt off."

"Oh, no you don't you go first, tell me the big surprise."

"I've got a big surprise for you," Jack said opening the fly to his jeans.

"Really, is it just for me."

"Ah huh."

"Tell me the big surprise."

"I'll make you a deal. Take off the shirt and I'll take it out."

"No, I want the surprise."

"First the shirt, then the surprise."

Eilis looked at him. She loved him so much. Reaching for the bottom of the shirt she pulled it over head exposing herself to him. Jack's eyes went wide. They were beautiful. She was beautiful. Eilis reached down putting her hand inside his shorts. Holding him she took his member out as he gazed at her. She stroked him. "Tell me," she whispered.

Jack took a breath as if to speak, no longer able to contain himself he ejaculated. Eilis squealed in surprise as Jack moaned with pleasure. Then both panicked as her parents came into the house upstairs. Eilis grabbed the sweatshirt she kept near the washing machine and put it on. Jack was desperate. Sitting on the couch covered in his own semen he grabbed the tee shirt to clean himself. "No, not the shirt, Eww," Eilis whispered in protest. Jack buttoned his jeans quickly. "We're home, we bought ice cream," Eilis heard her mother call from the top of the stairs.

"Ok, mom we'll be right up." Eilis had her hair in a pony-tail quickly and she saw the wet spot on Jacks jeans. "Stay here," she commanded. Walking up the steps she said, "I'll get the ice cream Jack put on another stack of 45's. Hi, mom we were danc-ing. How was the movie?"

"Very nice," her mother replied. She sniffed discreetly while she helped Eilis with the ice cream. "We should talk later honey," her mother said.

"All right Momma," Eilis replied.

Eilis took a bowl of ice cream down to the basement to share with Jack.

"That was close," Jack laughed.

"It's not funny. My mom suspects something. She wants to talk to me later."

"Oh, how about your father?"

"He was sitting in his chair in the living room. My mom may not say anything. I hope that wet spot on your lap dries before you leave."

"We can say I spilled ice cream. What flavor is it?"

"Butter pecan."

"Next time, I'll be more careful. We've never gone that far before. You owe me though, you've seen mine. I get to see yours now."

"No, you owe me. Tell me the big surprise, or I swear I'll pull that thing off of you."

427

"Ok, I guess you're right." Jack ate some ice cream from the bowl. "Well, I'm waiting."

"All right. Remember I told you about the book I read about the Marines in the Pacific? There was a character in the book. His name was Pedro Rojas. That's what I'm going to do."

"Wait, you want to be a Mexican in the Marines?"

"Yup, but I won't be in the Marines. I'll be in the Navy."

Eilis looked at Jack. She knew he was holding something back. He had a devilish look in his eyes. "Jack, it's time to go. You know how your grandmother gets if your late," Eilis's mother called down the stairs.

"Ok, Mrs. McDevitt, I'll be right up."

He and Eilis went upstairs. Her mother was in the kitchen. "Where's daddy? Eilis asked her mother.

"Upstairs getting ready for bed. You be careful walking back to your grandparents' house, Jack. Give my love to Kay."

"I will," Jack answered.

He kissed Eilis again on the porch. No one noticed the stain on his jeans.

"I'll see you tomorrow. Love ya!" Jack left and Eilis went back inside.

"I'm going to get a shower, mom."

"Ok, honey, I'll be up soon," her mother replied. Eilis finished her shower and changed into pajama's. She was thinking about what Jack said. What was the name of that book, she thought. She got into her bed and was about to put the light out when her mother knocked and came into her room. She sat on the edge of the bed and said, "Now then."

Birds chirped in the trees. It was so peaceful here in the mornings. Duong enjoyed sitting here in the garden. Every morning after breakfast one of the staff wheeled him out to the garden. The malaria was gone. His head had healed as well as the shoulder.

He had limited use of the left arm. Part of his deltoid muscle had been removed because of the infection. After he ate his lunch he had to endure the painful therapy of moving his arm as much as he could. He had gained back some weight. He thought about the Army Captain who came to see him yesterday. For Duong, the war was over. His injury meant that the Army wanted to discharge him. He pleaded his case to the Captain. He wanted to stay in the Army. He had valuable experience. He would be an asset to train new recruits. He believed that passing his knowledge and experience on to new men would help to save lives. The Captain was impressed and promised to make an appeal on his behalf. The second phase of the Tet Offensive was winding down. Another phase had been planned. More young men would be going south to fight. He read newspapers that indicated that the people of the United States were in revolt over their participation in the war. President Johnson was not running for reelection. The papers showed violent protests in American cities. Perhaps the end was near.

A week later the Army captain returned and informed him that he would be posted at his old base in Ky Son. He was scheduled to be released by the end of the week. Transportation would be provided and Duong retained his rank of Senior Sergeant. Training young men to survive in the jungle and fight in the war would be a life saver for Duong. Discharged from the Army he would have nowhere to go. He could not return to his old village in the south and all he ever knew since leaving it was the Army. This was now his home, his family and his life. He embraced it.

Once he was discharged from the hospital, he made his travel arrangements to Ky Son. Arriving there he marveled at how much the base had changed. It had grown and the number of troops there amazed him. He was directed to report to the training battalion. Handing his orders to a clerk he was shocked when the clerk gushed with excitement.

"It is an honor to meet you Phan Duong. The Major has been awaiting your arrival," he said.

The clerk took Duong to another building that was next to it. He saluted a Major and informed him that Senior Sergeant Phan Duong had reported for duty. The Major was pleased to see Duong as well. "Welcome Sergeant, it is a privilege to meet you. I am Major Trinh Ty. My clerk will see to your baggage and show you to your quarters. We have all heard of your dedication and courage. For now, rest from your travel and we can start first thing in the morning. Do you have any questions?"

"No sir, I am pleased to be here."

"Good, I look forward to introducing you to the staff of this battalion. Recruits arrive every day now. We begin training them in four days. I will see you in the morning."

Duong was escorted to his quarters by the clerk. It was a small hooch that included a desk a cabinet for his uniforms and a bed. Duong was tired from travelling and after unpacking lay on his bed to sleep.

It was hard to walk. Hands of his dead comrades reached from the ground grabbing at his feet. More hands reached and grabbed at him from the gate. The stone walls rose high into the sky. The gate was black. He could not see inside. He fought to release himself. He saw the helicopter diving straight at him. It had the head of a white eagle. Fire and smoke from the rockets and machine guns swept over him.

He sat up startled and awake from the nightmare. Sweat covered his body. He staggered to the door way. The cool night air washing over him. Looking through the tops of the trees he could see the faint glow of dawn. He dressed himself and walked to the mess area that the clerk had shown him the day before. There was tea and rice with fish. The troops preparing the food ignored him. He sat at a table and ate his breakfast. While drinking the last of his tea major Ty entered the mess. His first day of his new life was about to begin.

CHAPTER 36

YOUNG MEN, BAD DREAMS

The graduating class of Saint Joseph's Preparatory High School tossed their caps into the air. Jack had finished very high in his class and was eager to start his new life. Keeping the bargain that she made Hope signed his papers when he enlisted in the United States Navy. He was seventeen and would be finished his training sometime near his next birthday. In just two weeks he would report to the military induction center at 401 North Broad Street and be taken to the US Navy's Great Lakes Recruit Training Center. The graduation party would be later that afternoon at his grandparent's home in Media.

Jack changed out of his cap and gown and went outside to the back yard. A cooler filled with beer and soda sat next to a table filled with snacks. His grandfather was busy filling up the Weber barbeque grill with charcoal briquets. It was getting warmer, but high elm and maple trees around the yard kept the early afternoon sun at bay. Out in front of the house his Uncle Mike and Aunt Susan arrived with Hope his mother and grandmother Colleen. They were the first guests to arrive. Soon after Maggie and Kevin arrived with Dorothy and Steve. Everyone greeted each other outside in the yard and took seats on folding lawn chairs set up around the yard. Jack sat with his mother and Uncle Mike when the McDevitt family came out of the house and stood on the back porch. Kay greeted Eilis' mother and father and introduced them to the other guests. Eilis finally appeared wearing a white linen shift dress. Her hair was down below her shoulders and getting longer. Seeing her Jack took a deep breath. Mike said in his ear, "You, dumb ass, you're going to leave that girl here all summer while you go play sailor?"

Walking down the steps into the yard she had everyone's eye.

Jack's mother beamed, "Eilis you look beautiful."

"Thank you." She knew everyone and greeted them all warmly leaving Jack as the last. Hugging and kissing his cheek she saw a man she did not know on the back porch. Then she heard Maggie cry out, "Oh my God, oh my God." Walking down the steps into the yard Maggie threw herself into Dylan's arms. "Far out, it's my Uncle Dylan.," Jack told her excitedly.

"The one from the CIA, in Vietnam?" Eilis asked.

"Yea."

Dylan made his way around the yard hugging and kissing the women and handshaking and back slapping the men. He finally made his way to Jack and Eilis. "Hi, Uncle Dylan," Jack said greeting his uncle.

In his best Humphrey Bogart imitation Dylan said, "Go away kid, ya bother me." Taking Eilis by both hands he kissed her on the cheek. "You are as pretty as everyone says you are. It's so nice to finally meet you Barbara."

"Barbara, who's Barbara? My name is Eilis," Eilis replied.

"Whoops, sorry kid you should have told me," Dylan said with a devious grin.

"Haha, very funny," Jack said hugging his uncle.

"Congratulations kid. Sorry I missed the big show, my flight was delayed," Dylan told Jack.

"Who's Barbara?" Eilis asked.

"Uncle Dylan this is my girlfriend Eilis." Jack emphasized Eilis.

"Oh, of course now I remember, Barbara was a brunette."

"Hello, so nice to meet you. Who's Barbara?" Eilis asked tauntingly Looking at Jack playing along with Dylan's' game.

"There's no Barbara. Uncle Dylan tell her there is no Barbara."

"Oh man, look I didn't mean to get you in a jam. I'm gonna go get a beer," Dylan said apologetically and walked to the cooler.

"Barbara?" Eilis asked.

"Baby, there is no Barbara. That's just my uncle. Really, come on, you know I love you, only you."

"Hah, you sailors are all the same. I think I'll go talk with your grandmother," Eilis said mockingly annoyed as she turned and walked away.

"Eilis!"

Jack looked over at his Uncle Dylan standing with his Uncle Mike, both enjoying his dilemma. He walked towards them.

"Enjoying yourselves? Jack asked.

Uncle Mike took a drink from the bottle of Ortliebs and asked, "Who's Barbara?"

He and Dylan laughed and then finally Jack joined in. "OK, very funny. You better set the record straight before the days over," Jack said poking his uncle in the chest.

Dylan replied, "No sweat, GI. She is number one round eyed girl. You're a lucky fella Jack."

"What's a round eyed girl?" Jack asked.

"Any western women that is not an oriental. Most of the women in country are slant eyed." Dylan answered.

"Is that some kind of Vietnam slang? Jack asked.

"For sure, newbie. Don't mean nothing. You gonna learn most rickie tick, or your shit is in a world of hurt. Take you down to the Ville get some numba one chop chop. Then find you a nice tea girl to love you long time, no short time, she give you numba one

boom boom. Make sure she clean or else no can go back to the world." Dylan said.

Jack looked at his uncle Mike and asked, "Did you understand any of that?"

"Some of it. A lot of things are the same over the years," Mike replied.

"So, what's it like?" Jack asked Dylan.

Dylan looked around to assure himself he would not be overheard and replied, "It's a cluster fuck. There's no way we can win. The communists have infiltrated the Saigon government. Most of the ARVN forces are useless. Some of their officers are good, and command great units, but there is no way they can fight off the entire NVA by themselves. Corruption is rampant. You think our politicians are bad, they could really learn from the Viets. I'm telling you, I believe within five years the commies will take over, shortly after we are gone."

"You mean we lose?" Jack asked surprised.

"Yeah kid. We lose. Nixon is already pulling out ground troops. The 9th Infantry Division will be sent home later this summer with the 82nd Airborne leaving by the end of the year. Next year several of the separate infantry brigades will be sent home as well. We scale back and turn over everything to the ARVN, and Charlie builds up his bases in Laos and Cambodia. After we leave, Charlie will go through the country like a hot knife in butter."

Jack was stunned. How can this be he thought? "You are messing with my head, right? I mean, lose. We can't lose. We have to save those poor people from communism. Laos, Cambodia and Thailand will all be next.

The domino effect. They have no aircraft. They don't even have tanks or artillery. How can we lose?"

No tanks or artillery, huh. Tell that to the Marines at Khe Sanh. Charlie, has it all. Yes, we do control the air, but old Chuck he's smart. He keeps all his heavy infantry support weapons hidden away. I'm telling you Jack, when this is all over you'll see NVA tanks rolling in the streets of Saigon."

"I can't believe that." Jack said stubbornly.

"All right, I'll make you a bet. Vietnam will be unified under the communist government of Hanoi before... ah the end of 1975. How's that? Twenty buck's say's I'm right," Dylan offered.

"Don't take the bet Jack. Remember he's CIA. They know stuff, we don't," Mike added.

"You got a bet. In fact, I got twenty bucks that says your wrong and...

We win and South Vietnam keeps its independence. Like North and South Korea." Jack said with defiance.

"Far out, double or nothing. Put some skin to it," Dylan replied extending his hand. Jack shook it confident he was $40 richer. "How about you Mike, you want some of the action?" Dylan asked.

"Nah, I would feel bad taking the kids money."

Dylan asked, "So what's the deal Jack? Why are you in such a hurry to get to the Nam? What could be so important to you that leaving that pretty girl of yours home alone with Jodie doesn't stop you?"

"Who's Jodie?" Jack asked.

"The guy that replaces you when you're gone. Do you really think that Eilis will sit home alone waiting by the fire for her hero to return? She's young, very pretty and from what I can tell smart. Guy's everywhere will be after her."

"She wouldn't do that. We love each other and she understands and accepts my decision. She would never betray me," Jack replied defiantly.

Mike added, "We have pretty much exhausted the reasons why Jack feels so compelled to do this. I have to say, he's been very adamant about fulfilling this...dream for years now."

"So, what's he gonna do when he winds up in the Nam, and his dream becomes a nightmare? And it is a nightmare. Look

Jack, Vietnam is beautiful country. It's people, and I mean the real people are sweet, generous and hardworking simple people. They don't really care about who's in charge or what the government ideology is. All they want to do is live in the same village as their ancestors and work hard to feed and provide for their families. That's why we can never really win. The Chinese, British, the French and the Japanese have been telling them what they can and can't do under force of arms for decades. They want to be left alone. They want their independence. And they will have it under force of arms. I see my mother and father waving for me. The damage is done Jack. You already signed the papers. I hope you don't live to regret it." Dylan left Mike and Jack. Jack was confused. His Uncle Mike was right about one thing. The CIA knew more than everyday Americans. Mike interrupted his thoughts, "Jack, there is some things that can't be controlled no matter how much we try. You won't be seeing some of the ugly stuff about this war from a ship at sea. Just keep your nose clean, do your duty as best you can, and when you come home think about what's more important to you. Make sure you write to Eilis every day so you will always be in her thoughts. If things for you two are meant to be...then everything will work out for the best."

"Thanks Uncle Mike, I will." Jack walked towards the house and catching her eye gestured for Eilis to follow him. The two of them met on the front porch and Jack embraced her. She returned his hug but sensed something was wrong. "What is it Jack?"

"I have no right to expect you to be...well faithful to me while I am away. I know you say that you support my decision. I just want you to know I don't expect you to be stuck at home."

"Where is this coming from Jack. I know there is no Barbara. That's just your uncle being funny and me playing along. I love you. I told you a long time ago I would always support you."

"I know you did, but there is something else. You can't tell anyone please," Jack pleaded.

"Jack, what is it, I promise I won't tell anyone."

"When I enlisted in the Navy, I signed up for Hospital Corpsman Training and Vietnam. I won't be on any ship. I'll be assigned to a Marine unit as a medic in Vietnam."

"That's it. Jack, I know who Pedro Rojas is, Battle Cry the book."

"You knew."

"Of course, silly. I like to think that you and I are Danny and Kathy. I will worry about you though. Just come home safe and sound. I'll be here."

"I love you, Eilis. I always will." He kissed her then. Laughter from the party interrupted them and they went hand in hand returning to the back yard. As they walked down the steps Eilis said, "One things for sure. When your mother finds out, she will kill you."

Jack thought about what she said. If he survived Vietnam his mother would shower him with hugs and kisses upon his return. Then she would kill him.

They were all so young. Very young. Duong had become a part of all of this when he was just fourteen. Some of the new recruits to be trained looked as if they were not much older. Conscripts was a more accurate description. Many of these young boys did not enlist. They were drafted. Duong remembered well the lesson's he was taught in the jungle camps where he had lived. Many US troops were drafted and not professional soldiers. As such they were undependable. In practice, he learned the opposite. Drafted or not the helicopter soldiers he encountered in the battle of the Ia Drang fought bravely against his brothers at LZ X-Ray. Despite the fact that Duong and his men overwhelmed them days later at LZ Albany, they fought like tigers. The Marines at Hue and the Citadel were just as fearsome. Then there were those small quick firefights in the jungle. He marveled at how the Americans fought so hard not so much to defeat Duong and his men, but to rescue their dead and wounded.

Standing now in front of the formation with Major Ty, Duong was introduced. "The man responsible for your training is a hero of the people. He has fought against the Americans and the ARVN. He was at the 'Forest of Lost Souls' (Battle of the Ia Drang) and the Citadel in the city of Hue. During the first phase of the people's offensive he was separated from his company. Wounded and alone he made his way many kilometers without food and water back to our forces in Cambodia. During his trip, he successfully evaded detection from the 'Eagle Head' American unit with their helicopters and their forces on the ground. He will teach you how to survive in the jungles of the south. He will teach you how to fight the enemy. Listen and learn from him. His teachings will save your life and the lives of your comrades. With his knowledge given to you we will win the final victory and unite our country and send the Americans home in defeat. His name is Senior Sergeant Phan Duong."

Duong looked over at the men, boys really in the front row. "Platoon leaders have been given your assignments. Upon dismissal take your platoons to the designated training areas. Company dismissed," he turned and saluted Major Ty. Then as the new trainees moved to the places they were meant to be Duong followed the first platoon. At this class, the men were familiarizing themselves with the SKS rifle. Many of them looked up from the weapon in their hands at Duong. Some of them were wide eyed with admiration. He spoke to all of them quietly and with patience. He was teaching them the little things that would help them survive. He talked about what each class was learning. This one was the SKS rifle. He taught them the little things he had learned from others as they fought in the south. "Everyone is a student and everyone is a teacher. Learn the responsibilities of each man in your unit. Learn here how to function with your weapons. You must take care of each other. I learned this from the Americans. They will stop at nothing to rescue a wounded or man killed. Use this passion against them. In the south, we would set up ambush sights at places where the helicopters could land. Then we would wound some of them. When the helicopters would land to take the wounded away we would attack them just as they were landing. The Americans would fight back, but we would slip back into our tunnels evading them. Remember to get close to them. They have very accurate artillery fire."

He looked into their faces as he spoke. They were focused on his every word.

It had been a long day. Still he found the work to be rewarding. It was not that these young boys admired him. It was that they were so attentive to what he was telling them. Maybe they would be the turning tide. He lay on his bunk and soon fell asleep. The one thing he never told his young men was that the terror would always return. It would come back to him in the night when he was most vulnerable and could not control it.

The hands were back. Clinging to his legs and feet he could not move. In the darkness of the gate surrounding the walls he watched helplessly as the Marines came. The men he left behind fought bravely but were eaten alive by the tanks. They screamed in agony as their bodies were pulled apart, pieces of their flesh hanging from the huge jagged teeth of the tanks. Then they came to feast on the carrion, they're scattered and crushed bones picked at by the Marines. He shouted but no one heard him. The weapon in his hand so heavy he could not lift it. Then a large burly Marine turned towards him. He had belts of machine gun ammunition crossing his chest. His face under the helmet was the mask of death. His thickly muscled arms pulled a huge stone from the wall. With every step he appeared taller, and holding the stone over his head stood high above Duong dropping it on him.

He woke on the floor. He had flung himself out of his bed. He was covered in sweat. He was shaking. He sat there on the floor weeping in silence. Tomorrow he knew that he would be looking into the faces of many dead men. So many had already died. Never to return home they're families told only that they were missing. He would remember the names and the faces. He would remember their bravery. Accepting their own deaths so that he and others could escape. They were the true heroes of the people. When the final victory was won, monuments in their memory and honor would be erected. The largest monument of all would be a free and united Vietnam.

A few days after Jacks graduation party, Dylan sat in the kitchen drinking coffee with his mother and Aunt Colleen. He was telling them his opinions of the war in Vietnam and how he felt it had all been a mistake. "The one thing that I marvel at is how the whole country seems to be aware and obsessed with the war. I mean it's everywhere, even if it is mostly negative. Was it like that here in the second world war?"

Colleen answered, "Well sort of. I mean everyone was working towards the war effort. We had scrap metal drives, clothing drives and War Bond drives. We collected all kinds of resources to be reused for the war effort. The troops wore their uniforms. Military people could be seen all over town. But the troops had a lot of support then, sadly now it's different."

Dylan replied, "I have noticed the contrast. After getting off the plane in San Francisco, I saw all the hippies there. They were actually cursing at our troops coming home. Some of the names I could not repeat here. I saw a pretty young girl with flowers in her long hair in a sun dress spit on an Air Force Captain. Unbelievable and at the same time the rest of the country is getting on with their everyday lives as if there is no war. I shudder to think what they would do to me if they knew what I was doing there."

"What are you doing there? Maggie asked.

"Mom, you know I can't tell you specifics. The company runs its own operations. Sometimes I think our agenda and purpose is in contrast with the military. MACV is obsessed with body counts and how many weapons captured. As for us, we are just trying to hold the government together. The corruption level would blow your mind."

Hope added, "Well at least I was able to convince Jack to forget the Army and the Marines. Now if he goes he will be on a ship at sea, far away from the jungles."

"I see you've never heard of the brown water navy."

"No, what is it?" Hope asked.

"The Navy has patrol boats, mostly in the Delta. They patrol the rivers. They work very closely with the 9th Infantry Division. Landing craft and fire support vessels support the divisions operations. Soon they will be working with the ARVN units."

"Oh, that crafty little…"

Colleen interrupted, "now Hope, let's not think the worst."

Dylan asked, "What is Jack's M O S going to be?"

"M O S, what is that, I've heard the term before." Colleen inquired.

"Military Occupational Specialty. Or in layman terms his job," Dylan replied.

"I don't know. He had to take a bunch of tests prior to his enlistment. He was told there would be more tests during basic training. Is that how the Navy assigns the M O S?" Hope asked.

"Usually that's true. Let's not get ahead of ourselves. It's a big world. The Navy will send him where they want him. He could wind up cruising the Mediterranean," Dylan explained.

Colleen sighed, "One could only pray."

Sunday morning started out cool with a pleasant breeze. This was Jack's last day as a civilian. Tomorrow he would be on his way to Chicago. He had mixed feelings. Part of him regretted joining the Navy. He had really focused on the Army or the Marines. The Navy came out of left field. Still he had made the deal with his mother and the government. There would be no turning back now. Yesterday the family had a going away party. He wanted to spend his last day before he left with Eilis. They planned on going to the zoo. It was one of the favorite things Eilis loved to do. He dressed and went downstairs to the kitchen for breakfast. His mother heard him getting up and as always had timed his breakfast right on time as he came into the kitchen. Sitting at the table he wolfed down the three eggs and scrapple that Hope had prepared. "You might want to take a breath between bites, Jack." Hope complained.

"Sorry Mom, I have to go get Eilis." He wiped his mouth and drank half of the cup of coffee, kissed his mother on the cheek and headed for the door. He was gone in a flash and Hope was left standing there alone. She sat and started to cry. Colleen arrived home from early mass and found Hope crying at the table. "Do all of this now and not tomorrow. His departure should be positive, not negative. All smiles in the morning no tears. Just be happy and proud for him."

"I will Mom, but it is just so hard. You never cried when Daddy left?"

Hope asked her mother. "Not in front of him. But those were different times. You have prepared him his entire life to grow up and be a good man. Now you have to let him go so he can do it."

"That's a lot easier said than done."

"I did it for you, and you'll do it for him. Dear God, I'm getting to good at this, saying goodbye to someone you love as they run off to play soldier."

Jack jumped off the trolley and started walking towards her house. Eilis was waiting on the porch. She wore a full-length granny skirt with sandals. She wore her long hair parted in the middle hung well below her shoulders. They walked quickly back to the trolley stop. On Sunday mornings, the layover was longer and they boarded the same trolley Jack had come in on. Jack was nervous, but Eilis put his mind to rest by talking about the zoo. They had been there many times. Reaching the 69th Street Terminal they took the elevated line to 63rd Street and walked north to Girard Avenue. The trolley from there would take them right to the zoo. Eilis was excited as Jack purchased the admission tickets. Passing through the entrance gates jack watched as Eilis tried to get a peacock to come to her. The birds roamed the grounds freely, and on occasion the males would spread their tail feathers. Walking hand in hand down the main path they purchased a bag of peanuts. They always went straight to the elephant house. There was one spot where guests could reach out and toss peanuts into the waiting mouths of the elephants. Jack had conflicting emotions. Part of him loved her more the way she marveled at the animals. Another part was saddened because he was leaving her. She was upbeat and happy today. Determined that their last day together would be a happy one. Tomorrow would come, she could not stop it, so there was only today.

After the elephant house, they stopped in the large cat house. Eilis always thought it was sad to see such massive beasts caged up. The first cage they came to held a large male lion. Eilis growled at him. The lion lay on the cool tile of his cage, head erect staring at nothing and panting. He ignored her. "I don't think he is very impressed with your growl," Jack said to her. "He's just playing hard to get," she laughed. Leaving the lions, they walked past cages holding jaguars, leopards and servals. Then they approached one of her favorites. It was a male snow leopard. The soft looking white fur was dotted with silver and light gray spots. Eilis had named him 'Frosty'. The large cat looked right at her as if knowing he was special to her. "Look at him Jack. He is so pretty. Yet at the same time he is thickly muscled. Look at his massive paws. Those powerful shoulders. The long tail bouncing back and forth. I just want to hug the stuffing out of him." She was beaming and happy to see the large powerful predator. "And he would love to eat you." Jack laughed.

She turned to him. Wrapping her arms around his neck she looked deep into his eyes. "No, he would never do that. He knows I love him. He is the only lover I could ever have beside you Jack Randall." Frosty got up. He started pacing the front of his cage. Keeping his eyes on Eilis he paced back and forth. "I think he's jealous of you Jack." She giggled.

"He should be. Jack kissed her. It was one of the most passionate kisses the two had ever shared. Frosty quickened his pace. Back and forth he moved. The huge wide soft paws patting against the tiled floor of the cage. Then the keeper arrived from around the corner. Throwing a large piece of beef that had been butterfly cut till it was almost flat between the bars and the floor the cat lunged and at it. "Ha, Jack laughed, he's not jealous of me. You've been replaced by a steak." Eilis punched him in the chest and skipped away. "But we are still lovers." She laughed.

Jack watched the big cat gnaw on his meal. "You will never replace me. Enjoy your steak." Jack said to the cat as he chased after Eilis. The leopard ignored him.

They had lunch at the zoo and walked the grounds until late afternoon. Then they took the trolleys back to her home in Media. They bought a pizza after getting off the trolley and walked to her house. Knowing this would be Jacks last night with Eilis her mother had made arrangements to visit with her sister in Chester. They would be home by ten. Jack took the pizza and some sodas down to the basement. Eilis went to her room to change. When she came down stairs she was wearing an oversized tee-shirt and a pair of shorts. They sat together on the couch eating pizza and drinking their sodas. Jack had put a stack of 45's on the record player.

"Are you nervous about tomorrow?" Eilis asked. It was the first time today the subject had come up. "A little. I know one thing, I am really going to miss you." Mel Carters voice came from the record player.

"Hold me, hold me, never let me go, until you've told me, told me,"

Jack and Eilis fell into each other arms. Shifting their bodies, they lay side by side on the overstuffed old couch. Kissing her neck, he had his hands up under her shirt. Before the record was over she lay on top of him, shirtless, their hips grinding slowly at the pace of the music.

She unbuttoned his shirt and pants. He was reaching with both hands fighting the button and zipper of her shorts. Once he had them open his hands reached inside her shorts holding her butt, squeezing her and pushing her hips harder into him. Then he turned her back unto her side and reached into the front of her pants. Finding her he slipped his finger inside the moist place he wanted to be. Her breathing changed and her hips started moving faster. She took a breath and then her body shuddered. Eilis rolled over on top of him. Pulling at his pants she found what she wanted. Kissing his chest and stomach she surprised him when her mouth found him. His hips raised into the air off the couch as his orgasm seized him. Laying together catching their breath they continued kissing and touching each other. Sexually this is a s far as they had ever gone together. Jack made an attempt to push her shorts off, but she stopped him. "No Jack. When I finally surrender to a man it will be as his wife, and not on an old couch in my parent's basement."

"All right, this was very special. I'm really going to have something to look forward too. I love you Eilis, I always will." The records had finished. The silence in the room was deafening. "What time is it?" Eilis asked. "Nine fifteen. It's time for me to go."

They both dressed and cleaned up. Jack and Eilis went out on the front porch to say their goodbyes. After the final kiss, she watched him walk up the street, then he turned the corner and waved, he was gone. She had promised herself not to cry as they said goodbye to each other. Now that he was gone she burst into tears running up the stairs she fell on her bed and sobbed. Still crying she knew her parents would be home soon. She drew a bath and sat in the hot tub weeping. The memory of Jack turning the corner as he waved goodbye still locked in her mind. Unknown to her then, she would never see her Jack again.

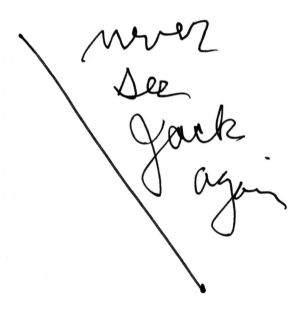

CHAPTER 37
NEW TRAVELS

Getting off the train in Chicago, the Navy had buses waiting. Jack was in the second of eight buses that would take them to the Recruit training center where they would learn to be sailors. He kept to himself the memory of his last night with Eilis fresh in his mind. After arriving at the base, he was ushered into a large room and took a seat. The Master Chief addressing the men informed them all that there would be another round of physicals. There would also be several hours of IQ tests. Under no circumstances was anyone permitted to have a car on the base and none of them were allowed to drive any vehicle on base no matter how many licenses they had. In the next few days they would be getting haircuts, uniforms and billet assignments. The actual basic training course would start on Monday.

The next three days before the weekend had kept everyone busy. As promised they had another physical first thing Wednesday morning followed by more general knowledge and IQ testing that afternoon.

On Thursday morning, everyone got a haircut. Once leaving the barbers there was a lot of head rubbing and laughter. After lunch, they were all marched to a large warehouse. They were all issued a sea bag and stopping along each station was issue new uniforms. Underwear, socks, bell bottom dungarees and shirts, dress blue and dress white uniforms and the infamous pee coat and Navy dixie cup. In addition, they were also given a ball cap. With the heavy and full sea bags, they marched back to the reception barracks and were to change into their dungarees. Civilian cloths would either be mailed home or donated to a local charity. On Friday mornings formation, they started looking like sailors. That afternoon they would be assigned their individual basic training classes and assigned to the barracks where they would spend the next eight weeks.

Jack had to learn a new language. In the Navy, walls were bulkheads. Doorways were called a hatch. The head was the bathroom. On Friday afternoon after lunch they met the men who would train them to be sailors. They were assigned new barracks, received instruction on how to pack their foot lockers and bulkhead lockers. They were given instructions on how to make a bed or a rack. Then they had their evening chow. That night some of the men wrote letters home others gathered in groups getting to know one another. Some of those conversations went late into the night.

On Saturday morning Five AM came hard fast and noisy. Chiefs in khaki uniforms banged empty trash cans with old broom handles and screamed at the new boots to get out of their beds. Men who were to slow to rise whether on top or bottom of the two-tiered bunks found themselves on the floor when the bunk was turned on its side. One boot complained that basic was not supposed to start until Monday. He regretted his comment.

They were told once everyone was up that they had just ten minutes to shave, shower and dress into their ball caps and dungarees. Then they were to fall into formation in front of the barracks. Anyone that was late would live to regret it. No one was late. Marched to the mess hall the men were fed breakfast. They were told there was busy day in front of them. "Eat heartily, the mess chief is sensitive about his cooking," they were told. With everyone fed, they formed up and began the first of the daily one mile run that followed breakfast. Many of the men especially the smokers left their breakfast on the road. Exhausted they returned to the barracks and still in formation were now assaulted verbally by the Chiefs because they had left the barracks in disarray. Bunks that had been overt turned remained where they were. No one had made a bunk. The head had water on the floor, towels scattered, and some of the sinks still had the water running. Toilets had not been flushed. The entire barracks was a disgrace. They spent their day cleaning up and getting the barracks ready for inspection. By the end of evening chow, they were exhausted.

The barracks looked as clean as it was the day they arrived. They were told that this was what their living quarters would look like each day before they came to morning formation. Church services were posted on a bulletin board in the day room. Sunday afternoon was free time. Monday morning the real work would begin.

"Surprise!" Caroline was startled. She was going home and retiring from the company after more than twenty years of service. The party was in her honor and was attended by other US personnel and Vietnamese employees of the embassy. Dylan was there as well. He was going to miss her. Returning from his leave home he had been back in Saigon for just two weeks. Nothing had changed much. Nixon's new plan of Vietnamization was just getting off the planning table. US troops came and went. Men in new jungle fatigues walked past other men in dirty crusted uniforms. They would soon change into crisp new khaki's and go home. The new guys would learn they had just 364 more days before they too could return to the world.

The party was well organized. Caroline received presents and they had a cake baked for her. The crest of the CIA right there on top. She had spent the last week with Dylan. She shipped most of her belongings home. Her apartment now occupied by someone else. She was excited to be going home. With the exception of some leave time when she first arrived in Vietnam she had not been home in over ten years. She loved it here. She loved the people. Caroline was starting to agree with Dylan. This war was lost, the communist would win. She did not want to be here when it happened. It had been a wonderful and exciting time of her life. It was however, time to go home.

"This will be the first thanksgiving at home in a long time. Imagine real turkey, stuffing and cranberry sauce. Pumpkin pie and ice cream. Breyers ice cream, Breyers! Not that shit we get at the embassy. When do you think you will call it quits here? You could retire or get a posting anywhere in the world," she asked Dylan as they lay in bed together.

"Me, I'll stay to the bitter end, then maybe I'll retire and write a book. That would scare the crap out of a lot of people. I just wonder how much longer. I wonder what happened to the Bo sisters. I imagine they are in Phenom Penh with their father. Funny as big as the world is, how small it can be. So, are you going to chase down some poor bastard and make him marry you?"

"Oh no, my darling. I shall wait by the door, night after night, for my man to return from war," Caroline said then laughed out loud at her own joke.

"Me come home with numba one mama san. You see," Dylan laughed.

The morning she left he drove her to the airport in a jeep. Her flight was going to Honolulu. She would spend a few days there, before booking a flight to LA or Frisco. She had time on her hands. She was in no rush. They said goodbye, promised to write and her flight left on time. Dylan stood on the tarmac as her flight lifted off. In one way, he loved her. He knew however he was not in love with her. The sex was great and he was going to miss it and her. He had no idea when he would see her again. Ok he thought to himself as he left the airport. Time to find numba one girl for chop chop, and boom boom.

Caroline sat by the window in first class just behind the cockpit of the Pan American commercial flight. As the aircraft lifted off she watched the country she fell in love with fall away. Below she could see off in the distance the huge base at Long Binh. Turning north the lush green jungles below were broken up by small villages surrounded by rice patties. She would always remember the beauty of this country. Then she saw the scars on the land she loved. Bomb craters patched the earth. Visible even from 20,000 feet and climbing it was the last reminder of the sadness and despair endured by the people that lived such simple lives there. Smoke and flames from napalm bombs could be seen on top of a mountain as war claimed more of the land below. Then the aircraft banked to the right and all she could see was blue sky. When the plane leveled out the South China Sea glistened as sunlight reflected off its waves. "Good morning, would you like more coffee?" The stewardess asked her breaking her thoughts. "Yes please, how soon before you serve breakfast?"

"We can cook up some eggs and bacon in just a few minutes. How would you like your eggs?"

"Sunny side up. Thank You."

"I'll be back in just a few minutes," the stewardess said leaving her for the galley. She thought about Dylan. She would miss him. Then she thought what I need to do is find a rich old man and marry the bastard. She was smiling broadly when the eggs and bacon arrived.

"Can I get you anything else?"

"Do you know any rich old men?" Caroline asked.

"Honey, if I did we would not be having this conversation. Enjoy your breakfast."

"Thank you, I will."

They looked older now. There was a confidence about them. Or maybe it was determination. Duong stood before his first class to finish its training. From here they would be going south, a trip that was long and exhausting not to mention dangerous. Reports were that the US was bombing the trail south on a daily basis. He had prepared them as best he could. They were still in awe of him. The affection went both ways. They were as ready as they could be. Duong knew however, the horrible things that they would see and do would be with them the rest of their lives. The luckier ones would be killed, for them the horror and the haunted faces of men they fought with would be gone. They together would invade the dreams of those who survived. He said goodbye to each of them as they mounted the trucks that would take them into Laos down the now infamous trail.

The trucks brought new men in with them. They looked as young and innocent as his first group. Squad leaders barked commands to get them to form up. Confusion, fear and apprehension showed on their faces. The training would be repeated. Weapons, camouflage, booby traps, and night movement exercises. Class room sessions on tactics used by the enemy. Of course, the required communist political classes. Duong, felt they were waste of his time. The focus of these young men was to fight and stay alive. Politics was never a concern. They were fighting for the independence of the entire country. One Vietnam, determined to find its own destiny without any foreign power overseeing what they did as a united country. Freedom. The one wish and goal of all people. Kings, Emperors and Presidents would come and go, but for each person to be free was eternal.

Finally, they were assembled at attention. Major Ty came out of his office to address the troops. He would give his speech praising Duong for his service. When he finished, the troops would settle in to their quarters, be issued equipment and weapons. The task of staying alive and killing other men would begin immediately.

San Francisco was the hippie capital of the world. Haight Asbury in the middle of the city was where the happening was. Tom Brady had arrived a few years ago. His quest to find Michael was long behind him. Music, drugs and the anti-war movement was where he found comfort. Politicians were the enemy. The man was the enemy. Tom was the oldest of his little group of friends. His hair was long and getting grey. He grew a beard that was already turning white. The drugs took their effect on his body. He weighed 130 pounds and had very little body fat. He was still drawing and found that tourist liked to buy his more psychedelic works. He made enough money to keep a room over a store on Haight Street. Today was no different. Several people camped out on the floor, and getting out of bed he had to tip toe over the sleeping bodies. He took a shower and by the time he finished his sleep over guests were starting to get up.

The plan today was too hang out in Buena Vista Park. Everyone gathered their belongings and the small troop made their way to the park. Once there the group rolled joints, and met with other people. Before long the air was thick with the aroma of marijuana. Someone had brought guitar and he began playing and singing the popular songs of the day. The event although not formally organized turned into a happening. By the early afternoon there were more than fifty people in the park dancing singing and lounging on the grass. Tourist came by to watch as they made their way around the city. The mood was festive and peaceful. Before long many left the park making their way east toward the down town area protesting the war. Tom stayed in the park selling his drawings and paintings. Today was a good day with bright sunshine and temperatures in the sixties.

Tom was considered to be the old man of the group. He had many sexual relationships with anyone that showed an interest. One of his favorite partners was a girl named Melodie. She had run away from her home in Nebraska. At sixteen she was thin with waist long hair. She stayed mostly with Tom but the two did not have a formal relationship. Free love and the sexual revolution had long been a way of living. Melodie knew about Toms history and was fascinated by his experience in Cuba.

She could also sing and played the violin. It was the only possession she cherished. She hung out with Tom and played and sang songs.

Tourist and others would drop coins or paper money in her violin case. Between her playing and Toms art work they had a good day. At the end of the day they collected their money bought some food and wine returning to Tom's room. Living together they made a good team and usually had more money than the rest of the group they hung out with. It was simple life and both of them seemed content to share their lives.

Melodie had run away from her home, because her mother's boyfriend had started to molest her. Her father had been killed in an automobile accident when she was twelve and her mother had numerous boyfriends. The last one was the worst. Somehow, she had managed to hitch hike her way west and wound up in the city by the bay. Tom met her in Golden Gate Park one day. She was dirty and hungry. She had no place to stay and slept in the parks around Haight Asbury. When she first saw, him he looked out of place because of his age. He walked up to her and asked if she was hungry. Reaching into his backpack he gave her a sandwich that she devoured. "My name is Tom. Do you have a place to stay?"

"No, I stay here in the parks."

"You can hang with me if you want. No strings attached. It's not safe for you here in the parks."

"But, I'll be safe with you, right. Look man I'm not into the whole daddy thing."

"It's cool. Really, I'm not looking for sex or anything. Come with me. What's your name?"

"Melodie."

"Great name. Look Melodie, it's better to find someone to hang out with. A lot of people stay with me from time to time. Like I said no strings. You can get cleaned up have place to crash and a steady supply of food."

Having no real choices, she agreed and found that Tom was cool. Back at his place she showered and was able to get some clothes that had been left by others. Now she had someplace to live and just as Tom had said there were no strings. Over time they got to know each other's history. She had been there for more than a month when she first slept with him.

With boot camp behind him, Jack would remain at Great Lakes for his hospital corpsman training. He was not alone. Several of his boot camp buddies would also attend courses there. Friendships that would last a life time were made. Many of the men training with Jack would be assigned to Naval hospitals or to the Fleet serving on ships. Volunteers like Jack would go on to Camp Lejeune for Field Medical Training or FMT, with the Marines. For now, they were training on how to tend to hospital patients and assisting doctors and nurses. They learned all of the basics. Testing blood pressure, taking temperatures, cleaning and dressing surgical wounds, moving patients and dispensing medications. The paperwork that was part of the training was extensive. During his time in Illinois, Jack and Eilis exchanged letters. He kept all her letters and she did as well. Finishing high school, she found a job at the Courthouse in Media. She worked for the Delaware County Sheriff's Office, as a file clerk processing warrants. She enjoyed the work and kept contact with some of her girlfriends from school. She often visited with Jacks grandparents. His grandfather the Judge, now retired had helped her get the job she had. She was looking forward to Jack getting home soon. His last letter indicated with just two more weeks to go he would be going to North Carolina and then on to a permanent posting. He was not fooling her. She knew that posting would be with the Marines in Vietnam. His mother and grandmother were happy that he chose the job he was training for. What they did not realize was that Jack had deceived them. He had volunteered to be a corpsman and Vietnam.

With just a week to go before finishing his training he was summoned to the Master Chiefs office. He was a burly man with a nose that had seen a few fist fights. The closely cropped hair on his head looked like a brush. Knocking on the hatch frame he was ordered to enter. Memories came back to Jack as the Master Chief sat behind his desk shuffling some papers with a large cigar clenched in his teeth. The aroma of that cigar filled the room. "Stand at ease, Randall. The next class was filled for FMT, alphabetically. You and anyone with a last name starting with a P or later missed the cut. So, here are your options. One, stay here pulling details for a month until the next FMT. Two, go home on leave for thirty days, then go to FMT. What's your pleasure?"

Jack thought for just a second. This was no surprise. The scuttlebutt they all heard was true. If Jack went home on leave from FMT, he would have to face his family about his volunteering for Vietnam as a corpsman assigned to a Marine combat unit. Going home now meant he would get home for some of the holidays and be able to go to FMT and then on to Vietnam. He had already decided on the latter. "Master Chief, I choose to go on leave and be assigned to FMT after return to duty." He said looking straight ahead.

The Master Chief took a long pull on his cigar blowing the smoke across his desk in Jacks direction. "Very well, Randall. Your orders will be cut and waiting for you at BUPERS (Bureau of Personnel) day after graduation. Good luck, now get the hell out of my office."

"Aye aye, Master Chief," Jack bellowed coming to attention and leaving the office. Jack was happy with his choice. Returning to the barracks after evening chow he wrote a letter to Eilis, and his mother. He let them both know he would be home for Thanksgiving. One more week and he would be back with Eilis. Time could not have crawled any slower.

Two weeks before the Thanksgiving holiday Hospitalman Jack Randall walked out of 30th Street Station and looked east to the city sky line. He was home. William Penn still stood atop the City Hall tower. Finding a cab, he put his sea bag into the trunk and gave the cabbie the address of his house on Ogden Street. They had graduated on a Wednesday and he picked up his orders the following day. He was on a train from Chicago before lunch time. He arrived a day later in the evening in Philadelphia. He remembered that Friday nights the family often had a cheese steak dinner from Beatos. A cheese steak sounded great. Based on his letters he was not due until Saturday, so he was early. He paid the cabbie and walked into the home he had known since he was a baby. Dropping the sea bag, his mother screamed with delight and hugged him so hard he had a hard time getting his breath. His grandmother was on the phone with the steak shop. "Make that three mushroom cheese steaks with fried onions," she said. Then she ran to greet Jack. "My goodness, look at you. They put some weight on you. I don't like the hair. Why do they cut off all the hair?"

"I can start to grow it back some now Grandma. One more training assignment then I'll have a permanent posting," Jack replied hugging his grandmother.

"Are you hungry? I ordered an extra steak," Colleen stated.

"I'm starved. A cheese steak sounds great."

"Good. Come into the kitchen, the steaks will be here soon. Do you want a coke or a beer?"

"Coke is fine, Ma. It sure is great to be home."

Then Hope asked the question he knew he would have to answer carefully. "Your home for a month then where are they sending you?"

"North Carolina, for field medical training. After that it's up to the Navy.

For now, I'm home, I'm hungry and just happy to be here."

The delivery man showed up with the steaks and they sat down to eat.

Jack took his first bite as the steam came off the sandwich, "Oh my God. That is so good," he said with a mouthful of steak.

Hope replied, "Don't talk with your mouth full."

CHAPTER 38
A LIFE GONE FOREVER

The month went quickly. He was amazed at how the thirty-day leave had passed. But it had been worth every minute. Eilis was working but they spent every weekend together. Jack's Uncle Mike and Aunt Susan had come up from the shore for Thanksgiving dinner at Kevin and Maggie's. In Media, the dinner was hosted by John and Kay Randall and was attended by Hope and Colleen as well. Jack and Eilis had to make three stops on the big day to see everyone. His grandfather had let him use his car and the first stop they made on the holiday was to Kevin and Maggie's house. Arriving late in the morning Maggie had prepared hors d'oeuvres. They had to pace themselves knowing that there was going to be two more dinner stops. Mike was happy to see him. Steve and Dorothy were also there with their twin boys, Joe and Tommy.

Both of Dorothy's boys were excited to see Mike and Susan. When Jack and Eilis arrived, the boys became more excited, as Jack was wearing his dress blue uniform. He and Eilis had to pose for numerous photos with other family members and friends throughout that day. The last images of a happy time that would be forever gone.

Another surprise was that Caroline Grindell was home. She had retired from the CIA. She had worked for the agency since it had been formed. She had substantial savings and a healthy pension. She stopped by and told everyone the story of how she had seen Tom Brady in San Francisco.

No one had any news from Cuba on the fate of Michael Costigan Jr. It was presumed he was dead but a body had never been recovered. Tom was a 'professional hippie' as Caroline put it living on his drawings and shacked up with a sixteen-year old run away named Melodie. Jack had met him as a boy and always thought there was something a little off about Tom.

The conversation with his Uncle Mike came back to him, as he sat on the train heading to North Carolina. "So, what does the Navy have in store for you Jack?" They were sitting out in the yard smoking cigars and drinking beer. It had been a nice day, with sunshine and around sixty degrees. I have to report back for training in North Carolina. Once I finish that I'm at the Navy's disposal."

"You going to Vietnam?" Mike was looking right at Jack when the question was asked. Jack could never lie to his Uncle. "Yes."

"The training in North Carolina. What's it for? Based on your stripes and insignia, you're no apprentice."

"The school is called FMT, field medical training. I spend four weeks with the Marines at Camp Lejeune."

"Then your off to Vietnam. I don't think this is what your mother is expecting."

"No, she's not. Look there is still a chance I could be assigned to a battalion aid station. Nothing is guaranteed that I will be in the jungle with the Marines. Everyone will know in another five weeks. For now, everybody is happy for me. Let's just leave it there."

Look kid, I went to bat for you. I was the one keeping the wolves at bay. Your mother went along with this Navy deal thinking you would not be running around the country getting shot at. When she finds out, I'll be the one here at home holding the bag. I have to admit though, you pulled the wool over everybody's eyes. Does Eilis know?"

"She has known all along."

"Wow, I have to say then the girls a keeper. Just do me one final favor, Jack. Do not get yourself killed over there. Your mother and grandmother will never forgive me."

The train wheels turned over and over, clickity clack, clickity clack. It was true. He had deceived everyone. Maybe he should have waited till he was eighteen. Then he could have made up his own mind and done what he had always wanted to do. The Navy wasn't bad, he kind of liked it.

The medical training, he accomplished was top notch. He could make a life for himself doing this. I wonder if Eilis would agree to it. She had been a little standoffish. He thought about that first Saturday when he arrived home on leave. He took the trolley out to Media. Dressed in civilian clothes that were a little tight in the shoulders, chest and arms he was fooling no one. The haircut gave him away. He remembered the dirty looks people his own age gave him.

Arriving on her front porch, her father was coming outside. "Holy smoke, how are you doing boy? You look great. I see Navy chow agrees with you. When did you get home?"

"Late yesterday, Mr. McDevitt. I came out first thing to see Eilis."

"Well she's inside with her mother. Me I'm off for a round of golf with the boys. We can catch up later, welcome home Jack."

"Thank you, sir." Jack walked into the house and found Eilis at the kitchen table with her mother. She was wearing a robe over her pajama's and her hair was up in curlers. "Hello, ladies. Got a cup of coffee for a young sailor?"

"Jack, oh my goodness, I'm so happy to see you," Fran McDevitt said hugging him. "Don't look, don't look," Eilis screamed running for the stairs. "That girl I swear," Fran stated. I'm afraid she may be a few minutes, you want some cream or sugar in your coffee?"

"Just cream please. She knew I would be home today. Why is she surprised?"

"Well she was expecting you later this afternoon or this evening. How are you Jack, you look great."

"Thank you. I'm all right. Funny though, I got some dirty looks from some kids I saw coming out. I guess the haircut screams military."

"Well, you know. Ever since that offensive last year and the attacks they showed on the news every night, most people think we should get out of the war." They sat and drank the coffee and talked then Fran got up to tend to the breakfast dishes. Hearing Eilis coming down the stairs Jack met her in the dining room. She was just as pretty as the day he first saw her. Her hair was still a little wet but he could not have cared less. Taking her into his arms he kissed her. Then there was a very long hug. "I've missed you so much," he told her.

"I missed you too. Let's go sit on the porch and catch up."

"Ok."

"Mom, we'll be out front," Eilis called to her mother.

Once outside she punched him hard on the arm. "Ow, hey what's that for?"

"For surprising me in my PJ's and my hair in curlers," she smiled tauntingly.

Taking her in his arms he told her, "I don't care, I missed you."

He remembered the rest of that day they sat and talked. After lunch, they walked down to the park. She sat on the swing and he pushed her. Each time she went up her hair flowing back in the air. She laughed and he did too. That day they were just two people in love with each other. Children living in a moment of innocence about to be dragged into the ugliness of war and reality.

After they left Kevin's house on Thanksgiving they drove home to the home where Eilis had spent her entire life. Her mother had dinner ready early. Her father complained about missing the football on TV, but sat at the table and ate like a hungry lion. Jack and Eilis put small portions on their plates, another dinner was waiting across town. Talk about the war was avoided. Everyone knew what was coming, but just maybe if it was ignored long enough it would just go away. After dinner, the walked across town to Jack's grandparent's house. Another dinner of smaller portions then Jack and Eilis walked outside on the front porch. "I'm stuffed. I don't think I could eat anything for a week," Jack said.

"Don't forget there are three houses with left overs," Eilis replied.

"Oh no, those houses are on their own. I'm not going to be making any visits for the rest of the weekend."

"You know we have to stop at your Aunt Maggie's house to-morrow. I'm sure she will have plenty of food left."

"Yes, I still want to go to her house but no more talk of food. I'm trying to find a way for us to have a little alone time. You know just the two of us," Jack said holding her. During their traveling, Jack remembered stopping in the park on Lemon Hill or at Strawberry Mansion. He wanted to be with her. She had been receptive to a point but once things started getting too physical she put a stop to it. They were so busy visiting friends and family there just was never a good time. Eilis had to work during the week, and Jack saw her on the weekends. He thought with the longer holiday weekend there would be an opportunity. "Is that all you ever think about? Isn't it enough that we are together? You're going away next week and you are going to be gone for more than a year. The last couple of months have been hard. I go to work and I come home. I go to the movies with my parents or my girlfriends. In some ways, I have become a social outcast."

Looking out at the passing scenery, Jack remembered how the rest of the weekend had gone. They went to the parade and Maggie's house afterward, but something had changed. They had not fought but like two boxers waiting for the bell they were both ready. Jack had the idea that Eilis would wait for him to return. That she would be honest and faithful to him. It was apparent that that was not what she had in mind.

They had fun at the parade. They were across the street from the Gimbels Department store. The city fireman that played the role of Santa Claus climbed the ladder waving at the crowd. The Christmas shopping season had begun.

He walked her home that night. It was late and the November chill had returned. Arriving at her home she turned to him on the porch and said goodnight. He would pick her up the next day for the parade at eight in the morning. Walking back to his grandparents' home alone he was confused. What had he said? What had he done?

Despite his complaints, the previous day Jack found that by the time he returned to his Aunt Maggie's house he was famished. It had been spring like again during the day. He was outside in the yard with his Uncle Mike, Kevin and Steve. Lunch with leftovers from the day before was over and it was time for beer and cigars. "I'm trying to figure out what makes a girl tick," Jack said.

"When you find out let me know," Kevin replied.

"Are the two love birds having trouble building the nest?" Steve asked.

"A little hard to build a nest together if the trees are separated by an ocean. Let me guess, Eilis is giving you a bit of the cold shoulder because your leaving again," Mike offered.

"Yea, that's it. She like...she's ok with going to see people or going places. But, as soon as you know things get a little lovey dovey she shuts down," Jack said concerned.

"I know how you feel. I had the same kind of problem with Dorothy after her attack. It took a lot of patience, but we worked through it," Steve said.

"Did you ever think about this from her perspective? After all she's just eighteen. You're running off to fight in a war. You two are not married. She doesn't know if you're even coming back. You two are far too young for this shit. You may be asking too much from her," Kevin said.

"So, what am I supposed to do, let her go, just break up with her?"

"The dining car will be open for dinner in ten minutes, sir." The conductor was advising all of the passengers. He was hungry. Jack remembered the long and very quiet ride home from Media that night. His mind had been in turmoil. The conversation with the other three men that he had known and looked up to all his life had been fresh in his mind. She sensed something was wrong. She could feel it. They had said goodnight on her front porch. They had told each other that they were in love. He knew that they were, but there was something driving a wedge. That something was miles down the track in North Carolina. Or maybe it was just him, he thought. This was his dream. His desire. Why? What was it that drove him to this? He went to the rest room and then to the dining car. This could be his last civilian meal. The train would arrive in Fayetteville around nine that night. From there it would be a few more hours by bus to the Marine base.

He decided on the chicken and dumplings. Jack washed it down with a coke and had apple pie and coffee. Ordering more coffee, he lit a cigar. His Uncle Mike had given him an entire box of Partagas Toro's. The cigars were Cuban acquired by Mike years before the embargo. They had been a gift to him from Michael Costigan. Smoking the cigar, he thought about his family history. His grandfather had been in WWI. His father in WWII and Korea, where he and his mother met. He was killed she was wounded. Now here he was on his way to Vietnam. When does it end he thought? He heard the stories from his grandmother and his Uncle Mike about how the war had changed his grandfather. How it ruined his marriage with his grandmother. Would Vietnam ruin things with he and Eilis, or had that already happened. He spent those last hours on the train in the dining car, drinking coffee and smoking another cigar.

It was a cold December night in North Carolina. He retrieved his sea bag from baggage and made his way outside to get a cab to the bus station. He pulled up the collar on his pea coat to keep the cold air off his neck. He was lucky, he had arrived at the bus station in time to get the last bus that night going to Lejeune. The coffee had made him restless. He could not sleep. Alone with his thoughts the only sound was the tires of the bus and the snoring of Marines coming back from leaves. He wondered how many of them would be going to Vietnam with him.

Getting off the bus Jack asked directions to the unit that would be conducting his next four weeks of training. He learned that there was a van outside that would take him to his unit. Finding the van, he was the only one going to FMT.

He checked into the orderly room with his orders. He was assigned a bunk, given linens and a blanket. He decided to make the bed in the morning. Other sailors were asleep in the squad bay of the barracks. Slipping off his shoes he lay on the bunk and was able to get some sleep.

The next morning, he woke and followed the crowd to chow. Jack learned that his training class was scheduled to start the next day. He would have the rest of the day to square away his gear. When he returned to the barracks he found he had a new bunk mate. His name was Dennis Miller and he was from Iowa. Dennis showed Jack a mimeographed page of information about the training they were all about to undergo.

Reveille was at 0500. After chow, they were marched to supply and were issued new fatigues, a pistol belt with a canteen, a two-magazine pouch and holster for a .45 pistol. Returning to the barracks they changed into the new fatigue uniforms and then went to lunch. In the afternoon, they went to a class room. Each man was given a Combat Corpsman Bag. Sometimes referred as a Unit One or a U1. The rest of the afternoon was spent studying the contents of the U1.

The Marines were fanatics. Despite their crazy reputations, they were knowledgeable about their weapons and tactics. Jack was learning on how to keep them alive under the worst of conditions. The one instruction they were told over and over was to stop the bleeding.

Sitting on a bench in the park, Dylan waited for his asset Nguyen Tam. Tam entered the park and sat next to Dylan. He had information that the 33rd NVA Regiment was moving south and would be operating in Long Khanh Province and had already set up intelligence units in Xuan Loc. For Dylan, this was the confirmation he was looking for. Leaving Tam, he returned to MACV to get the information to the Army unit stationed in that area. The 199th Light Infantry Brigade had arrived in Vietnam in 1966. Under no one's command except MACV the Brigade was used as a reaction force wherever it was needed. Now it was based in Long Binh. Part of the brigade was running operations out of a (FSB) Fire Support Base named Nancy. Located in Long Khanh Province it was just north of the town of Dinh Quan. Dylan knew the place well. He had been here before looking for Vang Bo. He met with the CG (commanding general) and gave him everything he had on the 33rd NVA Regiment. This was a hardcore battle-hardened unit that had participated in some of the major battles between the NVA and US forces. Their arrival in the AO (area of operations) of the brigade was a concern. A new push or possible assault on Saigon was suspected. In addition, the 199th had another FSB at the base of Signal Mountain. Fire Support Base Mace was protected by the 3rd Battalion 7th Infantry Regiment that was part of the brigade. Signal Mountain was a communications hub for all of the units in the area. Operations to look for the base that would be used by the NVA was launched by members of the Brigades 4th Battalion 12th Infantry Regiment, based at FSB Nancy.

It had been some time since Dylan was here last. The FSB brought with it the usual suspects. Black marketers', dope peddlers, prostitutes and the gypsies of Vietnamese society following the rich Americans wherever they went. Soldiers needed haircuts and their uniforms cleaned. Those lucky enough to have permanent quarters hired house girls to clean them.

Most of the house girls were elderly women, but a few of the younger ones had other duties. All of this economic activity was a boom for any village or hamlet. American capitalism had infected the Vietnamese people and the people with power gorged themselves on the riches of corruption. Dylan returned to his empty apartment in Saigon. He could have retired with Caroline but he decided to stay. Despite its setbacks, he too loved the country and its people.

The intel he got from Tam was good. The brigade's operations picked up and there were numerous engagements in and around Xuan Loc. Some prisoners yielded additional information. There was no doubt that the 33rd NVA Regiment was operating in the 199th's AO.

Back in his apartment he showered and crawled into bed. He missed her. He could go home but he felt that doing so would leave his work unfinished. He needed sleep. Meetings scheduled for the morning would cover the possibility of a ARVN and US invasion into Cambodia. COSVN, (Central Office for

South Vietnam) the command structure for the NVA and Viet Cong would be the main target. Capturing or destroying the 'Bamboo Pentagon' would be a major turning point in the war. The North Vietnamese sanctuaries in Cambodia if destroyed may just end the war. The next day at his office he learned that Bob Tevenson had gone home. He was curious to know if Bob had finally stretched the rules too far. One thing was for sure, American units would no longer be directly involved with company operations.

The air in the back of the aircraft was stifling. Officers and NCO's were the first ones off the plane. It had been a long and boring flight, that lasted more than twenty-four hours. They had made two stops, one in Anchorage Alaska and one in Guam. The last stop was here, at Tan Son Nhut. Exiting the plane Jack looked forward to a breath of fresh air. It was hotter and more humid outside the aircraft. There was a peculiar odor in the air. Marine and Navy personnel were separated and marched to a waiting C-130, that would take them to Da Nang. They stood on the tarmac in the blistering hot sun while Air Force crew members loaded their luggage on the plane. Name, rank, and serial number was checked off a list as they boarded the air craft. They were sitting on cargo netting on each side of the plane, their luggage stacked in the middle. The air on this plane was worse than the commercial aircraft they had just got off. The back hatch was raised and the C-130 started to taxi towards the runway. The noise during takeoff was deafening. Before long the plane banked sharply and the air got cooler as they gained altitude headed north over the South China Sea. Landing in Da Nang a few hours later everyone retrieved their luggage and was assigned to a transit unit. From there they would receive a permanent assignment. A Marine Corporal advised them to take note of all of the bunker locations in the area they stayed. Enemy rocket and mortar fire was frequent and without warning. Even the barracks had sandbagged entrances built around the doorways. He was here. Just like his grandfather and father before him, Jack Randall was in a war zone, serving his country.

Jack learned that he was to be assigned to the 1st Battalion 26th Marines. He would report to his unit in a few days. For now, he was assigned to an aid station on the base. He introduced himself to several Marines, but they always referred to him as 'Doc'. It was something he would be accustomed too. Another corpsman who would be leaving for home in just a week helped him pack his U1 bag.

The bag itself was pre-packed and included everything he had been trained with at FMT. PO3 Mike Rans added three more large battle dressings and two additional medium sized battle dressings. He also added two extra rolls of adhesive tape and an extra pair of scissors. "It's more weight to hump but it'll be worth it." He also gave Jack two extra .45 magazines for his pistol. Rans had been assigned to 1st Battalion 4th Marines at Dong Ha. He had two Purple Hearts. Soon, Jack would be heading for the same base. He had more questions to ask than he could remember, but Mike answered them all. "Just remember your training. Take care of yourself first. A wounded corpsman is no help to anyone. Try to look like the rest of the Marines in your unit. Charlie likes to shoot officers, corpsman and RTO's. (radio operators) Get yourself an M-16. Charlie knows that anyone without a rifle is someone special."

"What's it like?" Jack asked.

"It's different for everyone. I've seen guys that pull the buttons off their shirt to get closer to the ground. Other guys walk around like they're at a picnic. The officers will most likely tell you to stay put and not to move until they tell you. Fuck em. When you hear CORPSMAN UP, you go. Take care of your Marines and they will take care of you. Shit gets to deep you holler, GUNS UP. Always keep your wounded man between you and Charlie."

"Ever have someone die?"

"It happens, but just do your job. Focus on that. Guy's will ask you to write their wives or parents. Most of the time they want relief from the pain. Use those morphine packs on guys that will make it. Dead Marines feel no pain. Oh, and one-real important thing..."

"Stop the bleeding," Jack said interrupting Mike.

"Well yeah, but remember this. If you see a Marine digging the heel of one boot on the toes of the other boot, he's got jungle rot on his feet. Make sure the keep their feet dry whenever they can."

"Thanks, Mike." Jack had a lot to learn. Mike told him that there would be other corpsman with his company. They would become a close-knit group. They would help him along the way. "You play cards Jack?"

"I have. Why?"

Rans pulled out a deck of cards and put some MPC (Military Payment Script) on the table. "Five card stud, Jacks or better."

Two days later Jack Randall was on a CH-53 helicopter on his way to Dong Ha. The DMZ was just a few miles away. Landing at the base he found his way to the Battalion Aid Station for 1st Battalion 26th Marines. His company was out in the field sweeping the hills around Khe Sanh. The NVA and the Marines had been fighting over these hills since the beginning of the war. They were due back to the base later that day. Jack had already stored his gear where they would be quartered during a three day stand down on the base.

For now, Jack was assigned to the aid station. The next morning the NVA fired rockets into the base. Jack was walking from his sleeping quartets to battalion aid when the first rocket hit. He dove into a sandbagged mortar pit for cover. Marines around the base ran about seeking bunkers for cover. The rocket fire stopped and Jack heard calls for a corpsman. He had his U1 bag with him and ran towards the wounded Marine. The doctor from the aid station was already there when Jack ran up. He was a Major and was on his second tour as a battalion surgeon. The wounded Marine had shrapnel wounds up and down the front of his body. He had been close to the first of the rocket salvos. The Major had used the Marines belt as a tourniquet on his upper arm. His lower arm was a mess of exposed bone and torn flesh. Jack had seen photos of wounded men during his training but this was the real thing. The man moaned as he drifted in and out of conciseness. Jack looked over and treated the more serious wounds with help from the doctor. With the help of two other Marines that had brought a stretcher they began to carry the man to the aid station. Then another barrage of rockets hit the base again. They were by the landing strip of the base as the new attack began. There was a steep gulley between the runways and they all stumbled into it escaping the deadly shrapnel. Jack felt a sting on the back of his neck as he rolled over unto his back, but thought nothing of it. When the rockets stopped, they picked up the wounded Marine and went to battalion aid. It was early morning but it was already hot and humid. Jack was still adjusting to the heat. When they reached the aid station Jack was covered in sweat. He could fell it running down his back. Placing the wounded man on a gurney one of the other corpsman saw the blood on the back of Jacks t-shirt. "Randall, you've been hit sit down over here."

"What, where? I don't feel nothing." Jack said surprised.

"Back of your neck. Shrapnel wound. Not serious, brace yourself, this is gonna sting."

The corpsman poured hydrochloride from a bottle to flush the wound. Then using a probe looked for any foreign matter. Major Burns who had been with him during the attack took a quick look. "Looks good Billy, stitch him up."

"Yes sir. Ok Jack, I'm gonna give you a local and then stitch you up. Looks like five or six should be enough."

Jack was sitting on a stool watching as the other corpsman and the Major treated the wounded man they had brought in. He was awake and comfortable despite being covered in bandages. A medivac chopper was on its way to take him to Da Nang. Billy came back with a tray and two hand held mirrors. He handed one to Jack and said, "Here ya go take a look." Jack adjusted the mirror so he could see his wound. Just under the hair line on the left side he saw the open wound. The bleeding had stopped and Jack could see a piece of skin hanging off of it. Billy gave him the shot to numb the area. "I'm cutting off that big piece of skin Jack, then I'll stitch you up. You'll have a nice scar to show your grandkids. Worst thing about these wounds is the possibility of infection. Nam is one big dirty place."

Finished, Billy admired his work. "Not bad if I do say so myself."

Jack looked in the mirror at the stitching. "You do nice work Bill."

"Hey, this was not my first time. I could be a plastic surgeon. Want me to fix that nose?"

"What's wrong with my nose?"

"Too aristocratic," Billy replied putting a fresh bandage on Jacks wound.

Major Burns approached to let Jack know he would be staying at the aid station for a few days so they could watch him for infection. He could still work and there were always patients to care for. Marines came in everyday to have boils lanced and packed, jungle rot on their feet, fevers from the start of malaria and a variety of insect bites that got infected. there was also the delivery of wounded Marines from the field, that were not serious enough to be taken to Da Nang.

His first month in Vietnam he had earned a Purple Heart. He had yet to see combat, but that would change soon. His company had stayed one night and was taken to Wonder Beach for a little

R&R. He had yet to meet anyone, other than his platoon leader and sergeant. They would be back in three days. While there the Navy shelled the Marines on R&R at the beach. Fortunately, there were no serious injuries.

Jack was on duty when a young Marine limped into the aid station. He was just in from the field. Like most Marines he had not had a shower in some time and was quite ripe. The problem was his feet. He sat on a gurney and Jack unlaced his boots and helped him take them off. The leather on the boots had dried blood that had soaked through. He winced in pain, Jack winced from the smell. It was over powering. He put on a surgical mask and looked at the young Marine's feet. The left was the worst. Blood had dried around the socks and clung to the open wounds.

Billy came over to help. "Phew, all right what we need to do is soak his feet in a hydrochloride solution until everything gets soft. Then we can get the socks off," Billy said. He showed Jack how to prepare the solution with warm water and set two trays on the floor. They helped the Marine unto his feet and then sat him on a stool. Then Jack took the Marines information for his report and the Marines medical file. About an hour later Jack started cutting off the socks. The solution inside the tray was pink. The toes were the worst. Fibers from the socks had been soaked by blood from the sores and clung to the skin and had embedded itself into the wounds. Using tweezers and a soft sponge soaked in fresh solution Jack removed the fibers from the wounds. The Marine winced in pain. During the process, a Sergeant, Jack had already met entered the aid station. "Yo, Bobby I see you're gold-bricking again. What's the prognosis Doc? He ever gonna have children?"

Jack looked up in surprise, "Bobby? I thought you said your name was Charles?"

"It is, Guys in my squad call me Bobby." The Marine answered.

"That's right Doc, this here is Bobby Bootcamp. A fine poster board example of a hardcore Marine. This here is yours I believe. Next time you decide to get wounded and spend time here at Battalion Aid make sure you bring your own shit. We had to hump all this crap for you."

The Sergeant dropped a ruck sack with all of Jacks gear. "I wondered what happened to my stuff." Jack replied as he looked in the ruck sack. "This is my stuff but the rucks not mine. This thing looks like shit."

"Casualties of war, Doc. How long before Bobby gets back on duty?"

"If he keeps his feet clean and dry, couple of days," Jack replied.

"Outstanding, we have 'Sparrow Hawk' duty next five days. See you back at the tents, Bob," the sergeant said leaving the aid station.

"What's Sparrow Hawk?" Jack asked Charles.

When we come in from the boonies we either have bunker perimeter defense or Sparrow Hawk. As Sparrow Hawk we respond to any section of the base that is overrun or about to be overrun," Charles answered. The doctor came over to look at the feet. All of the fabric from the socks had been removed and the sores although all open had stopped bleeding. "Ok private, keep those feet clean and dry and no boots or socks for a couple of days. Wear these slippers if you have to go anywhere. Come back day after tomorrow and I'll check you out. Jack, it was nice to have you but you have to go to your unit. I'm sure I'll see you now and again, good luck."

"Thank you, sir. See you around Billy."

Billy shook hands with Jack, Yea, take care Jack, I'll see you around."

Jack and Charles left the Battalion Aid Station and walked to the tent area that would be occupied by Delta Company. Jack took a cot next to Charles and the two men talked, getting to know one another. Charles Gallagher was from Glassboro NJ, a small town in Gloucester County. It was twenty miles from Philly. He had enlisted in the Marines and liked it. He was considering making a life in the Corps. He told Jack he was given the name of Bobby Bootcamp because the first time Corbett his squad leader saw him his boots were shined and his fatigues were still starched. Jack learned that 1st Platoon was a good group of guys. He and Charles became fast friends, and he would meet the rest of the men later as they drifted back into the tent. Gallagher was a point man by choice, he and Corbett had come to the understanding that if he walked point, he would not have LP (listening post) duty. Jack told Charles about himself and his family. Charles was surprised that his family was involved with the Red Arrow rapist story. He had seen all the newspaper stories. The continued talking and Jack asked, "Why don't you like LP?"

"It spooky as shit. The first time I had to do it they sent me out with Corbett to show me what I was supposed to do. But let me start at the beginning."

CHAPTER 39

LIFELONG MEMORIES

Hope handed the telegram to Colleen. It was short, direct and on point. Jack had sustained a minor injury during a rocket attack. He was treated and returned to duty. "Great, first month he is there and he gets hurt," Hope complained. "It does say the injury was minor. He was back at work, and his last letter said he was working at the Battalion Aid station on base. That sounds better than walking around in the jungle, Colleen replied. "I know. Let's, hope he stays there. I knew there was some kind of catch to this whole Navy thing. Why couldn't he be on a hospital ship, or any ship for that matter. I know what medics do. They get right into the thick of it. I've seen the bravery they have."

"Yes, and your son is one of those men. Be proud of him. I know I am. I know Jack will come home Hope. I believe it. Don't ask me how I know, I just do."

"I hope your right, Mom, I really do."

The plan was to go out to Media for a visit with the Randall family. They would be bringing the news contained in the telegram. The weather had been colder but the sun was out and the threat of snow was a few days away.

The drive out on the Baltimore Pike was pleasant. New stores and houses were being built as the new suburban communities were growing. They arrived in time for lunch and before the meal began they shared the telegram with the Judge and Kay. They were concerned but relieved that the injury seemed to be minor. Eilis arrived and shared a letter she had received that gave more information about Jacks injury. Hope was not happy to learn that he had been carrying a wounded Marine during a rocket attack when he was wounded. Yet at the same time she was proud of her son. She knew what his job was, she had always marveled at the dedication and courage these men had.

Eilis stayed for lunch and then left to meet up with friends for a movie. Colleen asked, "I wonder how those two will get along when Jack comes home? Eilis seems a bit distant."

"I think she has learned to get on with her life. She is far too young to be standing by the home front while her lover is off fighting in a war," Kay said.

The Judge added his own opinion, "What about Jack? You think when he meets some young pretty thing while he's away, that he will be honorable about it. Don't forget my son fell in love with a young girl while he was away. What was the name of that German girl...Greta or Gretchen something? He had a girl back home at the time. Penelope Marson from Granite Run. Then when he went to Korea he met Hope. Very happy he did by the way."

"Was he seeing someone when he was in Korea?" Hope asked.

Kay answered, "No dear, he was not involved with anyone. We were quite surprised by his meeting you. You were all he could write about in his letters home."

"Times are different now. When my Jimmy was in France I waited for him. Today these young people all talk about free love. Some young girls give themselves away like they are handing out candy. It's just shameful. I think Eilis is a good Catholic young lady. I don't see her as the type to engage in sexual activity outside of marriage." Colleen offered.

Hope gave her mother a side glance, "Oh I think even proper young girls do things they are not supposed too."

The judge excused himself. The conversation was going in a direction that made him uncomfortable. "I'll be having my coffee and cigar in my office ladies."

Kay laughed, "John you're a big sissy. We are all grown adults, there is no need to be embarrassed." Once he left Colleen asked Kay, "Did his honor act like a gentleman when you two were dating?"

"When we were young, his honor was after me all the time. He was like a cat after a canary." Sometimes I fought him off... and sometimes I didn't."

Jack listened intently as Charles told him the story. "We were air lifted by helicopters into the hills around Khe Sanh. We had been humping all day and it was getting late. Our platoon was walking right point flank when 2nd Platoon opened up on some NVA. They got five of them as soon as they opened up. We had all just come out of a tree line into an area of high grass and scrub brush. This was the first time I ever was in a fire fight. It didn't last long all of the NVA left before it got too intense. Trust me I'm not complaining. The LT decided that we would set up our NDP (night defensive position) about a hundred yards back into the tree line. I'm getting myself together when Corbett comes over and tells me to bring my weapon some water and some frags. He has a prick 25 (PRC 25 Radio) with him and we walk back out to where the tree line ends. We had already stripped the dead NVA of their weapons and other gear. We sit down next to a tree and Corbett tells me we are the LP for the night. Our job is to alert the company of any enemy movement before they get to our lines. Normally this is a one-man operation, but because I'm the new guy, he's there to show me what to do and what not to do. I'm telling you Jack once it got dark it was real spooky. Your mind plays tricks on ya. Your eyes see things that aren't really there and the whole time I was scared shitless. So, we sit there for hours when they show up."

Jack interrupted, "The NVA came back?"

"Oh, yeah. They came back to pick up their dead. I mean there was NVA guys and women. Some of the women we could hear them crying over, you know Uncle Joe or whoever. Then this one NVA guy walks over towards us. He stops and looks right at us, I mean he is like ten meters away." Charles replied.

"So, we sit there and watch each other, nobody moves or says anything. He knows we are there, we certainly know he's there. The rest of the group is carrying off the dead. There is like dead silence. You could have heard an ant fart it was so quiet. My heart is pounding in my chest, I don't think I took a breath for the ten minutes they were there. The NVA guy is holding his AK across his chest held by his left arm. He looks like a guy on a hunting trip. Then he just turns away and leaves, like ok guys, see ya later. He fades off into the grass and the radio breaks squelch twice. It sounded to me like a bomb went off it was so loud. I like to jump out of my skin. I hate fuckin, LPs."

"That is some heavy shit man," Jack replied.

"Tell me about it, I hated doing the fuckin things."

"Isn't point man more dangerous?"

"I guess, but at least you're not on your own. I mean there is a whole company of Marines behind you. Right behind you. On LP, there back a way. This goddamn tent is hot. I need to go outside and get some air."

"Ok, look I gotta go over and get my gear. I'll be back in a little bit. You like cigars?"

"Beats me never really had one." Jack handed Charles a cigar from his pocket. "These are Cubans. My uncle used to live in

Havana before Castro. He gave a box to my other uncle and he gave them to me." Jack used a punch at the head of the cigar and gave Charles a lighter. "Try it, you'll like it."

Jack left to go to his old quarters for the rest of his stuff. Charles went outside and sat on top of a bunker. He lit the cigar and puffed on it. Not bad he thought. The sun was getting low in the sky. Charles had grabbed a six pack of Hamm's from a cooler in the tent. He opened a can with a church key and looked at his feet. Inside the toes the skin was very red. Sores covered the instep and the ball of his foot was still very sore were the toes started. He drank his beer and puffed on the cigar, remembering his first night on LP alone.

They had been humping for days between Con Tien and the DMZ. Signs of NVA activity was everywhere. That day they came across a cooking fire in a small patch of jungle. A pot containing rice and boiling water had been found. Based on the amount of rice in the pot the Marines guessed that three NVA scouts had been there for dinner. The enemy was all around and had so far been allusive. The Marines set up they're NDP in the jungle and Charles was eating from a C-Ration can when Corbett approached him. He had a radio with him. "Bob, you got LP tonight."

"Fuck me, why?"

"Your turn asshole, grab you're shit and let's go."

Corbett led Charles back to the area where they had found the cooking fire. Corbett set the radio down next to a large tree that had elongated roots growing into the ground. "This looks like a good spot. Company RTO will call you soon for a commo check. After that every hour, you get two squelches send one back if you're ok. Three fast one's means there's movement. Use your frags. You fire your weapon the NVA will see the muzzle flash and then your fucked. Any questions?"

"No."

hear

"Good, see ya in the morning, I'll be out to get you at dawn."

Corbett left and Charles looked around. He was on the edge of the jungle. He could see across an open area with grass and termite mounds. Small trees here and there. The sun was getting low. It was still hot and humid. He had a two-quart canteen and a can of turkey loaf. He had forgotten the spoon. He walked behind the tree a few yards and urinated. Returning to the tree he took one last look around while he had enough light. He felt very much alone.

The jungle is a living growing thing. A variety of species call it home. This is where they live and die, each contributing something back to advance their own species and to benefit others. During the day it has one personality, at night something different. Sound travels better at night. Even here he could here sound, from behind him he knew was created by his fellow Marines. The jungle and its creatures also knew he was there. His was a species that brought thunder, destruction, fire and death wherever they came. His was a species that killed for love, jealousy, anger and sport. He was not supposed to be there, but he was, and he was alone.

Looking up at the sky it was now a getting a darker blue. It would be dark soon. He would be here for almost twelve hours, alone. He had no idea what the weather would bring. He had a towel and a poncho with a liner. He checked his gear, one two-quart canteen, one can of turkey loaf no spoon, eight spare mags of M16 ammo and four frags. One radio and plastic covered handset. His only link to reality. As if on que the handset came alive, "LP 1, this is Pro Devil 3, commo check, over."

Charles grabbed the handset and squeezed the talk button once.

cue

"Roger LP 1, Pro Devil 3 out." Just like that he was now on his own.

The jungle came alive as he sat down nestled in the roots of the big tree. It was filled with sounds as the jungles day shift left and the night shift arrived. Birds flew from branch to branch. Insects crawled over everything. Flying insects would also fly around. Mosquitoes would soon arrive in squadron formation and Charles was the target. Small creatures and some larger one's moved about. Taking off his helmet he removed the bottle of bug juice from the band. Pouring it into his hands he rubbed it on his face and neck. Then he poured more and rubbed the stuff into his ears. Mosquitos always attacked the ears. The buzzing sound came in stereo as they attacked each side of his head. He put his towel over his head and put the helmet back on. The towel and the bug juice would give him some relief from the buzzing of the mosquitos. His senses came alive. The pupils of his eyes opened wider as it got darker and his hearing became more acute. He was becoming a part of the jungle at night.

He opened the can of turkey loaf with his P38. No spoon meant he had to finger the food out of the can. It tasted funny as he realized he still had bug juice on his hands. Fuck it, don't mean nothing. Finishing the turkey, he took a drink from the canteen. He settled in to start the first time he would pull LP duty by himself. This very long and maddening night and many more like it, would haunt him the rest of his life. Off too his left something moved across the ground. It slivered its way into the high grass in front of him. Snake. There were lots of snakes. Constrictors and vipers galore. Cobras lived here as well as the two-step viper. Spiders, scorpions they were all here. Looking up at the sky it was very dark now. Stars were everywhere. He never saw stars at night like this at home. Home. The air above him screamed as the flare round exploded over the open grass to his right. High in the night sky it floated down slowly on its para-chute. The wind blew it off to the right further away from him but the shadows out in the grass and the small trees and termite mounds came alive. All sorts of things moved among those shad-ows. His pulse quickened and his heart pounded in his chest. His eyes and his mind played with his sanity. C'mon Gallagher, get it together he thought. I'm a United States Marine. Those guys behind me are counting on me. I'm they're first line of defense. They're lives are in my hands. I have a duty.

RAUARW. What the fuck was that?

Straight ahead, but how far. Every pore on his skin tingled. He had a sickening feeling in his stomach. The adrenalin raced through his body. It sounded like a leopard like in the movies. Or maybe a tiger. There was a tiger once, back in 1965 or 66. A man eater. It liked Marines. They had a special task force to kill it. They got it one night when it jumped a Marine in a bomb crater. The jungle was quiet now. No birds, no bugs it's like someone turned off a switch. No sound. It was spooky, then a sudden rush of something in the grass squealing as it died. Then the grass rustled again and whatever was out there ran back into the jungle to his right. Whatever it was it had made its kill and would now feed on the flesh. Someone hit the switch. The sounds of the night returned. Time is his enemy now. Alone with the jungle each minute passes so slowly. A jet flies overhead, a freedom bird heading back to the world. Phfewt, phfewt.

The handset squawks twice. It sounds like it is broadcasting through loud speakers. He keys the handset once. He feels as if he has been there all night, but only an hour has passed. At least ten more hours to go. He would do another ten or so LP's.

They were all like that he remembered. The NVA never came but the threat was always there. It played with a man's sanity, it challenged his courage. The bravest men can only take so much. On the last LP, he would do he returned to his company's position. He found Corbett, sitting drinking his coffee. He walked up took a knee and looked Corbett in the eye and said, "That's it. No more LP duty. I'll burn shit, walk point, hell I'll let you reach around to give me a choke and stroke, but I will never do another LP." Corbett looked at him and without any reaction replied, "All right Charles, no sweat." It was the first and only time Corbett called him by his given name.

The cigar burned his fingers and he dropped it as Jack found him on the bunker. Between his memories, the cigar and the sudden appearance of Jack, Charles was rattled. "Jesus Christ," he exclaimed.

"You ok Charles? How did you like the cigar?"

"Good...it was good. Get all your gear?"

"Yup, it's all down in the tent."

A loud group of men walked down the road towards them. Charles announced, "Here comes the rest of the inmates. C'mon I'll introduce ya."

The company of men had finished their training. Duong was proud of them. They had applied themselves and the training they had would help them in the coming months. Living in the jungles took its toll on everyman. The recent phases of the TET Offensive had taken a heavy toll on the units already in the field. So much so that even Duong would be making the trip south with them. It would be a difficult trip for him. The Americans bombed the roads south almost daily. Once there they would be sent into the hills around Khe Sanh. The large base had been abandoned by the Americans, but the surrounding areas were still heavily occupied. The enemy had bases in Quang Tri, Dong Ha and Con Thien.

He and his men would be operating against the Americans and the ARVN there.

The new company commander was a man that was related to a party official in Hanoi. He was incompetent. His name was Captain Diem Tho.

He was aristocratic. Basically, he left the training regime to Duong, who would later find out the man could barely read a map let alone plot a course. Duong had seen this type of man before. Generally, they were careless and that would lead to good men getting killed. The long trip south would take several weeks. If they were lucky an American bomb would take care of him. During the long trip, Captain Diem showed little regard for the safety or health of his men. Most of the trip was taken by truck. When the men were marching some of them had foot problems. They're pain and discomfort was of little concern for Diem.

Duong had his own physical problems. His surgery had left him with limited use of his arm. He found it was difficult to carry and use a rifle effectively. The easiest to handle was the K50M sub machine gun. He also had a pistol a Luger P08 captured from WWII. Because he participated in the physical training alongside his troops he was prepared for the trip south. It also increased the admiration and respect his troops had for him. He knew he could be effective with his troops, he was not very confident in Diem.

CHAPTER 40
LIFELONG FRIENDSHIPS

They climbed down off the bunker and went into the tent. Jack met a host of characters that made up the first squad of first platoon. One of the more prominent was John DeFelice nicknamed Hollywood. He wore aviator sun glasses and the story was he never had been seen without them. Even on missions in the bush Hollywood wore them. He was the M60 Gunner. He greeted every new man that came into the platoon the same way, "Bring me a dirty belt of ammo and jam my gun, I'll shoot ya in the fuckin face." This was accompanied by jamming a .45 under the new man's nose. Corpsmen were not required to carry M60 ammo. Hollywood's only welcome was, "Nice to have ya Doc. You need me, ya holler GUNSUP. Me and my 60 will come mow the grass."

Jack also met Winston Parker, Steve Heinz, Sam Woodward and Terry Segura. "Hollywood seems to be some kind of nut case," Jack said to Charles. "Oh yeah. Let me tell you, once the old man came in to talk to us after a mission. He gave us the ra ra good job Marines speech. Now this is a Marine Colonel. The old man was done and said if any of us needed anything we should let him know. So, Hollywood raises his hand and the Colonel asks what do you need Marine? Hollywood looks around at us and says, Colonel I really need a blow job."

"He asked a full bird for a blow job?" Jack asked shocked.

"Well, maybe not from the old man, but the Colonel looks at him hard then turns to the Sergeant Major and says, get this man's mother over here asap."

"C'mon man you're pulling my leg."

"I shit you not. That man does not have all his ball bearings greased, but there is no one else I want with me when the shit hits the fan."

Another man entered the tent and spotted Charles talking to the new man he heard about. Shaking hands, he introduced himself as Doc Cahill. Cahill was assigned as the company corpsman. He was from Texas. He asked for Jacks U1 bag and checked the contents. "Billy over at battalion aid checked it too. He added some bandages and an extra pair of scissors," Jack told him.

"Cool, Billy's a good man. Looks like you got it all Jack, guard those scissors with your life, it's easy to lose a pair out in the bush."

Delta Company spent the next few days on the base and then were told to get ready to go back out. They would be inserted by choppers in an area known as the Rock Pile. Jack had remembered that he needed an M16 and asked for one. He was told that there were none available but that he would get one eventually. Aside from his ruck sack and U1 bag Jack had his .45 and five magazines, each loaded with seven rounds. His Uncle Mike had taught him how to shoot and Jack qualified in the Navy as an expert with a pistol. He liked the .45and was used to it, he shot his uncles often. The operation they were going out on was a company sized mission to patrol and keep the enemy on their toes. Jack learned that letting the NVA get a foot hold anywhere was bad. Once they entrenched themselves they were hard to get rid of. They were airlifted on CH-53 helicopters each bird capable of transporting an entire platoon. The choppers landed in a clearing that had been prepped by artillery fire. The LZ was quiet once the choppers left. Jack hunched over from the weight of his rucksack looked at a large pyramid shaped mountain 800 feet high. With sheer jungle covered cliffs all around it was occupied by US Marines and Army units with sophisticated equipment used to track the NVA. The Rock Pile was north of Highway 9 that ran parallel to the DMZ. Jack and his company had been inserted between the Rock Pile and the DMZ to the north. They started marching west. There were other mountains around them with some as high as 2000 meters. Unlike the Rock Pile these were scalable. They were also the favorite hideaways for the NVA. The mission for Delta company was to seek out the enemy and destroy his ability to use these mountains as a staging area for their operations.

Sitting in a defensive position on one of the mountains surrounding the Rock Pile the NVA heard and spotted the choppers bringing the Marines into their area. NVA scouts reported the landing and the direction of travel the Marines had taken from the LZ. Duong and his company moved towards an area with high ground and good cover and set up a hasty ambush on a small ridge overlooking a long field of high grass. Scouts were following the Marines and kept them under observation reporting back to the company. Based on this information Duong repositioned his men. The Marine column would pass them to the south. Captain Diem set up his mortar team behind the company's position beyond a clump of trees. Planting a long stick in the high grass where the Marines would pass they used it as a target point and the mortar crews set their sights and waited. Once the ambush started they would rain mortar rounds down on the Americans. He also had a .51 caliber machine gun. The Marines came within 100 meters of the kill zone when they suddenly stopped. The first Marine on point was talking to another Marine. The long column of men sat in the high grass resting as two more Marines came to the front of the column. The Marines were talking when Captain Diem ordered his .51 caliber machine gun crew to open up. Duong protested the order and the crew hesitated. Diem's argument for the order was that two of the men were high priority targets. An officer was on the radio and a corpsman was with them. An officer, radio operator and a corpsman were more important than the point man. Diem silenced his senior sergeant and ordered the machine gun crew to fire. The big gun fired a short burst hitting the intended targets. The large caliber bullets tore into the officer, and the radio operator and corpsman. The mortar crew had instructions to fire when the rest of the company did. Because the Marines were not in the kill zone those rounds impacted with no effect. The rest of the Marine company responded and came on line to the left and right of the point position. Duong watched helplessly as the Marines on the far southern line adjusted their positions to bring effective fire on the NVA positions. NVA mortar rounds continued to fall harmlessly in the kill zone. The Marines knew where Duong and his men had set up their positions and called in effective artillery fire. Duong knew that the artillery fire would be deadly to his men. He ordered a retreat back to the hills. Captain Diem was furious. He screamed counter orders to his men who did not obey. Screaming at his men to follow his orders he turned his anger on Duong. Facing him Diem screamed in his face. Duong pushed his Captain back, drew his pistol and shot him in the head. Artillery fire now cut off his escape route and one round took out his mortar crew. Duong repositioned his men leaving one platoon to cover his company's retreat. Instead of escaping to the west he and his men would have to move to the north. As his company retreated to the north Duong stayed with the one platoon that would cover the retreat. Another corpsman was tending to the wounded Marines. Duong ordered four men to charge the forward Marine position and to kill the corpsman and the four other Marines as they attempted to move the wounded to the rear of the firing line. Then Duong and his men left their positions and headed north as the American artillery shifted towards them. Ordering the four men to attack the Marines was hard for Duong. He knew that they might not be able to retreat and rejoin the company. He also knew the Marines would stop at nothing to save their wounded comrades. The four men he chose were good soldiers. Losing them would lay heavy on his mind. As he moved north with the platoon he prayed for their safety. Making their escape the platoon caught up to the rest of the company. Suddenly the small arms fire stopped as the American artillery pounded the old NVA positions. This fire fight was over. Duong felt no shame or guilt over killing Diem. The man was incompetent, and would only cause higher casualties. Those men who saw what happened would keep it to themselves. They knew their greatest chance for survival was with Duong.

Dylan looked over the table with a large area map of III Corps in Vietnam and the bordering country of Cambodia. The planning stages were almost complete. The US Army was going to invade Cambodia and search out the military headquarters of the enemy known as the Bamboo Pentagon. COSVN had always been a high priority target. What MACV did not know was the long-time headquarters for VC and NVA military operations was abandoned. The base was located on a rubber plantation across the border in Cambodia just northwest of Tay Ninh. Relocating COSVN and the people there was easy. The NVA also has huge stores of weapons, ammunition, medical supplies and food in Cambodia. Moving everything before the American invasion of Cambodia was impossible. COSVN learned of the coming assault just weeks before it happened.

Huyen Trang had learned of the assault from a US Air Force Colonel that talked in his sleep. She had been living in Saigon with the officer. Originally, he hired her as a maid to keep his off-base apartment clean. Seducing him was easy. Trang was still a very attractive woman despite living years in the jungle. The Colonel always drank too much at the hotels and often came back to his apartment in a drunken stupor. Trang would also give him tea laced with a little opium.

During the early years of the American war Trang operated from a safe house in Khe Sanh. When the siege of the Marine base began she made her way south, travelling amongst refugees fleeing the VC and NVA during the Tet Offensive. Upon reaching Saigon she lived with her cousin, Nguyen Tam. Tam was an asset for Dylan Brogan. He was also a double agent.

It was Brogan that helped her get cleared by the employment office in the embassy. Hung had provided the necessary documents and she was soon hired as a maid to cook and clean for high ranking officers. She was working for her fourth employer. Passed on by officers leaving and new officers arriving Trang had excellent references. Her latest employer was on his second tour. He commanded a logistics unit. Many of the documents he brought back to his apartment contained valuable information. Even the most secret of operations had to be supplied. Weapons, ammunition, clothing and special equipment were listed for a variety of units. Flights moving the equipment or even the operatives themselves had to be scheduled. Time schedules, destinations, it was all there. Most of the documents were unclassified.

Trang would give the information to Tam. Tam would give intelligence to Hung and Brogan. The 33rd NVA Regiment operating in the Xuan Loc area showed up in logistical documents ordering extra supplies for the 199th Infantry Brigade. Tam had given the intelligence to Brogan and the American military responded. Troops on the ground had to be supplied.

When Trang discovered the excessive movement of ammunition, gasoline, diesel fuel, medical supplies as well as food and water to Tay Ninh, the only conclusion was an operation attacking COSVN. The area around Tay Ninh had been relatively quiet since Tet. So why the extra supplies. Additional documents showed equipment and supplies for certain units along the Cambodian border. The stage was set.

The chopper lifted off the LZ and gained altitude. The higher it went the cooler it got. Sitting in the big noisy machine on the ground as the sun beat down on it turned it into an oven. Charles along with the rest of the Marines was already soaked in sweat. Sitting across from Hollywood, Charles watched the machine gunner. Despite the heat he was still wearing the aviator sun glasses. The big M60 sat with its muzzle on the floor and was propped up by the tripod legs. Hollywood was wiping the gun down as if it were a naked girl. He looked up and smiled at Charles. The chopper ride took just twenty minutes and as it banked to land they could hear the prep fire from artillery. The big bird landed softly as the back ramp lowered and the Marines were out the door. Small grass fires burned from the artillery as the Marines made their way into the high grass. Corbett gave Charles his azimuth heading and he checked his compass and set out. He was travelling west. The rest of the company followed in a single file of march. Charles walked methodically his eyes continuously scanning the horizon, and any small clumps of trees. He had been taught to look for things that seemed out of place. During the pre-mission briefing they were told the NVA were very active in this area, and to be on their toes. Charles had to concern himself with other things. Like booby traps and snakes. Insects flew around the grass like fighter planes. The sun was relentless. Sucking the fluids from your body and baking your brain inside of the helmet liner and steel pot he wore. The terrain here was made up of rolling hills. Coming over the top of a hill caused Charles to crouch as he reached the top. Standing straight up in the high grass as you reached the top was a sniper's dream. Coming down off the last small hill he reached a flat and grass free area of packed earth. An old termite mound was to his right. Dead ahead about 100 meters there was another larger cropping of trees and brush. They sat on a sloping hill no more than fifty meters high to the north. The hill ran east to west. Charles knew that walking past this hill on either side was a prime ambush site for the NVA. Still there was something else that made the hairs on the back of his neck stand up.

Corbett was crouched in the grass on the hilltop behind him. He held up his fist to stop the rest of the company. Marines took advantage of the break and sat in the high grass. Corbett watched Charles. He had taken a knee by the termite mound. He saw the hill running east to west just to the north. It was a good hundred meters away. His RTO came up behind him. "Six wants to know why we stopped," he said. Corbett took the handset and notified the Captain that the point man was checking something. "Devil dog 6, this is Spearhead 5 papa mike is watching the grass, over," Corbett said.

"Copy Spearhead 5." The Captain, frustrated waited for an update.

Corbett told his RTO to hold in place and made his way next to Charles.

"Looks like a good ambush site," Corbett said.

"Somethings not right. I don't like it. I can feel it," Charles replied.

"We could cut south get behind that ridge line. Let's see what the old man thinks."

Before Corbett could go back to his RTO, he saw the Captain, his RTO and the company corpsman Parker. They had just come over the hill top and approached Corbett and Gallagher. "What the hell's going on Sergeant?" The Captain asked.

"Sir, see that ridge line to the north about a hundred meters. It could be an ambush site. If the NVA are in there, they're gonna chop us up. I suggest we move south and continue moving west behind that ridge."

"Negative, I'll get some arty on that northern ridge…"

Charles still watching the terrain in front of him saw it. A single branch with no leaves on it stuck straight up right in front of his path 100 meters away. It did not belong there. He turned towards the Captain, "Sir…"

Winston Parker shoved Charles to the ground towards the termite mound.

Then he fell mortally wounded next to the Captain and his RTO. Corbett was shouting orders back to the company. Surprised Charles then heard the small arms fire coming from the northern hill. He never heard the rounds that killed his CO. Instinctively he called out, "Corpsman up." Turning back, he saw Jack coming over the top of the hill. Amazed he saw enemy mortar rounds detonating in the area where the branch had been. Charles knew they would have been ambushed.

Jack slid down the hill and grass and crawled over to the Captain. He was dead. The RTO was still alive but had a horrible looking wound on his shoulder. The radio he wore was mangled. Jack looked over at Winston. He was also dead, Jack grabbed the U1 bag from Winston and started treating the Captains RTO.

Delta company was responding as they maneuvered to the left and right of Charles. Using the hill top for cover they returned the NVA fire. Two Marines slid down the hill and removed the bodies of the Captain and Winston Parker. Artillery fire was hitting the NVA. Another Marine came down the hill and slung his rifle over his shoulder. Charles did the same and using Parkers

M16 as a seat started to carry the wounded RTO back over the hill. Then they heard the screaming.

Turning towards the sound they saw four NVA soldiers just ten meters away charging the Marines with their bayonets. Dropping the RTO Charles and the other man started to unsling their weapons. BLAM, BLAM, BLAM, BLAM. Stunned Charles looked to his left. Jack was on one knee, his .45 in his hand still smoking. The four NVA were all dead. "Holy shit, Doc!" Charles exclaimed. "Fuckin A, Doc. That's some hardcore shit," the other Marine said.

Jack walked over to the RTO and bent down over him. The wound that Jack had bound had opened up when he was dropped. The man had bled out. Charles picked him up and fireman carried him back over the hill to the other Marines on the line. The fire fight was over. American artillery continued to pound the now deserted NVA positions.

Coming over the hill his .45 still in his hand Jack saw the other Marines watching him. They said nothing. They had seen it. Their corpsman gunned down four NVA, with a handgun, wild west style. Hollywood had his canteen out, pouring water on the barrel of his M60. He looked up and smiled broadly, still wearing his sun glasses. Jack walked over to the bodies of the dead Marines. Lying side by side they had been wrapped in their poncho's waiting to be picked up and taken on the long journey home. The four dead NVA would lay where they fell. Stripped of weapons and equipment they're bodies would rot in the sun, picked at by animals, birds and insects.

Three Marines from Delta were going home. The rest of them swept through the brush and trees that had once been the NVA positions. The NVA had fled north towards the hills. One body was discovered in the trees. It was an officer. He had been shot in the head just above his eyes.

Corbett looked at the man lying on his back. Executed. He looked north. Somewhere out there an NVA soldier had deliberately killed his commanding officer. It explained why the NVA opened up prematurely. The officer was most likely an asshole. Then again, most offices were assholes he thought. The Marines also found what was left of the three-man mortar crew. Artillery had done a number on them.

The Lieutenant in command of 2nd Platoon was now the new CO. He wanted to order the company north after the NVA. He wanted payback.

Instead he had to keep his company in place to evacuate his dead and wounded. Charles and his squad set up they're NDP. The positions were tight five meters between men. The LT was not taking any chances on getting ambushed again. Corbett was setup close behind Charles. "You ok, Bob?" he asked using Charles nickname.

"Yea, no sweat."

"That was some shit with Doc Randall. He saved your ass, man."

"So, did Parker."

"I know. He was a good Marine. So are you. You saved the company today. The NVA would have kicked our ass good."

"Why did they open up? They had us."

"What did you see that got you spooked?"

"There was a branch, no leaves on it, just sticking straight up in the ground in the grass by itself."

"Target point for the mortar crew. If we had walked into that we would have been fucked."

They spoke no more as they sat in the grass. Charles was deep in thought about how close he had come to being killed. A selfless act by another man had saved him, just as he had saved a lot of them.

CHAPTER 41

THE OK CORRAL

They called him 'Doc Holiday'. The infamous dentist turned gunfighter and gambler from Tombstone Arizona. It was Hollywood that gave him the name. Delta Company would re-member the day as the firefight at the OK Corral. Jack hated the name. Watching helplessly as his Marines died in his care or were already gone before he had a chance bothered him enough. He had killed four men. He did not remember doing it, only the aftermath. He had watched as other Marines had brought back the weapons and equipment of those four men. Stripped of their identity and their dignity, the four bodies lay in the grass baked by the sun. He wondered if the NVA would return for them. He hoped they would. He was supposed to save lives, not take them. Corbett told him later that night had he not gunned them down, two more Marines and even he would have been killed. Jack turned it all over in his mind. He accepted what he had done as necessary. Having a name attached that glorified his actions bothered him more.

Back in the world, news of the invasion of Cambodia was another protesting point for ending the war. Demonstrations were held on college campuses around the country. Things got worse four days later when National Guard Troops in Ohio fired on demonstrators. The anti-war movement was reaching a fever pitch. Eilis was with her friends. They marched from City Hall to the Art Museum and back again. Police in riot gear followed the protestors. Frank Rizzo was the Police Commissioner in Philadelphia and had no patience with hippies exercising their constitutional rights protesting the war. Any lawless activity by the protestors would get an immediate police response. Along the march they chanted the slogans of the day. Eilis carried a poster stapled to a piece of lumber that said, "Suppose they gave a war, and no one came." Charolette Keyes had made the line from a Carl Sandberg poem infamous. It was her personal favorite. Once the official march was over people started drifting back up the Parkway towards the Art Museum. Eilis and her friends settled on the grass near the Joan of Arc Statue. She knew the area well, Jacks mother and grandmother lived just a few blocks away. The Brogans were closer on Olive Street. Her friends knew about Jack. They had all met him. They all wanted his safe return but they would not condone what he was doing. To them the war was an evil that must be stopped.

The girls had sat down to listen to a young man playing a guitar. He had a thick mustache and shoulder length hair. Dressed in faded jeans with sneakers, he also wore a t-shirt and a vest covered with ant-war buttons. He had a soft voice and Eilis found him interesting. The young man told Eilis and her friends his name was Peter, and that he was a disciple of Jesus. He sang the popular songs of the day and they all joined in. It had become a pleasant afternoon. Her friends decided it was time for them to leave. They would have to walk back to 30th Street Station to get the elevated train to 69th Street. Peter agreed to walk with them, but in reality, he was more interested in Eilis. Eilis offered no objection and encouraged his attention by being flirtatious. Her two girlfriends walked ahead of them to give them some space. "So, where do you live?" He asked her.

"In Media, with my parents. I work in the courthouse there."

"Wow, I never figured you for the establishment type."

"I don't see it that way, besides I need to see how I want to live my life."

"How about boyfriends? Is there someone special in your life or do you just go with the flow?"

"I had, that is to say I have a boyfriend. He is in the Navy."

"It's funny, you look like a child of peace, your protesting the war, but you work for the man and your boyfriends a military guy."

"What do you do? How do you live, where do you live?"

"Like I said, I am a disciple of Jesus. People help me. I stay wherever I am welcomed. I am free. I stay away from the man and his establishment."

Eilis thought for a moment then asked, "So how do you survive. If you have no home, how do you get food, water?"

"People provide man. Where ever I go, people provide. They share what they have and so do I. I sing songs and play my guitar. Some people give me money. I sit and play and they throw money into my case."

"Where did you grow up?"

"A small town up in north Jersey, called Mahwah. I used to hang out in the big city, but it is corrupt. There's like porn and prostitutes and some really perverted people there, it's a drag. So, I hitched myself down here to Philly, you know the city of brotherly love. It's cooler down here but the fuzz is really bad. They're like gestapo. I try to stay far away from them."

"Doesn't your family worry about you? Do they know where you are?"

"No way. My old man was in Korea during the war. When the man sent me his invitation to fight in his war, I left. No way was I going to be a part of the war. My old man threw me out. I've been free ever since."

They reached the station and the three girls dropped they're tokens in the box and went through the turnstile. Peter casually hopped over the turnstile and went down the stairs with the girls to get the train. When the train arrived, Eilis annoyed sat with Peter. "You know, for someone who is so anti-establishment you like to take advantage of what the establishment provides," Eilis stated.

"Whoa, hold on little girl. What do you mean?"

"I mean in some ways you actually steal from the establishment. You did not pay a fare to ride this train. You admitted to being a draft dodger. You accept money from people to buy food from the establishment, or business people associated with the establishment. Did you ever stop to think, by avoiding the draft, someone else had to take your place? That someone might go to Vietnam and be killed. I don't think that's right. My boyfriend is there. He's a corpsman. He helps wounded Marines. He goes into the villages and gives medical care to the people. According to you, he is the establishment. Maybe he's there because you're not."

"Girl, you are bumming me out. I thought you were cool. My mistake. Peace." Peter got up and got off the train at 63rd Street.

Still angry Eilis sat alone. Then she started to cry. Her two friends sat with her and comforted her. When they arrived at the 69th Street Terminal they boarded a trolley for Media, and went home. When Eilis got to her house she went upstairs to her room and wrote a letter to Jack.

The NVA had fled north. Duong and his company had escaped the American artillery with just a few wounded, all of them minor. They marched the rest of the day into the night. Duong knew the Marines would find Captain Diem. He did not care. He was concerned for the four men he sent to finish off the wounded Marines. The Marines would stay at the ambush site for another day to secure the area. They would also evacuate their own wounded and dead.

By midnight they reached an area Duong knew well. He told his men to dig fighting positions and to rest. The Marines would come he knew that. All he and his men had to do was to wait.

The next day was quiet day of rest. The fighting positions were complete and Duong went over the ambush plan with his squad leaders. Every man knew the escape routes, and their fields of fire. Ammunition was distributed and food and water was provided. Scouts were sent out to track the Marines, and to retrieve stores of supplies from hidden caches. The NVA was ready.

Charles watched as the helicopter arrived for the dead and wounded. Two Marines carried each of the poncho covered bodies of their fallen comrades unto the big bird. For them the war was over. The helicopter lifted off and left the Marines in the grass.

It was hard sleeping that night. Despite his exhaustion Charles thought about the day's events. There was nothing he could do but accept it all and move on.

The Marines wanted payback but were stuck where they were waiting for resupply. The re-supply chopper arrived after lunch and the men of Delta company started north. By mid-afternoon they were once again told to hold in place. They set up a defensive position and waited for instructions.

Corbett came back to his squad and let them know that the next day they would be heading north again as the left point flank company of the battalion. The old man knew that the Marines would be rotated back to the world soon and wanted to leave his slate clean. He was not going to leave a functioning enemy presence in his AO. Delta would be on the left flank, Charlie

Company on the right, while Alpha, Bravo and Echo Company would be the main column.

Early the next morning Charles and the rest of his squad could hear the choppers come in and insert the rest of the battalion a thousand meters away to the east. Soon word came by radio for the battalion to move out heading north. Terry Segura an FNG was assigned to be the point man.

"Wait how about I take the point and Terry can walk right or left flank of me as the terrain dictates," Charles said.

"You a fuckin general now. Since when did you become tactician?" Corbett replied.

"I can do it, I'll walk point," Terry offered.

"Negative newbie, you can walk flank for General Bootcamp here. Let's move out," Corbett ordered.

Charles and Segura walked side by side through the grass heading north.

"Ok, all you have to do is walk slightly behind me but off to the right or left about twenty meters or so. Keep your eyes open. Watch out for snakes the fuckers are everywhere." Charles informed Terry.

Another hot day in the sun was replaced by the shade of small forest. Getting out of the sun was a blessing as Delta kept moving north under the watchful eyes of the NVA.

Charles walked around a tree and found an area of open ground. There did not seem to be any human activity but it aroused his curiosity. Nice place to bed down for the night he thought as he continued on. The rest of the column followed the line of march. Radio instructions were given from the main column so that the three columns of movement stayed on the same heading and pace. The main battalion column was 1000 meters to the east with Charlie Company another 1000 meters further east.

As the point man, Charles could see that the wood line was ending and that they would have to cross a field of high grass and shrubs to another wood line 250 meters away. Before he broke out of the tree line he held up his fist to halt the company. Segura missed the hand signal and kept going almost stepping out of the wood line before Charles could stop him. Corbett came up to Charles and looked at the terrain. The wood line in front of him looped around to the west slightly. The eastern side was a hard L shape. "Terry, you stay on Bobbies left, I'll be on the right. Ten meter spread, five meters back. Move out," Corbett ordered.

They had been moving all morning and Segura had hoped they would have stayed in the woods for a lunch break. The main column was still moving so they had to go on. Crouching over, Charles stepped out of the wood line and headed for a downed tree about 200 meters away. The grass was chest high in places with large bushes spread around the open ground. The sun beat down on him again baking his head under his helmet. He used a towel around his neck to wipe the sweat from his eyes and face. He thought that he would walk to the downed tree then take good look at the tree line to his front. He reached within fifteen meters of the tree when he saw movement to his left. Two men in black pajamas had run into the high grass behind the tree and disappeared. Holding up his fist to stop the company, he looked to his right at Corbett. Using hand signal's, he indicated he saw two men moving east to his front. Corbett signaled to continue moving. The three-point men moved cautiously forward. Charles prepared to go over the tree stump.

The patience of the NVA was rewarded by the arrival of more Marines. Scouts reported the movement of the battalion in the three columns of march. Duong had been promoted to Lieutenant and had command of his own company after the death of Captain Diem. Hunkered down in a room underground he listened to the Regimental Commander reveal his plan on a map as he used a bayonet as a pointer.

"One of the three columns of Marines will reach comrade Duong's company dug into this tree line. This is where the first contact will be. There is only one landing zone for the American helicopters, here at this eastern point where the wood line turns south. Once we initiate contact the main column of Marines will start to move west to reinforce the company under attack. Waiting for them will be three companies along this ridge line 500 meters to their west. One company will be held in reserve here just north. They will act as a blocking force against the other Marine company further east. They may also be used to overrun the rear of the main enemy column. Two additional platoons will be provided to comrade Duong."

With no questions they all left via the tunnels. Duong picked up his two additional platoons and returned to his company dug in the woods. Along the way he placed one squad of seven men in a position that covered the landing area discussed in the briefing. He gave them instructions and left them. The rest of the men he wanted in place in the high grass and shrubbery to the west of the Marines as they crossed the open ground. This would catch the Marines in an L shaped cross fire. Movement of this column of Marines was quicker than expected. They were already in the kill zone.

Two of the NVA scouts dressed in pajamas saw the approaching Marines. Running into the high grass to their fighting positions the first Marine was only ten meters away. Grabbing their AK-47's the two scouts opened up on the center man and the man to the west. The first man was hit and fell behind the tree stump. The other man was lifted off his feet by the impact of the rounds and was screaming.

The other Marine returned fire but was hit by NVA fire now coming from the woods. Duongs initial plan fell apart by the

Marines early arrival but his soldiers were putting out a horrendous amount of fire. Green tracers from machine gun positions as well as automatic weapons fire from AK-47's raked across the Marines pinning them down. An entire platoon of Americans was in the high grass taking everything the NVA could give them. RPG fire peppered the wood line preventing the rest of the Marine Company from coming up to reinforce the trapped platoon. Duong saw there was still a chance his plan might come together. He ordered the two extra platoons to take up positions along the small ridge in the high grass to the west of the Marines. They would also be used as a blocking force should the rest of the Marines attempt to flank the wood line.

Over the din of the firefight the NVA could hear the screams of the wounded Marines. The trap had worked. Machine guns and RPG's continued a wall of fire into the wood line. To the west more AK-47 fire was slicing through the grass. The Marine platoon was in a cross fire.

Casualties were mounting. The familiar cries of 'corpsman up' could barely be heard over the gun fire, but the snipers knew what it meant.

They prepared themselves, knowing that they're targets would soon appear.

Watching the grass in front of him, Charles was about to step over the tree when he felt something hit him in the chest. Lying face down in the grass he found it was hard to breath. Blood seemed to fill his nose and throat. Then he heard the firing of weapons. The sound was deafening. Why was there so much shooting? There were only two of them. He thought. He half rolled over but the ruck sack he wore was in the way. Still trying to get his breath he saw LeCoin coming towards him then everything went black.

Dave LeCoin was the 3rd Platoon corpsman. He and Cahill had somehow made it through a gauntlet of fire to where the point position was. Cahill reached Segura who was yelling. Upon seeing Cahill, he started talking in a normal tone, "Doc, it hurts like hell. Am I gonna die?"

"Don't lie to me Doc. Help me, please." Cahill was on his knees pulling at the bandoliers and M60 ammo strapped across Segura's chest. Once he was past all that he fought with the flak jacket and utility shirt. Reaching inside to his chest Cahill saw three large welts were the bullets had hit. Not one penetrated the skin, slowed down by all the gear that Terry was wearing. "You, dumb fuck, you're not shot... look no blood," Cahill declared holding up his hand. "What? Are ya sure Doc. It hurts." "No shit asshole, of course it hurts now get your shit together and give me some cover fire."

"Cahill."

Looking over to his right Cahill saw LeCoin clutching his stomach. He had been gut shot and part of insides were exposed. LeCoin was trying to crawl back towards the wood line. "Get Gallagher, he's bad."

"Segura fire that weapon, cover me." Cahill half crawled and ran up to Gallagher. He was lying on his left side and still wearing his ruck sack. Cahill could see the pink frothy bubbles from his nose and mouth and Charles had a hard time getting air. Opening up his shirt he saw the hole. More bubbles, a sucking chest wound. This was bad. Cahill looked around and as he did an NVA soldier just ten meters away fired at him, spraying wood chips from the tree all over him and Charles. Ducking Cahill got up on his knees and fired a magazine at the NVA. He found Gallagher's weapon and removed the condom that Charles kept over his muzzle to keep it clear of debris. Looking it over deciding it was intact he put it on his finger and stuck it into the hole in Charles' chest. He moaned but his breathing improved. The NVA fired at him again and Cahill used Gallagher's weapon and emptied another magazine. The NVA fired again this time hitting Charles in the wrist. Blood and woodchips splashed into Cahills eyes. "Fuck this, GUNS UP, GUNS UP."

Reloading both Gallagher's and his own weapon he held the two M16's over the tree trunk and let loose. Getting back down he cut away the straps of Charles' rucksack and turned it over. Another round of AK-47 fire hit a can of peaches in the outside pocket. Now Cahill had bits of peaches all over his face. "Gallagher, you asshole, where the fuck did you get peaches," Cahill said as he bandaged the chest wound. "Guns up goddamn it." Looking back to the line he saw Hollywood, his M60 barking as he held on to a 200-round belt of ammo.

More wood chips and debris from the NVA flew into the air. "Hollywood, get that motherfucker!" The M60 let loose along burst.

Hollywood looked at Cahill with that grin of his and asked, "What's up Doc?" Cahill noted that Hollywood was still wearing his glasses. He was prepping another long belt. "Time to mow the grass," he yelled as the M60 tore into the NVA positions in the tree line.

Cahill shook his head and bandaged Gallagher's wrist. Using his body as a shield Cahill got ready to move the wounded man back from the line. Gallagher was hit again in the stomach. Getting him up on his shoulder Cahill ran crouched over back to the line. Then he saw Corbett fumbling with one hand to reload his weapon. "Corbett, give me a hand." Corbett came over and with the one good hand he had helped Cahill carry Charles back to the trees. Reaching the tree line, he collapsed exhausted and started to crawl. He saw a Marine and asked where the staging point was. It was the open patch of ground they had seen before. Reaching it he saw Randall tending to wounded Marines. "Jack... it's Charlie Gallagher...sucking chest wound. He took one in the belly too." Cahill explained out of breath. "Fucks sake Cahill, you ok? You look like shit."

"Yea, Corbett here has a bum wing. I'm going back up. Then Cahill saw Dave LeCoin lying on his back with no shirt on. His stomach was bandaged. He was breathing, a red M on his forehead told him Jack had given him morphine. He ran back up to the tree line as green tracers filled the air. Looking back, he could see them going back into the woods. Jesus Christ, he thought I was just there standing up.

The Marines had made an attempt to flank the NVA positions from the west, but ran into two platoons instead. The NVA were disciplined and opened up on the Marines when they were just feet away. Some of that fighting turned into hand to hand, before the Marines pulled back. Knowing they could not outflank the enemy as long as the NVA held the ground the Marines needed to maneuver through, they called on the next option. Artillery. The initial ambush had the NVA and 1st Platoon too close to use. But the NVA on the western side of the field was easy prey.

The 105mm howitzer crews were delighted to hear "enemy troops in the open." The artillery would chase out or destroy the NVA, opening up that ground for another attempt at the NVA flank.

Jack got the word that a medivac was inbound to pick up the wounded. So far, the Marines had been lucky. They had men that had serious wounds but no one had been killed, yet. He had seven men waiting when Cahill returned with a man with a leg wound. LeCoin and Gallagher were a priority. The other men that could walk would help the two corpsmen with the others. The big CH-54 came in from the south along the eastern edge of the forest. When it set down the back ramp was already open and the bird was facing northeast. The wounded were loaded on and the door gunner tossed an U1 bag to Jack. Jack ran back to the staging area ahead of Cahill. Cahill stopped at the edge of the wood line. The pitch on the choppers motor had changed. He turned to look.

Seven NVA soldiers sat through the vicious fire fight. They could hear the American artillery off to the west. They could also hear off in the eastern distance the battle raging behind them. Just as Lieutenant Duong had said the big helicopter came along the wood line from the south and landed not only in the spot he had pointed out but at the exact angle. They readied themselves. A group of marines had loaded wounded men on the big machine and had run back into the woods. The engine roared as the big bird lifted off the ground hovered for a second or two then started its turn to go back out the way it came in. It was then the seven-man squad fired their AK-47 rifles simultaneously. In less than three seconds the cockpit exploded as 210 AK-47 rounds tore the bodies of the pilot and co-pilot to pieces killing them instantly. The huge machine turned over on its side as it fell. The rotor blades spinning at full power tore into the ground sending broken steel and debris into the air. The engine screamed out in protest as it fought to maintain the speed it was set for as the big blades tore into the earth. Collapsing finally from its wounds the chopper fell with a loud thud as smoke and dust enveloped it.

The seven men congratulated each other, then set out to the other place Duong sent them. They would now harass the Marines from their rear.

Undetected they ran the 200 meters through the woods to the south before cutting across and coming back up north. The rear position of the Marines was just meters ahead.

Stunned Cahill watched the big bird go down. With the noise of the firefight in progress and the chopper itself he could not see or hear where the NVA were when they shot it down. Running back to the bird he saw bodies falling out of the back. The ramp had been partially closed when the chopper fell. Corbett and other Marines were pushing people outside afraid the chopper would explode. The door gunner had an M60 and was watching the area. Cahill ran up to the cockpit. He would never forget the site before him. Running back, he checked the two most seriously wounded men LeCoin and Gallagher. Both were still alive.

Jack had heard the crash. He was amazed to see the wounded men coming back into the staging area. It was getting crowded here. After the attempt to flank the enemy more wounded came in. There were also five poncho covered bodies.

The LT came by and ordered Cahill and Randall to stay in the staging area. Wounded would be brought to them. Jack and Cahill also learned that the main column of the battalion had run into a big NVA unit that had been dug in. They would not get here today to help. With everyone back into the tree line from the high grass the LT was raining artillery fire on the NVA positions. By the end of the day the NVA had broken off they're attack and had retreated to the east. Later that day a second medivac was called in. This time the bird never set down. Hovering a foot or so off the ground Marines had to throw the dead and wounded unto the ramp. Charles Gallagher was conscious. He watched mesmerized as Marines threw his broken comrades on the big chopper. Then it lifted off. Charles had no idea that this was his second helicopter ride of the day.

CHAPTER 42

NOTHING MAKES SENSE

For the next two days, the NVA and the Marines fought over ground they had both fought over before. It made no sense. Waiting for the choppers to take them back to Con Thien Jack sat against a tree. He like everyone else was filthy. He was also covered in blood. None of it his. Cahill sat across from him. They had lost thirteen men, and three times that many wounded. Delta Company was now combat ineffective. They had started out with 110 men. They came back with fifty-eight. The rest of the battalion was just as bad. Alpha, Bravo and Echo Companies took a beating against three companies of NVA that would be re-enforced by two additional companies.

"You look like shit, Jack," Cahill said.

"Well, I did something right today. I feel like I look."

"In a few hours, we gonna be drinking warm beer." Cahill added.

"I wonder where Charlie goes when we pull out to our bases?"

"Back into his holes and his tunnels, I guess," Cahill answered.

"You know the Marines and the NVA have been fighting in this area since the beginning of the war. You would think one side would finally win. We come here, pick a fight. Charlie gives us good as he gets, we leave and bomb the crap out of him. Nobody ever wins. We come back and we do it all over again. It's like no one wants us to win or lose," Jack said staring at a tree.

"Fuck it, don't mean nothin," Cahill said.

"Naw man, that ain't right. What the fuck are we doing here. Guys are getting fucked up or dead and for what."

"Sailor you sound like you've lost your patriotic dedication. What you need is some serious R&R. A little round-eyed pussy will straighten you right out," Cahill laughed.

"This shit ain't funny, man."

"Look Jack, lifers want to pin medals on themselves and the rich people want more money. It's that simple. You and me, we're just pawns on a big chessboard. Charlie, he just wants us and everyone else out of his country. Nixon wants to turn it all over to Marvin the ARVN. You really think he could go toe to toe with the NVA like we do? No way. Charlie will fuck him up in tee tee time."

Off in the distance they could hear the rotors. Choppers were on the way in.

The next couple of days were spent at Con Thien. While they were there they got themselves cleaned up, were given fresh uniforms and they were regrouped into three companies. The battalion was reassigned to the 9th Marine Division. Base security duty, and guarding bridges became the normal routine. The NVA was also regrouping. Those infamous hills around Khe Sanh were active once again. The ARVN had taken responsibility for the area but had gotten their ass kicked again. The Marines would be called on once again to clean out the NVA.

Jack was in the village assigned to a MEDCAP detail. He had a security team and he along with nurses and a doctor spent the day treating the inhabitants of the local village. He felt human again. He especially liked checking the children. Most had normal childhood aliments. Some however had sores that had become infected and a few were victims of booby traps or artillery fire. None of the injuries were serious. Almost all the inhabitants displayed some coughing hoping to get Cepachol lozenges. These were sold on the black market. Medicine was dispensed by the doctor. Jack checked heart rates and blood pressure as well as temperatures. Not all the children came with their parents. He learned that there were several orphans living in the village. One in particular was clearly an Amerasian. They Vietnamese called them, 'bụi đời' (dust of the earth) and they were largely ignored. This little boy was about five years old. He kept to himself. One of the mothers explained through an ARVN interpreter that the little boy slept in the woods outside the village. He ate food he found in the gardens and sometimes some of the other children gave him food. Today he was fighting with a C-Ration can. He was attempting to pull something out of the can. One of the Marines from the security detail approached him to help but he ran off behind a pen containing pigs.

Before long he returned to the road were the Marines were, and he was still trying to retrieve the contents of the can. Jack and one of the nurses watched him. One last final pull and the little boy pulled his prize from the can. He dropped it on the ground at his feet. Jack yelled, "Grenade" but it was too late. The grenade exploded as the little boy attempted to pick it up. He died instantly. The event shut down the MEDCAP. No one else was wounded, but the vision of the little boy enveloped by the blast of the grenade shook Jack. Returning to the base at Con Thien he got very drunk. Nursing a bad hang over the next day he learned that the company was going back into the hills to re-enforce the ARVN that very afternoon.

American air power had, as it always had made the difference. The ARVN units operating in the hills north of Khe Sanh had been soundly defeated. The NVA could not sustain the number of casualties that air power could inflict. As a result, the NVA was forced to break off their attacks on the ARVN before they could be wiped out. Duong and his company retreated back into the tunnels and underground bunkers. It was frustrating. Why bother to attack the enemy at all. The attack helicopters came first followed by jets that dropped massive bombs of high explosive and napalm. An entire platoon could be wiped out in seconds with anyone of these aircraft. Duong knew that he and his men could defeat the puppet soldiers, but not as long as the Americans were still there. Political pressure in the US called for the American president to end their involvement. American units were leaving Vietnam, but not at a pace to satisfy Duong.

The new tactics called for hit and run type ambushes. Attack the ARVN and escape back to their bunkers before the air power of the Americans arrived. This worked well, moral among his troops was high. Duong expressed his frustration with his commanders but orders were orders. The May attacks into Cambodia were repulsed by the NVA. The ARVN were pushing into their southern sanctuaries before the Americans arrived.

They heard of great success stories about defeating the puppet soldiers. When the Americans finally joined them, it turned the tide. The NVA lost many men, but the stashed supplies they lost cost them heavily. New supplies were coming south everyday but now the NVA hid these in new jungle sanctuaries in the north along the DMZ.

Then one day they heard the familiar sounds of rotor blades of the Marine CH-54 helicopters. Their old enemy was back. Another operation calling for ambushes was set in place. Duong and his men were ready. Leaving the tunnels and bunkers they set out for a large area filled with high grass and tall trees. The grass would give them concealment while the trees provided cover. The area would not be considered jungle, but more heavy woods. There were good fields of fire in the area the NVA set their ambush. Scouts reported where the Marines landed and what direction they were travelling. The Marines travelled west in two columns about 100 meters apart. As they entered the woods Duong and his men waited in the northern part of the wooded area that covered more than 1000 square meters. Other NVA units were set up in the south with some in between the two Marine columns.

Point elements of Jacks platoon ran straight into the waiting NVA. During the initial barrage of NVA fire, the Marines encountered enemy fighting positions all around their perimeter. The enemy seemed to be everywhere. Marines found themselves firing in all directions responding to enemy attacks. Most of the fight was in the south of the Marine columns. Green and red tracers crisscrossed the woods as fire from the NVA intensified. Jack was ordered to set up a staging area for the wounded that started coming in. Most of the wounded had gunshot wounds. Before he could get himself setup he had four badly wounded Marines. As he was treating these men two more Marines were brought in from the north. With six men suffering from severe gunshot wounds he was overwhelmed. Then the battle seemed to shift further south. The volume of fire from the north subsided. Four more Marines staggered into his perimeter. He now had ten men to care for. By the time he treated the wounds of the new arrivals he had a feeling of dread. He had no radio and seemed to have lost contact with the rest of his company. Three additional Marines made their way to the staging area from the north. Jack looked around and noted that most of the firing came from the south and the west. Using the last of his supplies from his U1 he treated everyone and took an inventory of weapons and ammo. Two of the last Marines that came in had their M16 rifles but no additional ammo. None of the wounded were in any condition to mount a defense. Two rifles with 20 rounds each and his own .45 with two spare magazines was all they had. Most of the men still had their canteens so water was not an issue. Jack hunkered down with his wounded men and started thinking about how to hook up with his company as movement was spotted to their north. Five NVA scouts had come upon his staging area and after exchanging fire with Jack from the two M16's and before long he was out of ammo. The enemy charged into the perimeter and Jack drew his .45 and killed two outright. The second round, stove piped in his pistol and before he could tap and rack the enemy was on him. He threw the pistol into the face of one man who screamed and fell. Another NVA tried to bayonet him but he was able to parry the thrust down and away from his body but it still caught him in the right thigh. Seeing the last of the attackers coming towards him he grabbed the NVA that had just got him in the leg and put him into a bear hug. Spinning the man to use him as a shield. The last man thrust his bayonet into his comrades back, but it went all the way through getting Jack in the stomach as well.

The NVA fired his SKS rifle as he withdrew his bayonet. The round went through his friend killing him and hit Jack in the stomach. Pushing the dead NVA into the last attacker he knocked him down and Jack grabbed his throat with both hands squeezing as hard as he could. He pounded the man's head into the ground as he tightened his grip. Blood came from the NVA's mouth as Jack pounded his head as he squeezed harder. The other NVA that Jack had hit with the pistol jumped on Jacks back getting him on a choke hold. Rolling over Jack was lying on top of his attacker. Jack reached behind and pushed his fingers into the wound on the man's face. He howled in pain as Jack rolled off him. Grabbing a helmet Jack hit the man over and over crushing his skull. The attack was over and Jack sat on the ground exhausted and bleeding from his wounds. Three of the wounded Marines Jack had treated and propped against a tree stared in awe, helpless and unable to come to his aid. "Holy shit, Doc, are you ok," one Marine said. Before he could answer a platoon of NVA came into the staging area and started to dispatch the wounded. Jack grabbed his .45 and tried to stand but was cut down by burst of automatic weapon fire, that caught him in the hip on his right side. An officer appeared and ordered his men to cease firing. The NVA had killed all the wounded Marines except for Jack and the three men propped against the tree. Jack crawled over to them as if to shield them from the enemy. The officer ordered his men south as he stood over Jack and the three wounded Marines. Once they left he looked hard at Jack. Jack looked up thinking this was it. He felt that he was going to die, but instead the officer said in a determined voice, "Rời khỏi đất nước của tôi, bạn không thể giành chiến thắng." Then without warning he pointed his weapon in the air and emptied his magazine. Then he left following his troops south. The four men sat together amazed that they had been spared. Jack was badly wounded. He sat against the bodies of his wounded men and soon passed out. Before night fell the fighting shifted to the west and Marines could be heard in the woods to the east. Helicopters were landing as well. PFC Carmichael holding unto Jack began shouting, "Corpsman up. Help. Corpsman up." A squad of Marines came into the staging area. Doc Cahill was with them. He checked Jack and found he was still alive. "Get these guys out to the choppers, now."

Doc barked.

Cahill fireman carried Jack and coming towards him other Marines began to help. The wounded men were all put on the chopper as Cahill started checking Jacks wounds. He got a bandage on his leg that had started bleeding again. The medivac chopper corpsman jumped off and helped Cahill get Jack on the chopper. "Take care of him Bob, he's one of ours," Cahill told him.

"No sweat, man, keep your head down," the man yelled over the noise of the engines.

The chopper corpsman plugged in his headset and told the pilot they were clear for lift off. The big bird lifted into the air and Bob Lange waved at his counterpart as Cahill stood watching the bird leave. Seeing another chopper coming into the LZ, Cahill saw the dead being carried out. They would be going home. If he made it, Jack would too. Cahill turned and ran back towards the fire fight. It was going to be a long night.

The Marines continued their push against the NVA. Before long the operation was over. Doc Cahill returned to Da Nang to finish his tour. Assigned to the hospital there his duties became perimeter defense and night ambushes with the Marines. He hated the Master Chief in charge of his unit. The man was a typical lifer. During the day Cahill was tasked with filling the 55-gallon drums with water, that the Master Chief and his cronies used for showers. He hated the detail. Filling the bucket from a water truck he had to climb the ladder to the top of the showers and fill each drum with fresh water. On his last night in Vietnam, Cahill could not sleep. He was fighting diarrhea. Then a thought occurred to him. He went to the latrine with his bucket and relieved himself. Then filling the bucket half way with water, he climbed the ladder and poured the foul-smelling mixture into one of the 55-gallon drums.

For the first time since arriving in Vietnam Cahill slept with a smile on his face.

Sitting at his desk in the embassy, Dylan read the initial reports and looked over the aerial photos of Son Tay. A raid to rescue American POW's was in the works. Back home in Florida at a secret location a full-scale model of the camp had been built. He wondered if the Green Berets handpicked for the mission would be able to pull it off. Drinking his coffee, he thought about home. He had not been there in over a year. Caroline had already gone home and retired. He missed her. He thought about their relationship. It was peculiar to say the least. The situation here in the country became questionable. The ARVN were given more and more responsibility for the combat operations, but were still supported by American air power and artillery. The NVA still had a viable presence in the country and despite operations by US units and the ARVN, no decisive gains could be measured. Maybe it was time for him to put in his papers. Go back to Langley and begin the outgoing process. It was almost lunch time. Another two-hour lunch at the hotel bar, with more booze than food. Maybe my liver will kill me, he thought.

Leaving the embassy, he walked to the hotel. Another hot and humid day. Sweat ran down the small of his back, it would collect on the .45 tucked into his pants at the small of his back. A lot of good it will do me, it is most likely rusted shut. He sat at the bar and ordered a beer and a club sandwich. The TV was on and tuned to the BBC channel. The news story was covering large protests back at home against the war. Dylan ate half the sandwich and finished the beer. An Army officer sat next to him as he ordered another beer. "Can't believe we're going home to this shit," he said.

"Getting short, Major?"

"Me, I'm on my third tour. The Brigades pulling out. We leave in September." Dylan looked at the patch on the officers left shoulder. It was the patch of the 199th Light Infantry Brigade.

"Another brigade heading home to the world. Pretty soon we will all be gone," Dylan replied.

"Actually, it's a numbers game for now. Members of my brigade that don't have enough time in country will be transferred to other units. Short timers in those units will be transferred to us. Same people going back to the world just under different colors. The Brigade goes back to Fort Benning but the number of people coming with us doesn't really change. All Washington is doing is shuffling the deck. Politics. That's the real enemy."

"Major, you sound like a man that has lost his sense of mission."

"Doesn't matter. Soon as I get back to Benning I'm going to resign my commission. I've seen too much bullshit for one lifetime."

"Can't say I blame you. I'm considering going home myself."

"Are you a contractor, or a reporter?" The Major asked.

"Company man, been here since the beginning. I've seen enough to know I've seen all I need. You may be right Major. It just might be time to go home."

"A spook, huh? Sometimes I wonder about you guy's. No offense. Too many secrets within secrets hidden in more secrets."

"Damn, after all this time, that's how that shit works."

Both men laughed, but there was nothing funny about it at all.

They could hear the choppers to the southeast. The Marines were coming. An entire regiment of crack NVA soldiers waited for them in the woods. Duong and his men started moving south. They were eager for another fight. The ARVN had been beat, but US air power saved them again. These were valuable lessons. If US support ever faltered the war would be over quickly. Vietnam would finally have its independence. One country, one people, one Vietnam without western influence or control. Soldiers from the north were giving their lives by the tens of thousands toward that goal. Today would be another one of those days. Young men dedicated to the cause defending their own country would never be defeated.

As Duong and his men moved south he had two platoons on either side. He sent five men forward to recon the area. He and his company reached the woods and set up a defensive perimeter against any US helicopters that might land troops in the field of high grass they just crossed. They had been there for over an hour and heard no reports from the scouts. Duong made his decision, they would head south. They marched south the fighting could be heard off to the south and to the west. His point squad had made contact up front. Then the firing stopped. He could hear men screaming and then he heard single shots of AK and SKS fire. He walked into a small clearing that had been a staging area for American wounded. His men had killed most of the wounded Marines. He ordered them all to cease fire. One of the Marines obviously badly wounded was attempting to reload a pistol. Duong fired a short burst hitting him in the hip. He fell, but still crawled to shield three wounded Marines by a tree. There was no fight left in them. They all had serious gunshot wounds. Wide eyed they stared at the entourage of enemy soldiers around them. Some were pointing their weapons at them, hatred in their eyes. Duong heard all of them. They wanted to kill the last four men and move on. He silenced their protests and ordered them south. "I will deal with these invaders myself. Join our comrades and defeat the Marines, like we defeated the ARVN. I will join you all soon," he ordered.

The NVA soldiers left running south. Duong stood over the wounded Marines. He looked over his shoulder at the carnage. Ten badly wounded Marines lay dead from gunshot wounds to the head. From what Duong saw many of them would have died anyway. Then he saw his five scouts. Looking at the Marines in front of him he surmised that only one man could have killed his men. He looked at Jack hard. He was looking back at Duong defiant but accepting his fate. The other three had fear in them. They said nothing. Duong saw the collar insignia on Jacks shirt. He was a corpsman. These men stopped at nothing to get to and treat the wounded Marines. Duong was now convinced that Jack had killed his men. The fighting was hand to hand. He looked Jack in the eye and said, "Leave my country, you cannot win." Then he fired his sub machine gun into the air and left. Running south he re-joined his men. The fire fight shifted west and that was where they went.

A Marine General walked into the ward at the hospital in Da Nang.

The doctors and nurses ignored him. They had seen this happen too many times. The General stopped at each bed pinning a Purple Heart to the patients pillow. For those that were awake he took the time to speak to each of them. When he got to Jacks bedside he pinned the medal to his pillow. Jack was heavily sedated. PFC Carmichael's bed was next in line. He spoke loud enough so only the General would hear, "That's Doc Holiday sir, he deserves more than just a Purple Heart. He saved us General, all by himself. He's the reason we all alive."

"That's right sir, just like Carmichael said." Another one of the surviving Marines that had come in with Jack said.

"What's your name son."

"PFC Jerome Carmichael sir."

"You say this man saved your lives. Tell me what happened," the General asked softly.

Carmichael told his story and the other two Marines gave the same account. The General was surprised the NVA officer had spared them. He was very curious as to what he said to Jack. The men called him Holiday but his chart said Randall. His aide reminded him about the fire fight the Marines referred to as the OK Corral a few months ago. The General remembered hearing the story. He had approved Jacks, Bronze Star. "All right men. My aide will get all the required information from each of you. I promise I will personally review this. In the meantime, I'm told all of you will be going to Japan soon and then home. Good luck and God bless," the General said before leaving.

All of the men Jack had been with all left Da Nang for Japan. Because of the different wounds and their severity, they had been separated to different wards. Jack would undergo surgery to repair the bones in his hip. He also had two stomach wounds that would heal in time. Jack would need to undergo physical therapy once his hip healed. Then he would be transferred to the Naval Hospital in Philadelphia.

Shortly after his arrival his family was permitted to visit with him. The bayonet wound in his leg had healed. The two stomach wounds had also fully healed. He went to physical therapy every day. He would need a cane the rest of his life.

CHAPTER 43

RETURNING WARRIOR

Hope and her mother arrived at the hospital in South Philly. Both were very anxious to see Jack. He had been progressing well. He would finish his own therapy sessions and help other veterans with theirs giving them encouragement. Today he would have his first visitors and sat in the garden waiting for his mother and grandmother. When they came through the door he was sitting. Standing to greet them he embraced his mother. His grandmother joined them. Both of them were crying. "Aw, come on Mom, don't cry. I'm ok, really. Look I gotta cane just like Uncle Dylan."

"Yes, and just as soon as you get better, I'm going to beat you with it," his mother cried.

They sat in the garden and talked. The Navy would keep him here for a few more months. Then he would get a medical discharge. His Navy days much to their delight was over. Jack learned that his Uncle Mike and Aunt Susan would be up to see him later that week. The Brogan's were all anxious to see him as well. He asked about Eilis, but neither Colleen or Hope had spoken to her in weeks. It had been a few weeks since his last mail as the post office tried to keep up with the changing addresses.

Even when he was at Con Thien it had been several weeks since she had written. The last couple of letters he did get from her were short and very general in content. He was starting to feel a disconnect in their relationship. The Randall's would be here later today, maybe they had seen or heard from her.

He sat with his mother and grandmother in the garden catching up with family news. Hope asked him about his injuries and Jack told her there was no permanent damage, other than the fact he would need a cane the rest of his life. A nurse came by to give him some medication and Hope was able to talk with her about his injuries. Looking at her son after her conversation she felt blessed he was still alive.

The Randall's arrived and Jack was thrilled to see them. They had not seen or heard from Eilis either, and Jack was worried. When visiting hours were over they all hugged him and promised they would all reach out to Eilis. Jack returned to his ward had dinner and went to the day room for the evening card game.

Her mother came out unto the porch where Eilis had been sitting. She sat with her daughter and said, "That was Kay Randall on the phone. She saw Jack today at the Navy hospital. His mail is all messed up and he is not getting his letters. Have you written to him, lately?"

"I guess the last letter I sent was a few weeks ago. How is he? Did Kay say how he was?"

"Kay said he looked well. He was in good spirits. He will have to use a cane, but other than that he is going to be fine. The Navy will discharge him in a few more months. Are you two, ok?"

"I suppose. It's hard. I'm here and he's on the other side of the world. Then you get the news about him being wounded and needing surgery. My friends all have their boyfriends here at home. They want me to go out with them to movies and dances, but I'm always the third wheel. Then there is the stupid war. Everyone is against it. When they find out you have a boyfriend fighting there you become an outcast."

"None of that is Jack's fault," her mother replied.

"No mom, you're wrong. It is Jacks fault. He enlisted, he wanted to go there. I just don't know how I feel anymore."

"Maybe you should go see him. You know you're going to see him sooner or later. Maybe that will help you."

The next day Eilis took the day off from her job at the courthouse and took the trolley to 69th Street. From there she caught the EL and transferred to the Broad Street subway. An hour and a half later she stood outside the main entrance to the Naval hospital. She was nervous. She remembered him yet at the same time she felt as if she was about to meet a stranger. She checked in at the main desk and was instructed where to go. Jack was waiting for her when she got off the elevator. He looked fine, the only indication he was hurt was the cane. He hugged and kissed her and told her how much he had missed her. Holding hands, he took her outside to the gardens and they sat on a bench. "I really missed you, how have you been? How's the new job?" He had a thousand questions the one lingering in his mind, he avoided asking, fearful of the reply.

"I'm ok. The new job is interesting. I file and read all the arrest reports from the previous day. I never knew there we're so many bad people in town. How did you get hurt?" He was quiet for a few seconds before he answered her, "It was nothing really. The Navy say's I'll be discharged soon. Then I guess I'll have to figure out what I'm going to do."

"Have you thought about that? You always felt that the military was going to be how you lived your life. I guess that's not going to happen."

The last sentence came out a little sarcastic and Jack noticed it. "I'm in no hurry, I'll figure out something."

They sat in silence for a few minutes. Then Eilis told him, "This past year has been hard. I was so lonely. My friends would want me to go out, parties, movies and dances. I always felt out of place. When you first left it wasn't so hard, but as time went on it got worse. I never went out with any of the boys that asked me. Not out of any duty to you, but...well I guess for my own self esteem. I had no desire to be the cheating girlfriend. I wonder sometimes if things between us will ever be like they were."

Jack was surprised. He had no idea what to say. He thought for a moment, then told her, "All I know is that I still love you. I missed you something awful. Sometimes at night I wondered why I was doing this. It was not what I expected. I mean, I thought I was there as the part of a plan to liberate people from Communism. Nothing could be further from the truth. All we did was fight the enemy over the same ground over and over again. They would kill us and we would kill them. It was just a meat grinder. So many people died, men women...children." Tears welled in his eyes, the memory of the little boy in the village coming back to him. He squeezed his eyes shut fighting to keep the tears back. He took a deep breath, composing himself. Eilis watched and felt sorry for him. For the first time since he had left she realized just how hard it was for him. In comparison, she felt that her feelings did not measure up to his experience. It was the way he hesitated and said children. Some of the anti-war protesters called returning veterans, 'baby killers'. "I'm sorry, I did not want to upset you. Maybe I'm being selfish. Let's try to put all of this behind us and start over again. Is there somewhere here that you could buy me a coke?"

"A coke, sure in the commissary."

"You've forgotten. The first time we met on the boardwalk, you bought me a coke."

"Oh yeah. Wow, that seems like a lifetime ago."

"It's only been a few years silly. I remember those first days we had at the shore. That I think was our happiest time. We were getting to know one another. There was no job, no war...just me and you on the beach that summer."

He took her hand and walked with her to the commissary. He leaned on his cane. He was getting stronger but long walks brought some of the pain back. "Does it hurt to walk? How long will you have to use a cane?" She asked.

"Doctors tell me I will always need a cane. Part of my hip bone was shattered, and a tendon in my thigh was torn up. Just call me 'gimpy'. One things for sure, I won't be any races any time soon."

They spent the day together repairing the relationship by re-living its happier days.

The mission failed. Dylan was reading some of the after-action intelligence reports about the raid on the Son Tay prison camp in North Vietnam. All of the men that pulled the mission off got back all right but without any POW's. They were the objective. He dropped the folder on his desk in disgust. The Green Berets found evidence that they had been there recently. Part of the intel revealed that the NVA sometimes moved POW's from camp to camp. Was this bad luck, bad intel or maybe the mission itself had been compromised. Sitting there in disgust, it was just in Vietnam would end in failure. American units were being withdrawn and more and more of the combat operations were conducted by the ARVN with US air and artillery support. The Son Tay mission was, labeled 'TOP SECRET'. Very few people in Saigon knew about it. The training for the mission took place in Florida on a secret base. The only points that leaks could have occurred was, Washington or Saigon. He had no faith in either.

For now, the NVA were preparing for another operation up north. Troops and supplies continued their progress down the Ho Chi Minh trail despite heavy US bombing. Dylan also knew that more American military units were scheduled to leave Vietnam as part of Nixon's Vietnamization plan. The light at the end of the tunnel was getting dimmer.

With the day over he left his office and walked back to his apartment on Gia Long Street. He had plans on going home for the holidays. Dylan learned that Jack had been wounded months ago and was at home recuperating. The Navy had already discharged him. He was looking forward to seeing him. He had another letter from Caroline, she had adjusted to retirement and was looking forward to travelling to Europe again after the first of the New Year. She indicated he should retire and join her. He gave it some thought, but decided no matter what was to happen he was here when it all began, and he would most likely be here when it ended. He spent another lonely night by himself. He was just so weary of it all, it seemed that no matter how much we gave the country never seemed to advance towards their stated objectives.

The next morning, he woke, showered and headed into the office. The usual stale pot of coffee and donuts were found in the small kitchenette.

He sat at his desk and made his flight reservations for going home. He hated connecting flights, he would rather go one way all the way. He found a direct flight from Tan Son Nhut to Washington DC. He would have to stay in country one day longer but it still got him home quicker than any of the other flights where he had to stop in Honolulu, Los Angeles, Chicago and then into Philadelphia. He could get a company car at Langley or rent one at Dulles. He decided to wait.

He sent a telegram home to his mother to let her know when to expect him.

With the approaching holiday's he decided he would do his Christmas shopping at home. He could get some good deals on cameras and other electronics at anyone of the base exchanges but he would also have to carry it all or check it with baggage.

The only thing he liked to travel with was a small canvas courier bag containing, a shave kit, socks and underwear and his .45 pistol.

Three days later he boarded his plane and settled into his first-class seat. The flight left on time and he settled in for a nice nap. In about twenty-four hours he would be in DC.

Since his discharge several weeks ago Jack had time on his hands. Idle hands make for the devil's workshop, and Jack was no exception. He drank too much. Eilis had her job and Jack would go and stay with his grandparents during the weekends. They began to settle into their old routine. He began to lose some weight and he had trouble sleeping. The booze helped but it was more from the excess. More than once he had passed out either in the backyard or the living room. When he was at his grandparents' home there was not much drinking there or at Eilis' house.

The two-young people had renewed their relationship but because of the drinking tension was growing. There was also something else. Jack did not seem to be Jack, Eilis noticed a change while he was still in the hospital.

He was more distant. She could not quite put her finger on it but it was there non-the-less. He had a coldness about him. It was if he lost any sense of apathy. He simply did not care. Before, Jack would stop and give money to a bum on the street, now he passed them as if they were not there at all. Then there was the anger. It could appear if out of nowhere and for no reason. He was also combative. Several times she saw him become confrontational with complete strangers over nothing. One of her girlfriends had seen him in a pizza shop get into a fight with two guys from the Pagan Motorcycle Club. The fight was brief leaving the two bikers seriously injured.

They planned a weekend at a Pocono Mountain resort with two other couples that Eilis was friends with. She thought maybe

531

if they got away to relax it would help him. They left late that Friday afternoon and drove up the Northeast Extension on the PA turnpike. One couple Frank and Annette had left earlier to open her father's cabin. Eilis and Jack sat in the back of Dan's car, while he drove and sat with Betty. They had two six packs of beer as they drove upstate. By the time they arrived Jack already had a good buzz going. They ordered pizza from the local shop in town and settled around the kitchen table eating and drinking. The hour was getting late and everything in town was closed. Frank had brought two cases of beer with him. Annette found the only bottle of liquor in the cabin. A full bottle of tequila.

Neither Frank or Dan had served in the military. Frank had poor eyesight and Dan was in college at Temple. The guys started drinking shots of the tequila, while the girls stuck with beer. Eilis noticed Jack was getting quite drunk and tried in futility to get him to slow down. Then Dan in his collegiate stupidity asked the forbidden question. "So, Jack how many babies were actually killed by our guys in Vietnam?"

"Dan stop, how could you ask him that?" Eilis said angrily.

"I don't mean any offense. I mean…for me I don't believe it. I really don't think we ran around killing babies. That's just the anti-war crowd trying to stir up bullshit that isn't true." Replied Dan apologetically.

Betty chimed in, "Wait what about that village…Me Lye or something. The Marines killed all those woman and children."

"That waz the fucckkin Army," Jack said angrily, his speech slurred.

"What difference does it make. Army, Marines, who cares they did it. Lined up those poor people in a ditch and shot em all," Annette offered.

"Let's change the subject," pleaded Eilis.

"Why, were all adults here. Nobody likes the war. We never should have gotten involved in the first place. I'm glad I didn't have to go. If I was eligible I think I would have headed to Canada," Frank said.

Jack looked at Frank, "Well that'z... just great. You run off to Canada to save your own asz, while some poor slob that takes your...place gets his balls shot off."

Frank got defensive, "Whoa, hold on their buddy..."

"Fvuck you, asshole."

"All right stop. No more talk about Vietnam," Eilis pleaded.

"My Lai, that was the village," Betty remembered.

"Be honest, Jack do you really believe we are doing any good there?" Annette asked.

"What would you know anyway? You were a goddamn corpsman. How much combat could you have seen passing out band aids," Frank demanded angrily.

Jack lounged across the table at Frank. The girls screamed. Eilis threw herself on Jacks back to try and get him to stop. Jack flipped her off his back unto the table locking his hands on her throat. She looked up into his murderous eyes and for the first time in her life felt absolute fear. Frank and Dan grabbed Jack and muscled him towards the door. "Open the fuckin door," Frank yelled. Annette opened the back door of the cabin and all three men tumbled outside. Dan managed to get inside as Frank hit Jack on the head knocking him down. Then he ran inside locking the door leaving Jack outside screaming at them in a rage. "You... fuckin pussiez, I'll fukin waste you mother fiuckkes."

Betty was holding Eilis. She was crying uncontrollably. "Jeses fhuggin Christ," Dan said, his voice also slurred. "He's a freak... lunatic!"

Eilis started to compose herself. She held her throat, it was sore and bruised. She looked out the window at Jack as he stumbled around the backyard of the cabin screaming at the woods. "C'mmon...fuckin pukeesz. I'm right here. No more...ammo, just fuckin shoot me! SHOOTME mothefuks," he collapsed then on his knees and wept.

Eilis watching from the window felt pity for him. Something happened to him and it was torturing him.

After sometime Jack seemed to calm down. He laid on the grass and pine needles in the yard and wept quietly. Inside Annette and Betty poured what little was left of the tequila down the drain. Frank and Dan sat at the table quietly drinking their beers. "Why don't we all just go to bed and sleep it off. You guys take the bedrooms, Jack and I will sleep down here,

Eilis suggested. The two couples went upstairs leaving Eilis. Eilis walked outside and approached Jack with some apprehension. "Jack, it's me Eilis are all right?" Jack rolled over on his back and then sat up. Wiping the tears and his nose with his hands he looked up at her. "Why am I out...here? Where did everybody go?" He asked.

"Do you remember what happened?" Eilis asked softly.

Jack thought for a moment then started to cry again, "They killed...em, all of em, xepdt for...me and three odder guys," he slurred.

Eilis looked at him. She felt sorry for him. Tears welled in her eyes as she explained, "No, Jack. Not Vietnam. Here, just a few minutes ago. You attacked Frank and Dan."

"Frank and Dan, who?"

"All right, let's get you back inside so you can go to sleep. She reached down to grab his hand and helped him up. Putting his arm over her shoulder she helped him inside. She helped him to the overstuffed sofa and helped him lay down. He seemed to go to sleep as soon as his head hit the sofa. She found a light blanket and after taking his shoes and socks off covered him. The odor from his feet was awful.

Finally, she got a sheet and covered herself as she sat in the lounge chair. She cried softly. She knew that this relationship with him would never work. He was so different. Eilis watched him sleep. His legs twitched and his body sometimes did too. Vietnam had destroyed him, she thought. Her Jack, the one she fell in love with existed no more, he was gone. Replaced by an evil that occupied his body. She was asleep after a few minutes.

Everyone was awake early the next morning while Jack slept. The two couples decided to go into town for breakfast and food shopping. Eilis stayed behind to wait for Jack to get up. She had been thinking about Jack and her. She asked Dan for his keys. When he did get up, she handed him a cup of coffee. "Any of that tequila left?"

"No, and there is no beer either, just coffee."

"It will have to do."

"Do you remember anything from last night?"

"I know there was tequila. After that…it is pretty much a blank."

"So, you don't remember this?" Eilis said exposing the bruises on her throat.

"NO, what happened?"

"You happened. You just don't know when to quit. Aside from the six pack of beer you drank on the way up, you drank must of the bottle of tequila by yourself. Then you attacked Frank, pinned me to the table choking me. I thought you were going to kill me. Frank and Dan managed to get you outside in the yard. You stayed out there yelling obscenities at the woods."

"I don't remember, honest. I'm sorry, ok."

"No, it's not ok. I don't know who you are. What I saw last night scares me. You scare me. I don't know what happened to you over there but all I know is you're not the same man I fell in love with. I cannot be with someone who at the drop of a hat wants to kill me."

"So, what does that mean? Your breaking up with me? That's not me last night, Eilis. I would never hurt you."

"But you did, and if not for Frank and Dan I might be dead. I looked into your eyes. What I saw…is not something I want to see again."

"So, what am I supposed to do? Where is everyone else? It's not like I can just walk home."

"They went into town for breakfast. I'll drive you to Scranton. You can get a bus home from there. Get yourself cleaned up. I'll wait in the car."

"Eilis, let's talk about this."

"No, my minds made up. We are done, and I don't want you here when everyone gets back."

He still had his house key and let himself in quietly. His flight left Saigon in the afternoon and it was now late at night here at home. He set his bags down and went to the refrigerator. He opened a bottle of Ortliebs and drank half of it. He looked in the dining room and found his father humidor, and was pleased it had cigars. He took a cigar into the kitchen and sat at the table. It was good to be home. He heard floor boards creak and saw his father. The two men embraced. "I didn't want to wake anyone."

"I heard the cab. Your mothers out like a light. How are you? You look like you lost a few pounds."

"I've been living on rice and chicken for too long. I'm thinking about packing it in Dad. We can't win this one. Nixon's bringing troops home. Without US support the Vietnamese will never be able to keep it together. In five years, it could all be over."

"Nixon needs to get a lot of troops home before the next election. If not, he may not get re-elected," his father added.

"Part of me wants to stay, see it all through. Then another part says, get the hell out now."

"Caroline retired. She is back from Europe. Which brings me to a question. When are you two going to put a peg in the wall and hang your hats on it.?"

"That's top-secret Dad, sorry, can't discuss that."

Kevin Brogan laughed at his son's answer, "Well, I have a deposition in the morning. It's good to have you home son."

"Great to be home, Dad. See you tomorrow."

They drove in silence. Eilis had made it clear there was no more to be said. Once he got off the turnpike she stopped for gas and asked for directions to the bus station. She paid the attendant for the gas and found the bus station. The directions had been perfect. She pulled up out front and stopped. She looked straight ahead and waited for Jack to get out of the car. He looked at her and knew she would never change her mind. He opened the door and went inside. The next bus to Philadelphia was an express and left in twenty minutes. He bought his ticket and boarded the bus. Sitting there he thought about what had happened. For whatever reason, he felt no remorse. He just did not care. When the bus left he fell asleep. The driver woke him in Philly.

CHAPTER 44

NEW YEAR, OLD MEMORIES

The mailman rang the doorbell. He had a letter that some-one had to sign for. Colleen signed the card and looked at the envelope. It was addressed to Petty Officer Third Class Jack Randall. The return address listed the Department of the Navy at the Pentagon. Hope was in the kitchen drinking her morning coffee. Jack was upstairs sleeping off another night of drinking. "This came for Jack, I had to sign for it."

Hope looked at the envelope. "I wonder what it is," Hope offered.

Colleen sat down with her coffee. "He drinks too much."

"I know. He should be going out to look for a job, or at least take advantage of the GI Bill and go to school."

"Maybe we should ask Mike to come up and talk with him," Colleen said.

"I don't see where that will hurt anything. Something hap-pened to him. He drinks to make it go away, but it won't. Mike just might be able to help. He seemed to be more at ease after Mike and Susan came up to see him after he came home. Should I call Mike or do you want to do it?"

"It might be better if you called. I know things are settled down between Susan and I but I don't want to push it."

"I think that ship has sailed. She was fine the last few times she was here."

They finished their coffee and Hope said, "You go wake up the drunken sailor, and I'll call Mike."

Hope made the phone call and Colleen went upstairs to wake Jack. He was tossing in his sleep. "Jack, wake up, Jack." She shook his leg and he sat up suddenly. "What…let me sleep."

"No, your mother said to get you up and there is a letter from the Navy downstairs."

"All right…all right, I'm up." Jack got up washed and dressed and went downstairs to the kitchen. His mother was on the phone and had just finished her call. She handed him a cup of coffee and set the envelope in front of him. Jack ripped it open and began to read.

PO3 Jack Randall,

This letter is to notify you that two officers from the NAVARB will visit you at your home of record on Wednesday the 27ʰ of this month at 0900 hours. If this time and date is inconvenient please notify my office at the number provided below.

Yours Truly,
Captain Gerald Reaney USN
Commander Officer, NAVARB

"What the fuck, over."

"Jack, please control your language." Hope scolded.

"What does the letter say?" Colleen asked.

He handed the letter to his grandmother. As she read it she asked, "What's NAVARB?"

Jack answered, "Navy Awards Review Board."

"Maybe it has something to do with your VA disability," Hope said.

"No, it has nothing to do with the VA. I don't know what it means. Besides why are they sending a couple of officers. I don't get it."

"Well, we'll know in two weeks, won't we," Colleen said.

"Yes, two weeks. Plenty of time for you to sober up and clean up. Get a haircut and a shave," Hope ordered.

"C'mon Mom. Let's not get into that again."

Hope replied, "But we will get into it again and while we're at it, you never said why that weekend just before Christmas with Eilis was cut short. The only thing you said was the two of you decided not to see each other anymore. What did you do Jack?"

"What makes you think I did something."

"Because since the Navy discharged you you've have been on one drunken binge after another. You are not acting like the son I raised."

"Let it go, Mom. Eilis and I are done."

"Well, I for one miss her. Whatever you did Jack, you should crawl on your hands and knees and beg her to forgive you," Colleen injected.

"There's nothing to forgive. Did you two ever consider maybe she did something."

"Never." The two women replied.

On the next weekend Mike and Susan came up for a visit. The women went downtown to go shopping leaving the two men alone. "So, what's the plan Jack. Are you looking for work? You thinking about going to school?"

"I'd like to get drunk, but my mother has a short leash on me. She threatened to throw me out on my ass. Now you're here to give me a good talking too. Plus, the Navy is sending a couple of brass hats to see me on Wednesday."

"What is that about?"

"I haven't the foggiest. Maybe they want me to be a recruiter. Hey guys come join the Navy, travel to far exotic lands, mingle with the native people and kill them all." Jack laughed at his joke.

"You sound bitter kid. How you sleeping?"

"Lousy. I have dreams, you know. Not good ones. You ever have dreams about France?"

"Still do. Somethings in life never leave you alone. You can't drown it in booze or kill it with drugs. You have to learn to deal with it. You have to talk about it Jack. If you bury it, all it does is erupt like a volcano. I know, I've been where you are."

"Right now, I'd rather not."

"That's fair. You should know that whenever you are ready, you can call me, ok."

"Sure."

"Now, what the hell did you do to Eilis? I told you Irish women are dangerous."

"Why does everyone believe I did something wrong? Maybe it was her."

"Yeah, right. No one believes that."

"Ok, but you can't tell anyone. I sort of got into a fight with a couple of her asshole fiends."

"Sort of a fight?"

"Not much of one, I mean after all the two guys walked away from it."

"Ah huh. In other words, I'm guessing you were hammered again."

"Yea, I had a few drinks. One guy starts talking about going to Canada and another is talking about baby killers."

"And that pisses off Eilis how?"

"Well she got in the way, I don't know."

"You hit her?"

"No…I sort of choked her."

"You sort of choked her. You, dumbass. Of all the things…"

"I don't care. I mean I really do not give a shit. She says she was faithful while I was gone, but the letters started getting shorter and far apart."

"So, she stops writing and you get pissed at two of her hippie friends and take it all out on her?"

"I know, sounds crazy. If you told me this would happen before I left for Nam I would have been heartbroken. Now, I don't care."

Wednesday morning at nine sharp the doorbell rang. Colleen answered the door and found two Naval Officers on the doorstep. "Good morning mam, we are here to see PO3 Jack Randall, the one with all the gold and ribbons said.

"Yes, of course please come in." Colleen showed them into the living room and offered them seats and coffee. They took the seats but declined the coffee. Jack came downstairs, dressed in slacks and a dress shirt. He had a fresh haircut and shave the day before.

"Good morning sir, I'm Jack Randall." The officers both shook his hand and they introduced themselves to Jack, his mother and grandmother. "I'm Commander Griffin and this is Lieutenant JG Morris." Everyone sat down and the Commander got right to why they were there. "Petty Officer Randall, our purpose here is to obtain your recollection of events that occurred last year on 19 July. You were assigned as a Corpsman to 1st Platoon Bravo Company. Your unit as well as other USMC units were inserted in an area north of Khe Sanh. During the march west, your unit entered a forest area and made contact with a large NVA unit. During the initial contact, your Platoon Leader ordered you to set up a staging area for the wounded. Do you recall these events?"

"Yes sir."

"Can you tell us in your own words what transpired after that."

"Well sir, wounded started coming in. I was by myself and I treated each man for his wounds like I was trained too."

"You treated the man with the worst wounds last. How many men were there in the staging area?"

"Thirteen, sir."

"Do you recall how much ammo you had, or what weapons were available to you?"

"Sir, the last three men that came into the staging area had two M16 rifles with each one having a single magazine. I had my sidearm and four spare magazines."

"Where was the rest of your platoon?"

"Sir, I believe at this point we were cut off and on our own. We had contact with the enemy and I exhausted all of the remaining M16 ammo."

"Please continue." The Commander urged.

Jack was nervous. Sweat had broken out on his brow. His hands began to shake. He was clearly upset. Hope took his hand to encourage him.

"Sir, we...were attacked. They came out of...the woods."

The Commander interrupted him, "Relax Jack. You're not in any trouble here. We just want to confirm from you what you remember, take your time."

"I shot two, then the pistol jammed. I fought with the other three...there was five of em...sir." Jack took a deep breath. Then they all came. One shot me. I tried to protect the wounded...I tried, but they shot them all," Jack was now crying. Hope and Colleen were crying. The Commander waited patiently.

Colleen left the room for tissues. Returning she gave them to Hope and Jack. "Commander, if I may. What is all of this about?"

"I think your grandson's recollection of the events of that day are consistent with the affidavits that were include with the commendation report. Thirteen men were under Jacks care. During that time, the position was attacked by five NVA soldiers that Jack engaged and killed. At that point having exhausted all of his ammunition, the position then was overrun by a platoon of NVA. Even though Jack was severely wounded himself and had just witnessed the execution of ten wounded Marines he still shielded the reaming three wounded Marines with his own body. The officer in charge of the NVA platoon ordered his men from the site and left Jack and the remaining wounded men."

Hope had regained her composure and asked, "So, what does all of this mean Commander?"

"Mrs. Randall, for his actions that day, your son will be awarded the Medal of Honor."

"NO." Jack said loudly. "I don't deserve it. They killed them all. I could...there was nothing I could do. I failed"

"This commendation was submitted by the Commanding General of the 9th Marine Division. You really want to tell a General he's wrong?"

"Sir...I don't deserve this. Lots of guys did things every day. They never got a medal. Why me? How about Cahill, he did lots of stuff."

"I never heard of anyone surrounding this action named Cahill. Look Jack, you were written up for this. It has been investigated and reviewed by people who look at these things very carefully. You would not be the first recipient of the medal to protest they were undeserving. Based on the reports and your testimony today, I would say what you did that day is justified and far and above and beyond the call of duty."

"So, what happens now?" Colleen asked.

"Jack will be notified by mail to report to the Navy Barracks in Washington. He will be custom fitted for a dress blue uniform and will be instructed when to report to the White House. Congratulations Jack and thank you."

The officers left and the three of them sat on the sofa. Jack was still upset, but his mother and grandmother consoled him.

During the rest of that morning Jack gave the details of that late afternoon north of Khe Sanh.

Dylan arrived back in Saigon, just as Operation Lam Son 719 was under way. ARVN forces supported by US artillery and air support crossed the border into Laos. Elements from the US 5th Infantry Division, 101st Airborne Division, 45th Engineers, 23rd Infantry Division and the 101st Aviation Group operated in the areas around Khe Sanh. They were forbidden by law to cross the Laotian border. Many of the air crews of the 101st Aviation were shot down, rescued and went back out again to support the ARVN forces. Once the ARVN began to withdraw the retreat turned into a rout. NVA forces were successful in defeating the South Vietnamese Forces, despite Nixon's statements that his Vietnamization program was working.

Nixon continued to bring more and more US forces home. The political atmosphere in Saigon was in turmoil. US bombing raids on North Vietnam continued and was a point of contention during the final days of the peace talks in Paris. The Viet Cong refused to recognize the South Vietnamese Government. In the northern most provinces the NVA had almost full control.

Dylan sat at his desk and was looking at the latest Stars and Stripes. Right there on the front page was a picture of President Nixon presenting the Medal of Honor to a very familiar sailor. He already knew about the Medal presentation from Caroline. She had written him shortly after getting the news herself. She was now in agreement that the war could not be won and urged him to retire. As much as he wanted too, he had decided to see it through to the end.

Mike and Jack sat on the steps of the Lincoln Memorial. Jack had since changed back into civilian clothes and the two men sat and talked about the day's events. "I still maintain I'm not worthy of the honor," Jack said.

"Doesn't matter now kid, the deed is done. You're going to have to clean up your life now. No more heavy drinking and fighting people."

"Ever hear of Ira Hayes?" Jack said.

"Yeah as a matter of fact I have. There's a lesson to be learned there, you know. You can't bring disgrace to yourself or the other members of the MOH Society. That medal you wear is not just for you. It's for the country Jack. It's for every man you served with"

"You mean the country that sent us over there. The country that lied and betrayed us. Have you seen the news lately? Marvin's getting his ass kicked again. How much longer do you think it will be until it all falls apart."

"I agree. They lied to us too. We were set up to get involved in France during the first world war. But, we went and did our duty. Your grandfather let the war destroy his marriage and himself. Your father did his duty in Europe during the second. He did it again in Korea. So, did your mother. She made it back and had you. You think your father gave his life so that we would walk away with two Korea's. He served, period. He believed in his country, right or wrong."

"So, how do you think it will all end?"

"If I were a betting man, I would say Nixon will end our involvement before his second term is over. The commies will win and Vietnam will have finally won its independence. Your Uncle Dylan believes that and he went back. He didn't have too, but he went back."

"What about the nightmares? What about the sense of guilt that I have that here I am living my life, a decorated hero, while all those other men died. They are the real heroes. How do I look myself in the mirror every day?"

"One day at a time kid, one day at a time."

Jack was thoughtful for a few minutes. "You know what I saw. I saw a kid, maybe five years old get blown to bits by a grenade. I don't think I can ever forget that."

"You never said anything about that before."

"I know...in a lot of ways I think I died with him. Vietnam changed me. It took everything I ever believed in that one day."

"You should see the guy I talk to. Why don't you move in with me and Susan? We can set up our appointments together."

"That might not be a bad idea. I need to get away. My mom's not going to like it."

"If it helps you get your life back together, I don't think she'll mind."

Jack broke the news to his mother and grandmother. Uncle Mike would drive up from the shore the following weekend. His mother protested, but he insisted it was what he needed to do.

Susan was happy to have him. She also told him she was very proud of him. For the first two weeks with Mike and Susan he did nothing. He sat on the beach most of the day and walked in the surf at night. He realized that walking with a cane restricted most of the jobs he was interested in. He decided that he would try his hand at owning his own business. He made all the preparations worked with the VA and a local bank and opened a cigar shop down town in Ocean City, just in time for the upcoming summer season. He named it after his grandfathers and called it 'JUDGE JIMS'. For the first season he barely got by, but made a small profit.

The next season he did better. He made enough money to rent the apartment above his shop. He moved out of Mike and Susan's and for the first time in his life he was on his own. He met a girl that was from South Philly. She was Italian, and her name was Carmella. He took his uncles advice and stayed clear of Irish women. Her family owned and operated several pizza shops on the boardwalks of Ocean City and Wildwood. They dated off and on for the next year.

During that second season, his grandmother Colleen passed away quietly in her sleep. She was buried with her husband, Jimmy and his parents Michael and Rose in New York. She left a tidy sum of money to her daughter Hope and Jack too. He bought a small cottage on the north end of town in Ocean City.

He found that living by himself suited him. Running his own business gave him control of everything. Like his grandfather Jack loved the smell inside the small walk in humidor. He kept all the shelves filled with boxes of cigars. Sometimes he thought about his Uncle Michael. The family never did learn his fate. His expertise would really be helpful now. He kept the shop open all year, but made the bulk of his revenue from April until October. He never told anyone about the medal. It was home in its case in his bedroom closet.

Jack kept a small TV in the shop and watched the news broadcasting a cease fire in Vietnam. Walter Cronkite told the viewers that American POW's would be returned soon. The news saddened Jack and on that day, he closed early. He sat on the beach and thought about his life. How the one event that lasted just a few months consumed each of the days of his existence. He was not alone. He thought about the men he served with. He thought about the men that were there before and after him. They all shared a similar burden. Like a bag of heavy rocks, they all carried it wherever they went.

The fifteen page, booklet was titled; STANDARD INSTRUCTION and ADVICE to CIVILIANS in an EMERGENCY. Dylan read through the document that had precise helicopter pick up points illustrated on the street maps of Saigon. The signal to evacuate would be broadcast on the AFR network indicating that the temperature in Saigon was 105 degrees and rising, followed by the song 'White Christmas.' Dylan put the book down. So, what happens if you don't have the radio on when the signal is broadcast, he thought. I guess you become permanent guest of the Hanoi Hilton. There's plenty of room. Supposedly all of the POW's are home, but we still list more than 2500 men as MIA. President Thieu had been back stabbed by Kissinger and Nixon. Nixon the crook of crooks had resigned rather than facing almost certain impeachment. The NVA, Viet Cong and ARVN units were to hold their positions. Resupply was allowed and the NVA took full advantage of the provision as agreed in Paris.

The booklet that Dylan had read was a proof copy. The final booklet would be released after the first of the year. The end was coming. Intelligence reports indicated that the current South Vietnamese Government could hold onto power for at least another year or possibly two. Getting the NVA to give up territory in the south that they now controlled was going to be a tough nut to crack. The US had promised to keep the ARVN supplied with the tools of war. The Soviets and the Red Chinese were supporting the NLF. The final solution Dylan thought would come down to who had the better army.

Intelligence reports from the field indicated the NVA was getting a steady stream of equipment and supplies. The ARVN were entirely dependent on the US. All US combat units had already been sent home. The South Vietnamese Government had assurances that US air power and re-supply of vital military equipment would be provide if the North restarted military operations in the south below the DMZ. It was all a lie.

After the Christmas and New Year holidays reports from sources in the northern most provinces indicated the NVA was moving Russian T-54 tanks and heavy artillery south. Just after the Tet celebration of 1975, the NVA started their final offensive. South Vietnamese troops caught off guard and in some cases poorly led collapsed under pressure from the NVA. Retreating

ARVN forces combined with thousands of refugees clogged the highways leading south. The US in early March began an orderly evacuation by air of US citizens still in the country. That would soon change. The CIA was caught off guard by the speed of the NVA advance. Activity in the embassy was chaotic. Non-essential personnel were ordered out of the country along with family members. Flights from Saigon were booked solid. The NVA had captured several northern cities including Hue and Da Nang.

Dylan was working eighteen-hour days collecting documents that could not fall into communist hands. Some of the paperwork was shipped to Langley or sent out by courier to ships gathering in the South China Sea. He was spending all of his time in his office and slept on the couch whenever possible. Aside from getting documents out of the country there were assets in the field that needed to be evacuated. Communication lines worked on and off. Saigon itself was now getting ready for a final defense. The knock on the door came on April 27th when the NVA fired rockets into the city.

Dylan needed to get back to his apartment. He had equipment personal items and paperwork there that he needed to get out. He drove out to his place with two Marines in a jeep. Reaching his apartment, he bundled everything up that he needed including his Thompson and .45 pistol. Loading the back of the jeep he jumped into the back with his possessions and returned to the embassy. He was ordered to stay on the grounds until further notice. Some of the paperwork and photographs he had was put into burn bags. The incinerator was operating at full capacity and some material was being burned in 55-gallon drums on the grounds. He never heard the radio broadcast of 'White Christmas' but he knew the US was leaving before the NVA arrived. During the chaos, he noticed his walking stick that had been with him since the Philippines was missing. The last place he knew he had it was at the apartment. Over the years it had become an emotional crutch. Physically he rarely needed it. The loss bothered him but he had more pressing matters.

For now, he was attempting to get some of the Vietnamese that worked for him onto the embassy grounds or to an evacuation point. Looking out his office window the Marines had their hands full, with close to a thousand Vietnamese attempting to get into the embassy. Then the news came that Xuan Loc had fallen into enemy hands and that Tan Son Nhut was under attack. The end was coming quickly.

He was a Major now. In command of an entire battalion of young soldiers who were about to see the enemy fall once and for all. Duong was proud of his men and his army. They had beaten the US military and the puppet regime they had propped up. Vietnam was on the verge of being a free and independent nation. For now, his orders were to secure the intersection on Gia Long street. The Russian T-54 tank sat in the middle and was an imposing site.

On his way, here he had seen uniforms, boots and weapons abandoned by the ARVN forces left to defend the city lying in the street. Some of the population cheered their arrival. He wondered as he rode in his command car if their welcoming cheers were authentic. He gave orders to his subordinate officer to have their men arrest any military age men with soft feet. The ARVN wore American supplied boots. Their feet would go soft. He looked at an older man, his feet were callused, the dirt showed under the toe nails. The ARVN would be easy to find. He knew the fate of these men that supported the puppet regime. Prison and in some cases execution.

The Citroen drove up to the intersection followed by a small truck filled with men in civilian clothing. The men were all armed with side arms and AK_47 rifles. The man in the back seat showed Duong his credentials. He was a member of the NLF, and an intelligence officer. The rank indicated he was a General and his name was Nguyễn Hung. "Good morning, comrade. These men are all with me. We will be searching the building down the street. Number 22. If we need you or your men, I will let you know," Hung said.

"Of course, General, the last American helicopter left from that building some time ago. Do have any news about our forces?"

"The Presidential Palace is now in our hands. The puppet regime has capitulated. The American War is over. We are victorious. Vietnam is now one nation."

Duong smiled broadly and he passes the news on to other men around him. There was much celebration. Duong thought, now that it was all over he would return to his village and try to find out his father's fate. Perhaps he was still alive.

Hung and his men searched the building at 22 Gia Long Street. They took photographs and then cataloged every item and piece of paper they found. This building housed officers of the CIA among other US agencies. They hoped to find evidence of people in the city that worked for the Americans. In particular they soaked to find the identities of agents that had worked against the cause. The people who had identified agents of the NLF that went missing, presumed dead or captured. There was but one fate for these traitors.

CHAPTER 45

RETRIBUTION & RETURNS

Travelling with a Passport of a Chinese Diplomat had its advantages. His first-class flight from Hong Kong to San Francisco was restful. Documents and a package had been sent to New York from Beijing as part of a diplomatic pouch. The contents would not have been seen by anyone until he arrived and inspected them. He stayed overnight in San Francisco and got an early morning flight to New York.

A driver was waiting for him at JFK and took him into the city. He had specifically requested that the driver not use any of the tunnels. He had no desire to ever be underground again. He was to be taken to the consulate in Manhattan. He marveled at the city as they crossed the famous Brooklyn Bridge. As they drove uptown he asked the driver to go thru Times Square. The driver complied and mentioned as they drove down Broadway that this was certainly the capital of American decadence. All along Broadway and 42nd Street there were XXX movie theaters and prostitutes walking the sidewalks. The modern-day Sodom or Gomora would seem to be alive and well.

They arrived at the consulate near the UN building. He would rest for a day before he would undertake his mission. Meeting with the Chinese MSS (Ministry of State Security) Intelligence officer in charge at the consulate he was assured everything was ready to go. They were happy to assist in any way. The man he wanted to see was under surveillance. His name was Robert Iako, and he lived on the upper west side across from Central Park in an apartment building on the tenth floor.

Since his return from Saigon in the wake of the defeat of all of South Vietnamese forces Dylan retired from the CIA. He went through the normal debriefing period and came home to Philadelphia. Both of Caroline's parents had passed over the years and left her the house on Olive Street. He moved in with her shortly after his retirement. Her sister Charlotte married a Congressman from Iowa. She was living on a farm near Fort Dodge.

It just made sense for both of them to live together. The sexual revolution of the sixties had opened the door to couples living together instead of getting married. Neither of them wanted to make such a commitment. Flush with money they saved over the years and their combined independent pensions meant they could travel wherever and whenever they wanted. Having just returned from a trip to Switzerland they settled into their normal routine while home. Each morning at eight they would walk along the Parkway towards City Hall and then back.

Walking east on the Parkway they were walking past the Rodin museum when Dylan became aware of two men across the Parkway taking pictures with a telephoto lens on a 35mm camera. "I think we're under some kind of surveillance," he said to Caroline.

"What? By who, or even better, Why?"

"I have no idea. There are two oriental men across the Parkway taking pictures. Every time we get near a statue or a landmark, they take a picture with us in it."

"I think you're paranoid. Why would anyone have us under the eye? We're retired for Christ's sake. I've been out of the community for a couple of years."

They walked around Logan Circle and started back towards the museum on the south side. The two men crossed to the north side and followed them as far as 22nd Street. Then the men walked north got into a car and drove off. "OK, that was weird. Maybe we should call Langley and let them know."

"No, we'll look like idiots. Besides let's wait until tomorrow to see what happens, Dylan said.

The next day and for several days after that, they did not notice anyone following them or taking their picture. Still as a precaution Dylan carried a .45 in his waistband. Returning to their home they had breakfast. They were scheduled to drive to the shore to see his Uncle Mike and Aunt Susan.

When they arrived, they had a late lunch on the beach. "Uncle Mike, how is Jack doing with the business?"

"Not too bad. I get a big discount, so I hope his success continues," Mike replied. Susan offered, "Isn't it funny that his great grandfather and grandfather had the same business."

"Yes, it is." Caroline responded. I wonder what ever became of his real Uncle Mike?"

"He retired in a beach house with a beautiful woman, that fights off other beautiful women," Mike answered.

"Not you, I mean his real Uncle Michael," Caroline laughed.

"I had some people at Langley look into it. We know Tom was arrested and jailed. Michael just disappeared into thin air. The Cuban's never had him. I guess we will never know," Dylan said.

Susan said, "Such a shame. He could really have helped Jack when he started out. Maybe cigars are in the blood."

Dylan asked, "Do you know if he is seeing someone?"

Susan replied, "He pretty much keeps to himself. He does see a woman from time to time. Pretty too. Her names Carmella.

Her family owns pizza shops here at the shore. Her fathers sup-posed to be connected to the Philly Mob. I forget the last name. What is it Mike?"

"Hell, I don't know. Vinnie Stugots!" Mike laughed at his own joke.

Susan cried, "Stop, that's terrible. It's all just rumors. We see him from time to time. I really thought he and Eilis would wind up together."

"I spoke to Hope at Maggie's the other day. She told me that Eilis is engaged to a cop in Media," Caroline said.

"Really."

Mike interrupted, "Ok, enough with the soap opera gossip. The kids doing all right. Who he sees and what he does is his business."

Susan added, "I'm worried that he keeps to himself so much. I knew a guy like that once. He was a real asshole."

"Oh, very funny," Mike replied

"Well it's very true. You did act like an asshole at times. You wanted to be alone, fly off the handle for the most ridiculous reasons. Now you get medicine and see the doctor. He's much better now."

"So, the therapy helps?" Dylan asked interested.

Susan replied, "Yes it does. Now he's just a normal everyday asshole."

The big Cadillac Brougham was waiting for him at the curb. His driver was an agent of the MSS. On the back seat was a large leather valise. Inside was a MK22 with a Mark III silencer. The US Navy Seals used these pistols in Vietnam. They were nick-named 'Hush Puppies'. Built on the Smith & Wesson Model 39 platform they had been effective in assassinating NLF officials and high ranking NVA officers.

They drove uptown along the west side of the park. Turning east on 63rd Street they went around the block and the big caddie stopped on 64th Street and parked. Right on time at 10 AM the young woman mail carrier stopped in the apartment building to deliver the mail. She was attractive and the deskman led her into the back of the mailroom to make her deliveries. The deskman liked to flirt with the attractive mail carrier. The man entered the lobby a minute behind her. He was well dressed with a suit and he wore tight fitting driver's gloves. He went behind the reception desk and pushed the button to open the elevator door. He was going to see someone in apartment 10D but pushed the button for the twelfth floor. Getting off on the twelfth floor the man took the fire stairs to the tenth floor. Stepping into the hall the man waited, listening. The hall was quiet and empty.

He walked down the hall to the first door on the left. The door indicated 10D. He knocked softly. An older oriental man answered the door and looked at the man who had knocked. He did not recognize his caller. There was a look of recognition on the man's face standing in the hall.

In his left hand, he held a valise. In the other a pistol. The man raised the pistol and fired a single shot. The pistol made a pfft sound, the only other sound was the slide re-cycling the next round from the magazine. His victim fell on his back, the back of his head blown out.

The man stepped into the doorway and moved his victim's legs out of the way so the door would shut. He put the pistol back into the valise closed the door and picked up the spent 9mm casing from the floor.

He went back to the stairs exiting on the seventh floor and pushed the elevator button. Reaching the lobby, the desk clerk had returned to his station. Noting the elevator came from the seventh floor he ignored the man as he exited the lobby. His

557

driver held the door and the man slid into the back seat. The driver turned north on Central Park West heading to the George Washington Bridge. They crossed the bridge and headed south on the New Jersey Turnpike. The man had one more person to visit.

Driving south on the turnpike the man in the back seat thought about all the research that had been done for him to accomplish this mission. He remembered sitting at his desk in the Presidential Palace in Saigon. The war was long over but there was still much work to be done. He was reading a list of items found in the building at 22 Gia Long Street. One of the cataloged items caught his attention. He picked up the phone and dialed a number.

The item he wanted was delivered to him by courier. Looking at it brought back so many memories. He set it aside and returned to more pressing paperwork. Opening the thick folder, he found that Robert Iako was born in the United States. His parents thrilled to be in America gave him an American first name. He did well in school and during the summer of 1941 was working for a building contractor in New York City. He was working his way through NYU. In July, he was working on a building on the lower west side building scaffolding. Part of the scaffolding failed and Robert fell seven floors to his death.

Other paperwork inside the folder showed that Robert had a healthy bank account and lived in an apartment building on the upper west side after the second World War was over. Someone had taken his identity. That someone was Major Bunta Sasaki of the Imperial Japanese Army. He was wanted for war crimes by the US, the Chinese, and the Vietnamese. Stealing the money and jewelry from his victims, Sasaki managed to escape during the British occupation and had somehow made it to the US. He lived a quiet and comfortable life. That had changed this morning.

Reaching Philadelphia, they turned off Pennsylvania Avenue going north on 25^(th) Street. Another right-hand turn was made onto Olive Street. The street was narrow and the big caddie barely made it up the street to a couple sitting on the front steps of their home. Dylan and Caroline sat and watched the big car come up the street. The caddie had diplomatic plates and drove half way up on the side walk. The driver got out and opened the trunk. Dylan saw he was armed, a pistol was in a shoulder holster. The driver went around and opened the passenger rear door and a small well-dressed man in a tan suit got out. He walked up to the steps and bowed. "Good afternoon, Sergeant Brogan. I have something for you."

At first Dylan thought he needed to go into the house for his .45, but then he recognized the man. "Jesus H. Christ, I don't believe it. Vang Bo."

"Who?" Caroline asked.

"Ah, you are Caroline Grindell. It is my pleasure to meet you," the man said.

"Caroline, you remember. The girls with the embroidery shop in Saigon. This is their father. We were together in Shanghai."

"You mean this man is…'Gayal'. She remembered.

"That is just one of many names I have used in my life." The driver reached into the trunk and gave Bo a long cardboard box. Opening the box Bo handed Dylan the walking stick, he had left in Saigon. "Shit, I don't believe it. How…where did you get it?" Dylan asked pleased.

"Your apartment on Gia Long Street. It was with all the other things we captured after you left. When I saw it. I knew you would want it back."

"Jesus, I don't know what to say. Please come inside. We should talk."

"Regrettably I cannot. I have a flight to catch. It is good to see you again, Brogan." The driver was standing by the rear passenger door waiting for Bo to get back in the car. "Today I have closed a long and bitter part of my life. There is one more thing I wish to give you." Bo reached into his pocket and handed Dylan the spent shell casing he had picked up off the floor in New York. "I don't understand, Bo. What is this?"

"This morning I gave an old enemy the other end of that. You should know that it pleases me that I was able to do a kindness as the last part of closing that life I leave behind. Returning your stick was the last thing to do. When I return home, I will spend the rest of my days bouncing grandchildren on my knee. I wish you luck old friend. We have both seen and done things that although necessary, no one should be compelled to do."

"I wish you could stay. There is so much I would like to talk about. I really felt bad when the Japs caught you...there was nothing I could do."

"I understand, and I do not hold a grudge. You had a duty, as did I. Consider it all as necessary to the final outcome. We had no choice."

Bo got into the car and the driver closed the door. Before the big caddie pulled away, Bo said through the open window, "Live a peaceful life, my friend. It will be hard but we both deserve it. Try to put the past behind you. Become a new man and forget that we are Creatures Born of War."

Vang 30 — sat on
old tree stump P 32

P. 289 John Wayne
cedo Ray
Battle Cry

397 — Ham ð
motherfuckers
not ham ð eggs

P. 403 Water Gunboite
war not Winnable
404 already lost war,
Tet offensive

Made in the USA
Columbia, SC
16 October 2017